SAP PRESS e-books

Print or e-book, Kindle or iPad, workplace or airplane: Choose where and how to read your SAP PRESS books! You can now get all our titles as e-books, too:

- ▸ By download and online access
- ▸ For all popular devices
- ▸ And, of course, DRM-free

Convinced? Then go to **www.sap-press.com** and get your e-book today.

SAP® SuccessFactors® Employee Central

 **PRESS**

SAP PRESS is a joint initiative of SAP and Rheinwerk Publishing. The know-how offered by SAP specialists combined with the expertise of Rheinwerk Publishing offers the reader expert books in the field. SAP PRESS features first-hand information and expert advice, and provides useful skills for professional decision-making.

SAP PRESS offers a variety of books on technical and business-related topics for the SAP user. For further information, please visit our website: *www.sap-press.com*.

Amy Grubb, Luke Marson
SuccessFactors with SAP ERP HCM:
Business Processes and Use (2nd edition)
2015, 644 pages, hardcover and e-book
www.sap-press.com/3702

Kandi, Krishnamoorthy, Leong-Cohen, Padmanabhan, Reddygari
Integrating SuccessFactors with SAP
2015, 551 pages, hardcover and e-book
www.sap-press.com/3723

Masters, Toombs, Bland, Morgalis
Self-Services with SAP ERP HCM: ESS, MSS, and HR Renewal
2015, 345 pages, hardcover and e-book
www.sap-press.com/3585

Joe Lee, Tim Simmons
Talent Management with SAP ERP HCM
2012, 388 pages, hardcover and e-book
www.sap-press.com/3016

Luke Marson, Murali Mazhavanchery, Rebecca Murray

SAP® SuccessFactors® Employee Central

The Comprehensive Guide

Rheinwerk®
Publishing

Bonn • Boston

Editor Sarah Frazier
Acquisitions Editor Emily Nicholls
Copyeditor Melinda Rankin
Cover Design Graham Geary
Photo Credit Shutterstock.com/245722936/© Iurii Kachkovskyi
Layout Design Vera Brauner
Production Graham Geary
Typesetting III-satz, Husby (Germany)
Printed and bound in the United States of America, on paper from sustainable sources

ISBN 978-1-4932-1218-7

© 2016 by Rheinwerk Publishing, Inc., Boston (MA)
1st edition 2016

Library of Congress Cataloging-in-Publication Data
Names: Marson, Luke. | Murray, Rebecca. | Mazhavanchery, Murali.
Title: SuccessFactors employee central : the comprehensive guide / Luke Marson, Rebecca Murray, Murali Mazhavanchery.
Other titles: Success factors employee central
Description: 1 Edition. | Boston : Rheinwerk Pub., 2015. | Includes index.
Identifiers: LCCN 2015034358| ISBN 9781493212187 (print : alk. paper) | ISBN 1493212184 (print : alk. paper) |
ISBN 9781493212194 (ebook) | ISBN 9781493212200 (print and ebook : alk. paper)
Subjects: LCSH: SAP ERP. | Personnel management--Data processing. | Manpower planning--Computer programs. |
SuccessFactors (Firm)
Classification: LCC HF5549.3.D37 M37 2015 | DDC 658.300285/53--dc23 LC record available at
http://lccn.loc.gov/2015034358

Contents at a Glance

Dear Reader,

Like living organisms, companies both large and small function best when each limb, or individual moving part, can communicate with one another. You wouldn't want your brain to tell your leg to move, only to move your arm. You wouldn't want to take a vacation, only to come back and find that your boss thinks you've retired and are now living off your pension. Yikes.

Today, companies rely less on paper-pushing processes to manage these functions, and instead turn to sophisticated HR systems to pick up the slack. While SAP ERP HCM rules as on-premise king, many companies are looking to advance these HRIS processes further (higher) to the cloud. And in a cloud-based world, SAP Success-Factors Employee Central reigns supreme.

With this book, you'll learn how to implement and wield Employee Central functionality to fit your organization's mold, allowing you to streamline once cumbersome processes. Whether it's making sure the right people have the right access, or managing employee data and events, this guide will show you what it takes to keep your company—and your cloud HRIS system—up and running.

What did you think about *SAP SuccessFactors Employee Central*? Your comments and suggestions are the most useful tools to help us make our books the best they can be. Please feel free to contact me and share any praise or criticism you may have.

Thank you for purchasing a book from SAP PRESS!

Sarah Frazier
Editor, SAP PRESS

Rheinwerk Publishing
Boston, MA

sarahf@rheinwerk-publishing.com
www.sap-press.com

Contents

5   Extensibility 163

6   Foundation Objects 193

PART II Features and Functionality

9 Employee Data 299

PART III Integrating Employee Central with Other Systems

Foreword

I'm pleased to have the opportunity to write the foreword for *SAP SuccessFactors Employee Central*. While documentation, training, and various online learning channels enable customers and consultants to learn about SAP SuccessFactors and Employee Central, this book fills an important need. It provides a strong overview of the solution combined with practical advice from leading experts. Luke, Rebecca, and Murali have done a fine job with this book. It is readable, precise, and provides actionable guidance.

At the time of writing, more than 800 organizations are deploying Employee Central. Over the last year, the customer growth has been close to 100%. With more than 150 organizations over 10,000 employees deploying Employee Central, it is now well established as a leading core HRIS in the cloud.

The market has continued to shift to the cloud. Cloud computing for HCM is no longer a question of "if", but now a matter of when. The demand for information and guidance on how to move to Employee Central has grown dramatically. Organizations around the world are seeking new ways to manage their people processes. Employee Central has developed as a product over the years in response to this demand. We ship new functionality and enhancements every 13 weeks. Just in the last year we have seen major enhancements in Time Management, Global Benefits, Position Management, contingent labor, localization, new user experience (UX), major platform enhancements, stronger integration, and a host of other developments. The cloud model has enabled us to innovate at an unprecedented pace.

Customers also drive innovation. Whether it is new demands from new customers, or the wise words of long-standing customers, listening to the business requirements of our customers drives much of what we do. They share their best practices with us, allow us to incorporate these practices into our software, and share this knowledge with others. It would be remiss of me not to thank those customers here.

We also get to observe trends in the consumer software market, learn from them, and then deliver enticing experiences to enterprises. Simplicity remains at the center of what we do. Simple to use, simple to implement, and simple to operate, informs every investment decision.

Besides being well-timed, this book also offers a wide range of expertise. The authors are especially well qualified to develop this book.

Luke Marson grew up with HR software, with his father, Paul Marson, being one of the leading experts on SAP on-premise HCM. Over the past five years, Luke has become one of the leading consultants on Employee Central and SAP SuccessFactors, having implemented projects all over the world. He is a regular speaker at events, and writes on implementation and products on the SAP SCN site and LinkedIn. He works closely with SAP SuccessFactors product management in Germany and San Francisco, and he is a Certified Professional in Employee Central and an SAP Mentor Alumni.

Murali Mazhavanchery is the most senior product manager at SAP SuccessFactors working on Employee Central. He is the chief product expert, and has worked on Employee Central since its inception. He has been responsible for most of the decisions that have shaped the product, and his knowledge of the solution and how it should be deployed is unrivalled.

Rebecca Murray has spent more than four years delivering Employee Central implementations. She is a Certified Professional in Employee Central and a certified Dell Boomi AtomSphere developer. She teaches Employee Central Academy (mastery) classes for SAP Education and actively participates in planning course content. She has done numerous implementations at large and small firms, global and single-country.

I would like to thank Luke, Murali, and Rebecca for taking the time and applying their knowledge to write this important book.

Thomas Otter
Vice President, Product Management — Employee Central
SAP SE

Preface

HR at large can be broken into subcomponents. These are typically the "core" HR elements and activities (e.g., personnel administration, organizational management, actions, pay and benefits, management of employees, etc.), talent management (e.g., performance management, learning management, or succession planning), and workforce planning. HR analytics is another component that, although a subset of analytics, is still a component of modern HR.

Typically, these elements and actions of HR have been managed in an on-premise system, such as SAP ERP HCM. However, in recent years, trends have developed to leverage next-generation, cloud-based technology. For HR, SAP now offers SAP SuccessFactors Employee Central as its next-generation HR system. Employee Central is a cloud-based offering that integrates with on-premise and cloud systems, SAP and non-SAP systems. The functionality of Employee Central extends from handling employee's employment information to managing time entry and time off bookings, extended leaves of absences, global work assignments, employee benefits, self-services, and much more.

Objective

The purpose of this book is to provide a complete guide to Employee Central, covering a rundown of its features and functionality, implementation, configuration, extension, integration, and much more.

Once you have read this book, we hope that you have the knowledge to understand the inner workings of the solution, as well as knowledge of where to access more information.

Target Audience

The target audience for the book can be divided into two folds:

▶ *Customers* who are implementing or already using Employee Central (together or separate from other HR applications) that need to understand what features this powerful tool can offer and where it fits relative to their other key HR functionality.

▶ *Implementation consultants* who need to understand how to configure Employee Central based on a customer's requirements, and, once they're done, how to leave it in users' hands for daily HR processes and maintenance.

Structure of the Book

This book is divided into three parts: Part I: Foundation, Part II: Features and Functionality, and Part III: Integrating Employee Central with Other Systems.

This book begins by introducing the cloud context in which Employee Central has arisen as SAP's next-generation HR system, and how it fits into SAP's HR roadmap. Part I, Foundation, teaches the foundational concepts of Employee Central's implementations such as using Foundation Objects, extensibility, and data importing.

In Part I, Foundation, the following topics are covered:

▶ **Chapter 1: Employee Central Basics**
Beginning with basic definitions of key terms, this chapter broadly covers Employee Central's objects, data structure, operation, features, UI, and integration with the rest of the SAP SuccessFactors suite. Understanding what these terms mean, how the system is designed, and how the pieces relate to one another is key to all subsequent chapters, as well as your overall understanding of Employee Central.

▶ **Chapter 2: Implementation Steps and Considerations**
Before beginning an implementation project and configuring any Employee Central functionality, both customers and consultants need to understand what's ahead and what they can expect. This chapter will cover important items and activities to consider, how a project is structured and operated, the SAP SuccessFactors project implementation methodology, and what roles each "actor" in an implementation will undertake. Then it outlines post-implementation and administration steps and resources.

▶ **Chapter 3: Role-Based Permissions**
Role-Based Permissions (RBPs) are integral to Employee Central since they structure who has access to which information and actions. This chapter focuses on the RBP framework in an Employee Central context and will give

you a basic understanding of what RBPs are, how they work in Employee Central, what the extent and limitations of applying RBPs are, and the types of scenarios and roles to create them.

▶ **Chapter 4: Events and Workflows**
This chapter will cover how events, Event Reasons, and workflows work in Employee Central. After reading this chapter, you should have a thorough understanding of the events in an employee lifecycle, how to create customer-specific Event Reasons, how to apply workflows to these employee events, and how to configure workflows.

▶ **Chapter 5: Extensibility**
This chapter will cover all aspects of extending Employee Central, or moving beyond standard system setup. It will cover the Metadata Framework (MDF), Rules Engine, and extensions created on SAP HANA Cloud Platform (HCP).

▶ **Chapter 6: Foundation Objects**
This chapter will discuss the creating and managing of Foundation Objects that are used to populate employee data. It will build on the concepts discussed in previous chapters and show specific use cases for using the MDF to create and manage Foundation Objects.

▶ **Chapter 7: Data Imports and Data Migration**
Each implementation will require importing and migrating data to Employee Central. This chapter will cover the data import options, specific rules and formats of data imports, migration techniques from SAP ERP HCM and other systems, and explain how to successfully ensure that data is imported smoothly and successfully. This is the last "foundational" chapter before the book looks at specific features and functionality.

The bulk of the book, Part II, Features and Functionality, is dedicated to walking through Employee Central features and functionality from employee data to managing contingents and everything in between, and teaches both how to use and configure these functions.

The following topics are covered in Part II:

▶ **Chapter 8: Position Management**
As the first look at Employee Central features, this chapter will cover what Position Management is, why it is important, how it can be used, how it is set up, and how it works. We will also cover the different options that are available when setting up and using Position Management.

▶ **Chapter 9: Employee Data**
Managing employee data through an employee's lifecycle is one of the key use cases associated with Employee Central. This chapter will cover hiring and rehiring, terminations, transfers and promotions, reclassifications, changing job and compensation information, Employee Self-Service (ESS), and Manager Self-Service (MSS).

▶ **Chapter 10: Employee Time, Absences, and Benefits**
Another key piece of Employee Central is managing employee time sheets, paid time off, leaves of absence, and employee benefits. This chapter demonstrates how employees, managers, and HR administrators can manage positive and negative time, time off, leaves of absence, and benefit programs and enrollment.

▶ **Chapter 11: Global Assignments**
This chapter will cover all aspects of the Global Assignments functionality. It will cover the features and functionality behind global assignments, management of global employees in both home and expatriate positions, and using global assignment rules.

▶ **Chapter 12: Contingent Workforce Management**
This chapter will cover the features and functionality behind Contingent Workforce Management and how to manage external contractors and other temporary workers who require HR interaction and management, but who are not part of the permanent workforce.

▶ **Chapter 13: Mass Changes**
In this chapter, you'll discover how to use the mass changes feature to perform large-scale data changes for sections of the workforce. We'll look at the Manage Mass Changes tool, discuss best practices for using it, and look at the configuration involved in implementing it.

▶ **Chapter 14: Advances and Deductions**
This chapter will cover the features and functionality behind both advances and deductions. It will teach how they can be used together to issue advances against compensation payments and how those or other advances can be automatically collected.

▶ **Chapter 15: Employee Central Payroll**
Employee Central Payroll enables Employee Central customers to manage payroll capabilities. This chapter will cover its functionality, and how employees

can maintain payroll and tax information in Employee Central. The Employee Central Payroll-related integrations are discussed in Part III.

▶ **Chapter 16: Other Features and Functionality**
This chapter will cover the remaining transactions and processes not covered in previous chapters: concurrent employment, alternative cost distribution, document generation, and more. After reading this chapter, you should have a thorough understanding of all available transactions and processes in Employee Central and how to set them up.

▶ **Chapter 17: Reporting**
Consultants and customers need to know what possibilities are available for reporting based on Employee Central data, including legacy ad hoc reporting and Employee Central Advanced Reporting. After reading this chapter, you should have a thorough understanding of how reporting works, what reporting options are available, and how to create and schedule reports.

▶ **Chapter 18: Mobile**
SAP SuccessFactors has an app! This chapter discusses the Employee Central functionality that can be managed via the app, such as Time Off and ESS and MSS capabilities.

Finally, Part III, Integrating Employee Central with Other Systems, teaches how to integrate Employee Central with systems such as SAP ERP and other third-party solutions, and concludes our book.

The following is covered in Part III:

▶ **Chapter 19: Integration**
Employee Central fits into a larger HR picture. This chapter will give an overview of integrating Employee Central with SAP ERP applications, related cloud applications, and third-party vendors such as Benefitfocus and WorkForce Software. This chapter will discuss how Employee Central integrates with other applications, and what integration opportunities and limitations to anticipate.

▶ **Conclusion**
To conclude, we'll return to the big picture and recap concepts we've covered throughout the book. In addition, we'll provide resources for further learning.

We hope that with this book you will gain a complete understanding of the Employee Central module, its implementation, features, and integration possibilities.

SAP SuccessFactors Employee Central is a next-generation, core HR solution that enables organizations to flexibly manage all of their HR needs while providing a system of engagement that aligns with the user interface and user experience expectations of the modern workforce.

Introduction

Employee Central is the core HR system of the SAP SuccessFactors HCM Suite and provides a complete set of end-to-end core HR capabilities for enterprises that wish to leverage the cloud for their HR needs. Employee Central is an innovative, evolving, and flexible solution that can meet the business requirements of organizations of all shapes and sizes, and places a strong emphasis on globalization.

SAP SuccessFactors HCM Suite

For more details on the SAP SuccessFactors HCM Suite, including background of SAP SuccessFactors and its technical architecture, see *SuccessFactors with SAP ERP HCM: Business Processes and Use* by Amy Grubb and Luke Marson (2nd edition, SAP PRESS, 2015).

Although Employee Central shares a strong overlap with SAP ERP HCM for common core HR functionality, SAP has no intention to rebuild SAP ERP HCM in the cloud. In many cases, organizations find the early 1990s SAP ERP HCM core system cumbersome and outdated. Employee Central aims instead to offer fresh ideas and new methodologies for how core HR processes are run in the twenty-first century.

Employee Central is a Software-as-a-Service (SaaS) solution, meaning it benefits from being hosted in the cloud and is multitenant, so all customers are always on the most recent release. In addition, new releases and patches are pushed automatically—often with no effort required from the customer.

As previously stated, *globalization* is a core strength of Employee Central. The solution caters to global businesses, while it has localizations for legal compliance and reporting in seventy-one countries and in thirty-five languages.

As one would expect from a core HR system, Employee Central offers a wealth of functionality to ensure that it meets the needs of every company. This functionality enables organizations to manage employee data, provides access to that data via self-service capabilities, and enables various actions to be performed. The effective-dated platform within Employee Central ensures that historical data changes can be viewed, tracked, and audited. Various other capabilities provide users with the ability to manage benefits, time recording, time off, and their own data with built-in workflow options. In addition, administrators can manage employees who have multiple jobs, who go on assignment to other countries, or who are contingent workers.

The functionality available in Employee Central includes the following:

- New hire and rehire processing
- Terminations
- Transfers and promotions
- Job and compensation changes
- Job and position reclassifications
- Employee Self-Service (ESS) and Manager Self-Service (MSS)
- Workflows and events
- Position Management
- Payroll (with Employee Central Payroll)
- Benefits
- Time Management
- Global assignments
- Concurrent employment
- Contingent Workforce Management
- Mass changes
- Advances and deductions
- Alternative cost distribution
- Pensions Payouts
- Extensibility (custom objects and custom applications)
- Robust permissions framework
- Reporting

Frequent releases also mean that enhancements and new functionality are provided on a regular basis. We will touch on this soon, but first we'll take a look at some of the business drivers for using a core HR system in the cloud.

Business Drivers for HR in the Cloud

There are many advantages to moving core HR to Employee Central, and there are also some key benefits of using a multitenant SaaS solution, such as the following:

- No upgrades or patches
- No hardware
- Reduced maintenance
- Regular releases
- Always on the latest version

The time and money saved when considering these perks can be quite substantial, but aren't always the main drivers for moving your core HR to the cloud. Although they are certainly key factors, there are also other business drivers that can provide great value to your organization.

In addition to the multitenant and cloud-based features of Employee Central, there are also business drivers specific to using Employee Central. Business drivers such as hard *return on investment (ROI)* indicators, reduced *total cost of ownership (TCO)*—which can typically be between three and five times less than on-premise—and the need for fewer IT staff maintaining the systems are one set of benefits. However, there are also "soft" ROI indicators, such as the following:

- Ease of use/user experience
- Localization
- Mobility
- New ideas and modern design
- Built-in self-service and workflow approvals
- Extensibility
- New functionality

▶ Speed of innovation

▶ System of engagement

Coupled with the need to upgrade an aging on-premise HRIS (or for customers without a current HRIS), there can be a compelling business case for many organizations to make the move to Employee Central. The next section discusses how SAP's strategy and roadmap enable customers to make this move.

SAP SuccessFactors Strategy and Roadmap

SAP's strategy is to build out a feature-rich and feature-complete core HR system that reflects twenty-first century business practices and modern technology advances while not replicating SAP ERP HCM functionality in Employee Central. Due to the nature of HR technology, there will always be a large overlap in the type of functionality available in both systems and in competitor systems.

However, SAP works to design parallel functionality in a way that befits how it is used by enterprises today. In some areas, SAP ERP HCM offers richer functionality, and in others, Employee Central is superior. Over time, SAP plans to have superior functionality in Employee Central, but it is worth remembering that it took SAP almost twenty years to create a robust SAP ERP HCM system, and so it will take time for there to be parity in depth and richness of functionality. With that said, moving to Employee Central can bring great benefits not found in SAP ERP HCM.

From the outset, SAP has focused on the areas it knows best: globalization, enterprise-grade features, and flexibility. That said, each of these areas has been approached from a new perspective by SAP product management. For example, customization is no longer a feature of the cloud; it has been replaced by extensibility capabilities. We will touch on what this means in Chapter 5.

Due to the ever-changing nature of SAP's evolving and fluid roadmap for SAP SuccessFactors, it is almost impossible to provide roadmap information in this book that will remain relevant and up-to-date during its entire lifetime. However, SAP has confirmed that their short- to mid-term roadmap focuses on enhancing globalization, reporting, time management, benefits, and Contingent Workforce Management functionalities. Integration is also a continuous part of the overall roadmap for both Employee Central and the SAP SuccessFactors HCM Suite as a whole.

> **SAP SuccessFactors Integration**
>
> For further details on the integration with SAP SuccessFactors HCM for SAP or third-party vendors, see *Integrating SAP SuccessFactors with SAP* by Vishnu Kandi, Venki Krishnamoorthy, Donna Leong-Cohen, Prashanth Padmanabhan, and Chinni Reddygari (SAP PRESS, 2015).

SAP releases a public roadmap for SAP SuccessFactors HCM Suite — including Employee Central — each quarter on SAP Service Marketplace. This roadmap should be consulted for an overview of what SAP plans to release. It should be noted that SAP is not committed to releasing functionality on the roadmap, but provides instead an indication of those areas that it is considering for investment during the calendar year and beyond. The roadmap can be found at *http://service.sap.com/roadmap*. There, click the PRODUCT AND SOLUTION ROAD MAPS button and then click the LINE OF BUSINESS button.

Licensing and Release Cycle

The licensing and release cycles for Employee Central (and SAP SuccessFactors) differ from that for SAP ERP HCM. In this section, we will take a look at these cycles.

Licensing

Employee Central is licensed on an annual subscription basis with a fee per employee in the system. A contract length of three or five years is not uncommon. There are no additional fees, and the license currently includes a subscription for the Dell Boomi AtomSphere or SAP HANA Cloud Integration (HCI) middleware platforms for integrating Employee Central with other systems, such as SAP ERP or a third-party solution. At some point in the future, it is possible that Dell Boomi AtomSphere will no longer be offered to new subscribers of Employee Central.

Release Cycle

SAP SuccessFactors provides four releases per year for Employee Central, known as quarterly releases. Each quarterly release may contain a mix of new features, major enhancements, minor enhancements, and bug fixes. Releases are named for the quarter in which they are released and so are called Q1, Q2, Q3, and Q4. However, historically each release has a four-digit code denominating the two-digit year and two-digit month of the release, and this code may remain in common usage for some time. For example, the May 2015 release was called b1505, and the August 2015 release was called b1508.

Quarterly releases are first released into a preview environment, a month before the production system. This enables you to review new features and functionality prior to release in production, which can be useful for universal features (see below for definition). Table 1 details the typical quarterly release cycles.

Release	Test	Production
Q1	February	March
Q2	May	June
Q3	August	September
Q4	November	December

Table 1 Quarterly Release Cycles

These releases are pushed into the system automatically and require no effort from the customer.

New features are split into the following three types, each of which affects a customer differently:

▶ **Opt-in**
Opt-in features involve customers proactively enabling features if they wish to use them. This is usually performed in the Upgrade Center in OneAdmin.

▶ **Opt-out**
Opt-out features involve customers proactively disabling features if they do not wish to use them.

▶ **Universal**
Universal features are enabled for all customers and cannot be disabled. These are often communicated well in advance and are focused on stability or user interface enhancements.

Now that we've looked at the licensing parameters and release cycle of SAP SuccessFactors, next we'll provide an example of key enhancements released over the past few years.

Key Enhancements

To give some idea of what sort of enhancements have been released in the past and at what speed innovations are coming, Table 2 provides a brief overview of the key enhancements released in the last few years.

Release	Feature
Q3 2012 (b1207)	Mass Changes
Q4 2012 (b1210)	Position Management
Q4 2012 (b1210)	Global Assignments
Q3 2013 (b1308)	OData API
Q4 2013 (b1311)	Income Tax Declarations
Q2 2014 (b1405)	Global Benefits
Q3 2014 (b1408)	Concurrent Employment
Q3 2014 (b1408)	Employee Central Service Center
Q4 2014 (b1411)	Payroll Time Sheet
Q2 2015 (b1505)	Contingent Workforce Management
Q3 2015 (b1508)	External Event Framework

Table 2 Recently Released Key Enhancements

It is also worth noting that some major enhancements—including those mentioned previously—continue to be further enhanced in each release.

Summary

In this introduction, we provided a look at what Employee Central is and gave some background on the solution, features, functionality, business drivers, strategy, roadmap, licensing, and release cycle. In the following chapters, we will begin to dig deeper into the concepts of Employee Central, aspects of implementation, extensibility, features and functionality, and integration.

In Chapter 1 we will begin our Employee Central journey with a look at the basics and foundation needed to get started.

We hope that you find this title informative and useful in your cloud core HR journey, both as a foundation and as an ongoing reference.

Luke Marson
Murali Mazhavanchery
Rebecca Murray

PART I
Foundations

Employee Central offers a solid hire-to-retire system for the requirements of a modern workforce. However, such a robust offering has a number of different pieces that you should understand before jumping into the solution processes.

1   Employee Central Basics

Employee Central belongs to a suite in which individual components can operate independent of one another. It is not a requirement that a customer enable Employee Central to use the talent management, workforce analytics, or mobile applications in the suite. This offers a unique value proposition to the customer: start anywhere and go anywhere. Customers can choose to deploy Employee Central where the business imperative is most urgent.

When such a system is implemented, it becomes important to understand the nuances of the suite to deliver the maximum value to the customer. The SAP SuccessFactors system is designed to be a self-service application. This design manifests in many ways, such as in the term *user*, which equates not only to a user logging into the system, but also to a worker.

Detailed Configuration

For detailed configuration instructions, view the handbooks provided on SAP Service Marketplace, available at *http://service.sap.com/ec-ondemand* and *http://help.sap.com/ hr_ec*.

Provisioning is the part of the system that enables features with a cost implication. Sometimes, switches for specific features that have no cost impact to the customer are placed there as well. Customers do not have access to Provisioning, although some settings can be enabled by Customer Support or through the Upgrade Center. Troubleshooting should always begin with Provisioning. If the Provisioning settings are not set correctly, the system will not work as expected.

Understanding the different moving pieces of Employee Central and its key terminology is vital for building a foundation before transitioning to more advanced topics. This chapter discusses the basic terms, components, and elements that you need to understand in order to configure and administer Employee Central. We'll begin with a discussion of Employee Central's global reach.

1.1 Globalization and Localization

Employee Central is a global HR system. It comes with localizations for over seventy countries and features over thirty-five different languages (with full translations for standard-delivered fields).

In the Employee Central world, localizations include country-specific fields, picklists, validations, rules, reports, features, and more. This enables organizations to manage employees across different geographies while maintaining a global template of processes.

Some examples of localizations include the following:

- National ID formats and data input validation:
  - Documento Nacional de Identidad (DNI) for Argentina
  - Tax File Number (TFN) for Australia
  - Cédula de Identidad y Electoral (CIE) for Dominican Republic
  - National Insurance Number for UK
  - Social Security Number (SSN) for USA
- Address formats
- Legal entity data fields:
  - CUIT for Argentina
  - NAF Code for France
  - Certificado de Identificación Fiscal (ESP) for Spain
  - Federal Reserve Bank ID for USA
- Job classification data fields:
  - Asco Code for Australia
  - Occupational Classification for Canada
  - INSEE Code for France

- ‣ Inail Code for Italy
- ‣ Standard Occupational Classification Code for UK
- ▸ Personal information data fields:
  - ‣ Naturalized Citizen for Brazil
  - ‣ Name of Father/Husband/Legal Guardian for India
  - ‣ Military Certificate Number for Jordan and Lebanon
  - ‣ Iqama Number for Saudi Arabia
  - ‣ Professional Category ASM for Switzerland
- ▸ Job information data fields:
  - ‣ Occupational Code for Brazil
  - ‣ Labor Protection for China
  - ‣ New Calculation Average PPU for Czech Republic
  - ‣ Working Time Directive for UK
  - ‣ EEO Job Group for USA
- ▸ Reporting information:
  - ‣ Summary of Recent Employee Events (My Simplification) for Argentina
  - ‣ Work and Residence Permits (MoMi) for the Netherlands
  - ‣ Employment Equity Workforce Analysis (EEA2) for South Africa
  - ‣ Affirmative Action Plan (AAP) for USA
  - ‣ Equal Employment Opportunity analysis (EEO) for USA
- ▸ Picklists:
  - ‣ Military Certificate Status in Egypt
  - ‣ Counties in the UK
  - ‣ States in the US
  - ‣ Contract Type by country
  - ‣ Pay Scale Type by country
- ▸ Validations:
  - ‣ National ID
  - ‣ Bank Account
  - ‣ Address

We'll touch on globalization and localization features at various points throughout the book. Now that you understand the breadth of Employee Central's reach, next we'll discuss the building blocks of Employee Central: data models.

1.2 Data Models

The data model structure of Employee Central is built around several object types that interact with each other. Figure 1.1 shows the full logical object model structure of Employee Central.

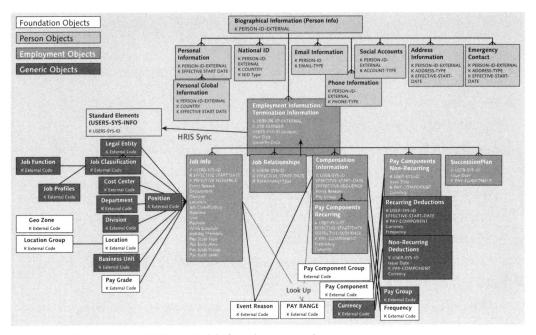

Figure 1.1 Logical Object Model of Employee Central

The objects in Figure 1.1 are color coded for the four different types of objects used in Employee Central:

▸ **Foundation Objects**
Foundational objects used to populate Employment Objects; see Section 1.4 for more details.

▸ **Person Objects**
Objects related to the person, such as Personal Information or National ID card information.

▶ **Employment Objects**
Objects related to a person's employment, such as Job Information or Compensation Information; multiple employments could exist if an employee has a concurrent or global assignment.

▶ **Generic Objects**
Objects created in the Metadata Framework (MDF), including common objects such as positions and some Foundation Objects; see Section 1.8 for more details.

Not shown in the diagram is the user object, which represents the user account (whether or not you use Employee Central). When using Employee Central, the user account is the basis of an employee. The system creates the user account automatically when an employee is hired and the appropriate data is populated into the User Data File (UDF). The Employee Profile reads and displays data from the UDF. When Employee Central is not used, the UDF is the employee record for the SAP SuccessFactors HCM Suite. The UDF stays up-to-date with HRIS Sync, which we cover in Section 1.10.

Four XML data models define the data structures in Employee Central:

▶ Succession Data Model

▶ Corporate Data Model

▶ Country-Specific Succession Data Model

▶ Country-Specific Corporate Data Model

Data models are XML-based, although some of their elements can be maintained in various screens in OneAdmin in Employee Central. We'll cover those elements throughout the book.

Let's take a brief look at each of these models now.

1.2.1 Succession Data Model

The Succession Data Model contains the definition of every element and entity in Employee Central. The Succession Data Model, contrary to its name, is not an entity relationship model; it is an XML file that contains the field properties and the user interface (UI) definition.

Historically, user elements and fields were the single place to define user attributes. *User Sys Info* — sometimes used interchangeably with the Employee Profile — is the canonical data of a person, user, and worker. In simple terms, it represents a current snapshot of all person and employment data. For processes that do not need effective-dating, it represents employee data. HRIS Sync keeps the data in sync between the elaborate structure of Employee Central and the snapshot.

When adding Employee Central in a talent instance, augment the Succession Data Model in the following manner:

1. Add all of the items between the background elements and the custom filters (tab elements, HRIS elements, and actions).

2. Add `dg-filters` between `element-permission` and `view-template`.

3. Add `hris-sync-mappings` at the very bottom after `view-template` and before `final/succession-data-model`.

4. Review any custom fields (1–15) for changes.

5. Update the standard elements that have picklists added.

6. Remove the field requirements of the standard elements, because now they need to be updated through Employee Central.

7. Load the XML in Provisioning, as shown in Figure 1.2.

8. Be sure the admin users are set up in the UDF.

Figure 1.2 Import/Export Data Model in Provisioning

1.2.2 Corporate Data Model

The Corporate Data Model contains the Object Definitions of the Foundation Objects. This includes the fields, labels, picklists, and so on found on each object. Since the Q4 2014 release, Foundation Objects have been migrated away from the Corporate Data Model to the MDF. As a result, the Corporate Data Model includes some Foundation Objects, whereas others are managed through the various MDF screens in OneAdmin.

The Corporate Data Model also defines associations between Foundation Objects and Generic Objects. An *association* is a relationship between two objects. SAP SuccessFactors Recruiting also uses the Corporate Data Model for the job code entity-based requisitions.

We'll cover Foundation Objects in Chapter 6 and the MDF in Chapter 5.

1.2.3   Country-Specific Succession Data Model

The Country-Specific Succession Data Model defines country-specific local attributes and behaviors. This includes country-specific fields for HRIS elements found in the Succession Data Model and those HRIS elements that are purely country-specific in nature, such as National ID. This data model is split up by country and includes a number of different elements:

▶ **Global Information**
The localized fields that are part of the Personal Information portlet.

▶ **Home address information**
Defines the address formats used for an employee's address.

▶ **National ID**
Defines the ID type and display format for national IDs, such as Social Security number; it is important to note that the system stores the data with the formatting.

▶ **Job, compensation, and employment information**
A field on the Job Information portlet may be defined as a country-specific field; it is important to note that a custom field defined in more than one country should have the same label, picklist, required, and visibility attributes across all countries. The Compensation Information and Employment Information portlets are also found in the Country-Specific Succession Data Model.

1.2.4   Country-Specific Corporate Data Model

The Country-Specific Corporate Data Model will—after the migration of the Job Classification object to the MDF—contain the country-specific formatting of the Location only. At one point in time, the Company (Legal Entity) and Job Classification local were defined in this data model. Legal Entity and Job Classification have been migrated to the MDF. Only the Corporate Address (tied to the Location object) is defined in the Country-Specific Corporate Data Model.

Now that we've looked at the main data models found in Employee Central that form the foundation, next let's look at Employee Central's UI-based module.

1.3   OneAdmin

OneAdmin is the UI-based configuration module designed for system administrators, HR administrators, and (in some cases) managers to perform various administrative activities. In the system, OneAdmin is called the Admin Center, and was previously called Admin Tools. In 2015, SAP released Next Gen Admin, which features a new UI and additional features and improvements for easy access to features and for monitoring administrative and system activities.

Much of the configuration performed in Employee Central—including for objects in the Succession Data Model and Country-Specific Succession Data Model—occurs in OneAdmin. Once all of the Foundation Objects are migrated onto MDF, the Corporate Data Model and Country-Specific Corporate Data Model will cease to be, and all configuration will be possible in OneAdmin.

Common OneAdmin configuration and maintenance activities include the following:

▸ Creating and maintaining Foundation Object data

▸ Modifying employee data objects and importing data into them

▸ Tracking stalled workflows and changing routes of workflows in flight

▸ Managing security

1.4   Foundation Objects

Foundation Objects is a collective term for the elements that define the foundational structures used to populate employee master data. They are classified into four groups:

▸ Organizational structures

▸ Job structures

▸ Pay structures

▸ Miscellaneous/other Foundation Objects

We will cover Foundation Objects in detail in Chapter 6, but we'll run through these various structures briefly now.

1.4.1 Organizational Structures

Legal Entity, Business Unit, Division, Department, and Cost Center make up the basic structures of the enterprise. Location is also used as an organizational structure element. You can create additional custom objects based on your organization's structure. The hierarchy of the organizational structures is as follows:

- **Legal Entity**
  This is at the top of the organizational hierarchy. It controls all country-specific behavior. In the Employee Central organizational management design, Legal Entity serves regulatory purposes and is specific to a country by definition.

- **Business Unit**
  This is at the top of the business hierarchy. Typically, Business Units tend to be organized either geographically or by lines of business (LOB). In some cases, it is a combination of both. It is best to leave Business Units and Legal Entities independent of each other, as they serve two disparate purposes.

- **Division and Department**
  Division follows below the Business Unit. A Department is a people unit.

- **Cost Center**
  This is a financial unit and is typically maintained in a finance system. Frequently, there is a link between Cost Centers and Departments. In the case of SAP ERP Financials, a delivered integration will feed the cost centers directly to Employee Central. It is a best practice to keep the Departments and Cost Centers separate, as finance cost center restructuring is very common and will likely cause changes to security, reporting, and workflow configurations if cost centers drive those processes.

In addition, as many levels of the organizational structure may be defined to create the structure necessary to support the organization.

1.4.2 Job Structures

Job Classification is the basic unit of the job structure. Job Functions and the Job Profile Builder make up the remainder of job structures.

The following describes each of these structures:

- **Job Classification**
  Job Classification defines the elements of a job, such as pay grade, level, standard working hours, employee class, and so on. Job Classifications have global

and local attributes, meaning that they have country-specific values and country-specific fields. Country-specific values can include job title; the field is valid for each country, and the value in each country may be different. Country-specific fields exist only in one country, for example FLSA Status for the USA, Standard Occupational Classification Code for the UK, and so on.

▸ **Job Functions**
Job Classifications are grouped into Job Functions, which are used to group Job Classifications into direct labor vs. indirect labor or administrative, professional, operational, and so on. You can use this attribute in reporting.

▸ **Job Profile Builder**
Job Classifications are used in conjunction with families and roles to provide integrated talent management (see Figure 1.3). They also form the basis of the Job Profile Builder. The Job Profile Builder creates a rich job profile that includes family, roles, certifications, competency, education, physical requirements, skills, interview questions, and so on. Job Profiles can be driven by Job Classification or by positions.

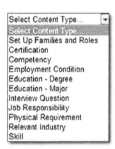

Figure 1.3 Elements of a Job Profile, Including Families and Roles

1.4.3 Pay Structures

Pay Component, Pay Component Group, Pay Range, Pay Grade, Frequency, Currency, and Pay Scale Structure make up the pay structures. The following list describes these elements:

▸ **Pay Component**
This is the unit of compensation administration. Compensations and deductions both share the Foundation Object. Pay Components are either recurring or nonrecurring. Likewise, they are either target or actual. Recurring pay targets may be used for nonrecurring payments, which enables reporting of targets vs. actuals. Pay Components can be units, amounts, or percentages.

- **Pay Component Group**

  Pay Components are grouped into Pay Component Groups, which you can use to create annualized compensation and to enable the creation of salary packages for employees. They also may be used in compensation planning, in which the basic pay is multicomponent. Pay Component Groups are always annualized and expressed in terms of one currency.

- **Pay Range**

  This is used to define the range of pay for a given period, with a min, mid, and max point created. Pay Range is used to calculate the Compa Ratio and Range Penetration.

- **Pay Grade**

  Pay Grades (also simply known as Grades) classify people into levels. Job Classifications are tied to Pay Grades, and a Grades itself has a Pay Grade Level that is used to identify the relative level of the Grade. This attribute can distinguish a promotion vs. a demotion from a lateral move.

- **Frequency**

  This is a non-effective-dated Foundation Object that contains the annualization factor. When the annualization factor is 0, then standard hours for the employee are used.

- **Currency**

  This provides an effective-dated list of currencies. The conversion rates associated with these currencies are not yet effective-dated.

- **Pay Scale Structure**

  This enables Pay Component values for employees to be defined based on a fixed pay structure. This is often used for unionized employees, for whom collective bargaining and contractual agreements exist to control employees' pay on a scaling basis.

1.4.4 Miscellaneous Foundation Objects

Other miscellaneous Foundation Objects exist and are mainly used for workflows. These include:

- **Workflows**

  This is used to define the route of the workflow. Workflows have approvers, contributors, and CC roles. Contributors can comment on a workflow, but cannot approve them. CC roles are notified after the workflow is completed. In some cases, workflows are set up with CC roles only.

▸ **Dynamic Role Assignment**
This provides a rule-based assignment of an approver based on foundational attributes. Using dynamic role assignment, you can define different approvers for different populations. For example, Controller could be defined for any combination of Business Unit, Legal Entity, Department, Job Classification, Grade, and so on.

1.5 Employee Interface, Information, and Maintenance

This section looks at the tools provided by SAP SuccessFactors and Employee Central for UI capabilities, access to employee information, and managing that information.

1.5.1 Employee Profile

The Employee Profile is a snapshot of a person, employment history, talent, and learning information. In the case of effective-dated entities, it represents a snapshot of the current effective record. This is also referred to as the UDF.

The Employee Profile consists of three parts:

▸ User information
▸ Background portlets
▸ Talent information

With the release of the People Profile (see Section 1.5.2), the latest iteration of the SAP SuccessFactors UI, the Employee Profile has effectively merged into Employee Central.

> **Further Resources**
>
> We will not be covering the Employee Profile in this book, although it is covered in detail in *SuccessFactors with SAP ERP HCM: Business Processes and Use* by Amy Grubb and Luke Marson (2nd edition, SAP PRESS, 2015).

1.5.2 People Profile

The People Profile is the latest version of the SAP SuccessFactors UI. This user interface uses SAPUI5 technology to bring the SAP Fiori experience to SAP SuccessFactors. The salient features of this UI are as follows:

- Consumer-grade user experience (UX)
- In-context employee, manager, and professional UX
- Single dashboard experience
- Responsive and role-based UI
- Improved navigation and information discovery
- Flexible and extensible administration
- Coherent and efficient profile data entry

With this UI, Employee Central and the Employee Profile merge into a single application. Figure 1.4 shows an example of the People Profile.

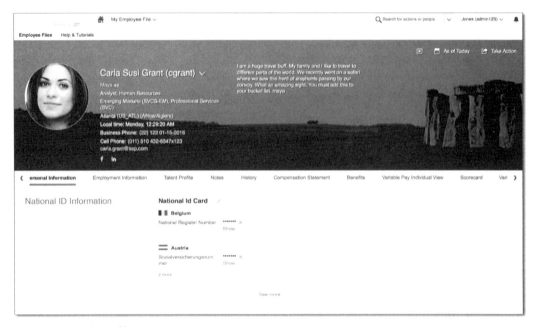

Figure 1.4 People Profile

1.5.3 Quickcard

The quickcard is accessed via the SEARCH box at the top of the screen (typically to the left of the user menu), from the Org Chart, or from the MY TEAM tile on the homepage if the user is a manager.

Figure 1.5 shows the expanded quickcard after searching for a specific employee. Typically, only the top third of the quickcard shows. The TAKE ACTION hyperlink is located below DIRECT REPORTS. Clicking it expands the full menu of options.

Figure 1.5 Quickcard

All actions and Employee Files views are displayed in the quickcard menu. Other available views and actions from modules other than Employee Central are also available, such as viewing the Variable Pay Statement.

1.5.4 Employee Files

Employee Files is where employee data is viewed and maintained by all users. It has built-in self-service capabilities for employees and managers, which are all controlled by Role-Based Permissions (RBP). Employee Files show both Employee Central and non-Employee Central screens (known as *views*). Several views are used for Employee Central:

- Personal Information
- Employment Information
- Pending Requests
- Payroll Information
- Time Sheet
- Time Off
- Manage Time Off
- Employee Benefits

Customers only using Employee Central, but who wish to display education, skills data, and so on, can leverage the Employee Profile view as well. If a Generic Object has been created with the Configuration UI, then that can also be viewed in Employee Files.

We'll discuss these screens in more detail in Chapter 3, Chapter 9, Chapter 10, and Chapter 18.

1.6   Transactions and Self-Services

Employee Central prides itself on having fully inclusive self-service capabilities. Unlike some other HR systems (particularly on-premise HR systems), no special self-service portal is required to access self-service transactions. In fact, Employee Central is designed with self-service principles included and uses a simple but robust mechanism to control self-service access and actions.

Employees, managers, HR administrators, or any other user group can be provided self-service access via the RBP framework. Self-service transactions are provided the same way, and users with this level of access can use the TAKE ACTION menu in the PERSONAL INFORMATION screen or EMPLOYMENT INFORMATION screen to run a transaction or action. Transactions can also be accessed via the quickcard.

Depending on the system configuration and features enabled, transactions can include changing Job Information, Compensation Information, and Employment Details, giving a spot bonus, sending someone on global assignment, giving an advance, terminating an employee, and more.

1.7   Events and Workflows

As you would expect of a core HR system, Employee Central uses events, Event Reasons, and employee statuses for the lifecycle of an employee. Event Reasons drive both the event and the status of an employee.

When taking an action for an employee—depending on the type of action—you can select an event and Event Reason. The employee's status will be driven by the Event Reason selected. If required, Event Reasons can be dynamically derived by the system based on rules. This means that managers and other users using self-service do not need to select the Event Reason manually, promoting better accuracy for historical data changes. We'll cover this topic in detail in Chapter 4.

Workflows can be applied to specific employee events. A workflow in Employee Central applies controls around transactions. It enables approval chains to be defined with various types of approvers and auditable history. The workflow rules were defined in an XML file until the Q2 2015 release, when the ability to define workflows in the business rules was released.

Workflows support pushback to the initiator, inflight changes with route recalculation and without route recalculation, delegation, and more. The route change without recalculation enables a final check before confirmation, during which any errors can be corrected by a professional user. Workflows are covered in detail in Chapter 4.

1.8   Extensibility

Employee Central provides a means for extensibility, allowing users to move beyond the standard system setup. Employee Central uses the MDF, Rules Engine, and extensions created on SAP HANA Cloud Platform to achieve as expanded setup.

The MDF is a set of tools for building SAP SuccessFactors applications. The MDF contains an object and a UI definition and is the framework on which all new Employee Central functionality is built. Position Management, Time Off, Employee Benefits, deductions, advances, and income tax declarations are examples of functionality built on the MDF.

The MDF is also the platform for extensibility of the application. Customer-specific objects may be defined in the MDF. At this point, Employee Customers may add up to twenty-five parent custom objects within their subscriptions.

A core set of Employee Central objects are not built on the MDF. These objects are being migrated to the MDF in a phased manner, starting with the Foundation Objects. This project is referred to as *EC2MDF*. Many of the Foundation Objects have been migrated, but at the time of writing (December 2015) some objects have not yet been migrated.

Objects and fields defined by the customer are automatically prefixed with `cust_` in order to separate delivered objects from customer-defined objects. These custom objects can be added into Employee Files, used by administrators, or even used as lookup tables. Many use cases exist for creating custom objects.

The *Rules Engine* is used to enforce business rules behavior. The Rules Engine enables validation, defaulting, and similar behaviors. Rules may be attached to objects or fields by means of triggers such as `onInit`, `onChange`, and `onSave` for objects defined in the MDF and for non-MDF objects as well.

The Rules Engine also contains a list of functions for specific purposes, ranging from mathematical functions to date/time functions to derivation functions and more. Functions are constantly added. Typically, Time Management or Position Management drive them, but more and more general functions are added to enable specific types of processing.

Almost all delivered business logic in Employee Central moves through the Rules Engine. Rules can be used to set data, raise errors and warnings, and trigger events. Rules are triggered on online transactions as well as offcycle batch transactions. Offcycle batch processing was introduced in the Q3 2015 release, and over the next few releases there will be significant enhancements to these capabilities.

Besides the MDF and Rules Engine, further extensibility can be found with SAP HANA Cloud Platform, on which you can build Employee Central extension applications. These extension applications enable you to build custom applications and functionality and embed them in Employee Central so that to the end user they seem part of the Employee Central offering.

1.9 Business Configuration UI

The parts of Employee Central that are not on the MDF can be configured using the Business Configuration UI (BCUI). The person- and employment-related objects that form the core of Employee Central can be configured here.

The types of changes that are typically performed through the BCUI include the following:

▸ Changing the picklist attached to a field

▸ Changing the reference type of a field

▸ Enabling or disabling a custom field

▸ Changing the field label and/or the translations of the field label

▸ Changing the HRIS Sync mapping to the Employee Profile

Figure 1.6 shows the Job Information portlet in the BCUI, and Figure 1.7 shows details of the POSITION field on Job Information.

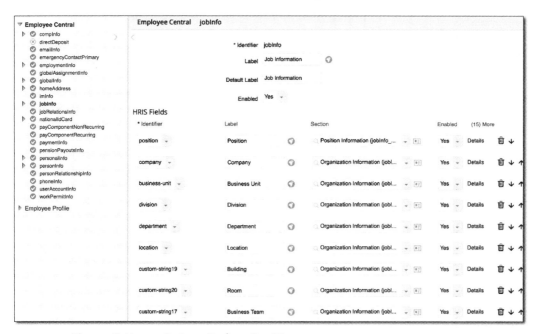

Figure 1.6 Manage Business Configuration UI

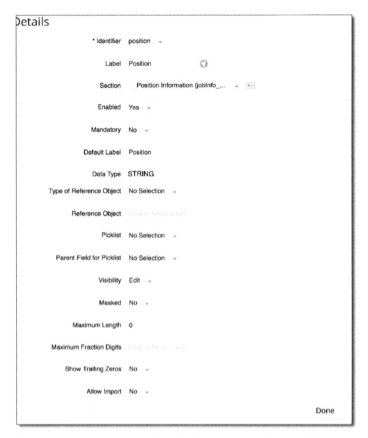

Details

* Identifier	position
Label	Position
Section	Position Information (jobInfo_...
Enabled	Yes
Mandatory	No
Default Label	Position
Data Type	STRING
Type of Reference Object	No Selection
Reference Object	Click to focus to edit
Picklist	No Selection
Parent Field for Picklist	No Selection
Visibility	Edit
Masked	No
Maximum Length	0
Maximum Fraction Digits	Click to focus to edit
Show Trailing Zeros	No
Allow Import	No

Done

Figure 1.7 Details of the Position Field in Job Information in BCUI

We'll cover the BCUI in detail in Chapter 9, Section 9.5.3.

1.10   HRIS Sync

HRIS Sync is a process that creates a snapshot of current data from Employee Central in the UDF and keeps this data synchronized when changes are made to data in Employee Central. This snapshot is used in the Employee Profile and by many of the talent applications in SAP SuccessFactors.

HRIS Sync runs in two modes: real-time and offline. The real-time synchronization is executed whenever a prospective change is made. The offline process runs as a scheduled job to process any future-dated transaction that has become effective.

HRIS Sync is delivered out of the box for the standard fields, such as first name, last name, department, division, and so on. A section in the Succession Data Model called `custom-sync-settings` may be used to override the delivered sync or add custom sync mappings.

Additorial Resources

For more information on the fields that are synchronized in real time, refer to SAP Note 2172427 (HRIS Sync—Data Synchronization From EC to EP).

1.11 Reporting

Reporting in Employee Central comes in three forms:

▸ **Ad hoc reporting**
Schema-based reporting tool for building queries on the fly and making reports available to other users.

▸ **Advanced reporting**
In-depth reporting tool that provides over seventy standard reports and provides an intuitive user interface to build simple and complex reports with the Online Report Designer (ORD). It is built on Operational Data Store (ODS) technology.

▸ **Employee Delta Export**
Employee Delta Export is designed to export a delta of employee data from Employee Central to be used with small country payrolls. This is covered in Chapter 19, Section 19.10.

We'll cover reporting in more detail in Chapter 17.

1.12 Deployment Models for SAP Customers

SAP SuccessFactors has four deployment models: *Talent Hybrid, Side-by-Side, Core Hybrid,* and *Full Cloud HCM*—all of which are shown in Figure 1.8. Employee Central uses *only* the Core Hybrid, Side-by-Side, and Full Cloud HCM deployment models. The Talent Hybrid deployment model is not used by Employee Central in SAP SuccessFactors since only the talent modules are used, rather than the HRIS (Employee Central).

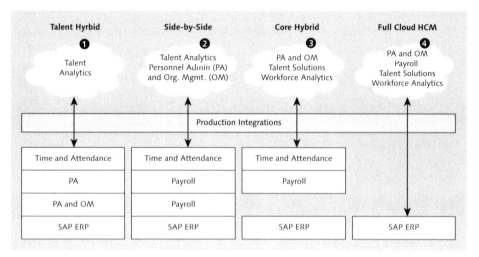

Figure 1.8 SAP SuccessFactors Deployment Models

In the *Full Cloud HCM* deployment model, all HR applications are in the cloud with some other processes in SAP ERP, such as sales distribution or materials management. In this deployment model, other processes may exist in third-party solutions.

In the *Core Hybrid* deployment model, core HR and talent applications are in the cloud with some other HR processes (such as time and attendance and/or payroll) in SAP ERP. In this deployment model, other processes may exist in third-party solutions other than SAP ERP.

In the *Side-by-Side* deployment model, the existing SAP ERP HCM system is retained and Employee Central is added to the landscape for existing and/or new employee populations. For an example use case, let's say that an existing subsidiary or newly acquired subsidiary has no HCM system and is put into an instance of Employee Central instead of the existing SAP ERP HCM system, which could be a costly exercise. Another possible use case might be that a "big bang" implementation of Employee Central is not feasible or possible, but introducing Employee Central brings strategic value.

There are numerous reasons that a company may choose the Side-by-Side model. It may be that a customer wishes to take advantage of new innovations while retaining the existing SAP ERP HCM investment or that the customer wishes to roll-out Employee Central across the organization for MSS or ESS while keeping HR administrators using SAP ERP HCM. Two types of Side-by-Side deployment model exist (see Figure 1.9):

▸ **Consolidated**

In the consolidated scenario, Employee Central is used as the system of record for all employees, but some processes are still performed in SAP ERP HCM. In this scenario, data is replicated back to SAP ERP HCM.

▸ **Distributed**

In the distributed scenario, employees are split across Employee Central and SAP ERP HCM. Access for all employees is through Employee Central, but all changes are made in the respective system in which the employee belongs. For employees mastered in SAP ERP HCM, a UI mash-up exists to access on-premise functionality through Employee Central. Figure 1.10 shows an example of this.

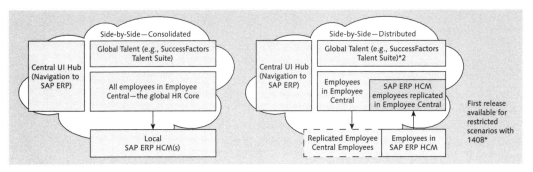

Figure 1.9 Consolidated and Distributed Scenarios

Figure 1.10 SAP ERP HCM Screen in Employee Central

In order to understand which deployment model might work for you, examine the decision tree in Figure 1.11 to review the most appropriate options.

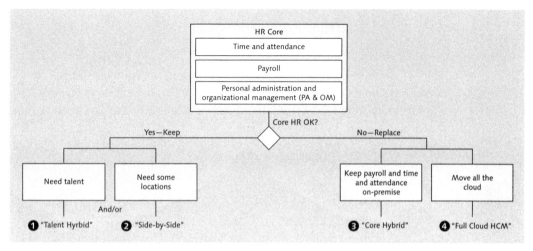

Figure 1.11 Decision Tree to Choose Deployment Model

1.13 Summary

In this chapter, we covered the basics of Employee Central. We looked at the concepts of globalization and localization, the various data models, and extensibility and deployment models for integration. Throughout, we discussed common elements of Employee Central, such as events and transactions, as well as the People Profile and OneAdmin.

We hope that this brief introduction has provided some insight into the topics that lie ahead. In the next chapter, we'll take a look at implementation steps and other implementation aspects that you'll need to consider as you implement Employee Central in your organization.

Proper preparation can ensure a successful implementation. There are several steps and considerations to review prior to starting an Employee Central implementation and several items to track during and after implementation.

2   Implementation Steps and Considerations

People who are excited to implement Employee Central often say they want to hit the ground running. People who are overwhelmed by the process are often hesitant to get going. In both cases, we need a clear-cut path to follow so that our runners don't trip and our distressed friends can see the light. Having a tried-and-true project plan, a formally defined project team, and a series of defined steps to follow to completion will help us successfully implement Employee Central.

In this chapter, we will examine the proper steps for getting started with an Employee Central implementation, including pre-work and kick-off. We will discuss the concept of the project team and member roles, and we will review SAP's project methodology: *SAP Launch*. The chapter ends with information about post-go-live maintenance and support resources.

2.1   Implementation Considerations

We need to think about and understand several things before embarking on an Employee Central implementation. We need to be able to answer questions such as "Who is involved?" and "What will each person be doing?" We must give thought to the idea of balancing scope with timelines and resource availability. This section highlights the steps we need to take during a project lifecycle and what things a project team should think about while in its infancy.

2.1.1   Project Checklist

The *project checklist* contains a series of steps that a project manager and/or lead consultant should complete prior to beginning an Employee Central implementation. Getting things moving is the first step and a signal to all involved that the sales cycle is over and the project implementation portion is about to begin.

The checklist is geared towards the implementation team, but there are overlapping activities for customer participants as well. The project checklist is divided into four main categories with subtasks. The following is a high-level overview of the project checklist; a full copy is available for implementation consultants through the SAP Partner Portal:

- ▶ Internal kick-off meeting and transition from sales to professional services:
  - ▷ Review documentation gathered and produced during the sales cycle
  - ▷ Review the scope of work (SOW) to ensure full understanding of project commitments
  - ▷ Engage technical resources if they are required
- ▶ Set up SAP Business ByDesign or other project planning solutions:
  - ▷ Set up initial project plan including start and end dates
  - ▷ Confirm project tasks and time estimates, including time estimates and resources when known
  - ▷ Secure project resources
- ▶ Set up project initiation documentation/repository:
  - ▷ Set up a repository for project documentation (e.g., SAP Customer Share-Point)
- ▶ Introductory call with implementers/customer:
  - ▷ Arrange a call to introduce the customer team and the implementation team
  - ▷ Deliver full kick-off presentation to customer team to highlight the project scope and timeline
  - ▷ Review the SOW to ensure expectations will be met
  - ▷ Help customer enroll in the Customer Community and register for Project Team Orientation (PTO) training

2.1.2 Project Team Structure

A good project team is essential for a smooth implementation, but just as critical to a project's success is a thorough understanding of each team member's role and responsibilities. Work cannot be performed in a vacuum. Implementation team members must bring a solid understanding of the system's capabilities and best practices recommendations to the project. Customer team members must contribute their business drivers and understanding. Table 2.1 shows the expertise brought to the table by both customers and SAP SuccessFactors team members.

Customer Team	SAP SuccessFactors Team
▶ Business drivers	▶ Product expertise
▶ Implementation objectives	▶ Best practices
▶ Overall project management	▶ SAP SuccessFactors HCM domain knowledge and experience
▶ Current process and system knowledge	
▶ Management and business issues	▶ Proven implementation expertise
	▶ Expert technical skills

Table 2.1 Customer Team and SAP SuccessFactors Team Skills

A solid project team structure must be determined and communicated to all team members. The following team member structure suggestions have proven successful:

- **Implementation team**
  Members of the implementation should be knowledgeable about Employee Central and be familiar with best practices setups and scenarios. The implementers should be able to guide the project team in making decisions.

- **Implementation project team leader**
  This individual must work closely with the customer project manager to ensure that the scope remains constant and consistent and that all team members are working towards project completion. He or she must keep work on track and escalate issues as needed.

- **Main functional consultant/solution architect**
  This person is responsible for the requirements gathering and configuration of the Employee Central solution. He or she also works hand-in-hand with the customer during testing and training to ensure a smooth transition. In the event of additional functional consultants, this main resource may act as more of a solution architect. A solution architect performs the same outward facing role as a

lead consultant but does not participate in much of the system configuration. He or she performs quality assurance reviews as the project progresses.

- **Additional functional consultants**
  Depending on the size and scale of the project, additional consultants may be needed to assist with configuration, data load preparation, and documentation.

- **Lead technical consultant**
  This individual is responsible for the technical activities required for the project, including integration, interfaces, and any Single Sign-On (SSO) functionality.

- **Functional/technical liaison**
  In very large projects or projects with numerous interfaces, a liaison may help organize data and ensure that consistent data values and codes are used across all systems.

- **Customer team**
  Members of the customer team should be knowledgeable about their business processes and have a clear vision about the future desired state of the Employee Central solution.

- **Overall project manager**
  The overall project manager has day-to-day oversight of the project and is responsible for keeping all team members in alignment with project goals. He or she is also responsible for the project budget and for resource gathering as needed. This individual often keeps track of project planning documents and organizes meetings between parties.

- **Business lead**
  The business lead is the head customer representative who is a specialist in the area being implemented and has the ability to make day-to-day decisions regarding requirements. This person is often in line to become an administrator or primary HR user within Employee Central.

- **Business specialists/generalists**
  Business specialists and generalists provide good insight into current and future vision states of the company's business. These people actively participate in requirements gathering and testing to help ensure that the planned vision is being realized.

- **Technical team members**
  These individuals are traditionally members of the company's Information Technology (IT) group. They are necessary to the project because they can

confirm network and computer availability, help with firewalls and SSO, and provide SFTP sites when needed. Their level of involvement depends on the size and scope of the project.

▸ **Auxiliary team members**
Other participants may be needed during various phases of the project cycle. Common examples include company trainers, internal auditors, change management specialists, and communications specialists.

▸ **Others**
In addition to the previously listed team members, the customer team should have project sponsors and a steering committee to help drive the vision and the need for change across the organization. Often, a project sponsor from the implementer team will be a member of the steering committee to ensure continuity between the teams.

Project Managers

In the initial days of implementing Employee Central, the customer traditionally provided the project manager. With the increased functionality of Employee Central and the overwhelming business need to exchange data with advanced time and payroll systems, we often see a dedicated project manager assigned to the team from either the customer or the implementer. With so many moving pieces, you may need a dedicated resource with experience in managing a large-scale, multi-system solution.

Project responsibilities should be doled out during the kick-off meeting. Some items may be specifically called out in the SOW, such as end user training and materials, but other items may still be up in the air. Resources should be assigned to create project documentation, maintain and update the documentation, produce administrator training materials, and so on. You don't want to begin a project with a series of assumptions about responsibilities. Every task should be planned for in a detailed project plan.

Keeping a project team on task and working towards common goals can be an overwhelming task. SAP has developed a best practices methodology to help project teams work together and achieve milestones.

2.1.3 Project Methodology

Employee Central is implemented according to the SAP Launch methodology. SAP Launch is the project implementation methodology used for all of SAP's

Software-as-a-Service (SaaS) implementations. It breaks the implementation into four phases and designates a series of activities and deliverables for each phase. Using a standard approach to implementation helps ensure quality and consistency from project to project. SAP Launch uses best practices templates and predefined content to help accelerate implementations, from discovery all the way to go-live. The SAP Launch methodology consists of four phases:

1. Prepare

2. Realize

3. Verify

4. Launch

At the end of each phase is a *quality gate (q-gate)* that acts as a checkpoint to ensure phase completion.

SAP Launch was previously known as *BizXpert*, a methodology exclusive to SAP SuccessFactors implementations. In August 2014, this method became applicable to all SAP cloud solutions and was renamed SAP Launch to denote the change.

In this section, we will review the four phases of the SAP Launch method, beginning with the prepare phase.

Prepare

In the *prepare* phase, the project team works to thoroughly understand the project scope, role definitions, timelines, and budget (see Figure 2.1).

Let's go over the key tasks of this phase:

▸ **Internal kick-off meeting takes place within the implementation team**
The team begins the project checklist, and the project manager meets with the sales team for official transition and to become acquainted with the project and its scope.

▸ **Project planning and resource booking**
Both the customer team and the implementation team begin to acquire and secure appropriate resources. The teams direct some effort to planning a timeline and major milestones.

▸ **Project Team Orientation**
The customer team attends PTO training (see Section 2.4.1).

▶ **Kick-off meeting**
The customer team and implementation team come together to meet and learn about expected responsibilities and desired outcomes.

▶ **Requirements gathering workshops**
The implementation team leads a series of workshops to help determine system requirements.

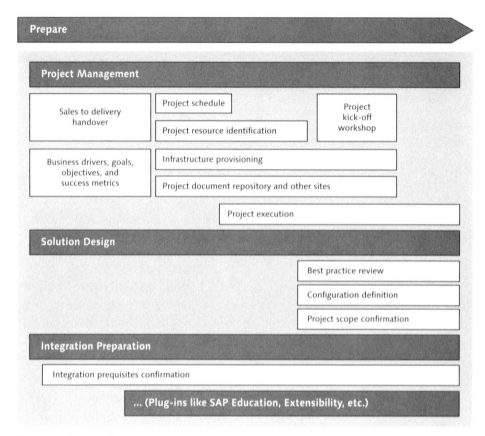

Figure 2.1 Prepare Phase

To pass the q-gate for the prepare phase of the project, all stakeholders agree to the scope of the project. Change orders may be needed for activities beyond the scope.

Realize

During the *realize* phase, the solution is configured, reviewed, and tested a series of three times. Each time through the process is called an *iteration*, and each project has three iterations. During this phase, the solution is not only built but is fine-tuned to meet the customer's requirements. Project management activities continue during this phase (see Figure 2.2).

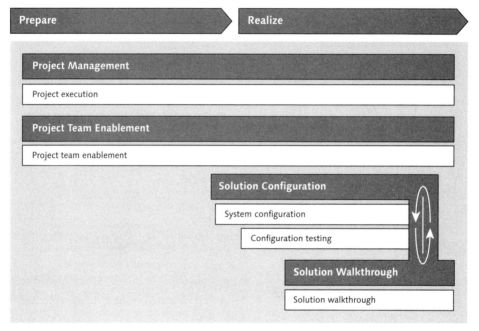

Figure 2.2 Realize Phase

Typical activities during this phase include the following:

▸ Configuration and refinement

▸ Data migration

▸ Integration work

▸ Custom report creation

▸ Initial admin training

▸ Iteration testing

To pass the q-gate for the realize phase of the project, all stakeholders agree that the solution has been satisfactorily configured to meet the requirements that were given. The system is ready for final testing, including testing of interfaces and data flow.

Verify

The *verify* phase of SAP Launch includes the final user acceptance testing (UAT), in which the customer performs a final round of testing. Not only is the solution tested in a standalone manner, but all integrations and touch points are tested as well. This means that any interfaces built for other systems should be tested in a real-life manner during this phase (see Figure 2.3).

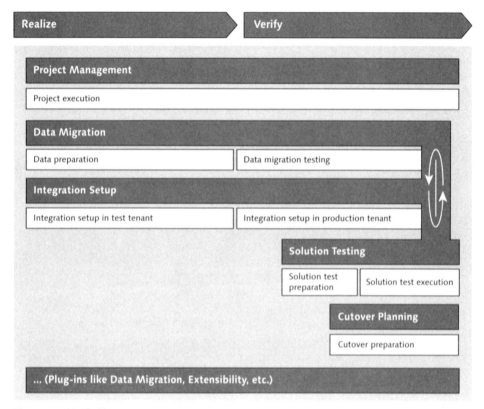

Figure 2.3 Verify Phase

Typical tasks during the verify phase include the following:

▶ UAT

▶ Integration testing (end-to-end with all data points participating)

- ▶ Robust administrator training
- ▶ End user training for managers, employees, and business partners
- ▶ The initial creation of a cutover/go-live plan

To pass the q-gate for the verify phase of the project, all stakeholders agree that the system is ready for go-live and that the end users, administrators, and HR persons are ready to use the system.

Launch

The *launch* phase of the project begins with the preparation of the production environment, ramps up with the move of configuration from the development and test environments into production, includes the import of employee data into production, and ends with the active use of the system (see Figure 2.4).

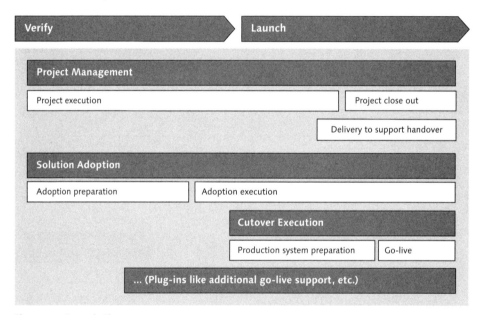

Figure 2.4 Launch Phase

Typical launch activities include the following:

- ▶ Revision and execution of the cutover/go-live plan
- ▶ Handover of the system to the customer
- ▶ A predetermined period of support by the implementation team

- Transition of the customer to the SAP SuccessFactors support team
- Completion of the project

To pass the q-gate for the launch phase of the project, all stakeholders agree that the cutover is complete.

2.1.4 Project Delivery

With the scope defined, the team assembled, and a methodology in place, the only thing left for us to do is to deliver the solution. Project delivery is not just an end result; rather, it is a project-long process whereby we constantly work towards goals, track and measure progress, and celebrate milestones. We use a project plan, tracking tools, and documentation to help us along this process.

When implementing Employee Central, we have a series of documents available to us to assist with the tracking and measuring process. These documents are part of the *SuccessFactors Delivery Toolkit*, a bank of templates and collateral that helps us meet and document the milestones in SAP Launch. Examples of these template documents include the following:

- Project Kick-Off
- Customer Welcome Kit
- Project Plan
- Configuration Workbooks

  System requirements are gathered and documented within the Configuration Workbooks. Employee Central has multiple workbooks to choose from, depending on the scope of the project:

    - Foundation Objects
    - Employee Data
    - Event Reasons and Transactions/Workflow
    - Time Off
    - Basic Profile
- Status Report Templates
- Meeting Note Templates
- Sign-Off Templates for the four q-gates

The SuccessFactors Delivery Toolkit is available for implementers from the SAP/ Partner Portal via the menu path HCM Cloud Partner Services • Implementation • Launch Delivery Toolkit.

2.1.5 Working with Third-Party Providers

Depending on the scope and nature of your implementation, you may need to work with third-party providers. This is fairly common with Employee Central implementations, because time, benefits, and payroll solutions from third parties are supported. A third-party solution may already exist and only require integration, or it could be a part of a larger HRIS transformation implementation. Regardless of the scenario, we will need to engage the third party that produces the solution and work closely with both functional and technical representatives to fully understand data needs and connectivity options. If Employee Central supplies demographic data to a third-party system, then Employee Central must contain the third party's required data fields. Do not forget to take third-party requirements into account during your own requirements gathering processes.

> **Important!**
>
> Do not delay establishing contact with third-party providers. Many of them will offer helpful tips for data setup and exchange. You must ensure that you gather and store all data necessary to support their processes if their data will originate in Employee Central.

Now that we've looked at the various implementation considerations and SAP Launch methodology, next let's discuss setting up Employee Central.

2.2 Setting Up Employee Central

The set up required for Employee Central involves a number of steps, and each should be considered carefully. In this section, we will begin by looking at the setup checklist provided by SAP SuccessFactors for implementation. We'll then look at the tasks that must be completed in Provisioning and OneAdmin to connect all of the dots.

2.2.1 Setup Checklist

SAP SuccessFactors has a recommended fourteen-step implementation sequence that should be used when implementing Employee Central. The fourteen steps represent the key tasks and areas of configuration that should be completed to have a fully functioning Employee Central solution. The steps should be implemented in order, and each step should be completed before moving on to the next because there are numerous dependencies involved. Most of these steps are the responsibility of the implementation consultant, but customer involvement is key in some areas.

Let's review the fourteen-step sequence:

1. Activate Employee Central and its supporting components by completing the Provisioning setup under COMPANY SETTINGS.
2. Create a super admin in Provisioning.
3. Configure and import the Corporate Data Model.
4. Configure and import the Succession Data Model.
5. Configure and import the Country-Specific Corporate Data Model and the Country-Specific Succession Data Model.
6. Import the picklists template.
7. Create your Foundation Objects.
8. Configure and import the Propagation Rules Data Model.
9. *Optional*: Configure and import the Event Reason Derivation Rules Data Model.
10. *Optional*: Configure and import the Workflow Rules Data Model.
11. Set up Role-Based Permission (RBP).
12. Import employee data.
13. Set up and run HRIS Sync as a recurring job.
14. *Optional*: Set up Leaves of Absence.

These fourteen steps should be considered the golden standard by which all Employee Central projects are implemented. Following each step in order will result in a thoroughly executed solution.

The first two steps contain activities that must be executed in *Provisioning*. Provisioning is the backend setup area available only to implementers. If you are an implementer, you should be sure to perform these actions when you first begin a project. If you are a customer, these steps should have been completed for you.

Let's review the activities and settings that should be completed in Provisioning for a new customer setup.

2.2.2 Provisioning

Provisioning is the backend area of SAP SuccessFactors in which modules and additional functionality are selected and activated for customers. Some options are preselected for us, and others must be manually applied based on the modules being implemented and the desired functionality of each module.

Employee Central is probably the most complex module to provision, because it contains multiple dependencies and offers numerous enhancements or optional pieces of functionality. As new functionality is released, new options may need to be selected or provisioned. Older options do not need to be deselected, because SAP SuccessFactors builds new functionality on the premise that older functionality will be added to or replaced.

This section assumes that the implementer has access to Provisioning. If you are an implementer and do not have the appropriate access, you should contact your onboarding manager for assistance. He or she will ensure you receive the proper training and request Provisioning access for you.

Once you are logged into Provisioning, select the company you are setting up and then choose EDIT COMPANY SETTINGS • COMPANY SETTINGS. This brings up the complete listing of assigned and available-to-be-assigned functionality. Each section has its own SAVE button, so sections should be filled out one at a time.

Provisioning settings should be made in the following areas:

▶ **Enable Employee Central V2 and dependent entities**
Dependent entities include Foundation Objects, Employee Profile, Generic Objects, Effective-Dated Data Platform, Role-Based Permission, Admin 2.0, Version 11 and Version 11 UIs

▶ **Enable Optional Functionality**
Time Off, Position Management, Alternative Cost Centers, Global Assignment, and Payment Information

▶ **Enable Employee-Specific Reporting**
Ad Hoc Report Builder and Standard Reports Bin, Employee Profile, Foundation Objects, Person and Employment Info, Job Information, Person and Employment Audit, Person and Employment Export, Recurring Compensation Information, Non-Recurring Compensation Information, and RBP reports

▶ **Document Attachment Functionality**

- ▸ **Web Services**
  Employee Central SOAP APIs and others (as needed)

Employee Central Provisioning Settings

A complete listing of Employee Central Provisioning settings are available for implementers in the Employee Central Master Implementation Guide, which can be found at *http://help.sap.com/hr_ec?current=hr_compensation*. This guide is updated each quarter to reflect module changes and should be consulted each quarter to ensure that updates are accounted for. The guide is available on the SAP Service Marketplace, referenced in Section 2.4.2.

2.2.3   Admin Center

The Admin Center of SAP SuccessFactors is the main area for system administrators to monitor and maintain Employee Central and other SAP SuccessFactors modules. This area allows for the maintenance of Foundation Objects, system settings, and employee data. Access to different sections of this area is controlled through RBPs (see Chapter 3).

Admin Center History

Prior to the 2015 Q3 release, the Admin Center was known as Admin Tools. The Admin Center still contains Admin Tools, along with additional functionality. Admin Tools has been available in its current form since 2011. Prior to 2011, Admin Tools was available with a different look and feel. This setup is sometimes referred to as *Old Admin Tools*. Although a handful of legacy customers continue to use Old Admin Tools, it has become obsolete as of Q3 2015 and is not supported for general use.

There are currently two supported versions of the Admin Center: OneAdmin and Next Gen Admin. OneAdmin is a standalone version, whereas Next Gen Admin functions as an add-on or enhancement to OneAdmin. They are both supported in a single system, and each individual admin user can choose which version he or she prefers to use.

OneAdmin

OneAdmin is the core area of the Admin Center. In OneAdmin, administrators have the ability to make changes to modules—such as Employee Central—and to maintain employee and foundation data. It is the area we traditionally think of when we hear the terms *Admin Tools* and *Admin Center*.

The following applications are supported in OneAdmin (see Figure 2.5):

▶ ADMIN TOOLS

   ▷ COMPANY PROCESSES & CYCLES

   ▷ MANAGE EMPLOYEES

▶ TOOL SEARCH

▶ UPGRADE CENTER

▶ MY (ADMINISTRATOR) FAVORITES

▶ NEWS & UPDATES

▶ RESOURCES & MATERIALS

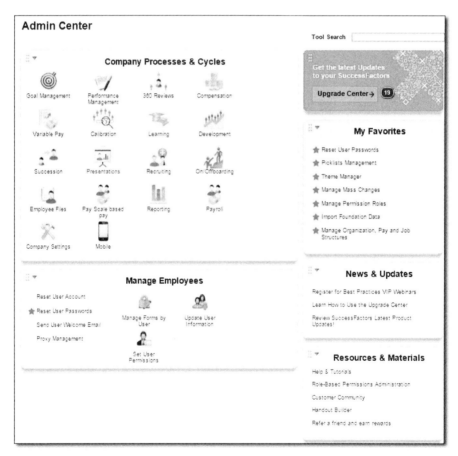

Figure 2.5 OneAdmin

Next Gen Admin

Next Gen Admin was introduced in Q2 2015. It serves as an augmentation piece for OneAdmin. Next Gen Admin contains portlets and analytics including the following (see Figure 2.6):

▸ ADMIN ALERTS

▸ SCHEDULED JOBS

▸ PAGE VIEWS

▸ EVENT CALENDAR

▸ TOOLS

▸ INTEGRATION CENTER

▸ UPGRADE CENTER

Each portlet can be accessed and drilled into for more information.

Figure 2.6 Next Gen Admin

Administrators who use Next Gen Admin can switch back and forth between Next Gen Admin and OneAdmin by clicking on the SWITCH BACK TO link on each screen, as shown in Figure 2.7.

Figure 2.7 Switch between OneAdmin and Next Gen Admin

Setup

In order to use Next Gen Admin, RBPs and the Action Search feature must be enabled as prerequisites. RBP must be activated by an implementer or SAP SuccessFactors support. The Action Search feature can be enabled by that same party or by applying the appropriate upgrade from the Upgrade Center. See Section 2.4 for more information about the Upgrade Center.

Once these two items are enabled, we can apply the Next Gen Admin upgrade to our system by applying the Next Gen Admin update from the Upgrade Center in Admin Tools. Navigate to ADMIN CENTER • UPGRADE CENTER • IMPORTANT • UPGRADES. Select the upgrade titled NEXT GEN ADMIN and click APPLY. The system will first check for the two prerequisites mentioned previously. If both have been met, then you can choose to apply the update. If the update is successful, you will receive a confirmation message, as shown in Figure 2.8.

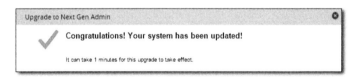

Figure 2.8 Successful Application of the Next Gen Admin Upgrade

Congratulations! You've completed your Employee Central implementation and are ready for the next steps. In the next section, we will discuss the post-implementation considerations and ongoing administrative tasks in Employee Central.

2.3   Post-Implementation and Ongoing Administration

If you're an implementer, then you should ensure that your customer is fully trained and comfortable maintaining the system. In this section, we will discuss the use of SAP SuccessFactors support for customers, and post-implementation maintenance for system health.

2.3.1   SAP SuccessFactors Support

After an agreed-upon period of post-go-live support, implementers should complete the project close-out documentation (see Section 2.1.4) and transition customers over to SAP SuccessFactors support.

The process of transitioning to SAP SuccessFactors support should begin approximately four weeks prior to go-live. This allows enough time for making introductions, sharing documentation, and conducting orientations. Once go-live completes and the implementation team rolls off the project, the SAP SuccessFactors support team will be the customer's primary point of assistance.

There are three levels of support available, and each level has a slightly different transition and use process. The support site can be accessed by all customers by going to *support.sap.com*. Once there, the following support cases are available:

- ▶ **Enterprise Support, Cloud Edition**
  The implementer should introduce the customer to the Enterprise Support process by sending an orientation email with a link to the *SuccessFactors Support Resource Kit*. This kit contains information about the support process, how to get assistance, anticipated response times, and how to receive product updates.

- ▶ **Platinum/Premium Experience Plan Support**
  The implementer should first contact the customer success manager and arrange for a check in four weeks prior to go-live. The implementer will bring the customer success manager up to speed on the status of the project. The implementer will also send the customer a copy of the SuccessFactors Support Resource Kit. At an introductions meeting, the customer success manager will meet the customer, and avenues for ongoing support and product updates will be reviewed at that time.

- ▶ **Preferred Care Support**
  Preferred Care Support begins at the start of the project implementation, so no transition process is needed.

If you're a customer, in addition to knowing how to contact support, you may have additional post-go-live maintenance activities that you may need or want to perform within the system. We discuss these activities in the next section.

2.3.2   Post-Implementation System Maintenance

Employee Central was built with flexibility and ease of use in mind. The system can accommodate restructuring and mass data changes well. As your organization changes shape and size, so too can Employee Central. When mass data changes need to be made, the system can assist by accepting data in multiple manners.

Here are a few of the most commonly performed system maintenance tasks, with references to instructions:

- Adding and editing Foundation Data:
    - Use the Manage Organization, Pay and Job Structures area of the Admin Center for small to moderate changes (see Chapter 6, Section 6.5.2).
    - Import Foundation Object templates for large changes (see Chapter 6, Section 6.5.1)
- Reorganizing teams and groups of employees:
    - Use the Manage Mass Changes tool (see Chapter 13)
- Monitoring and advancing stalled workflows (see Chapter 4, Section 4.3)
- Monitoring scheduled jobs and page views (see Section 2.2.3 on Next Gen Admin)
- Updating RBPs (see Chapter 3)
- Resetting passwords (see Section 2.2.3)
- Helping with reporting (see Chapter 16)

All of these post-implementation administrative tasks should be considered after go-live to ensure a smooth transition and continued upkeep.

In the last section of this chapter, we will provide customer-specific and implementer-specific resources for Employee Central implementations.

2.4   Implementation Resources

Various resources are available to assist implementers and customers during all phases of a project and well after go-live. Resources are tailored to the specific type of user/audience so as to give direct and relevant information. Let's review some of best and most useful resources for customers and implementers in the next sections.

2.4.1 Customer Administrator Resources

Customers have an array of resources available before, during, and after Employee Central implementations. These resources include the following:

- Customer Community
- Cloud Learning Center
- Upgrade Center
- Support Team/Representative

Let's look at these various resources in detail.

Customer Community

The Customer Community is available for customers prior to the start of an implementation. This site links customers to other customer users and offers documentation, discussion forums, best practices documents, product information, and links to training, among other things. This is a wonderful place for initial resources and for ongoing information and product updates. The Customer Community site can be accessed directly from the main SAP SuccessFactors website or by navigating to *http://community.successfactors.com*. It is recommended that customers register for and join the community and continue to use it as long as they are customers. Checking back frequently will keep you informed of planned and released updates.

Cloud Learning Center

The TRAINING link at the top of the Customer Community website will direct customers to REGISTER FOR TRAINING and then to the CLOUD LEARNING CENTER. Within the Cloud Learning Center, there are links for module training classes, including the PTO session. These sessions help prepare customers to actively engage in project requirements gathering and discussions by teaching basic concepts and definitions and by calling out decision points that may need to be made. The Cloud Learning Center also contains links for ADMIN TRAINING COURSES and JOB AIDS.

The Employee Central PTO training course and other trainings can be found by selecting the EMPLOYEE CENTRAL link from the homepage, as shown in Figure 2.9.

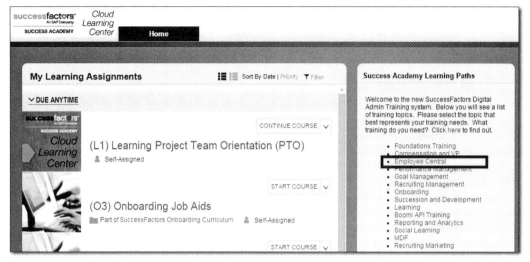

Figure 2.9 Cloud Learning Center

Upgrade Center

The Upgrade Center is another resource that is helpful to customer administrators after implementation. The Upgrade Center is discussed in Section 2.2.3 and provides notice of updates as well as the ability to activate them.

Support Team/Representative

Another resource available to customers post-implementation is the SAP Success-Factors support team. Many Employee Central customers, depending on their chosen level of support, have designated support representatives to help them navigate post-go-live activities, including maintenance and updates.

2.4.2 Implementer Resources

There are also numerous resources that exist to assist implementers. The most commonly used resources include the following:

- SAP Service Marketplace
- SAP/Partner Portal
- SAP Jam groups
- Internal Release Readiness (IRRs) Sessions and Documents

Let's walk through each of these resources now.

SAP Service Marketplace

The SAP Service Marketplace (*https://service.sap.com*) is the main online resource for all SAP implementers. It contains official documentation, configuration guides, and links to other internal resources. There is a specific breakout for cloud products, and within this breakout you can drill down to find information on SAP SuccessFactors and Employee Central. Additional information can also be found at the SAP Help Portal (*help.sap.com*).

SAP/Partner Portal

The Partner Portal (or the internal *SAP Portal* if you are an SAP employee) contains useful information about project methodology, collateral for presentations and trainings, and links to other sites and collateral. On an online bulletin board, implementers can ask and answer questions about Employee Central and configuration scenarios. The website can be found by navigating to *partners.successfactors. com* and is shown in Figure 2.10.

Figure 2.10 SAP/Partner Portal

SAP Jam Groups

Several SAP Jam groups exist to help implementers tackle roadblocks and ask configuration questions. There are groups specific to Employee Central (such as the EC Enablement Group) and groups related to auxiliary topics, including integration (e.g., SAP SuccessFactors Integration for Partners) and Product Updates (e.g., SuccessFactors Quarterly Releases for Partners). Often, specific groups have closed memberships. Asking a colleague who is already a member for an invite or posting on the bulletin boards or on the Partner Portal can be effective ways of joining these groups.

Internal Release Readiness Sessions and Documents

Internal Release Readiness (IRR) Sessions and Documents are vitals tools for staying up-to-date on new functionality and current best practices. Implementers should attend and review quarterly releases to make sure they are keeping pace with new enhancements and are able to recommend the best course of action for customers. Information about IRR can be found by joining the SuccessFactors Quarterly Releases for Partners SAP Jam group mentioned in the previous subsection.

2.5 Summary

In this chapter, we examined activities that should take place prior to starting a project, during implementation, and post-go-live. We explained that proper planning and preparation is just as essential to a project's success and that having a properly staffed team with well-defined roles is a good beginning step to launch a project. Appropriate support and maintenance after implementation ensures a consistent and properly functioning solution.

In the next chapter, we will examine RBPs and determine how they can be used to simplify system and module access.

Role-Based Permissions (RBPs) form the foundation for permission and access to all the major components of Employee Central. They provide the framework for dynamically controlling what different users can see and do.

3   Role-Based Permissions

A complete Human Resources Information System (HRIS) needs a dynamic means for controlling access and authorizations across its complete system offering and entire user base. Employee Central uses the RBP framework to meet this requirement.

RBPs are an essential part of Employee Central. In this chapter, we will look at what RBPs are, their functions, how they are created, how they control access to areas of the system, and how certain business scenarios and requirements will drive the expansion of roles.

3.1   Overview

RBPs are the driving force behind each end user's personal system experience. RBPs control which menu options and tiles are presented on the homepage as well as specific access control within each SAP SuccessFactors module. They are the reason that a regular employee sees different options than a manager or administrator. RBPs are used across all modules within the SAP SuccessFactors suite and are an absolute requirement for Employee Central customers. Some modules have additional module-specific permissions settings outside of RBP, but Employee Central permissions are contained within the RBP framework. Let's take a look at some basic RBP elements.

Role-Based Permission Framework

The RBP framework is the current best practices solution for controlling permissions in SAP SuccessFactors. It is a required element for all new customers and is absolutely essential for Employee Central. Legacy customers, including those running Employee Central v1.0, may be using the former framework, known as Administrative Domains.

This framework is no longer supported and has been replaced with the RBP framework. Customers wishing to implement Employee Central or upgrade from Employee Central v1.0 must first switch to the RBP framework.

3.1.1 Groups and Roles

The main premise behind the RBP framework is the creation of groups and roles. These two elements allow us to tailor the user experience at an employee-level granularity. The next two sections look at groups and roles in greater detail.

Groups

A *group* is a collection of employees with similar characteristics bundled together for the purpose of assigning permissions and authorizations. We define groups when we have clusters of employees who need certain permissions. We also define groups to indicate which groups of employees certain users should have visibility into or control over. This type of group is informally referred to as a *target population*. The setup of all groups follows the same format, and groups and target groups can be used interchangeably in different roles.

Roles

A *role* is a list of access/permissions that members of a group will have when they access the system. Within each role, we define who should be given the role, what permissions are included, and what, if any, target groups are applicable. Roles and groups are tied together in the role definition, as shown in Figure 3.1.

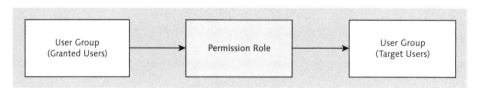

Figure 3.1 Groups and Roles

3.1.2 Administrators

There are two main types of administrators involved in the setup and maintenance of RBPs: *system (security) administrators* and *super administrators*. Depending on

84

the size of your organization, these administrative roles may fall to the same person or persons, as is sometimes the case for smaller companies. Larger companies should consider delegating these responsibilities separately to assist with segregation of duties.

Security Administrator

A *security administrator* controls admittance to the system and permissions access to specific modules and fields for various users and groups. These tasks are all accomplished by managing permission groups and roles—a key task for security admins. To accomplish these tasks, security admins access MANAGE PERMISSION GROUPS and MANAGE PERMISSION ROLES under MANAGE EMPLOYEES • SET USER PERMISSIONS in the Admin Center (see Figure 3.2). You will learn more about groups and roles in Section 3.2.

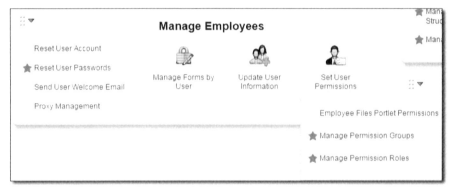

Figure 3.2 Manage Permission Groups and Roles

Security admin assignments are made and maintained by super administrators, who we will discuss next.

Super Administrator

When speaking in terms of permissions, super administrators are persons who control who can be a security admin. These users have access to MANAGE ROLE-BASED PERMISSION ACCESS under MANAGE EMPLOYEES • SET USER PERMISSIONS in the Admin Center (see Figure 3.3).

Figure 3.3 Manage RBP Access in the Admin Center, Available Only to Super Admins

With this access, the super admin maintains a listing of security admins and also has the ability to designate other individuals as fellow super admins. To add a new security admin, follow the menu path MANAGE EMPLOYEES • SET USER PERMISSIONS • MANAGE ROLE-BASED PERMISSION ACCESS and then click ADD USER. On the MANAGE ROLE-BASED PERMISSION ACCESS screen, select ADD USER to designate a person as a security admin. If you want someone to also be a super admin, select the ALLOW ACCESS TO THIS PAGE checkbox for that user, as shown in Figure 3.4. Remove a user from the security admin and/or super admin role by deleting that user's row and/or by deselecting the checkmark.

Admin Center

Back to Admin Center

Manage Role-Based Permission Access

Use this page to specify who can manage Role-Based Permission in the system. User with Role-Based Permission Access privileges will be able to manage permission roles and assign users to those roles.

⊕ Add User   Revoke Permission

	First Name	Last Name	Allow access to this page
☐	System	Admin	✔
☐	admin	3	✔
☐	Emily	Clark	☐

Figure 3.4 Manage RBP Access

> **Tip**
>
> An implementation consultant should designate one or more persons to be the initial super admins before completing an implementation. Customers that no longer have access to their implementation partner or don't know who the super admins are can open a support ticket with SAP SuccessFactors and will be able to receive help in determining who has this access and making new assignments.

3.2 Creating Groups and Roles

Now that we've explored what permissions may be needed to help support the Employee Central setup, let's look at how groups and roles are configured in the system.

Setting up RBPs is a three-step process:

1. **Defining groups**
   Be sure to include both permission receiver groups and target groups.

2. **Creating roles**
   Go through and assign all of the needed permissions and views for the role.

3. **Assigning roles to groups**
   More than one group can be assigned to a role with the same or different target groups.

In the sections that follow, we will walk through these three steps and their corresponding configurations.

3.2.1 Defining Groups

Groups are defined and maintained by navigating to ADMIN CENTER • MANAGE SECURITY • MANAGE PERMISSION GROUPS. Click on the CREATE NEW button to create a new group.

> **Tip**
>
> The system can infer multiple known groups using already assigned relationships. Groups do not need to be created for the following populations because the system can inherently determine them:

- All employees
- Managers
- Second managers
- Matrix managers
- HR managers
- Custom mangers

We'll now begin walking through the process of defining a group:

1. Begin by giving your group a name in the GROUP NAME field. It should be something descriptive and meaningful.

2. Next, choose your group members. Start by identifying what characteristics tie the employees together. Are they all in the same department or location? Choose the identifying characteristic from the dropdown menu under PICK A CATEGORY, and enter in the specific values in the CONDITIONS section. To choose all accountants, for example, set CATEGORY to JOB INFORMATION—JOB and set CONDITION to ACCOUNTANT. Click the SAVE button to complete your setup.

3. We can also use multiple characteristics chained together. If you want all accountants in the Atlanta office and the Beijing office, click ADD ANOTHER CATEGORY for JOB INFORMATION—LOCATION and set the values to ATLANTA and BEIJING. This way, an accountant working at either location would be included.

4. We also have the option of using distinct people pools to pull in another grouping of unrelated employees. If you click ADD ANOTHER PEOPLE POOL, you can specify including all IT managers in Munich, for example. In this scenario, all accountants in Atlanta, all accountants in Beijing, and all IT managers in Munich would be included in the group.

5. From time to time, we may need to exclude certain people from our defined groups. Assume that you want to include all of the people listed previously, but not if they work in the Client Service department. Under EXCLUDE THESE PEOPLE FROM THE GROUP, select the DEPARTMENT field from the CATEGORY dropdown. In the values area, enter in "Client Service." Now, your group will leave out those persons in the Client Service department. Figure 3.5 shows a complete picture of how this scenario is configured in the system. Click the UPDATE button in the top-right corner to see the group population.

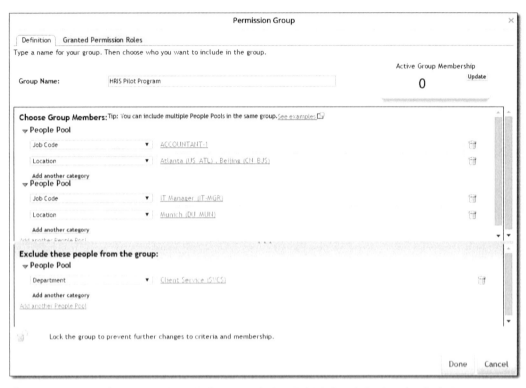

Figure 3.5 Compound Permission Group Definition, Including Multiple People Pools and an Exclusion

The group definition you just created uses employee characteristics to bundle its members together. This type of group is referred to as a *dynamic group*, because its membership changes based on the characteristic changes of individual employees. If a member has the data characteristic required to be in the group, then the employee is placed in the group. If the employee's data changes and lacks the data characteristic required, then he or she will be removed from the group without intervention from a security admin.

In a *static group*, the members of the group are manually assigned and unassigned. Static groups are created in the same manner, but instead of specifying a universal characteristic such as department or location, we choose user or username. Static groups require manual maintenance and updates as its members move around the organization and therefore are not a preferred option. However, there will be times when static groups are the only option available, especially when defining niche groups and roles in the system to be granted to only a few individuals.

A common use scenario for group creation is to gather employees together by country, location, or department. These groups can then be used as target populations during role setups. For example, if you want to give HR generalists in Poland the ability to manage HR tasks for all employees in Poland, you will need two separate groups:

▸ HR generalists in Poland (In the JOB field enter "HR Manager" and in the COUNTRY field enter "Poland", with both set in the same people pool.)

▸ All employees in Poland (In the COUNTRY field, enter "Poland.")

3.2.2 Creating Roles

Roles are defined and maintained by navigating to ADMIN CENTER • MANAGE SECURITY • MANAGE PERMISSION ROLES. Click on the CREATE NEW button to create a new role.

The following steps walk through the process of creating roles:

1. Begin by giving your role a name in the ROLE NAME field. It should be something descriptive and meaningful. Also, be sure to include a description; it will help administrators in the future who may need to make updates. Figure 3.6 shows the starting point for creating a new role. Let's create a Manager Self-Service (MSS) role as an example.

Figure 3.6 First Step of Role Definition

2. Next, add the permissions you want to assign to your group members. Click on the PERMISSION... button and make the relevant selections for this role. Consult Section 3.3 for help determining what permissions are needed for particular Employee Central roles. To assign a permission, select the checkbox in line with the field for the permission to which you are granting access.

3.2.3   Assigning Roles to Groups

We complete this last step in RBP setup within the role definition. Assign groups and roles together by clicking on ADD... under GRANT THIS ROLE TO..., as shown in Figure 3.6. A popup appears in which you are asked to complete the following steps:

1. Select who should receive this role. You have a few choices available:

   ▸ Use a *permission group* (created in step 1, Section 3.2.1). Select more than one, if needed.

   ▸ Use one of the system-known groups mentioned in step 1, Section 3.2.1: managers, HR managers, everyone, or so on.

   ▸ Choose whether this role should be extended up to each recipient's manager, and if so, how many levels up.

   ▸ For this MSS example, grant this role to ALL MANAGERS.

2. Determine the TARGET POPULATION or the group(s) of employees that this role should be extended over.

   ▸ Select a group that was previously defined in MANAGE PERMISSION GROUPS, or select DIRECT REPORTS. You can also employ a combination of those two options in complex scenarios.

   ▸ For this MSS example, the target population is GRANTED USER'S DIRECT REPORTS. This selection will permit managers to view and edit data for their direct reports. You can also select how many levels down a manager can drill into his or her chain of command. Figure 3.7 shows the completed view of our MSS assignment example.

3. If you're setting up an HR manager or payroll-related role, consider checking the box marked EXCLUDE GRANTED USER FROM HAVING THE PERMISSION ACCESS TO HIM/HERSELF. Checking this box prohibits a user from making administrative changes to his/her own record and helps ensure compliance protocols are followed.

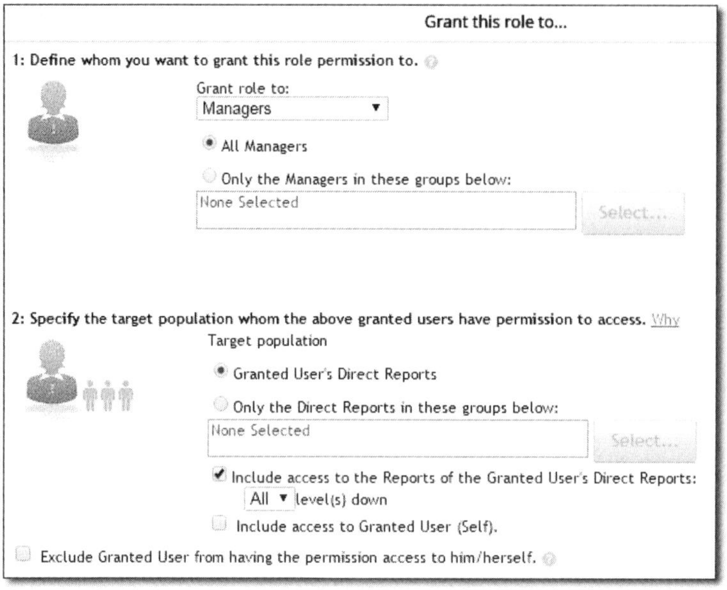

Figure 3.7 Completed Role Assignment for Basic MSS

Multiple Assignments

We can make multiple assignments to a single role by repeating this section and the steps above multiple times; continue clicking on the ADD... button in Figure 3.6 to add multiple assignments. If, for example, you defined an HR Administrator role and want to assign that role to HR admins in Poland to manage employees in Poland *and* to HR admins in Argentina to manage employees in Argentina, you can make two assignment entries for the same HR Administrator role. You do not need to create a separate role if the permissions are the same and only the groups are changing.

3.3 Permissions

The complexity and magnitude of Employee Central requires a security framework of equal form, and the RBP framework meets this standard. RBPs are designed to give Employee Central granular field-level access control and country-specific capabilities, and to manage effective-dated entities—all within a single framework.

Permissions for Employee Central and other modules can be found in ADMIN CENTER • MANAGE PERMISSION ROLES. Follow the steps from Section 3.2.2 to create roles.

Before diving into the process of creating groups and roles, let's look at the most commonly used areas of RBPs as they relate to Employee Central.

3.3.1 Common User Permissions

It's easy to get lost in the setup and maintenance of RBPs for general Employee Central users. There are many data fields maintained in Employee Central, and many of them can be permissioned individually; that makes for a lot of checkboxes! Let's see if we can break down some of the key areas and simplify the process.

Employee Data

Employee data may be the most cumbersome area for managing permissions. On the PERMISSION SETTINGS screen, and select EMPLOYEE DATA (see Figure 3.8).

Fields here are specific to the Employee Profile, Employee Central, and fields that overlap both areas. At its base, EMPLOYEE DATA contains fields viewed and maintained in the Employee Profile. When Employee Central is enabled, its non-effective-dated fields are added to the bottom of this permission set. The fields from HR Information down to the bottom of the page relate directly to Employee Central. The complete listing of fields is broken out in the remainder of this section and includes the following:

- HR INFORMATION
- EMPLOYMENT DETAILS
- GLOBAL ASSIGNMENT (IF ACTIVATED)
- HR ACTIONS
- FUTURE-DATED TRANSACTION ALERT
- TRANSACTIONS PENDING APPROVAL
- VIEW WORKFLOW APPROVAL HISTORY
- PAY COMPONENT GROUPS
- PAY COMPONENTS

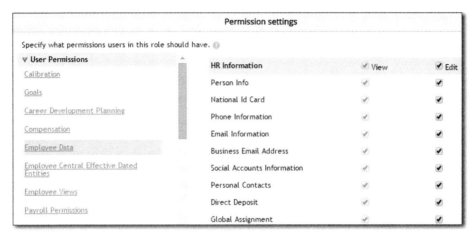

Figure 3.8 Non-Effective-Dated Employee Central Fields, Found in the Employee Data Permission Category

Because these data fields are non-effective-dated—meaning no history is stored—we can only view or edit these data fields (see Figure 3.8):

▶ VIEW
The data field or portlet is visible to the user. No history is maintained.

▶ EDIT
The data field or portlet can be edited by the user. No history is maintained.

In the following subsections, we will walk through the common settings found here for managing permissions for employee data.

HR Information

The HR INFORMATION permission settings are conducted at the *portlet level*. This means that giving someone view or edit access to this item includes all of the data fields defined with the portlet. More information on Employee Central portlets and fields can be found in Chapter 9. The common portlets in this area include:

▶ PERSON INFO

▶ NATIONAL ID CARD

▶ PHONE INFORMATION

▶ EMAIL INFORMATION

▶ BUSINESS EMAIL ADDRESS
This is broken out individually to allow for changes to a personal email addresses while leaving the business email addresses intact.

- SOCIAL ACCOUNTS INFORMATION

- PERSONAL CONTACTS

- DIRECT DEPOSIT
  Newer implementations may have this object defined under MDF OBJECTS.

- PAYMENT INFORMATION
  Newer implementations may have this object defined under MDF OBJECTS.

- GLOBAL ASSIGNMENT

- WORK PERMIT INFO

- LEAVE OF ABSENCE

- SPOT BONUS

- SPOT BONUS EDIT ACTION

Employment Details

This section refers to the Employment Details portlet available in Employment Information (see Chapter 9). These permissions are made at the field level and include hire and termination fields:

- EMPLOYMENT DETAILS MSS
  An EDIT option here permits users to make changes through the TAKE ACTION button, which includes a configurable workflow typically given to managers.

- EMPLOYMENT DETAILS EDIT
  An EDIT action here permits users to directly make changes without workflow approval; typically given to HR managers.

- HIRE DATE

- TERMINATION DATE

- ORIGINAL START DATE

- OK TO REHIRE

- PAYROLL END DATE

- LAST DATE WORKED

- REGRET TERMINATION

- ELIGIBLE FOR SALARY CONTINUATION

- ELIGIBLE FOR STOCK

- STOCK END DATE

▸ SALARY END DATE

▸ BENEFITS END DATE

▸ BEGIN SALARY CONTINUATION

▸ END SALARY CONTINUATION

▸ UPDATED HIRE DATE

▸ ATTACHMENT

HR Actions

This section includes permission settings for actions in the system. Permissions here are typically assigned to HR managers and in part to regular managers. The following permission settings can be found in HR ACTIONS:

▸ UPDATE EMPLOYMENT RECORDS
Indicates whether a user should have access to the TAKE ACTION button, which is typically reserved for MSS functionality.

▸ VIEW HIGHER GRADES
The permission for a user to see grades higher than his/her own in the TAKE ACTION screens; numerical pay grades must be used and assigned for this permission to function.

▸ HIREACTION
The permission to add a new hire.

▸ REHIREACTION
The permission to rehire a former employee.

▸ TERMINATE/RETIRE
The permission to terminate or retire an employee.

▸ PLANLEAVEOFABSENCEACTION
The permission to plan a leave of absence.

▸ RETURNLEAVEOFABSENCEACTION
The permission to end a leave of absence.

Future-Dated Transaction Alert

In this area, you control whether a user can view a future-dated transaction alert. If you select VIEW, a hyperlink alert (see Figure 3.9) will display next to the portlet in question, indicating that there is a future-dated change planned. The following elements are effective-dated and eligible for future-dated alerts:

- ▶ PERSONAL INFORMATION

- ▶ ADDRESSES

- ▶ JOB INFORMATION

- ▶ COMPENSATION INFORMATION

- ▶ JOB RELATIONSHIPS

- ▶ DEPENDENTS

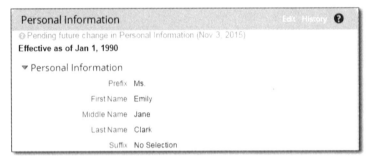

Figure 3.9 Future-Dated Transaction Alert in the Personal Information Portlet

Transactions Pending Approval

In this area, you control whether a user can see a proposed change that is still pending approval. If you select VIEW, a non-hyperlink alert will display next to the portlet in question, indicating that there is a transaction pending approval. The alert is not clickable, and no further information about the pending change and approval chain is available.

If you select EDIT, a hyperlink alert (see Figure 3.10) will be displayed instead. Clicking the hyperlink shows information about the proposed transaction that is pending approval.

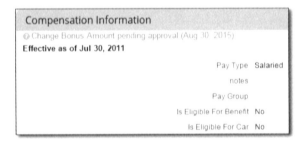

Figure 3.10 Hyperlinked Transaction Pending Approval Alert

View Workflow Approval History

The VIEW WORKFLOW APPROVAL HISTORY settings allow you to view workflow approval histories for your effective-dated portlets. If a data change has been made and a workflow was involved, the system saves this information. Selecting VIEW will allow users to see the workflow history in the HISTORY section of each of the following portlets:

▸ Personal Information

▸ Addresses

▸ Job Information

▸ Compensation Information

▸ Job Relationships

Pay Component Groups

This section lists all of the Pay Component Groups (see Chapter 6, Section 6.2.3) defined in your system. Since Pay Component Groups are system-calculated amounts, you cannot edit them. If you select VIEW here, then users will have the ability to see this Pay Component Group on the Compensation Information portlet.

Pay Components

This option lists all of the Pay Components defined in your system. If you select VIEW here, then users will have the ability to see this Pay Component on the Compensation Information portlet. If you select EDIT, then users will have the ability to add, edit, and delete values for this Pay Component within the Compensation Information portlet, subject to workflows if configured accordingly.

Employee Central Effective-Dated Entities

The next section down is EMPLOYEE CENTRAL EFFECTIVE-DATED ENTITIES (see Figure 3.11). Although this is a long section, it's broken down into categories (complete field listings for your system can be viewed directly in your system or in your Configuration Workbooks):

▸ Personal Information

▸ Addresses (available at the portlet level, not the field level)

▸ Job Information

- Compensation Information

- Job Relationships

- Dependents (only relevant if you are using Dependent Management)

Every field found in these portlets is available for permissioning. You can create a customer-specific end user experience with this level of granularity. You can have fields available just for HR managers, have other fields tied to MSS, and keep employees up-to-date on their basic records.

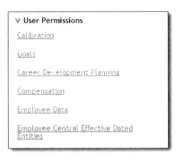

Figure 3.11 Menu Path for Employee Central Effective-Dated Entities

Let's look at the permission options at the individual field level. Because this section contains your effective-dated fields, you know that historical records are involved. The following available permission choices are enhanced to reflect this:

- VIEW CURRENT
  View the current record/field.

- VIEW HISTORY
  View all historical records/entries.

- EDIT/INSERT
  Create a new entry.

- CORRECT
  Correct an erroneous record without creating a new entry.

- DELETE
  Remove an entry completely.

In addition to field settings, you can also make portlet action settings. Each portlet listed has the first two rows/entries set aside for action settings (see Figure 3.12):

▶ ACTIONS

This row controls what views or changes can be made within the history view and outside of the TAKE ACTION button for effective-dated portlets. It controls what a user can do when clicking a record's HISTORY button:

▷ VIEW CURRENT allows you to view the current record.

▷ VIEW HISTORY allows you to view historical records.

▷ EDIT/INSERT allows you to INSERT A NEW RECORD within the history view, thereby bypassing workflow approval (typically reserved for HR managers).

Figure 3.12 Portlet Action Settings for Job Information

▶ EDIT LINK

This row controls what portlets can be changed using the TAKE ACTION button:

▷ EDIT/INSERT can use the TAKE ACTION button to propose a data change for the fields you have EDIT access to and route the proposal through your defined workflow process.

For Personal Information portlets for which TAKE ACTION is not applicable, this setting instead includes an EDIT link on the portlet face. An edit made in this manner will still route through the workflow process if defined (see Figure 3.13).

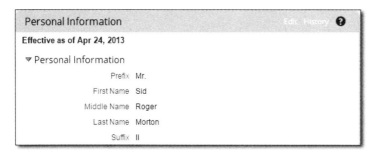

Figure 3.13 Portlet View for Personal Information, Showing the Edit Link

This sample is a best practices arrangement for Employee Self Services (ESS). An employee can view current and historical records and can propose changes through the EDIT link, subject to workflow approvals.

Employee Views

Employee views are the various employee records that you can see listed under the EMPLOYEE RECORDS dropdown within EMPLOYEE FILES. An example is shown in Figure 3.14.

Figure 3.14 Sample Public Profile, Including Commonly Used Employee Views

When selecting EMPLOYEE VIEWS, choose the views each user group should have access to when reviewing data, as shown in Figure 3.15. The SAP SuccessFactors modules enabled and the configuration steps taken determine which views are shown in the RBP listing for selection.

At a minimum, Employee Central users should have some access to Personal Information, Employment Information, and Pending Requests. If additional features such as Time Management are in place, then additional views may be needed.

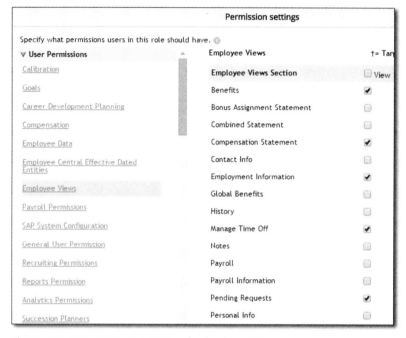

Figure 3.15 Basic Permission Settings for Employee Views

Miscellaneous Permissions

Various miscellaneous permissions may need to be enabled depending on the functionality implemented. We will not cover this section in detail but keep in mind that permissions can be set here for both standard and custom-created MDF objects. The permission settings are the same in this section as in other sections (VIEW/EDIT for non-effective-dated entities and HISTORY/CURRENT/EDIT/CORRECT/DELETE for effective-dated entities). One new addition is the ability to set IMPORT/EXPORT permissions at the object level.

Metadata Framework Foundation Objects

MDF Foundation Objects are permissioned in this section. This is essential for users to be able to view and select MDF Foundation Objects within the system. The permission settings are the same in this section as in other effective-dated entity sections: HISTORY, CURRENT, EDIT, CORRECT, and DELETE.

3.3.2 Administrator Permissions

On the administrative side, there are several permission areas that help you update and maintain Employee Central. Whether you need to add a new location in the Foundation Tables or set up and monitor integrations, you can make the relevant permission settings using RBPs. This means that you can tailor administrative roles based on need and use. A time administrator can have access to manage holiday calendars, whereas a global HR manager can oversee the job catalog. Both can operate in Admin Tools without total administrative access.

The following are some of the most commonly assigned administrative permissions in Employee Central and their uses:

▶ MANAGE USER
   Several key Employee Central settings are made for managing users:

   ▷ ADD NEW USER: To hire new employees into the system

   ▷ MANAGE PENDING HIRES: To hire accepted candidates from SAP SuccessFactors Recruiting or SAP SuccessFactors Onboarding

   ▷ REHIRE INACTIVE EMPLOYEE: To rehire inactive employees through the Admin Center

   ▷ INCLUDE INACTIVE EMPLOYEES IN THE SEARCH: To show the INCLUDE INACTIVE EMPLOYEES checkbox during searches

   ▷ IMPORT EMPLOYEE DATA: To import Employee Central-related employee data into the system

   ▷ MANAGE WORKFLOW REQUESTS: To monitor and control in-process and completed workflow notices

   ▷ MANAGE WORKFLOW GROUPS: To create and maintain workflow groups for ESS and MSS

▶ MANAGE COMPENSATION
   You only need to worry about one setting here, which is to give an admin the

103

ability to update currency conversion rates with the MANAGE CURRENCY CON-VERSION RATE TABLES setting. Pay Component Groups will not function without this table in place.

▶ MANAGE INTEGRATION TOOLS
This section contains a listing of permissions needed to set up and maintain external integrations. You can also find permissions for monitoring and usage statistics here. Commonly used protocols such as SFAPI and OData API are included.

▶ MANAGE MASS CHANGES
This section allows you to give access for implementing mass changes using the *Manage Mass Changes* tool. More information can be found in Chapter 13.

▶ MANAGE FOUNDATION OBJECTS
There are two important settings here:

▷ IMPORT FOUNDATION DATA: To import Foundation Data into the system using the Admin Center

▷ IMPORT TRANSLATIONS: To import foundation translations into the system using the Admin Center

▶ MANAGE FOUNDATION OBJECT TYPES
In this area, indicate which Foundation Objects your admins have the ability to create or maintain. Because Foundation Objects are effective-dated, you will see the expanded edit options here:

▷ VIEW

▷ CREATE

▷ INSERT

▷ CORRECT

▷ DELETE

▶ METADATA FRAMEWORK
The three most commonly used selections are as follows:

▷ CONFIGURE OBJECT DEFINITIONS: To create new objects and picklists for use in the MDF

▷ MANAGE DATA: To create instances of data based on MDF objects

▷ CONFIGURE BUSINESS RULES: To create rules and logic statements and set up workflows for use in Employee Central

- MANAGE BUSINESS CONFIGURATION

  This section has only one permission: SUCCESSION MODEL ELEMENTS. This allows an admin to access the MANAGE BUSINESS CONFIGURATION area, in which changes to the Succession Data Model and Country-Specific Succession Data Model can be made in real time.

3.4   Scenarios for Creating Roles

When it comes to Employee Central, we usually start by thinking about the core best practices roles:

- **Employee on Others**

  Allows all employees to view the directory, Org Chart, and Public Profiles.

- **Employee Self-Service**

  Allows the employee to view basic self-data and update Personal Information.

- **Manager Self-Service**

  Allows managers to perform basic management tasks and possibly run team reports.

- **HR Manager**

  Allows HR managers to actively manage their areas of responsibility, including new hires, entering transactions, and approving manager initiation proposals.

- **HR Administrator or General Administration**

  Allows HR administrators to manage large populations of employees or employees spread across the organization, including running global reports that include head count reports and often the upkeep of the Foundation Tables.

- **Super Administrator**

  Allows for full administrative access for system maintenance and health purposes and to assist with global reporting, if needed.

Beyond these roles, we encounter scenarios in which additional or supplemental roles are needed. This often stems from a need for segregation of duties on the HR team side. Instead of employees being supported by a centralized HR team or an individual HR manager, we frequently encounter cases in which localized HR teams manage their own local areas. In such cases, you can create groups for the local HR teams and groups for the target local employees and tie them together using a role. Often, you can use the same role and multiple assignment statements—each with its own permission group and target group.

You can also create additional roles as needed for auxiliary persons. You may have a need for people outside of HR to have more than just basic access to the system. Examples of auxiliary roles include IT managers, payroll administrators, time keepers, benefits administrators, and finance team members.

3.5   Summary

In this chapter, you learned about RBPs, how they relate to Employee Central, and how to create them within the system. They are a dynamic way to control access to and within the SAP SuccessFactors platform.

In the next chapter, we will discuss events and Event Reasons and explore how they relate to employee history and workflow approvals.

Employee Central manages the various employee events that occur during the lifetime of an employee. Multiple reasons can be created for each event. Coupled with workflows, this provides an automated way to manage events and have them approved in a robust process.

4   Events and Workflows

An employee will typically undergo several different events throughout his or her lifetime at an employer. This process begins immediately with a Hire event, and may include any number of other events, such as Transfers, Promotions, Pay Changes, and Terminations. Employee Central manages each of these events and provides customers with the ability to define multiple Event Reasons for each event. These Event Reasons identify the specific reason that an event took place.

Although not always directly linked, events and workflows can work mutually to enable approval of data changes created by an event prior to the event being committed to the employee's record. These workflows typically arise in ESS and MSS scenarios. *Workflows* ensure that employees and managers enter the correct data, but also—more importantly—enable compliance with decisions that may have financial and legal implications.

In this chapter, we'll look at the events provided in the system and how Event Reasons can be created and used. We'll then take a look at workflows in detail, covering the concepts and objects that enable workflows to operate, how and where workflows are triggered, the workflow process, and general administrative activities.

Before we examine events and Event Reasons, we should first briefly look at the different *employee statuses* that employees can have.

4.1   Employee Status

Employees can have an employee status that identifies their active or inactive status within the organization. Employee Central provides nine employee statuses:

- ▸ Active

- ▸ Unpaid Leave

- ▸ Paid Leave

- ▸ Retired

- ▸ Suspended

- ▸ Terminated

- ▸ Furlough

- ▸ Discarded

- ▸ Dormant

The employee statuses provided in the system cannot be changed, but the label of each EMPLOYEE STATUS can be changed (e.g., *Paid Leave* could be renamed to *Paid Leave of Absence*).

The EMPLOYEE STATUS can be displayed in an employee's Job Information portlet and is also visible in the HISTORY screen of that portlet. The EMPLOYEE STATUS field is shown in the JOB INFORMATION section in Figure 4.1.

Figure 4.1 Job Information Portlet

4.1.1 Active versus Inactive

All employee statuses consider the employee still to be active within the organization, with the following exceptions:

- ▶ Retired
- ▶ Terminated
- ▶ Discarded
- ▶ Furlough

When an employee has any of these four statuses, he or she is considered to be inactive. If Employee Central is integrated with other systems, such as a payroll or a benefits system, then the employee may become inactive in those systems as well when their status changes to one of these inactive employee statuses.

Retired is used with the Pensions Payouts feature, which is covered in Chapter 16, Section 16.5.

4.1.2 Employee Status Changes

The employee status of an employee cannot be changed manually: It is always changed by an Event Reason. Event Reasons can have an employee status assigned, although it is not mandatory. When an event occurs for an employee and an Event Reason is selected (either manually or automatically by the system using an Event Derivation), then the employee's status will change to the status assigned to the Event Reason. If the Event Reason has no employee status assigned, then the employee's status will remain unchanged. Let's look at two examples:

An employee with an Active status receives a salary increase using a customer-specific Event Reason, called *Annual Salary Increase*. The Annual Salary Increase Event Reason has no employee status assigned, because a salary increase doesn't change the status of an employee. Therefore, the employee's status remains as Active. A few months later, the employee decides to leave the company, so an administrator performs a termination in the system with a customer-specific Event Reason called *Resignation*. The Resignation Event Reason has Terminated assigned as the employee status. Therefore, the employee becomes inactive with the status Terminated. We will look more closely at how employee statuses are assigned to Event Reasons in Section 4.2.1.

Now that you are familiar with employee statuses, let's move onto looking at events and Event Reasons.

4.2 Events and Event Reasons

The system provides a standard set of events, and you cannot extend this set of events. This set of events is provided as a picklist. You can modify the event labels for each enabled language, just as other picklist labels can be renamed. Periodically, SAP SuccessFactors may introduce new events into the system.

Table 4.1 shows the standard picklist provided as of the Q4 2015 release.

Event	Code	Use
Additional Job	1	Defunct
Assignment	2	Defunct
Assignment Completion	3	Defunct
Job Change	16	Change in job
Completion of Probation	15	Available for manual use only
Data Change	5	Miscellaneous data change
Demotion	4	Change in job
Furlough	11	Leave of absence
Hire	H	Hire/rehire
Job Reclassification	9	Job reclassification
Leave of Absence	10	Leave of absence
Pay Rate Change	12	Compensation change
Position Change	13	Change in position or position reclassification
Probation	14	Available for manual use only
Promotion	8	Change in job
Rehire	R	Hire/rehire
Return From Disability	22	Leave of absence
Return to Work	23	Leave of absence

Table 4.1 List of Events

Event	Code	Use
Suspension	7	Available for manual use only
Termination	26	Termination
Transfer	6	Job and/or position transfer
Add Global Assignment	GA	Global assignment
End Global Assignment	EGA	Global assignment
Away on Global Assignment	AGA	Global assignment
Back from Global Assignment	BGA	Global assignment
Obsolete	OGA	Global assignment
Start Pension Payout	SPP	Pensions payouts
Discard Pension Payout	OPP	Pensions payouts
End Pension Payout	EPP	Pensions payouts
Start Contingent Worker	SCWK	Contingent Workforce Management
End Contingent Worker	ECWK	Contingent Workforce Management

Table 4.1 List of Events (Cont.)

Before you can use an event, it must have at least one Event Reason created; we will cover how to create Event Reasons in the next section. Typically, most processes require the system to be configured to read the appropriate event and Event Reasons or for Event Reasons to be selected manually. In some instances, events exist that either need to be assigned manually by an HR administrator or are legacy events (those marked as "Available for manual use only" in Table 4.1).

The events and Event Reasons selected are stored in an employee's history and can be viewed by users with appropriate permissions to view the history of the Job Information or Compensation Information portlets. This can be seen in Figure 4.2.

Typically, around half of Employee Central customers use Event Derivation in order to have the system automatically select the event and Event Reason based on the action performed by the user. This can be extremely useful for customers that use MSS, in which having the user select the correct Event Reasons has an impact on data integrity, triggering the correct workflow, and in some cases triggering integrations to external systems. We will cover Event Derivation in Section 4.2.2.

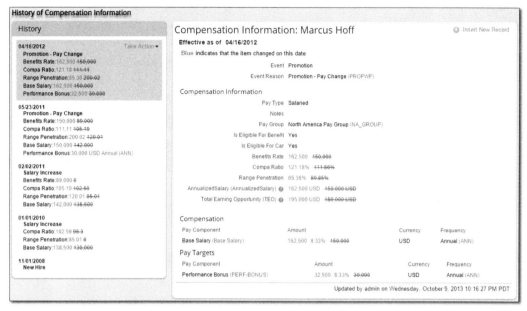

Figure 4.2 Compensation Information History for Marcus Hoff

Customers can choose to have users manually select the event and Event Reason instead when performing an action in the system.

Now, let's take a look at how Event Reasons are managed in Employee Central.

4.2.1   Event Reasons

An *Event Reason* describes why an event has occurred. For example, Resignation may be the reason for which a Termination event has occurred. For every event that occurs in the system, an Event Reason must be selected. As described in Section 4.1.2, an Event Reason can also change the employee status of an employee.

Although you cannot create events, you can create an infinite number of Event Reasons in the system. Event Reasons are Foundation Objects (we will cover Foundation Objects in detail in Chapter 6) and are therefore created in OneAdmin in EMPLOYEE FILES • MANAGE ORGANIZATION, PAY AND JOB STRUCTURES. We will cover this process later in this section. Please note that at some time in the future, Event Reasons will be moved onto the MDF and will then be managed in EMPLOYEE FILES • MANAGE DATA. Figure 4.3 shows an example of an Event Reason in the MANAGE ORGANIZATION, PAY AND JOB STRUCTURES screen.

Figure 4.3 Transfer—Department Change Event Reason

SuccessFactors provides 178 Event Reasons that you can import into the system, although these Event Reasons do not need to be uploaded if you wish to start from scratch or you can only use a selected number of the provided Event Reasons.

Table 4.2 provides a small selection of Events Reasons, their events, and the assigned employee status for some of the standard provided Event Reasons. As we discussed in Section 4.1.2, not all Event Reasons have an employee status assigned and this is reflected in the table.

Event Reason	Event	Employee Status
Internal International Transfer	Hire	Active
Loan from Parent Company	Hire	Active
New Hire	Hire	Active
Family and Medical Leave Act	Leave of Absence	Unpaid Leave
Long Term Disability	Leave of Absence	Unpaid Leave

Table 4.2 List of Event Reasons

Event Reason	Event	Employee Status
Unpaid Maternity/Paternity Leave	Leave of Absence	Unpaid Leave
Paid Maternity/Paternity Leave	Leave of Absence	Paid Leave
Lump Sum Merit Increase	Pay Rate Change	
Merit	Pay Rate Change	
Promotion	Pay Rate Change	
Job Reclassification	Pay Rate Change	
Normal Retirement	Termination	Retired
Vol Termination—Health Reasons	Termination	Terminated
Inv Termination—Insubordinate	Termination	Terminated
Vol Termination—Personal	Termination	Terminated
Inv Termination Non-Performance	Termination	Terminated
Transfer—Department Change	Transfer	
Reorganization	Transfer	

Table 4.2 List of Event Reasons (Cont.)

Event Reasons come into play whenever a change occurs in any fields in either the Job Information or Compensation Information portlets, or when certain transactions run. Such changes can occur through using the TAKE ACTION option and selecting CHANGE JOB AND COMPENSATION INFO (typically an MSS activity) or TERMINATION, or by inserting a new record in the HISTORY screen of either the Job Information portlet or the Compensation Information portlet (typically a HR administrator activity). The New Hire and Rehire transactions also involve selecting Event Reasons.

When a new employee is hired, the user can select any Event Reason created for the Hire event. The same is true for a Rehire transaction and Event Reasons created for the Rehire event.

The TERMINATION action enables the user to select the appropriate Event Reason from those created for the Termination event (see Figure 4.4).

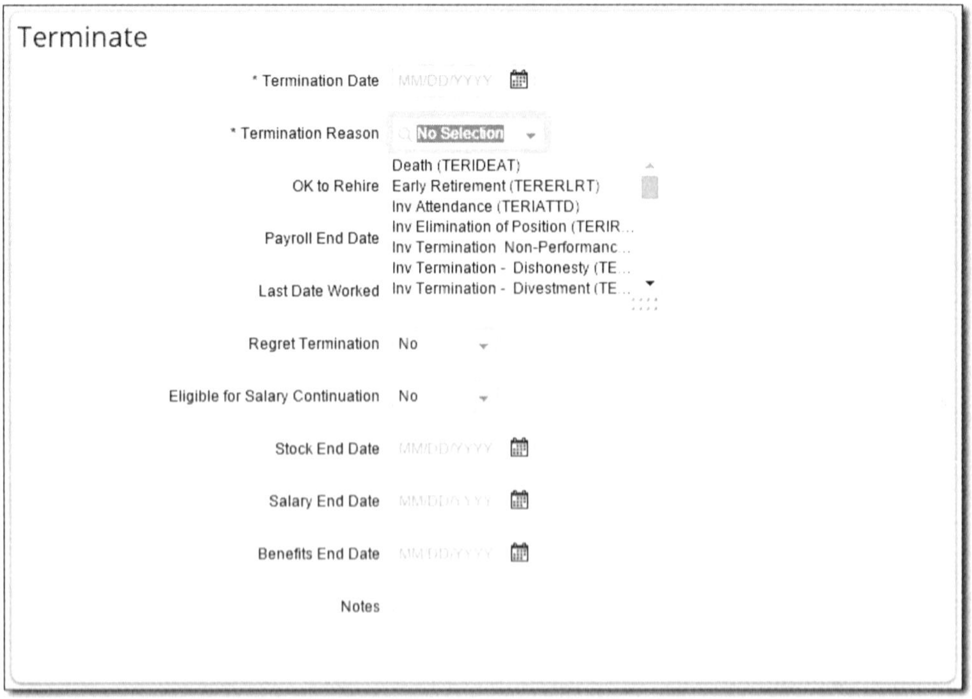

Figure 4.4 Event Reasons in the Termination Action

Event Reasons for the Termination events always link to the Job Information record and are viewable in the HISTORY screen of the JOB INFORMATION portlet. The Event Reason for the Termination event also appears in the EMPLOYMENT DETAILS portlet, as shown in Figure 4.5. The Event Reason for the Compensation Information will remain unchanged from the last change made prior to the termination.

Now that we've looked at when Event Reasons are used, we'll examine at the process of creating Event Reasons.

As mentioned previously, Event Reasons are created in OneAdmin in EMPLOYEE FILES • MANAGE ORGANIZATION, PAY AND JOB STRUCTURES. Remember, at some point in the future Event Reason objects will migrate to the MDF, at which time they will be created in Employee Files • Manage Data using a slightly different process from the one that we will discuss here.

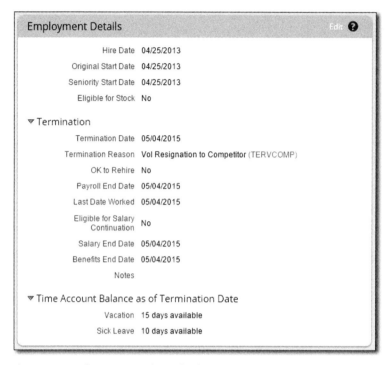

Figure 4.5 Employment Details Portlet for a Terminated Employee

To create a new Event Reason, select Event Reason from the list in the Create New dropdown. Enter the start date in the Effective as of date field (typically 01/01/1900), and then enter values for the following remaining fields, which can be seen in Figure 4.3:

▶ Event Reason ID
The Event Reason code.

▶ Event Reason Name
The name of the Event Reason.

▶ Description
An optional description of the Event Reason.

▶ Status
Whether the Event Reason is Active or Inactive.

▶ EVENT
The event for which the Event Reason is created.

▶ EMPLOYEE STATUS
The employee status of the employee after the event has occurred.

▶ FOLLOW-UP ACTIVITY IN POSITION
For a Position Management-related Event Reason, this determines if a POSITION RECLASSIFICATION or POSITION TRANSFER action should occur.

▶ PAYROLL EVENT
Used for integration to SAP ERP Payroll and Employee Central Payroll systems; enables a PAYROLL EVENT from one of these systems to be replicated instead of the event of the Event Reason.

▶ DISPLAY IN INTERNAL JOB HISTORY PORTLET
Used to indicate if Job Information records using this Event Reason should show on the Internal Job History portlet in the Employee Profile.

EVENT REASON ID, STATUS, and EVENT are mandatory fields. If you are not using Event Derivation, then the EMPLOYEE STATUS field must be left blank.

As a minimum, you should create Event Reasons for the following events:

▶ Hire

▶ Rehire

▶ Termination

▶ Leave of Absence and Return to Work (if Leave of Absence is used)

▶ Data Change

Once created, an Event Reason is available for use in the system. For Event Derivation, additional configuration is required, which we will cover in the next section of this chapter.

Event Reasons can be restricted by country by creating an association between the Event Reason Foundation Object and the Country Generic Object. Once the association exists, each Event Reason can be assigned to one or more countries. The Event Reason will then only be available for employees of a company that has the associated country assigned to it.

4.2.2   Event Derivation

Event Derivation—technically known as the youCalc event rules—is a feature in Employee Central that enables the event and Event Reason to be derived automatically within MSS depending on what field changes the user makes. This significantly reduces user error, which can impact data accuracy and integrity, the Job History portlet on the Employee Profile, and integrations triggered by the Event Reason.

Although Event Reasons are selected automatically with Event Derivations, any user with the appropriate permissions can manually change them in the HISTORY screen of the Job Information and Compensation Information portlets. Additionally, during a Termination action the user must still manually select and Event Reason for the Termination.

Event Derivation triggers when data changes via using the TAKE ACTION option and selecting CHANGE JOB AND COMPENSATION INFO. Any data changed in the Job Information, Job Relationships, or Compensation Information portlets triggers Event Derivation, although Event Reasons are not stored for changes to Job Relationships; they are merely cosmetic in nature when triggering a workflow.

Event Derivation is triggered by configurable rules. Until the Q2 2015 release, it was only possible to configure Event Derivation in the rules XML file uploaded in Provisioning. From the Q2 2015 release, customers have the option to have Event Derivation rules configured and triggered using the Rules Engine. We cover the Rules Engine in detail in Chapter 5, although we will look at configuring Event Derivation with the Rules Engine a little later in this section.

> **Important!**
>
> Customers can use either XML-based rules or Rules Engine rules for Event Derivation; a customer cannot use a combination of both. If a customer uses XML-based rules and wishes to use the Rules Engine, that customer must have the new method enabled in Provisioning and then recreate all Event Derivation trigger rules in the Rules Engine.

Once a change has been submitted—or if workflow is used, once the change has been approved by the last approver—the change is made to the employee data and the event and Event Reason are recorded against the change in the database. As mentioned previously, the event and Event Reason are then viewable in the HISTORY screen of the relevant portlet.

When using workflow, the Event Reason will be shown in the PLEASE CONFIRM YOUR REQUEST box that displays once the SUBMIT button is clicked (see Figure 4.7 ahead).

Let's take a look at how this works in practice. In Figure 4.6, the user selected the CHANGE JOB AND COMPENSATION INFO action for an employee and changed the DEPARTMENT from MARKETING to ALLIANCES.

> **When do you want your changes to take effect?** 05/20/2015 📅

> ## Job Information   ❓
>
> Position Information
>
> | | |
> |---:|:---|
> | Positions under Employee | No Selection ▾ |
> | Position | Sales Director, NE (DIR_SALESN... ▾ 🏢 |
> | Position Entry Date | MM/DD/YYYY 📅 |
> | Time In Position | |
>
> Organizational Information
>
> | | |
> |---:|:---|
> | * Company | Ace USA (ACE_USA) ▾ |
> | * Business Unit | Corporate Industries (ACE_IND) ▾ |
> | Division | Industries (IND) ▾ |
> | Department | Alliances (ALNCE) ▾   ~~Marketing (MKTG)~~ |
> | Location | Philadelphia, PA (US_PHL) ▾ |
> | Timezone | US/Eastern (GMT-05:00) ▾ |

Figure 4.6 Change of Department in an Employee's Job Information

Next, the user scrolls to the bottom and clicks the SUBMIT button. The workflow popup box (PLEASE CONFIRM YOUR REQUEST) opens (Figure 4.7). In this box, you can see the Event Reason for the change: TRANSFER—DEPARTMENT CHANGE.

Subsequent workflow approval screens, like the screen shown in Figure 4.8, display the Event Reason.

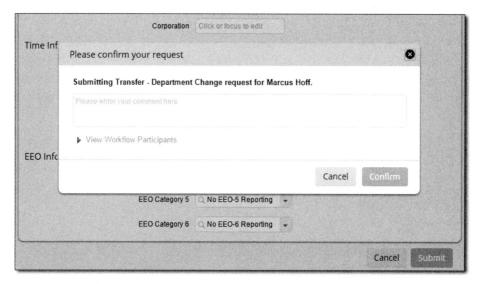

Figure 4.7 Workflow Popup Box

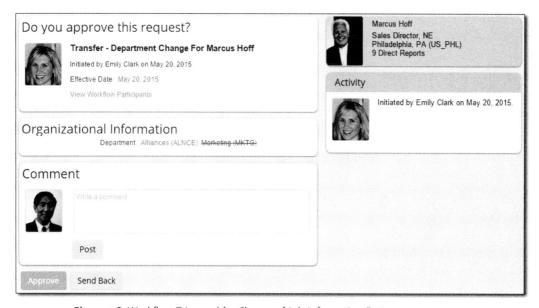

Figure 4.8 Workflow Triggered for Change of Job Information Data

Now that we've looked at how an Event Derivation works, we'll take a look at enabling and then configuring Event Derivation.

Configuring Event Derivation Rules

Event Derivation rules are configured in the Rules Engine, but some existing customers may have their rules configured in the legacy method via the rules XML. Customers may migrate to the Rules Engine-based Event Derivation at any time, but must consider that this requires building all of the existing rules in the Rules Engine manually.

> **Note**
>
> We will only cover configuring Event Derivation rules using the Rules Engine in this chapter. An experienced implementation consultant should handle changes to XML-based rules until you have migrated to Event Derivation using the Rules Engine.

Two steps are required to configure an Event Derivation rule:

1. Create a business rule that defines the Event Derivation trigger and the output Event Reason.
2. Assign the business rule to the appropriate portlet (Job Information or Compensation Information) on which it should trigger.

Let's run through these steps in detail. First, navigate to EMPLOYEE FILES • CONFIGURE BUSINESS RULES in OneAdmin to create the rule. Create a new business rule for the specific portlet (e.g., Job Information). The IF conditions should stipulate the trigger rules, whereas the THEN condition should set the WFCONFIG field to equal the Event Reason you wish to apply.

Let's take a look at a rule example. In Figure 4.9, you can see a business rule that sets the EVENT REASON field to TRANSFER—DEPARTMENT CHANGE. The IF condition is set to DEPARTMENT.VALUE is not equal to DEPARTMENT.PREVIOUS VALUE, so that field will trigger whenever the DEPARTMENT field value is changed in an employee's Job Information.

Once created, a business rule must be assigned to either the Job Information portlet or the Compensation Information portlet as an onSave event in OneAdmin via COMPANY SETTINGS • MANAGE BUSINESS CONFIGURATION.

Figure 4.10 shows our rule assigned to the DEPARTMENT field in MANAGE BUSINESS CONFIGURATION.

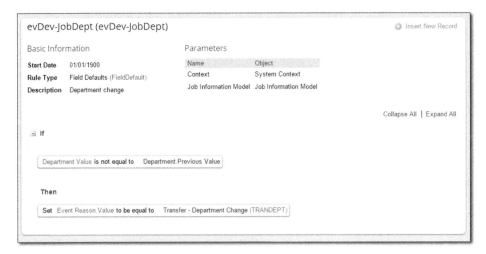

Figure 4.9 Department Transfer Event Derivation Rule

Figure 4.10 Assigning a Rule to a Field in Manage Business Configuration

Once the field is added, save your changes, and your Event Derivation trigger is complete!

Now that we've covered events and Event Reasons, let's turn our attention to workflows.

4.3 Workflows

Whereas Event Reasons define the reason behind a particular action or event, *workflows* provide the mechanism to ensure that such actions, events, or employee master data changes are adequately approved and auditable. Most organizations—including yours—use some form of approval chain for certain actions or data changes, and Employee Central has a robust framework to manage workflow approvals. Refer back to Figure 4.8 for an example of a workflow in flight.

Workflows approvals have one or more *approvers* assigned, and the workflow will route through each approver in order until the last approver has approved the workflow. At that point, the changes that are subject to the workflow become visible in the system (future-dated changes will be visible in HISTORY but won't become active until the effective date of the change is reached). We recommend that you keep your workflows simple, rather than creating large approval chains. The more workflows that have more approvers, the less likely it is for these workflows to receive approval as time goes on.

In addition to approvers, workflows can also have *contributors* and/or *CC users*. Contributors have the ability to view a workflow and to add comments to the workflow while it is active. CC users receive a notification upon the approval of a workflow. For each of these groups—approvers, contributors, and CC users—there are a number of different approver types available, which we will discuss when look at the Workflow Configuration. These approver types enable the system to derive the recipient of the workflow, such as the employee's manager or the employee's HR manager.

Workflows can be triggered on Generic Objects, effective-dated Foundation Objects, the New Hire, Rehire, and Internal Hire transactions, changes made to portlets on the EMPLOYMENT INFORMATION screen using the TAKE ACTION menu (including Global Assignments), or by using the EDIT button on the following portlets on the PERSONAL INFORMATION screen:

- NATIONAL ID INFORMATION
- PERSONAL INFORMATION (including Global Information fields)
- ADDRESS INFORMATION
- PAYMENT INFORMATION
- DEPENDENTS INFORMATION

The BIOGRAPHICAL INFORMATION, WORK PERMIT INFORMATION, CONTACT INFORMATION, or PRIMARY EMERGENCY CONTACT portlets on the PERSONAL INFORMATION screen do not support workflows.

Workflows also will not trigger when inserting or correcting a record on the HISTORY screen of a portlet.

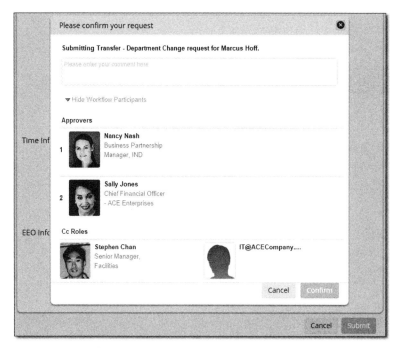

Figure 4.11 Workflow Confirmation Popup

Figure 4.11 shows the triggering of a workflow after making a change on the CHANGE JOB AND COMPENSATION INFO screen, accessed via the TAKE ACTION button on either the PERSONAL INFORMATION or EMPLOYMENT INFORMATION screen. By clicking the VIEW WORKFLOW PARTICIPANTS button, the user can see all of the approvers of the workflow before submitting it, as shown in Figure 4.11. The user also can add a comment.

Workflows, like Event Reasons, are Foundation Objects and are configured in OneAdmin in EMPLOYEE FILES • MANAGE ORGANIZATION, PAY AND JOB STRUCTURES. We will cover this process in Section 4.3.3. Workflow trigger rules are set up in the Rules Engine, although as with Event Derivation they used to be configured in an XML rules file prior to the Q2 2015 update. We will cover this in Section 4.3.4.

4.3.1 Approver Groups

In this section, we will discuss the two approver groups used in workflows: Dynamic Roles and Workflow Groups, and how they can be used to identify approvers, contributors, and notified individuals.

Dynamic Roles

Dynamic Roles dynamically determine the recipient, contributor, or CC role of an individual based on defined organizational attributes. For example, you may create a Dynamic Role called *Compensation Manager* through which you define the person responsible for approving compensation changes for each division. Figure 4.12 shows an example of a Dynamic Role.

The default attributes available for Dynamic Roles include the following:

- Company
- Business Unit
- Division
- Department
- Location
- Cost Center
- Job Classification
- Pay Grade

▶ Pay Group

▶ Position

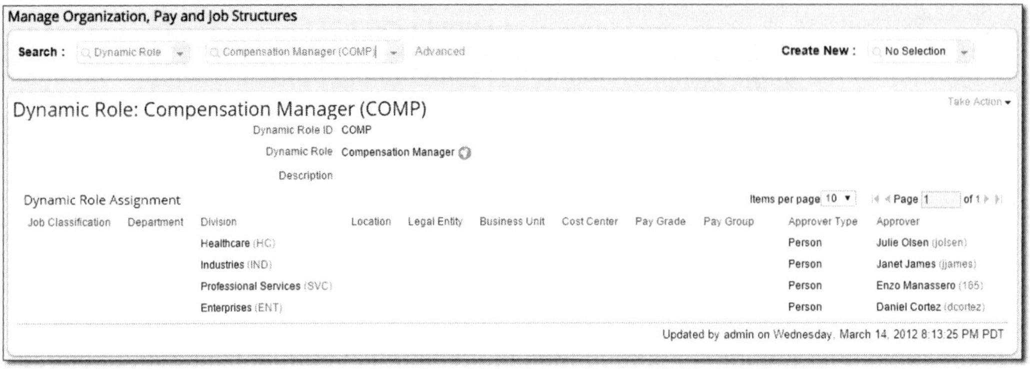

Figure 4.12 Compensation Manager Dynamic Role

You can add other Foundation Objects, such as Event Reasons and custom Foundation Objects.

For each attribute or combination of attributes selected, an approver is selected by approver type. There are three approver types:

▶ Person

▶ Position

▶ Dynamic Group

You can only use Dynamic Roles in workflows used for Employee Central objects and the Position object.

Dynamic Roles are Foundation Objects and therefore are created in OneAdmin in EMPLOYEE FILES • MANAGE ORGANIZATION, PAY AND JOB STRUCTURES. Use the CREATE NEW dropdown to create a new Dynamic Role, define the ID and name, and then select the various different attributes for each approver. In Figure 4.13, we created a new Dynamic Role called *Benefits Coordinator*. Here, we will define different approvers if the employee's organization assignment matches the following attributes:

▶ DIVISION is ENTERPRISES and LOCATION is ARLINGTON, VIRGINIA

▶ DIVISION is ENTERPRISES and LOCATION is ATLANTA

▶ DIVISION is HEALTHCARE

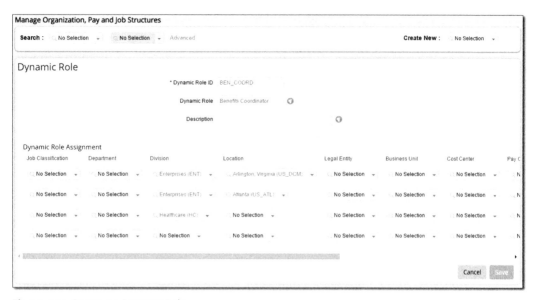

Figure 4.13 Creating a Dynamic Role

For each of these attributes, define an approver type and approver. Here, we will define a person for each attribute (see Figure 4.14).

Figure 4.14 Assigning Approvers to Attributes in a Dynamic Role

Now, click Save, and the Dynamic Role is created; you can see the result in Figure 4.15.

Figure 4.15 Benefits Coordinator Dynamic Role

Now that we've looked at Dynamic Roles, let's take a look at Workflow Groups.

Workflow Groups

Workflow Groups—also known as *Dynamic Groups*—are groups of individuals that all receive a workflow simultaneously. All members of a Workflow Group have the ability to approve the workflow, and the workflow will be available for approval for all group members until the first group member approves it. Once approved, the workflow is no longer available for approval by other group members. Figure 4.16 shows a Workflow Group.

You create Workflow Groups in the same way as Permission Groups, which we discussed in Chapter 3, Section 3.2.1. They use the same set of fields to include and exclude members.

Workflow Groups are also used for contributors and CC roles. For contributors, all members in the group will be able to comment on a workflow until it is approved. For CC roles, all members of the group will receive notification of the workflow approval.

To create a Workflow Group, go to OneAdmin and select Employee Files • Manage Workflow Groups. Click the Create Group button, enter the group name, and then select the inclusion and exclusion criteria as you would when creating a Permission Group. Click Done to save the group.

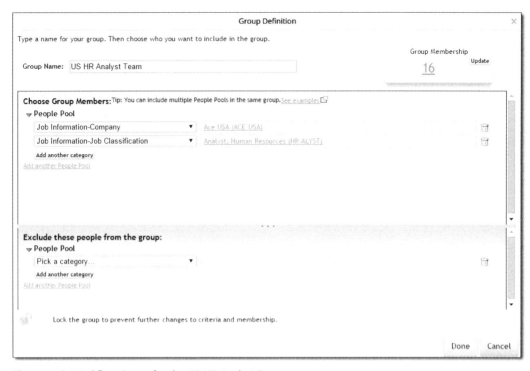

Figure 4.16 Workflow Group for the US HR Analyst Team

Now that we've looked at Dynamic Roles and Workflow Groups, it's time to look at the Workflow Configurations themselves.

4.3.2 Workflow Configurations

Workflows are defined by Workflow Configurations, which are Foundation Objects. Technically, a workflow is made up of several Foundation Objects:

- Workflow Configuration (wfConfig)
- Workflow Step Approver (wfStepApprover)
- Contributor Type (wfConfigContributor)
- CC Role Type (wfConfigCC)

A Workflow Configuration is broken up into four sections, represented by the objects just listed. These sections are as follows:

- ▶ Workflow attributes
- ▶ Approvers
- ▶ Contributors
- ▶ CC roles

Figure 4.17 shows a Workflow Configuration for a Promotion workflow.

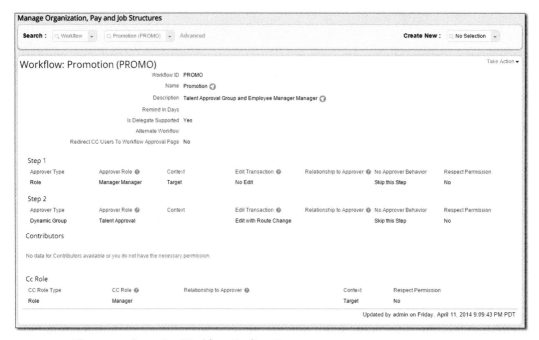

Figure 4.17 Promotion Workflow Configuration

In the sections that follow, we will look at each of these workflow sections in greater depth, including descriptions of both Foundation Object workflows and Generic Object workflows.

Workflow Attributes

The attributes used to define a Workflow Configuration and its overall behavior (not approval flow) are as follows:

- ▶ ID
  The unique identifier for the Workflow Configuration.

- NAME
  The name of the workflow.

- DESCRIPTION
  An optional description of the workflow.

- REMIND IN DAYS
  The number of days after which a reminder notification is sent to the current approver of a workflow (a reminder is sent on a recurring basis based on the value of the field). The REMINDER IN DAYS field is used if a reminder email should be sent by the system to the current approver of the workflow after a certain period if no action has been taken on the workflow. The value should be the number of days after which an email reminder is sent. A reminder email is sent every number of days until action is taken on the email. We will cover this in more detail in Section 4.3.7.

- IS DELEGATE SUPPORTED
  Determines whether a user can set up a workflow to be manually delegated or to be autodelegated in his or her To Do homepage tile. IS DELEGATE SUPPORTED is a Boolean field that enables the AUTO DELEGATION option and the DELEGATE option for approvers of a workflow. We will cover this in more detail in Section 4.3.8.

- ALTERNATIVE WORKFLOW
  Defines the workflow to use if a future-dated transaction already exists. For example, you are making a Job Information change for an employee on July 1, 2016. A Job Information change record already exists for August 1, 2016. In this scenario, it is possible to trigger a different workflow so that alternative approvers can approve the workflow. This could be desired so that HR administrators can review the change before it is approved, so that no duplicates or contradicting changes are made that are already in the future-dated record.

- REDIRECT CC USERS WORKFLOW APPROVAL PAGE
  Defines if CC users can access the workflow approval page or if they just get a notification.

Approvers

In this part of the Workflow Configuration, each approver step is defined. Every approver step must be approved before the workflow is approved. If the workflow cannot derive an approver, then the step is skipped, and if no approvers can be derived, then the workflow is automatically approved. For each approver step, there are several attributes to configure:

▶ APPROVER TYPE

The type of approver selected. There are a number of approver types that determine how the approver should be selected or derived by the system. These approver types are as follows:

▷ ROLE: A specific APPROVER ROLE

▷ DYNAMIC ROLE: An individual will be derived based on the criteria of the DYNAMIC ROLE

▷ DYNAMIC GROUP: A Workflow Group

▷ POSITION: The holder or holders will be selected

▶ APPROVER ROLE

Dependent on the APPROVER TYPE. Use the APPROVER ROLE field to select the value of the ROLE, DYNAMIC ROLE, WORKFLOW GROUP, or POSITION once the APPROVER TYPE is selected. When DYNAMIC ROLE, WORKFLOW GROUP, or POSITION is selected in the APPROVER TYPE field, the APPROVER ROLE field values will be a list of the respective objects. If ROLE is selected as the value of the APPROVER TYPE field, then the APPROVER ROLE field will provide the following list of approver roles that are used to derive the approver based on the employee who is the subject of the workflow:

▷ SELF: The individual that initiated the request

▷ MANAGER: The manager of the employee

▷ MANAGER'S MANAGER: The manager of the manager of the employee

▷ EMPLOYEE HR: The HR manager of the employee (as defined in the JOB RELATIONSHIPS portlet on the EMPLOYMENT INFORMATION screen)

▷ MATRIX MANAGER: The matrix manager of the employee (as defined in the JOB RELATIONSHIPS portlet on the EMPLOYMENT INFORMATION screen)

▷ CUSTOM MANAGER: The custom manager of the employee (as defined in the JOB RELATIONSHIPS portlet on the EMPLOYMENT INFORMATION screen)

▷ SECOND MANAGER: The second manager of the employee (as defined in the JOB RELATIONSHIPS portlet on the EMPLOYMENT INFORMATION screen)

▷ ADDITIONAL MANAGER: The additional manager of the employee (as defined in the JOB RELATIONSHIPS portlet on the EMPLOYMENT INFORMATION screen)

If an Approver Role is set as an approval step in a workflow but no user is assigned, then that step of the workflow will be skipped. For example, the approval step will be skipped if Employee HR is set as the Approver Role in a workflow but the employee who is the subject of the workflow doesn't have an HR manager assigned.

▶ Context
Determines whether this is the current Approver Type (Source) or future Approver Type (Target); only triggers if the approver changes as part of the data changes that trigger the workflow. Use the Context field when the value that is changed in the transaction is an Approver Role (excluding Self). There are two options:

  ▸ Source

  ▸ Target

For example, an employee's manager changes. If the Approver Role field value is Manager and the Context field value is Source, then the employee's current manager is selected as the approver. If the Approver Role field value is Manager and the Context field value is Target, then the employee's proposed new manager is selected as the approver.

▶ Edit Transaction
Determines whether the approver can edit data that is part of the workflow (Edit without Route Change), can edit the data and have the workflow reroute all the way through the approver chain (Edit with Route Change), or cannot edit any data (No Edit).

▶ Relationship to Approver
Determines whether the Approver Type is related to the initiator of the workflow (Initiator) or the subject of the workflow (Employee).

▶ No Approver Behavior
What should happen if the workflow reaches an approver that cannot be derived (e.g., a position with no incumbent, an employee has no manager, the employee's manager has no manager, there is no HR manager assigned, etc.); either the step is skipped (Skip this Step), or the workflow is cancelled (Stop the Workflow).

▶ RESPECT PERMISSION

Determines whether RBP permissions are respected (YES) or not (NO) for the user when viewing data in the workflow approval page.

Contributors

As mentioned, contributors have the ability to comment on a workflow during the approval process. Once the workflow is approved, contributors are no longer able to comment on it. Contributors have a similar but smaller list of fields as approvers:

▶ CONTRIBUTOR TYPE

▶ CONTRIBUTOR

▶ RELATIONSHIP TO APPROVER

▶ CONTEXT

▶ RESPECT PERMISSION

The CONTRIBUTOR TYPE and CONTRIBUTOR fields correspond to the APPROVER TYPE and APPROVER ROLE fields. The CONTRIBUTOR TYPE field has the same values as the APPROVER TYPE field, although for contributors there is an additional value available: PERSON. This value enables you to select an individual employee in the CONTRIBUTOR field.

CC Roles

CC roles have an almost identical set of attributes as contributors:

▶ CC ROLE TYPE

▶ CC ROLE

▶ RELATIONSHIP TO APPROVER

▶ CONTEXT

▶ RESPECT PERMISSION

Like with contributors, the CC ROLE TYPE and CC ROLE fields correspond to the APPROVER TYPE and APPROVER ROLE fields. The CC ROLE TYPE field has the same values as the APPROVER TYPE field, but also has the PERSON value as well as EXTERNAL EMAIL. The EXTERNAL EMAIL value enables a notification to be sent to a specified email address once the workflow is approved.

Before we move onto the workflow creation process, let's take a look at Foundation Object and Generic Object workflows.

Foundation Object and Generic Object Workflows

Foundation Object workflows have some limitations compared to workflows used for Personal Information or Employment Information data changes.

Workflows used for Foundation Objects only support DYNAMIC GROUP and POSITION as values for the APPROVER TYPE and CONTRIBUTOR TYPE fields. For CC users, the only values available for the CC ROLE TYPE fields are DYNAMIC GROUP, POSITION, PERSON, and EXTERNAL EMAIL.

You cannot edit or update active workflows. If the changes made by the initiator are incorrect, then the workflow must be rejected and the correct changes made by the initiator.

Workflows for Generic Objects do not support Dynamic Role as an Approver Type, Contributor Type, or CC Role Type. However, there is an exception for a Position object.

Next, we will look at an example while walking through the workflow creation process.

4.3.3 Creating a Workflow

Now that we've reviewed the various options available when creating a workflow, let's take a moment to look at an example of creating a workflow in action.

For our example, let's create a workflow for an employee change of position. In our workflow, we want four approvers: current HR representative, new HR representative, new manager, and the new manager's manager. We also want to notify the current manager and notify the IT helpdesk via its shared email inbox. The workflow should also have a three-day reminder.

First, let's define the attributes. These include the ID, name, and description of our workflow and the reminder, delegation, alternative workflow, and CC user redirection page. With exception of the reminder, let's use the default values. Figure 4.18 shows the attributes for our workflow, including the three-day reminder.

Manage Organization, Pay and Job Structures

Search : ⌕ No Selection ▾   No Selection ▾   Advanced   Create New : ⌕ No Selection ▾

Workflow

* Workflow ID	Position_Change
Name	Position Change
Description	Workflow for Position changes
Remind in Days	3
Is Delegate Supported	No ▾
Alternate Workflow	⌕ No Selection ▾
Redirect CC Users To Workflow Approval Page	No ▾

Figure 4.18 Attributes of Position Change Workflow

Next, let's define each of the approver steps. Add each step one by one, starting with the employee's current HR representative. For all approver steps, set the RELATIONSHIP TO EMPLOYEE field value to EMPLOYEE and the RESPECT PERMISSION field value to YES, but set different values for the EDIT TRANSACTION and NO APPROVER BEHAVIOR fields depending on the approver.

Figure 4.19 shows the four configured approver steps for each of the approvers we want in our workflow: current HR representative, new HR representative, new manager, and the new manager's manager.

Step 1

* Approver Type	* Approver Role	Context	Edit Transaction	Relationship to Approver	No Approver Behavior	Respect Permission	
Role ▾	⌕ Employee HR ▾	Source ▾	Edit without Rout ▾	Employee ▾	Stop the Workflo ▾	Yes ▾	🗑

Step 2

* Approver Type	* Approver Role	Context	Edit Transaction	Relationship to Approver	No Approver Behavior	Respect Permission	
Role ▾	⌕ Employee HR ▾	Target ▾	Edit with Route C ▾	Employee ▾	Stop the Workflo ▾	Yes ▾	🗑

Step 3

* Approver Type	* Approver Role	Context	Edit Transaction	Relationship to Approver	No Approver Behavior	Respect Permission	
Role ▾	⌕ Manager ▾	Target ▾	No Edit ▾	Employee ▾	Stop the Workflo ▾	Yes ▾	🗑

Step 4

* Approver Type	* Approver Role	Context	Edit Transaction	Relationship to Approver	No Approver Behavior	Respect Permission	
Role ▾	⌕ Manager Manag ▾	Target ▾	No Edit ▾	Employee ▾	Skip this Step ▾	Yes ▾	🗑

Figure 4.19 Approver Steps in Workflow

In a similar process, define the CC users, which are the current manager and the IT Helpdesk shared email inbox. Figure 4.20 shows the configured CC users.

Figure 4.20 CC Users in Workflow

Once you've finished the configuration, click the SAVE button to save the workflow. Figure 4.21 shows what our completed workflow looks like.

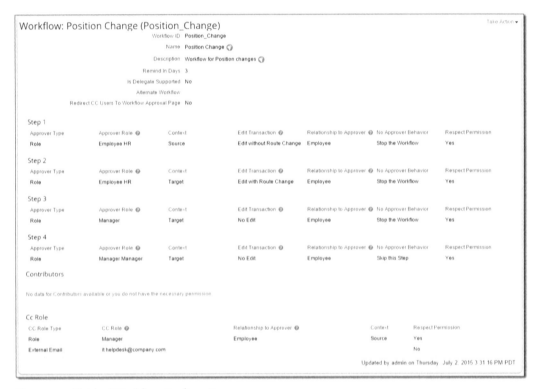

Figure 4.21 Finished Workflow Configuration

Now that we've set up a workflow, it's time to look at workflow triggers.

4.3.4 Creating and Assigning Workflow Triggers

No matter on which type of field or object the workflow is triggered, a business rule defines the trigger rule(s). The process is similar to creating business rules for Event Derivation. The key difference when creating a business rule to trigger a workflow is that the THEN condition should always set the WFCONFIG field of the base object to be the workflow configuration that will be triggered (for a Model object, it should be `wfConfig.Value`). Figure 4.22 shows an example of this type of business rule for an address change.

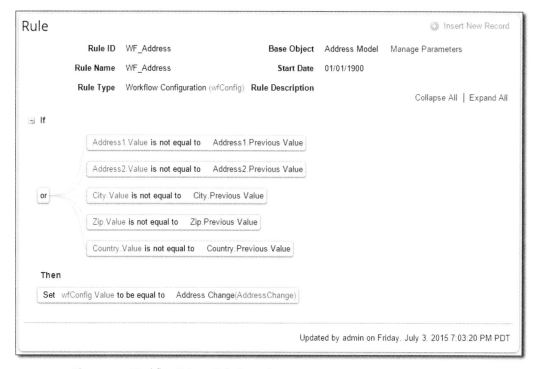

Figure 4.22 Workflow Trigger Rule Example

In order to compare new values to previous values for a field (i.e., identify if there has been a change), use the model version of a base object. For example, to compare address fields to determine change, use the ADDRESS MODEL base object instead of the ADDRESS base object.

138

We'll now look at the process of assigning workflows to trigger on different objects.

Personal Information and Employment Information Triggers

Workflows triggered on changes to Personal Information portlets using the EDIT button or to Employment Information portlets using the TAKE ACTION menu (including Global Assignments and Pensions Payouts) use Workflow Derivation, the same process that is used for Event Derivation. As with Event Derivation, workflows were triggered historically by creating rules in an XML file.

> **Important!**
>
> Just like with Event Derivation, customers can only use either the XML-based workflow rules or the Rules Engine rules—not a combination of both. If a customer currently uses XML-based workflow rules and wishes to use the Rules Engine, the customer must have the new method enabled in Provisioning and must then recreate all workflow trigger rules in the Rules Engine.

Business rules created for Workflow Derivation are assigned the same way as business rules created for Event Derivation, in OneAdmin in COMPANY SETTINGS • MANAGE BUSINESS CONFIGURATION. Assign these rules to the appropriate portlet as required.

Many workflows trigger based on specific Event Reasons, so the IF conditions of a business rule to trigger a workflow can reference an Event Reason, just like the New Hire example seen in Figure 4.23. These business rules are assigned immediately after the Event Derivation business rule on the MANAGE BUSINESS CONFIGURATION screen.

New Hire and Rehire

Workflows for New Hire or Rehire are assigned to the Job Information portlet in OneAdmin in COMPANY SETTINGS • MANAGE BUSINESS CONFIGURATION. A business rule for triggering a workflow for New Hire or Rehire should use the Job Information base object and have the IF conditions check if the EVENT REASON field is equal to any Event Reasons that you have configured in your system for hire or rehire. Figure 4.23 shows an example of a New Hire workflow trigger.

Figure 4.23 New Hire Workflow Trigger

Foundation Object Triggers

Foundation Objects can trigger workflows, whether traditional Foundation Objects or Foundation Objects that have been migrated to the MDF as Generic Objects. For Foundation Objects that have been migrated to the MDF, refer to the following section on Generic Object triggers. In this section, we will focus on traditional Foundation Objects.

Workflows for Foundation Objects trigger whenever an object is created, modified, or deleted. It is not possible to trigger a workflow on just one of these actions; a workflow will trigger on each of these actions as per the IF conditions defined in the business rule.

Business rules created for Foundation Objects require adding a parameter in order to define the workflow configuration. To do this when creating a new business rule, follow these steps:

1. Select the base object in the BASE OBJECT field.

2. Click the MANAGE PARAMETERS hyperlink.

3. In the CODE column, enter the value "FOWorkflow."

4. Enter a name in the NAME column; this will be relevant later.

5. In the OBJECT dropdown, select FO WORKFLOW.

6. Click APPLY.

Prior to clicking the APPLY button, the MANAGE PARAMETERS window should look like Figure 4.24.

Code	Name	Object
context	Context	SystemContext
FOWorkflow	FOWorkflow	FO Workflow

Manage Parameters

Add New Parameter

Cancel   Apply

Figure 4.24 Parameters for Foundation Object Workflows

After completing the rest of the business rule information, configure the THEN condition to set the Workflow Configuration. Select SET in the first dropdown, and click the + button next to the name you defined in step 4 in the second dropdown and select the field WORKFLOW INFORMATION. Select the Workflow Configuration, and click the SAVE button. Your business rule will look similar to that shown in Figure 4.25.

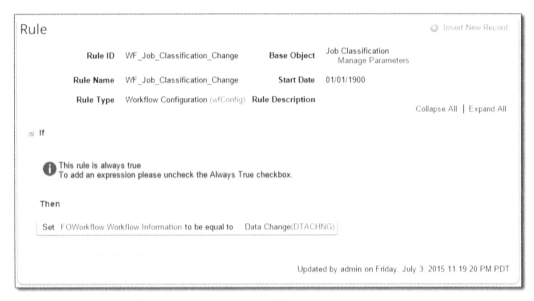

Figure 4.25 Business Rule for a Foundation Object Workflow

Workflows for Foundation Objects must have the business rule assigned to the object in the Corporate Data Model as an `onSave` event. An implementation consultant typically performs this process.

Generic Object Triggers

For Generic Objects—including Foundation Objects that have been migrated to the MDF and Time Off objects—create a business rule per the Personal Information or Employment Information workflows and assign it to the Object Definition.

Assign business rules created to trigger workflows to the object definition under RULES as a `validateRules` event. This might look like the example shown in Figure 4.26.

Figure 4.26 Business Rule Assigned to the MDF Object

Chapter 5 covers assigning business rules to Generic Objects.

4.3.5   Workflow Notifications

Once a workflow is triggered, an approver is notified of the workflow by email. In addition, the user can see the workflow listed in the To Do portlet on the homepage and also in the PENDING REQUEST screen in EMPLOYEE FILES. Depending on permissions, a user browsing the PERSONAL INFORMATION or EMPLOYMENT INFORMATION screens of an employee subject to a workflow may see a notification in the portlet(s) on which the workflow was triggered. We'll take a look at each of these notification possibilities.

Email Notifications

Email notifications are sent out automatically for a variety of workflow-related actions, including approvals, rejections, pending, comments, delegations, and more. We'll cover all of these shortly. You cannot turn off email notifications for workflows.

Manage email notifications in OneAdmin in COMPANY SETTINGS • E-MAIL NOTIFICATION TEMPLATES SETTINGS. There are fifteen email notification templates used by the system, as described in Table 4.3.

Workflow Email Notification Template	Scenario
Workflow Action Approval Notification	Workflow requires approval
Workflow Action Rejected Notification	Workflow has been rejected
Workflow Action Pending Notification	Reminder for pending workflow
Workflow Action Cancelled Notification	Workflow has been cancelled
Workflow Action Skipped Notification	Workflow has been skipped
Workflow Comment Posted Notification	Comment has been posted to workflow
Workflow Action Lock Down Notification	Workflow has been locked down by an administrator
Workflow Action Unlock Notification	Workflow has been unlocked by an administrator
Workflow Action Contributor Notification	Recipient is a contributor to a workflow that has been submitted for approval
Workflow Action Cc Role Notification	Notification that workflow has been approved
Workflow Step Approved Notification	Workflow step has been approved
Workflow Sentback Notification	Workflow has been sent back to initiator by an approver

Table 4.3 Workflow Email Notification Templates

Workflow Email Notification Template	Scenario
Workflow Action Delegate Notification	Workflow has been delegated
Workflow Action Delegate Revoke Notification	Workflow delegation has been revoked
Workflow Action Delegate Decline Notification	Workflow delegation has been declined by the delegate

Table 4.3 Workflow Email Notification Templates (Cont.)

You can modify any email notification template, and can change the following attributes:

▸ Priority

▸ Subject

▸ Body

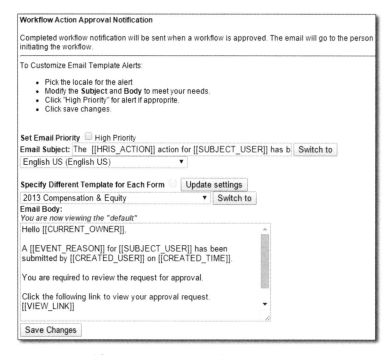

Figure 4.27 Workflow Action Approval Notification Email Template

The email subject and email body are configurable for each enabled language. Figure 4.27 shows an example of the WORKFLOW ACTION APPROVAL NOTIFICATION workflow email template.

As you can see in Figure 4.27, variable codes can insert dynamically determined values into the email that the template generates. Table 4.4 lists common variable codes used for workflow email notifications.

Variable Code	Definition
[[HRIS_ACTION]]	Type of action
[[ACTION_TYPE]]	Type of action for Foundation Object workflows
[[EVENT]]	Event for the action
[[EVENT_REASON]]	Event Reason for the action
[[EFFECTIVE_DATE]]	Date that the data change/action will be effective
[[VIEW_LINK]]	Hyperlink to the workflow approval page
[[SUBJECT_USER]]	Employee who is the subject of the workflow
[[SUBJECT_USER_ID]]	User ID of the employee who is the subject of the workflow
[[PERSON_ID_EXTERNAL]]	External ID of the employee who is the subject of the workflow
[[SUBJECT_USER_LEGAL_ENTITY]]	Legal Entity of the employee who is the subject of the workflow
[[SUBJECT_USER_DEPARTMENT]]	Department of the employee who is the subject of the workflow
[[SUBJECT_USER_COSTCENTER]]	Cost Center of the employee who is the subject of the workflow
[[SUBJECT_USER_JOBCODE]]	Job Code of the employee who is the subject of the workflow
[[SUBJECT_USER_JOBTITLE]]	Job Title of the employee who is the subject of the workflow
[[RECIPIENT_NAME]]	Recipient of the email

Table 4.4 Email Template Variable Codes

Variable Code	Definition
`[[CURRENT_OWNER]]`	Current approver of the workflow or the user that rejected a workflow
`[[APPROVAL_CHAIN]]`	Workflow approval chain up to the current approver
`[[CREATED_USER]]`	User who initiated the workflow
`[[CREATED_USER_EMAIL]]`	Email of the user who initiated the workflow
`[[CREATED_TIME]]`	The date and time when the workflow was initiated
`[[RECENTLY_APPROVED_BY]]`	The most recent approver of the workflow
`[[RECENTLY_APPROVED_BY_COMMENT]]`	Any comments by the most recent approver of the workflow
`[[RECENT_APPROVAL_DATE]]`	The date of the most recent approval of the workflow
`[[RECENT_COMMENT_POSTED]]`	The comment that was posted on a workflow
`[[RECENT_COMMENT_POSTED_BY]]`	User that posted a comment
`[[RECENT_COMMENT_POSTED_DATE]]`	The date that the comment was posted by the user
`[[SENTBACK_BY]]`	User that sent back the workflow
`[[SENTBACK_BY_COMMENT]]`	Comments by the user that sent back the workflow
`[[REJECTED_BY]]`	User that rejected the workflow
`[[REJECTED_BY_COMMENT]]`	Comments by the user that rejected the workflow
`[[DELEGATOR]]`	User who is delegating the workflow
`[[DELEGATEE]]`	User who has been delegated the workflow

Table 4.4 Email Template Variable Codes (Cont.)

Figure 4.28 shows the email generated by the system for the Workflow Action Approval Notification email template.

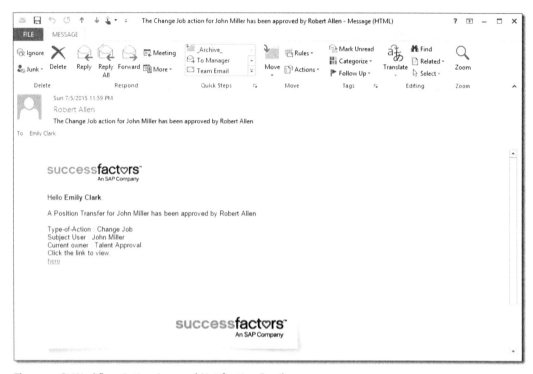

Figure 4.28 Workflow Action Approval Notification Email

Now that we've looked at workflow notification emails, let's take a look at how workflow notifications appear in the system itself.

To Do Tile

The To Do tile on the homepage highlights a variety of outstanding tasks and notifications for a user, including workflow notifications. All workflows that require action by the user appear in the To Do tile with their due dates. Typically, the due date for workflows is TODAY. By selecting a workflow in the To Do tile, a user can view the workflow approval page. Figure 4.29 shows the To Do tile.

Figure 4.29 To Do Tile

Pending Requests

The PENDING REQUESTS screen in the EMPLOYEE FILES menu provides workflow approvers and initiators—as well as contributors and individuals assigned as CC users—with the ability to view a variety of requests that they have submitted or are part of. The PENDING REQUESTS screen is broken up into four portlets:

► REQUESTS WAITING FOR MY APPROVAL
  Submitted workflows that require approval by the user

► REQUESTS STILL IN PROGRESS THAT I APPROVED
  Active workflows that the user has approved

► MY REQUESTS WAITING FOR APPROVAL
  Workflows that the user has submitted that are still active and waiting to be approved

► MY NOTIFICATIONS
  Workflows for which the user is a CC user

Figure 4.30 shows the PENDING REQUESTS screen.

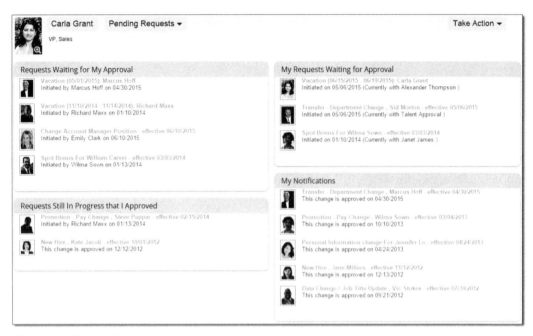

Figure 4.30 Pending Requests Screen

Access the WORKFLOW APPROVAL screen by clicking the appropriate hyperlink.

Portlet Notifications

If a user has the appropriate permissions, he or she will see a notification in a portlet in the PERSONAL INFORMATION or EMPLOYMENT INFORMATION screens on which a workflow has been submitted. This looks like the example seen in Figure 4.31. Once the workflow is approved, this notification will disappear.

Figure 4.31 Pending Workflow Notification in Job Information Portlet

Click the hyperlink to view the WORKFLOW APPROVAL screen.

Now that we've covered how users are notified of workflow requests, let's take a look at the approval process itself.

4.3.6 Workflow Approval Process

Once a workflow has been submitted and an approver notified, it's time for the approver to approve the workflow. An approver accesses the workflow approval screen from the hyperlink found in the email notification, To Do tile, or PENDING REQUESTS screen. The workflow approval screen usually looks like the screen shown in Figure 4.32.

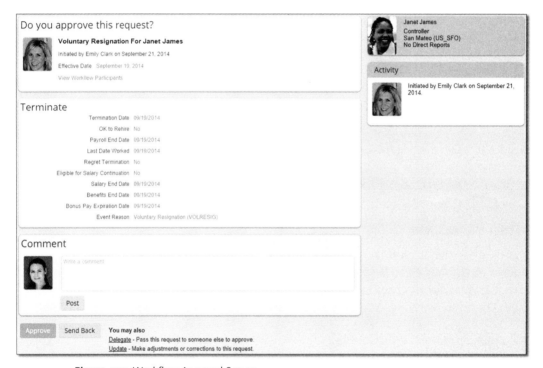

Figure 4.32 Workflow Approval Screen

The screen contains six areas (listed counter-clockwise):

▶ WORKFLOW OVERVIEW
Lists the Event Reason/action, initiator, date of submission, effective date of the action, and hyperlink to view the workflow participants.

▶ WORKFLOW DETAILS

Shows the data changes made that are being approved in the workflow (subject to permissions, if configured).

▶ COMMENT

Allows the approver or contributor to add comments to the workflow, which will appear in the ACTIVITY log.

▶ APPROVAL OPTIONS

Provides options for the approver to approve the workflow, cancel it or send it back to the initiator, delegate the workflow (if configured), or make changes to the data being approved (if configured), or for the initiator to withdraw the request. The approval options provide the approver with the ability to perform a number of actions on the workflow, some of which depend on the settings made on the Workflow Configuration covered in Section 4.3.2. These options include the following:

- ▸ APPROVE: Approves the workflow step
- ▸ SEND BACK: Sends the workflow back to the initiator
- ▸ DELEGATE: Allows the user to delegate the workflow to another user
- ▸ UPDATE: Allows the user to make changes to the data being approved
- ▸ WITHDRAW: Only available for the initiator; enables the initiator to cancel the workflow request

▶ ACTIVITY

Displays a log of all activities on the workflow, such as comments, approvals, and delegations.

▶ USER WHO IS SUBJECT OF THE WORKFLOW

Shows a brief overview about the user who is the subject of the workflow.

Once the approver has approved the workflow, it will move to the next approver in the approval chain. If the approver is the last approver in the approval chain, then the entire workflow is approved and the changes become active in the system.

Now, let's take a look at setting reminders for workflows.

4.3.7 Setting Reminders

Email reminders can be set up in the system by setting a value in the REMIND IN DAYS field in the Workflow Configuration(s) for which you would like email reminders to be sent. When set with a value (in days), the system will send an email reminder to the current approver of the workflow after the number of days defined in this field if no action has been taken on the workflow. The system determines "action" as activities such as adding a comment, changing an approver, and approving the workflow.

The reminder email is sent again after the same number of days and will continue to be sent out the number of days specified until action is taken. For example, if the value of the REMIND IN DAYS field is set to 5, then a reminder email will be sent five days after the workflow has been received by the approver. A reminder email will then be sent to the approver every five days until action is taken on the workflow.

The content of reminder emails are sent using the Workflow Action Pending Notification email template. If the workflow is sent back to the initiator and a reminder is triggered, the system will use the Workflow Sentback Notification email notification template. See Section 4.3.5 for details on workflow notifications.

In order to send reminder emails, a quartz job needs to be set up in Provisioning. Note that a global value can be set on the quartz job that is effective for all workflows, irrespective of what is put into the REMIND IN DAYS field of any workflow.

4.3.8 Delegation

Delegation of workflows is possible, enabling another user (delegatee) to receive and approve a workflow instead of the original approver (delegator). A delegatee can reject the delegation and return the workflow back to the delegator. Once a workflow has been delegated, it cannot be delegated further by the delegatee. If a delegatee becomes inactive (i.e., he or she is terminated or retires), then the delegation will be cancelled and the delegator will become the approver of any active workflows.

Delegated workflows appear in the delegate's TO DO tile and in the PENDING REQUESTS screen.

There are two types of delegation:

▸ Manual delegation

▸ Auto delegation

Enable both manual delegation and auto delegation for each workflow by setting the IS DELEGATE SUPPORTED field to YES on the appropriate workflow configuration.

Let's look at each type of delegation.

Manual Delegation

Manual delegation allows the delegator to manually delegate a workflow to a delegatee within the workflow approval screen by selecting the DELEGATE option at the bottom of the screen, as shown in Figure 4.32. The delegator selects the DELEGATE option and then selects the user to be the delegatee in the DELEGATE REQUEST popup window, as shown in Figure 4.33. The delegator then clicks the SEND button and is asked to confirm the action by clicking the DELEGATE button.

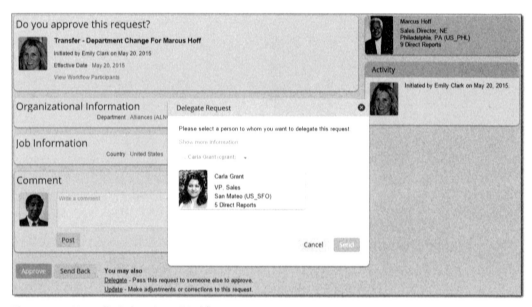

Figure 4.33 Manually Delegating a Workflow

After the delegator clicks the DELEGATE button, the delegatee will be made the approver of this step of the workflow, and a notification will be sent that the delegate has been delegated a workflow to approve. The email notification will use the Workflow Action Delegate Notification template. See Section 4.3.5 for details on workflow notifications.

Auto Delegation

Auto delegation automatically redirects an approver's workflows to a specified delegatee. This could be useful for an executive delegating his or her workflows to an executive assistant or a manager delegating workflows while on vacation, for example. Auto delegation is effective for all workflow approvals required after it has been enabled by the delegator and is not effective for existing workflows that require approval by the delegator. Any active workflows need to be delegated manually by the approver.

Set up auto delegation with the AUTO DELEGATE option in the MY INFO LINKS part of the MY INFO tile on the homepage (accessed by clicking the cog icon on the MY INFO tile), as shown in Figure 4.34.

Figure 4.34 My Info Links Tile

After selecting this option, the CONFIGURE DELEGATION OF WORKFLOWS popup window opens, as shown in Figure 4.35. Here, the user should select the DELEGATE MY APPROVALS checkbox and then find the user who will be the delegatee for all of the delegator's workflows. Once complete, clicking the SAVE button will save the delegation.

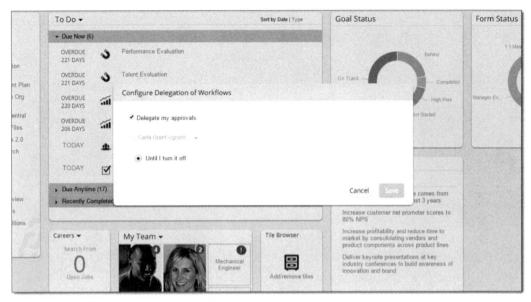

Figure 4.35 Configure Delegation of Workflows Popup

To cancel an auto delegation, select the AUTO DELEGATE option in the MY INFO LINKS part of the MY INFO tile on the homepage, uncheck the DELEGATE MY APPROVALS checkbox, and then click the SAVE button.

Now that we've covered delegation, let's look at the workflow audit trail.

4.3.9   Workflow Audit Trail

You can view the workflow approval audit trail for data changes in the Address, Personal Information, Job Information, Job Relationships, and Compensation Information portlets by navigating to the HISTORY screen of the portlet, selecting the appropriate record, clicking the TAKE ACTION button, and selecting the VIEW APPROVAL HISTORY option. The VIEW APPROVAL HISTORY option only displays for records approved by a workflow. Figure 4.36 shows the workflow approval audit trail.

Now, let's look at administering workflows.

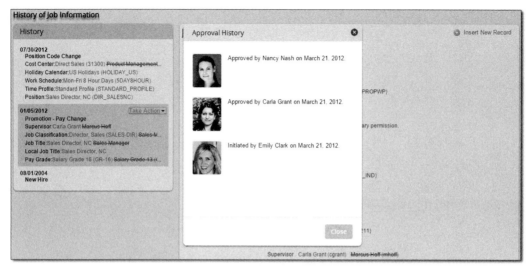

Figure 4.36 Workflow Approval History

4.3.10 Administering Workflows

There are several options in OneAdmin to administer workflows and associated configurations:

▶ MANAGE WORKFLOW REQUESTS

▶ MANAGE WORKFLOW REQUESTS WITH INVALID APPROVERS

▶ MANAGE WORKFLOW GROUPS

▶ INVALID USER IN DYNAMIC ROLE

▶ MANAGE ORGANIZATION, PAY AND JOB STRUCTURES

▶ Manage Data (for AUTO DELEGATE CONFIGURATION)

Let's briefly explore each of these options and their capabilities.

Manage Workflow Requests

The MANAGE WORKFLOW REQUESTS transaction provides administrators with the ability to administer active and inactive workflows in the system. It covers all workflows with a subject user (i.e., it does not show Foundation Object workflows). Access it from the EMPLOYEE FILES menu in OneAdmin. First, the MANAGE WORKFLOW REQUESTS transaction presents the user with the SEARCH WORKFLOW REQUESTS popup, which enables the user to select the type of workflows that he or she wishes to view. Figure 4.37 shows the popup and all of the search criteria. At least one search criteria must be selected, and any combination can be used.

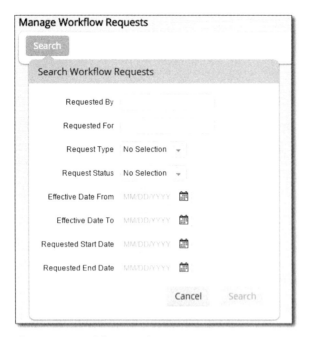

Figure 4.37 Workflow Search Criteria

The user can choose from the following search options:

▶ REQUESTED BY
Initiator of the workflow

▶ REQUESTED FOR
The employee who is the subject of the workflow

▶ REQUEST TYPE
The Event Reason that was triggered

▶ REQUEST STATUS
The status of the workflow; choose from the following:

  ▹ INITIALIZED: This is unused

  ▹ PENDING: The workflow is pending approval

  ▹ COMPLETED: Approved workflows

  ▹ REJECTED: Rejected workflows

- ▶ CANCELLED: Cancelled workflows

- ▶ LOCKED: Locked workflows

- ▶ SENTBACK: Workflows that have been sent back

- ▶ EFFECTIVE DATE FROM and EFFECTIVE DATE TO
  Date that the changes become effective once approved

- ▶ REQUESTED START DATE and REQUESTED END DATE
  Date the workflow was initiated

If PENDING or SENTBACK is selected for the REQUEST STATUS, then a new field is displayed: STALLED FOR DAYS. This field allows the user to search for workflows that have been stalled for a specific number of days. The value entered is the minimum number of days for which a workflow has been stalled. For example, if you enter "20" as the value, any workflows that have been stalled for twenty days or more will be displayed.

Now, let's go through a quick example. If you wanted to search for all active workflows that were pending approval, you would open the REQUEST STATUS dropdown, select INITIALIZED, and click the SEARCH button.

After you enter search criteria and click the SEARCH button, you will see a list of workflows that meet the criteria. Figure 4.38 shows a list of workflows that meet the example criteria.

Manage Workflow Requests						
Search				Items per page 10 ▾	◄ ◄ Page 1 of 1 ► ►|	
Requested By	**Requested For**	**Request Type**	**Request Status**	**Effective Date** ▲	**Actions**	**Stalled For Days**
Emily Clark	Brian Wilson	Start Pension Payout (S...	PENDING	02/23/2015	Take Action ▾	131
Carla Grant	Sid Morton	Transfer - Department C...	PENDING	05/06/2015	Take Action ▾	66
Emily Clark	Marcus Hoff	Transfer - Department C...	PENDING	05/20/2015	Take Action ▾	52
Emily Clark	Carla Grant	Add Address	PENDING	05/21/2015	Take Action ▾	51
Emily Clark	Matthew Moore	Add Address	PENDING	05/21/2015	Take Action ▾	51
Emily Clark	Caroline Clark	Add Address	PENDING	05/21/2015	Take Action ▾	51
Emily Clark	Caroline Clark	Add Address	PENDING	05/21/2015	Take Action ▾	51
Emily Clark	Position Account Mana...	Change Generic Object...	PENDING	06/10/2015	Take Action ▾	31

Figure 4.38 Active Workflows in PENDING Status

The table of results has several columns, many of which are included in the search criteria. View the workflow by clicking the hyperlinked value in the REQUEST TYPE column. There also are two columns to the right side of the table:

- ▶ ACTIONS
  A list of actions to take on the workflow

- ▶ STALLED FOR DAYS
  The number of days for which the workflow has been stalled (i.e., no action has been taken)

There are several actions available for each workflow. When you click the TAKE ACTION button in the ACTION column, a menu of six options opens. When you select an option, you will see a popup box in which to take the action. The six options are as follows:

- ▶ LOCK DOWN
  Lock down the workflow so it is no longer active

- ▶ ADD ANOTHER APPROVER
  Add an additional approver to the workflow

- ▶ CHANGE APPROVERS
  Change the current and any subsequent approvers

- ▶ REMOVE APPROVERS
  Remove any approvers after the current approver (the current approver cannot be removed)

- ▶ ROUTE REQUEST
  Reroute the workflow to a future approver

- ▶ DECLINE
  Reject the workflow

Figure 4.39 shows an approver change in progress after selecting CHANGE APPROVERS.

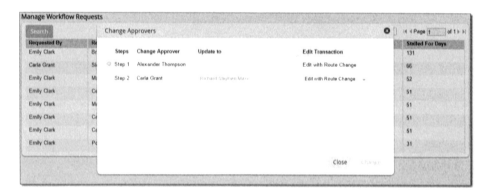

Figure 4.39 Changing a Workflow Approver

Manage Workflow Requests with Invalid Approvers

The MANAGE WORKFLOW REQUESTS WITH INVALID APPROVERS transaction located in the EMPLOYEE FILES menu in OneAdmin provides the user with a list of workflows that have an approver assigned who is no longer active in the system (i.e., the user has been terminated). Figure 4.40 shows the list of workflows with invalid approvers.

Manage workflow requests with invalid approvers								
						Items per page 10 ▼	◄ ◄ Page 1	of 1 ► ►
Request Type	**Invalid Approvers**	**Actions**	**Requested By**	**Requested For**	**Request Status**	**Effective Date** ▲	**Stalled For Days**	
Vol Termination - Sc...	Rebecca Lee	Take Action ▼	Janet James	Megan Gibbs	PENDING	01/31/2014	0	
Promotion - Pay Chu...	Linda Lewis	Take Action ▼	Richard Stephen Ma...	Steve Pappar	PENDING	02/15/2014	0	
Transfer - Departme...	Steven Thomas	Take Action ▼	Carla Grant	Sid Morton	PENDING	05/06/2015	0	

Figure 4.40 Workflows with Invalid Approvers

The list looks similar to the list shown in MANAGE WORKFLOW REQUESTS. As in that transaction, view the workflow by clicking the hyperlinked value in the REQUEST TYPE column. The list of actions in the TAKE ACTION menu are also the same. By using this menu, you can change the invalid approver or reroute the workflow to the next approver in the chain.

Manage Workflow Groups

Manage Workflow Groups in the MANAGE WORKFLOW GROUPS transaction covered in Section 4.3.1.

Invalid User in Dynamic Role

The INVALID USER IN DYNAMIC ROLE transaction displays a list of all Dynamic Roles with an inactive user assigned as an approver. The transaction is located in the EMPLOYEE FILES menu in OneAdmin.

The list (shown in Figure 4.41) has two columns, one that displays the Dynamic Roles with invalid approvers and one that displays the invalid user(s) in the Dynamic Roles.

Clicking on the hyperlink of the Dynamic Role opens it, as shown in Figure 4.42. Here, the invalid approvers can be viewed and corrected.

Figure 4.41 Dynamic Roles with Invalid Users

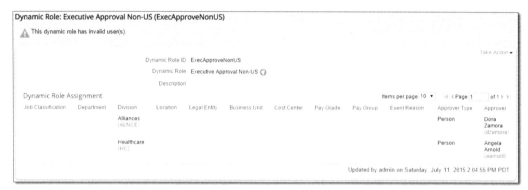

Figure 4.42 Dynamic Role with Invalid Approvers

Manage Organization, Pay, and Job Structures

Manage Workflow Configurations in the Manage Organization, Pay and Job Structures transaction is covered in Section 4.3.3.

Manage Data (Auto Delegate Configuration)

Configurations for each auto delegation can be viewed, modified, and deleted in OneAdmin in Employee Files • Manage Data. Select Auto Delegate Config as the object type in the Search dropdown and a selectable list of users that have enabled auto delegation will appear in the subsequent column. The list displays users with both active and previous auto delegations.

Once loaded, you can modify the Auto Delegation Configuration to add, modify, or remove an auto delegation. Figure 4.43 shows an example of an auto delegation enabled for Alexander Thompson.

Figure 4.43 Auto Delegate Config Object

Use the TAKE ACTION button to modify or delete an existing auto delegation. To create a new auto delegation, select AUTO DELEGATE CONFIG in the CREATE NEW dropdown, enter the necessary details, and click SAVE.

4.4 Summary

In this chapter, we examined employee status, events, Event Reasons, and workflows. We discussed how these concepts are used, when they are used, and how they are configured. We also demonstrated how they support the different processes in the system and enable employee history and approvals to be accurate and logical.

In the next chapter, we'll take a deep dive into the extensibility options in Employee Central and how you can leverage these to create new objects, screens, and applications for your system.

Inevitably, the behavior or functionality of HR applications need to be changed or extended beyond their delivered state. SAP SuccessFactors features a robust framework to adapt the standard Employee Central application.

5 Extensibility

Employee Central has the unique position of belonging to a suite in which individual components can operate independently of one another. This factor presents both a challenge and an opportunity. The product has to be adaptable to a seemingly endless combination of configurations.

The principle concept of extensibility in Employee Central is that there is no best practice. There are leading practices and practices optimized for the specific customer, and these tend to change over time. The 20–25% of customization capabilities that exist in legacy on-premise software are replaced by a set of extensibility features.

Although the standard Employee Central solution is highly configurable, the focus of extensibility is extending beyond the standard configurability. Extensibility really is about creating new functionality where it does not exist in the system. There are two focus areas for Employee Central extensibility:

- Metadata Framework (MDF)
- SAP HANA Cloud Platform (HCP)

Additional Resources

You can read more about extensibility in SAP SuccessFactors in Chapter 4 of *SuccessFactors with SAP ERP HCM: Business Processes and Use* by Amy Grubb and Luke Marson (2nd edition, SAP PRESS, 2015).

In this chapter, we'll take a look at the MDF in an Employee Central context and then discuss SAP SuccessFactors extensions that are built with SAP HANA Cloud

Platform. We'll also take a look at how to create custom objects, and how to create custom screens in Employee Files for these objects. We'll then look at the Rules Engine and creating business rules for different HR scenarios. Lastly, we'll look at how SAP HANA Cloud Platform can help bring your unique ideas to life.

5.1 Metadata Framework

The MDF is an extensibility framework that allows users to create, modify, and maintain custom objects, screens, and business rules within the SAP SuccessFactors UI. Although it contains enough complexity to handle complicated requirements, it's also simple enough for customers to learn and use without needing outside expertise. The MDF requires no coding, because everything is created via the UI.

The beauty of the MDF is that it enables customers to create objects without risking the safety and stability of their and other customer instances within the data center. Because the MDF uses metadata to influence a central set of technical system components instead of creating new technical components, the system is safeguarded and future-proofed to enable quarterly releases to be installed without adversely affecting customer functionality or operation of their instances.

Custom objects created using the MDF are called *Generic Objects*. The standard enterprise license of Employee Central provides twenty-five Generic Objects for customer consumption. This figure does not include objects delivered by SAP SuccessFactors in quarterly releases. Only the top-level object counts within the limit of twenty-five objects. If there are child objects—for example, for country-specific fields or for detailed data—these child objects are not considered against the overall count.

Generic Objects are defined through an *Object Definition*. The Object Definition defines various attributes about the Generic Object, including:

- Code, label, and status of the object
- Whether the object is effective-dated and to what extent
- If the object is visible to the API
- How the object version history is handled
- What workflow to use, how pending data is treated, and what To Do category to use for Generic Object workflows

- Fields, and which fields are searchable when searching for an object
- Associations with other objects
- Whether a different business key format should be used
- Whether the Generic Object is permissioned and which permissions category it is located in
- Business rules that should trigger from the object

Object Definitions can have up to two hundred custom fields, which can be of various datatypes. Some standard fields are delivered for Object Definitions — such as Name and Code — and SAP SuccessFactors-delivered Generic Objects may have a number of standard fields defined, depending on the nature of the Generic Object. Figure 5.1 shows the Object Definition of the Benefit Generic Object.

Figure 5.1 Object Definition of the Benefit Generic Object

This chapter will focus on Employee Central-specific elements of creating objects and screens rather than on the in-depth process. For the full definition of a Generic Object and how to create one, please refer to the *Metadata Framework* (*MDF*) implementation handbook found at *http://help.sap.com/hr_ec*.

Before we look at some of the specifics of creating a Generic Object, let's take a look at some of the use cases for Generic Objects to understand a little more about why and how they can be used.

5.1.1 Creation Scenarios for Generic Objects

Generic Objects are typically configured for one of the following purposes:

▶ **Custom Foundation Objects**
Generic Objects can be used to add additional org structure objects (e.g., a Sub-Division or Regional Location) or to add other Foundation Objects.

▶ **Custom Person or Employment Objects**
Objects can be created to add to Employee Files. There are many use cases, such as Tuition Reimbursement or Objects on Loan.

▶ **Business objects**
Data about business objects can be stored. For example, you can store data about different assets or detailed data on projects. This use case applies for SAP SuccessFactors to store benefits data and work schedules, for example.

▶ **Lookup table**
Generics objects can be used as lookup tables for other functionality. For example, you can look up workflows by attribute or user to run a check on attributes when running rules or calculations. Time Off uses lookup tables for storing seniority data.

▶ **Configuration table**
Tables to store configuration data for applications such as Time Off or global assignments are reasonably common. For global assignments, they may be screens of configuration settings, whereas for Time Off or Benefits, they could be objects that determine what time types or benefit programs are used.

As you can see from the sampling in the previous list, there are many custom and standard use cases for Generic Objects.

In Figure 5.2, a custom object for Tuition Reimbursement has been created as an ESS transaction in Employee Files. Employees can enter the details of tuition reimbursements they wish to claim, and the request will go through a workflow process so it can be approved by a manager and by HR.

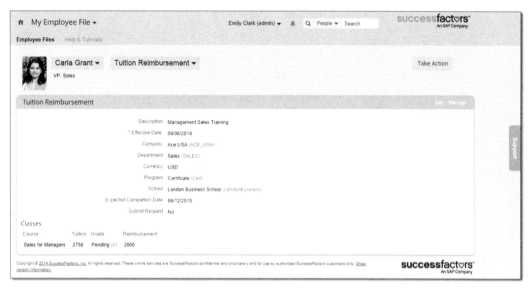

Figure 5.2 Tuition Reimbursement Object in ESS

Another example might include a Generic Object to use as a workflow lookup table within a business rule that triggers a workflow. Figure 5.3 shows an example of this type of custom object.

Figure 5.3 Workflow Lookup Table Generic Object

Before we take a brief look at creating a Generic Object, let's discuss parent and child associations, which will impact your Generic Object design.

5.1.2   Parent and Child Associations

Sometimes—particularly for self-service objects—it's normal to use a single object for an employee record and have a child object used to store multiple records for that employee record. For instance, in the Tuition Reimbursement example shown in Figure 5.2, two Generic Objects are used. One Generic Object is used for the Tuition Reimbursement object itself, and a second Generic Object stores each reimbursement request that is made.

This means that a single record can be kept for an employee for a fixed or permanent period, but multiple child records can be created as needed. The system also provides a logical method of storing transactional data against an employee. However, there are many use cases when one or more child Generic Objects can be used. It's worth looking at some of the SAP SuccessFactors-delivered Generic Objects to understand how such scenarios play out in practice.

5.1.3   Creating and Maintaining Object Definitions

Object Definitions are created and maintained in OneAdmin in Company Settings • Configure Object Definitions. On the Configure Object Definitions screen, users can either create a new Object Definition or view, maintain, or delete an existing Object Definition. Object Definitions for standard-delivered Generic Objects can also be viewed and modified here.

To create a new Object Definition, select Object Definition from the Create New dropdown located on the right side of the screen. To view, maintain, or delete an existing Object Definition, select Object Definition in the Search dropdown and then select the Object Definition to view in the adjacent dropdown box.

We're going to focus on creating an Object Definition. When viewing an existing Object Definition, the same screen and information can be seen as when creating an Object Definition. When viewing an Object Definition, you can also edit it, in which case you'll see the same screen as when creating a new Object Definition. In Figure 5.4, you can see the screen after selecting Object Definition in the Create New dropdown.

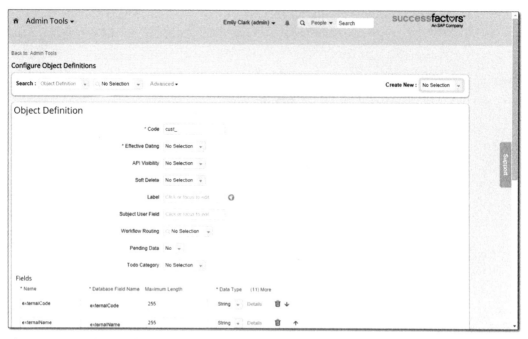

Figure 5.4 New Object Definition

Within the main attributes at the top of the OBJECT DEFINITION are several important fields:

▶ EFFECTIVE DATING
Defines the type of dating for your object. There are four types available:

  ▶ FROM PARENT: Used for child objects to inherit the effective dating value of their parent object.

  ▶ NONE: The object is not effective-dated (i.e., history is not saved when object data changes).

  ▶ BASIC: History is saved, but only one record can be created per day.

  ▶ MULTIPLE CHANGES PER DAY: Multiple historical records can be created through the lifecycle of the object data.

▶ API VISIBILITY
If your Generic Object data needs to be used for integration via an API, then set this field to either EDIT or READ ONLY, depending on which type of data access

you want for your Generic Object. You can set it to NOT VISIBLE if you don't want your data exposed to the API.

▶ WORKFLOW ROUTING
Used to route all Generic Object data requests to this workflow. If you plan on using conditional rules to trigger different workflows for different scenarios, then you should leave this field blank.

▶ PENDING DATA
Determines if data changes that are pending workflow approval are visible before or after the workflow is approved.

Conditional workflows are determined using business rules, and these rules are assigned towards the bottom of the Object Definition. We'll get to that shortly.

Under the main Generic Object attributes is the FIELDS section, which you saw back in Figure 5.4. There are a number of standard fields—most beginning with *mdf*—and many of them are system fields that should be left as is. The main system fields that you will need to use are described in the following list. Bear in mind that the name for some of these fields in Generic Objects delivered by SAP SuccessFactors may vary from those used when creating a Generic Object. You can change the NAME of the field, but the system automatically provides the DATABASE FIELD NAME.

▶ externalCode
The code of the object record. The DATA TYPE of this field can be changed to any number of different types, but two of the most common for Employee Central are as follows:

  ▶ USER: Used for Generic Objects that will be used in self-service.

  ▶ AUTO NUMBER: Used if you want the system to generate an ID for the object record automatically.

▶ externalName
This field is often left as is. In some self-service scenarios, it would be set to have no visibility because it doesn't make sense to name a record.

▶ effectiveStartDate
This field stores the start date of records for effective-dated objects.

▶ transactionSequence
If you are using effective-dating of MULTIPLE CHANGES PER DAY, then you need this field, and it should remain unchanged.

The name of the field in the NAME column is only the name in the Object Definition. The label of the field that displays in the UI is configured along with a number of other field attributes by clicking the DETAILS hyperlink, which you can see in Figure 5.5.

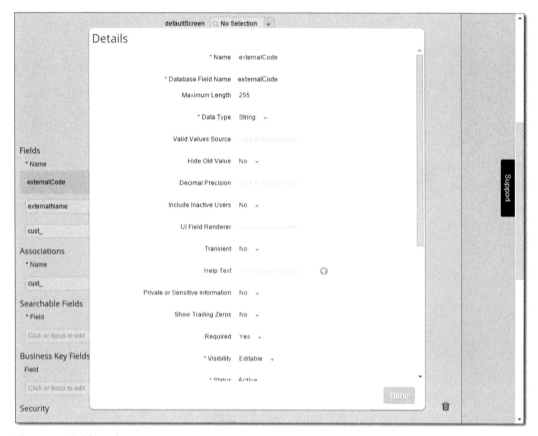

Figure 5.5 Field Attributes

We'll now look at the most important field attributes that you are likely to use:

▸ DATA TYPE
There are multiple data types available for a field. Many of them will be used regularly. Some of the most common that you will use are as follows:

  ▹ BOOLEAN: YES or NO field.

  ▹ DATE: Stores a date in the format of the user's locale.

- Picklist: An MDF Picklist (see Section 5.1.4).

- Translatable: A string field that can be translated into each language enabled in the system.

- Generic Object: A list of records for a specific Generic Object.

- Foundation Object: A list of records for a specific Foundation Object.

- Attachment: A field that holds an attachment.

- User: An employee in the system; used for the externalCode field in every ESS Generic Object.

▶ Valid Values Source
When the Data Type value is Foundation Object, Generic Object, or Picklist, then the code of that object should be entered here.

▶ Hide Old Value
Determines if the old value of a field should be shown with a strikethrough next to the field when the value has changed.

▶ Help Text
The help text to display alongside a field. This field can be translated for each language enabled in the system.

▶ Required
Whether a field entry is mandatory.

▶ Visibility
If the field should be visible in the UI. In some instances, it's useful to hide certain standard-delivered fields.

▶ Label
The name of the field in the UI. This field can be translated for each language enabled in the system.

The bottom two sections are also important:

▶ Rules
Determines if one or more rules will trigger when the field value changes.

▶ Field Criteria
When the Data Type value is Foundation Object, Generic Object, or Picklist, then this section can be used to determine matching criteria with the target object. This is often used for filtering records coming from the target object.

After the fields have been defined, you can create any associations to other objects as required in the ASSOCIATIONS section. If a child object has not yet been created, then skip this part and come back to it once you have created the child object. Associations have two main attributes once the child object has been selected:

▶ MULTIPLICITY

  ▶ ONE-TO-ONE: The Generic Object record can be related to only one other child Generic Object record.

  ▶ ONE-TO-MANY: One Generic Object record can be related to many records of the child Generic Object.

▶ TYPE

  ▶ COMPOSITE: The related Generic Object record can exist only as a child of a Generic Object record.

  ▶ VALID WHEN: The related Generic Object record can exist with or without the parent Generic Object record.

Both of these attributes are shown at the top of Figure 5.6.

In the SEARCHABLE FIELDS section found below the ASSOCIATION section, you can define all of the fields that can be used to search for the Generic Object in MANAGE DATA or for which the Generic Object is defined as a data type of a field.

The SECURITY section defines whether the Generic Object is going to be permissioned or will visible to any user with access to a transaction for which the object is consumable. The PERMISSION CATEGORY field can be used to define which of the available categories the field will be visible in when defining the permissions of permission roles.

The RULES section is the most often used. This section enables business rules defined in the Rules Engine to be triggered at certain points of the object lifecycle. The key trigger points used are as follows:

▶ INITIALIZERULES
  Triggers rules when creating a Generic Object record.

▶ VALIDATERULES
  Triggers a workflow after a Generic Object is saved.

▶ SAVERULES
  Triggers rules when saving a Generic Object record.

▸ POSTSAVERULES

Triggers alerts or notifications after a Generic Object record is saved.

Figure 5.6 shows many of the fields we just discussed.

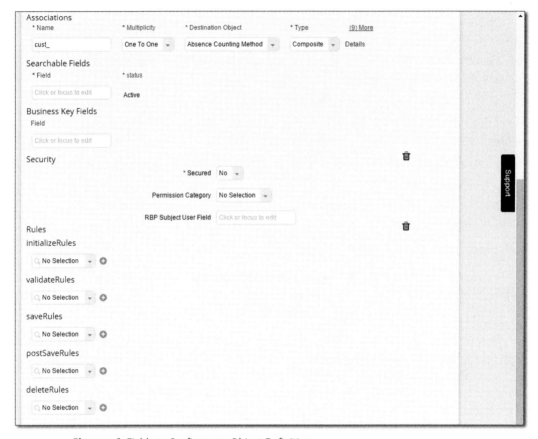

Figure 5.6 Fields to Configure an Object Definition

Once your Object Definition is complete, save it by clicking the SAVE button.

5.1.4 MDF Picklists

Generic Object picklists—known as MDF Picklists—are different from regular picklists. They are similar in nature to regular picklists, but they are created and managed through the UI in a manner similar to Object Definition creation.

MDF Picklists are created and maintained in OneAdmin in COMPANY SETTINGS • CONFIGURE OBJECT DEFINITIONS. There, you can either create a new MDF Picklist or view, maintain, or delete an existing MDF Picklist. You can also view and modify standard-delivered MDF Picklists here.

To create a new MDF Picklist, select PICKLIST from the CREATE NEW dropdown located on the right side of the screen. To view, maintain, or delete an existing MDF Picklist, select PICKLIST from the SEARCH dropdown and then select the MDF Picklist you wish to view in the adjacent dropdown box.

In this section, we're going to focus on creating an MDF Picklist. When viewing an existing MDF Picklist, the same screen and information can be seen as when creating an MDF Picklist. When viewing an MDF Picklist definition, you can also edit it, in which case you'll see the same screen as when creating a new MDF Picklist.

Figure 5.7 shows the screen after selecting PICKLIST in the CREATE NEW dropdown.

Figure 5.7 New MDF Picklist

We'll now look at the most important field attributes that you're likely to use:

▶ PARENTPICKLIST
Defines whether the MDF Picklist has a parent MDF Picklist that drives which values from the MDF Picklist are available for selection based on the value selected for the parent MDF Picklist. A common example is using the Country MDF Picklist as a parent MDF Picklist and then defining country-specific values.

▶ DISPLAY ORDER
Influences the ordering of the values that are defined for the MDF Picklist. There are three values available:

▷ ALPHABETICAL: Lists the values alphabetically.

▷ NUMERIC: Lists the values numerically.

▷ NONE: This displays the values in the order they are defined in the MDF Picklist and is the default behavior of an MDF Picklist.

▶ EFFECTIVE START DATE
The start date drives when the MDF Picklist values are available and is used to enable versioning of MDF Picklist values. We recommend entering "01/01/1900" for the date, which ensures that the MDF Picklist is always available for use.

▶ VALUES
This is where you can define the MDF Picklist values. There are four fields to complete:

▷ EXTERNAL CODE: This defines the code of the value.

▷ PARENTPICKLISTVALUE: If a parent MDF Picklist is used, then select the value from the parent MDF Picklist linked to this value. For example, if the parent MDF Picklist is Country and this value is for the United States, then select USA in this field. This means that the value will only be displayed in the UI if the Country value selected by the user matches the value defined in PARENTPICKLISTVALUE. Figure 5.8 shows an example.

▷ LABEL: The dropdown value seen in the UI. This is a translatable field.

▷ STATUS: Whether the value is active or inactive.

MDF Picklists are assigned to fields on Object Definition. The DATA TYPE of the field must be PICKLIST. At present, MDF Picklists can only be assigned to Generic Objects, not to Employee Central objects.

Figure 5.8 MDF Picklist with a Parent and Parent-Specific Values

When a Foundation Object is migrated to a Generic Object, the picklists assigned to fields of the object are converted to MDF Picklists. The picklists and MDF Picklists of the migrated Foundation Object are mapped by creating a record of the *MDF Picklist to Legacy Picklist Map* Generic Object.

5.1.5 Creating a UI for Maintaining Generic Object Data

When Generic Object data is accessed through self-services, it uses a *Configuration UI*. A Configuration UI enables a Generic Object definition to be configured and formatted for display to employees in Employee Files. Because the self-service user experience is important, the layout of the Generic Object fields that you wish to display for employees—and how you want to display those fields—may differ from the layout and configuration of the Object Definition that was created.

Configuration UIs present a variety of options to enable a flexible object layout when displayed in the Employee Central UI. Configuration UIs are created and maintained in OneAdmin in COMPANY SETTINGS • MANAGE CONFIGURATION UI. The Manage Configuration UI editor is a drag-and-drop, what-you-see-is-what-you-get (WYSIWYG) editor. The Configuration UI object enables the self-service

view of the Generic Object to differ from how the object is viewed in Manage
Data. This can be useful when you want to expose these objects to employees in
a more simplified fashion and remove more technical or administrative fields
needed by administrators.

In Figure 5.9, a Tuition Reimbursement object can be seen in Employee Files,
which is being rendered using a Configuration UI.

Figure 5.9 Tuition Reimbursement Object in Employee Files

On the Manage Configuration UI screen, you can either create a new Configuration UI or view, maintain, or delete an existing Configuration UI. You can also
view and modify Configuration UIs for standard-delivered Generic Objects here.

To create a new Configuration UI, select the Create New button located on the
right side of the screen. To view, maintain, or delete an existing Configuration UI,
select the Configuration UI in the Search dropdown.

When viewing an existing Configuration UI, the same screen and information can
be seen as when creating a Configuration UI. When viewing a Configuration UI

definition, you can also edit it, in which case you'll see the same screen as when creating a new Configuration UI.

After you click the CREATE NEW button, select a Generic Object in the SELECT BASE OBJECT field. Figure 5.10 shows the screen after selecting the base object. In this example, we've selected TUITION REIMBURSEMENT as the base object to create a Configuration UI.

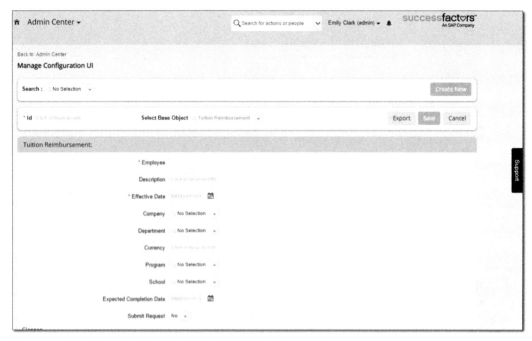

Figure 5.10 Creating a Configuration UI for Tuition Reimbursement

As you can see in Figure 5.10, the fields of the Tuition Reimbursement object were automatically rendered in the Configuration UI. Here, they can be renamed, removed, or hidden. Rules also can be assigned to fields here so that they only trigger when the object is maintained in self-service (e.g., by an employee and/or a manager).

You can change the layout of fields and add fields to sections (called *groups*). Groups can have titles and borders and also can be set to be collapsible in the UI.

Figure 5.11 shows the Configuration UI for Tuition Reimbursement that you saw in Figure 5.10 with a modified layout. In the example shown in Figure 5.11, the

COMPANY, DEPARTMENT, and CURRENCY fields have been put into a group called ORGANIZATION DETAILS that has a *flow* layout. Similarly, the three subsequent fields have also been put into a group with the flow layout.

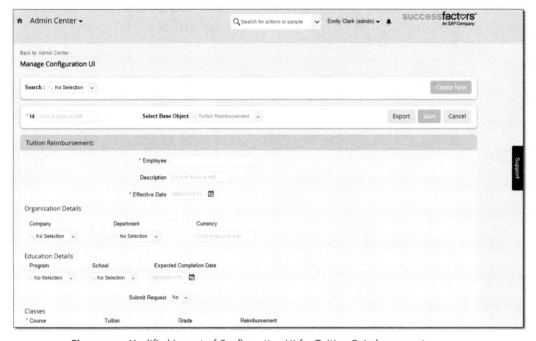

Figure 5.11 Modified Layout of Configuration UI for Tuition Reimbursement

After you create your Configuration UI, you can add it to Employee Files for access by employees and/or managers. We'll now discuss the process of adding a Configuration UI to Employee Files.

Configuration UIs are added to Employee Files in OneAdmin in EMPLOYEE FILES • CONFIGURE EMPLOYEE FILES. Once on the DESIGN EMPLOYEE FILES LAYOUT screen, select the ADD NEW VIEW button to begin the process. On the next screen (shown in Figure 5.12), click one of the INSERT PORTLET buttons. One of the top two buttons inserts the Configuration UI on either side of the screen. This can be useful to present multiple Configuration UIs on the same screen. If you are only inserting one Configuration UI, then you should select the bottom INSERT PORTLET button.

On the next screen, you will see a number of selections to add a new portlet. Click the CREATE & ADD button for the LIVE PROFILE MDF INFORMATION portlet name, found toward the bottom of the screen.

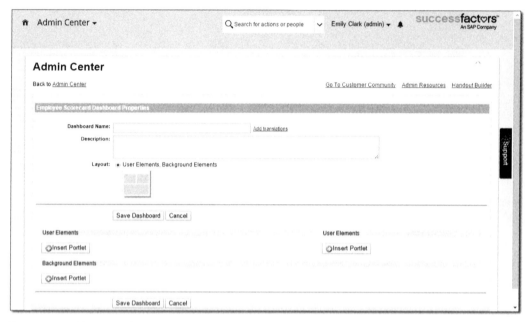

Figure 5.12 Adding a Portlet to a View

You will now find yourself on the LIVE PROFILE MDF INFORMATION screen. On this screen, enter a name and the following details:

▶ PORTLET TITLE
The name of the portlet

▶ PORTLET DESCRIPTION
An optional description

▶ MDF SCREEN ID
The Configuration UI

Click the SAVE button. On the next screen, select SAVE DASHBOARD. Back on the DESIGN EMPLOYEE FILES LAYOUT screen, sort your new view in the order that you want it and click SAVE at the bottom of the screen.

Once the view has been created, it must be permissioned in OneAdmin for the various permission roles that will have access to the view and the Generic Object. The view will be permissionable in the EMPLOYEE VIEWS permission category, and the object will be permissionable in the category defined in the Object Definition.

Once assigned, an employee or manager can access the Configuration UI by selecting the view in the EMPLOYEE FILES menu, as shown in Figure 5.13.

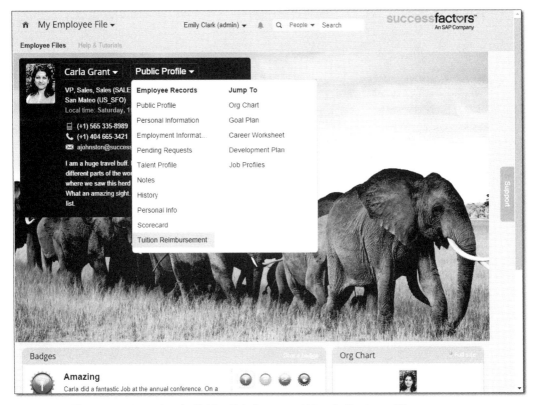

Figure 5.13 Accessing the Tuition Reimbursement View in Employee Files

The Generic Object then can be viewed and managed by employees and managers. We saw an example of viewing a Generic Object in Employee Files back in Figure 5.9. Now, let's look at how administrators maintain Generic Object data.

5.1.6 Maintaining Generic Object Data

Generic Objects are typically managed by employees and managers in Employee Files, as we've covered previously in this chapter. A workflow can be assigned to Generic Objects via business rules, which means that a conditional workflow can be applied for employees and managers when they edit data via self-services.

For administrators, Generic Object data can be managed through OneAdmin in EMPLOYEE FILES • MANAGE DATA. The MANAGE DATA screen will look similar to the screen used to create and manage Object Definitions and the screen used to create and manage MDF Picklists.

Generic Object data is created and maintained by selecting the Generic Object in the CREATE NEW dropdown located on the right side of the screen. To view, maintain, or delete existing Generic Object data, select the Generic Object in the SEARCH dropdown and then select the record to edit in the adjacent dropdown.

You will now see the object record. In Figure 5.14, we selected the Tuition Reimbursement record for an employee. You can view the history of all of the changes to this employee's Tuition Reimbursement record.

Figure 5.14 Viewing Tuition Reimbursement Object Data in Manage Data

Depending on the permissions of the user, he or she can be correct or delete each record by using the TAKE ACTION button or insert a new record by using the INSERT NEW RECORD button at the top right of the record.

Additional Resources

For more details on maintaining Generic Object data, refer to the *Metadata Framework (MDF)* implementation handbook found at *http://help.sap.com/hr_ec*.

5.2 Business Rules

The Rules Engine is a powerful part of the MDF that enables changes to behavior across Employee Central. The Rules Engine can be used for a variety of different purposes:

- Setting default values in the New Hire process
- Defining person IDs or IDs of other objects
- Propagating data
- Calculating the value of a field when a portlet loads or when data changes in a field
- Retrieving values from lookup tables
- Defining Event Reasons and workflows for self-service
- Setting up alerts and notifications

This is by no means a comprehensive list of use cases. The flexibility available to define rules, combined with the standard-delivered rule functions provided in the system, means that there are multiple ways to apply Rules Engine functionality across the system and for different use cases.

Rules use IF and THEN conditions to determine the trigger conditions and what will happen when the trigger conditions are met. ELSE and ELSE IF conditions can also be used to add in different multistep conditions. Both AND and OR operators are supported within rules, and many functions (such as mathematical, date/time, select/lookup, concatenate/substring, etc.) are provided for use in IF, THEN, ELSE, and ELSE IF conditions. You can have the THEN conditions always trigger when a rule is called, as is often used for field defaults or for field-level changes that trigger a rule.

Rules are effective-dated, meaning that a rule change can be future-dated. This could be important, for example, to set a new eligibility for a compensation or benefits enrollment in the future. Say that your compensation eligibility is going to change on the January 1, 2017. Instead of waiting until January 1, 2017, to make the change, you can create a new record for the rule with the date of January 1, 2017, for when the new record of the rule will go into effect.

Rules are created and maintained in OneAdmin in COMPANY SETTINGS • CONFIGURE BUSINESS RULES. On the CONFIGURE BUSINESS RULES screen, you can either create a new rule or view, maintain, or delete an existing rule. To create a new rule, select the CREATE NEW RULE button located on the right side of the screen.

To view, maintain, or delete a rule, select the rule in the SEARCH dropdown. When viewing an existing rule, the same screen and information can be seen as when creating a rule. When viewing a rule definition, you can also edit it, in which case you'll see the same screen as when creating a new rule.

After clicking the CREATE NEW RULE button, you must select one of three options:

▶ BASIC
   Create a rule from scratch.

▶ POSITION MANAGEMENT
   Create a rule specifically for a Position Management scenario.

▶ TIME MANAGEMENT
   Create a rule specifically for a Time Management scenario.

Once you've selected an option, enter the basic details on the right side of the screen, such as the RULE NAME, RULE ID, START DATE, and DESCRIPTION. Depending on the options selected, there may be additional fields available to maintain. Once you've entered the details, click the CREATE button to begin entering rule criteria.

Figure 5.15 shows the screen after clicking CREATE button.

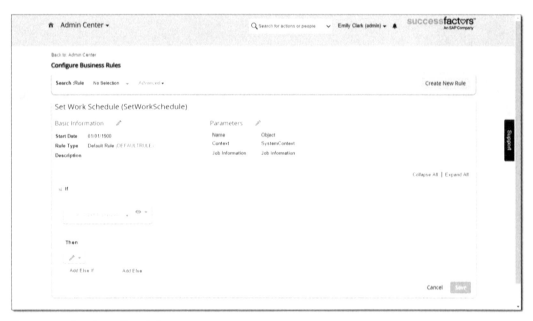

Figure 5.15 Creating a New Rule

To understand how a basic rule is created, let's look at an example. In the rule shown in Figure 5.16, the WORK SCHEDULE field in Job Information will be set to MON–FRI 8 HOUR DAYS if the EMPLOYEE CLASS field is set to CONSULTANT. This rule would be assigned to the EMPLOYEE CLASS field of Job Information, as we'll cover shortly.

The rule is constructed as such:

▶ **IF**
  EMPLOYEE CLASS is equal to EMPLOYEE or EMPLOYEE CLASS is equal to CONSULTANT

▶ **THEN**
  Set WORK SCHEDULE to be equal to MON–FRI 8 HOUR DAYS

This is a simple rule, but far more complex rules can be built for a variety of purposes.

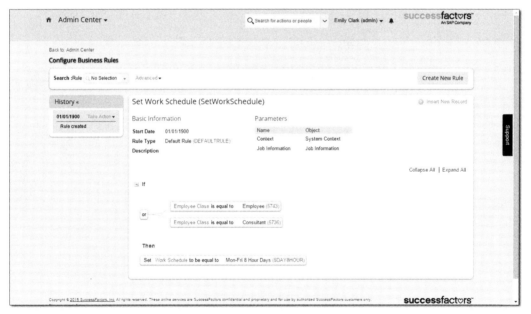

Figure 5.16 Rule to Set the Work Schedule Field

In another example, a rule validates the Payment Information portlet and provides an error message if it does not match the IF conditions (see Figure 5.17).

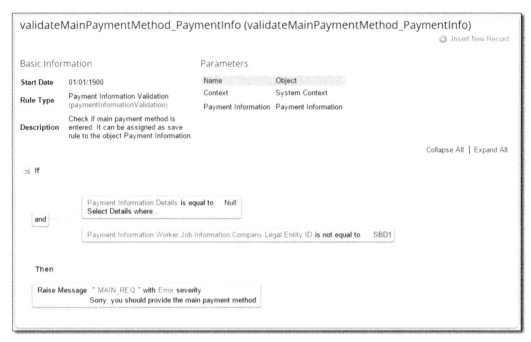

Figure 5.17 Rule to Validate Payment Information

The Employment Information and Employment Information Model objects are provided so that multiple Person or Employment Objects can be used in a rule. Each portlet in the PERSONAL INFORMATION or EMPLOYMENT INFORMATION screens can be used in a single rule.

Model objects allow the attributes of Employee Central object fields to be changed. These model objects exist for every Employee Central object. Model objects provide four attributes for each field that can be used in rules:

▸ PREVIOUS VALUE
  Used to select or set the previous value of a field.

▸ REQUIRED
  Used to set a field as required or not required.

▸ VALUE
  Used to select or set the value of a field.

▸ VISIBILITY
  Used to show or hide a field, or make a field read-only.

Rules can be triggered at the object level or the field level for both Generic Objects and Employee Central objects. For rules assigned at the object level, the following trigger points are available:

- `onInit` (Employee Central objects)/`InitializeRules` (Generic Objects)
  Triggers the rule when the New Hire transaction loads

- `ValidateRules` (Generic Objects)
  Triggers a workflow after a Generic Object is saved

- `onSave` (Employee Central objects)/`SaveRules` (Generic Objects)
  Triggers the rule when the portlet or screen (e.g., ADD NEW EMPLOYEE, EMPLOYMENT INFORMATION, or PERSONAL INFORMATION) is saved after being modified

- `onView` (Employee Central objects)
  Triggers the rule when the portlet loads

- `onEdit` (Employee Central objects)
  Triggers a rule to default the values for editable fields in the `paymentInfo` object in Employee Central

- `saveAlert` (Employee Central objects)
  Triggers a rule for an alert or notification

- `postSaveRules` (Generic Objects)
  Triggers a rule used for workflow for Generic Objects

Field-level rules are always assigned as `onChange` rules, which means that they trigger whenever the field value changes.

Rules are assigned in a number of ways, depending on the object:

- **Foundation Object**
  For legacy Foundation Objects in the Corporate Data Model XML and for Foundation Objects migrated to the MDF then on the Object Definition

- **Person or Employment Object**
  In the Manage Business Configuration transaction in OneAdmin

- **Generic Object**
  On the field of an Object Definition

Additional Resources

For more details refer to the *Configuring Business Rules in SuccessFactors* implementation handbook found at *http://help.sap.com/hr_ec*.

5.3 Extension Center

The Extension Center enables simplified creation and management of Generic Objects and their component parts, called *extensions*. The Extension Center offers a one-stop shop to create and maintain all MDF extensions. You can view and change a Generic Object and all entities that interact with that object—such as rules, workflows, and Configuration UIs. You can also create new entities. Figure 5.18 shows the EXTENSION CENTER homepage.

Figure 5.18 Extension Center

The Extension Center incorporates all of the transactions covered so far in this chapter so that users can perform those activities in a more guided and friendly user interface. It also contains different views of Generic Objects and related entities in visual or graphic formats to create a holistic view of your extensibility assets.

5.4 SAP HANA Cloud Platform

SAP HANA Cloud Platform is a Platform-as-a-Service (PaaS) offering that enables the creation of applications for many cloud and on-premise SAP systems, as well as non-SAP systems and mobile devices. Users can build extension applications for certain SAP products, such as SAP Financial Service Network, SAP S/4HANA, and SAP SuccessFactors.

SAP offers an SAP HANA Cloud Platform extension package for SAP Success-Factors that provides the tools to build extension applications for Employee Central. These extension applications inherit the theming of SAP SuccessFactors so that they look and behave like they are part of the SAP SuccessFactors system. By using the OData API, they can read and write data in Employee Central.

There are many use cases for extension applications. In some cases, the standard-delivered functionality or the MDF cannot meet your needs. When you need to create more complicated functionality, you or your partner can build applications for Employee Central. You can even buy Employee Central applications from an app store!

This functionality works in SAP SuccessFactors by creating applications on SAP HANA Cloud Platform. These applications are called *extensions*. Extensions are custom applications coded in Java or another programming language that leverage various UI technologies. SAP provides a software development kit (SDK) for the commonly used Eclipse development environment.

An extension called Networking Lunch is shown in Figure 5.19.

Figure 5.19 Networking Lunch Extension

The *Extensions Marketplace* provides a place to view, "test drive," and buy available extension applications. Access the Extensions Marketplace within SAP Success-Factors in OneAdmin via COMPANY SETTINGS • EXTENSIONS. Figure 5.20 shows the EXTENSIONS MARKETPLACE screen. All of the available applications are displayed. All seven extensions shown are available to test and/or purchase.

Figure 5.20 Extensions Marketplace

Additional Resources

You can read more about SAP HANA Cloud Platform in *Getting Started with SAP HANA Cloud Platform* by James Wood (SAP PRESS, 2015). Specifically, Chapter 11 covers extending SAP SuccessFactors with SAP HANA Cloud Platform.

In addition, for more information on SAP HANA Cloud Platform in an SAP Success-Factors context, refer to the *SAP HANA Cloud Platform, Extension Package for Success-Factors* implementation guide found at *http://help.sap.com/hr_foundation*.

5.5 Summary

In this chapter, we looked at some of the Employee Central-focused parts of the MDF. Although we didn't cover the low-level technical details, we did cover the key functionality that is important in an Employee Central context. We looked at the creation scenarios for custom Generic Objects, how they are related, how data is accessed in self-services, and how data is maintained by administrators. We also looked at the powerful Rules Engine and some examples of how it can be used.

We also discussed the Extension Center, a powerful solution that can bring together all elements of the MDF in one UI. Finally, we took a peek at SAP HANA Cloud Platform and how it enables extension applications to be created for Employee Central.

Now that we have the object model foundation in place, we should take a look at the Foundation Objects that define employee master data in Employee Central.

Foundation Objects are the building blocks of employee records within Employee Central. By creating a listing of data values from which to populate employee records, we are assured standardized data that is consistent and reportable.

6   Foundation Objects

Valid, consistent, and organized data is an absolute must for any organization looking to execute meaningful reports and simplify data entry processes. Having set values to choose from when populating a field provides consistency. Organizing these set values and giving them characteristics of their own takes this process further. In Employee Central, we accomplish this task by utilizing Foundation Objects.

In this chapter, we'll introduce you to the Employee Central Foundation Objects, beginning by walking through an overview of key terms and differences between regular Foundation Objects and MDF Foundation Objects (see Section 6.1). In Section 6.2, we'll dive into the different categories to define Foundation Objects. Then, in Section 6.3, we'll see how Foundation Objects work together through the use of associations and propagation. Section 6.4 will walk through the configuration of Foundation Objects before we finally move on to the creation and extension processes in Section 6.5 and Section 6.6, respectively.

Let's begin with an overview of the basics.

6.1   Basics

Foundation Objects are categories or structures for listings of data that are set up to be used across an entire company. Each object has a series of defining data fields associated with it that extends its characteristics. It's sometimes easy to think of Foundation Objects as index cards or card catalog entries from the library. Each object has a series of acceptable values, or cards. When you pick a card and examine it, you'll see additional characteristics of that card's value. These characteristics help further define an employee who is assigned an object.

Foundation Objects offer a single, pre-delivered list of values a user can select from when populating a data field. There are several benefits to using Foundation Objects in Employee Central, some of the most important of which are as follows:

- Eliminates the need for an end user to determine a free text entry for a field.

- Resulting standardized values can be easily reported on and/or used as report filters.

- Provides the ability to build in known associations between Foundation Objects, whereby one selected value helps drive available values in a second field.

- Provides the ability to have data propagate or autofill from one field to another based on the selected Foundation Object. This helps to streamline the data entry process because fewer fields need to be entered manually.

There are quite a few key terms to know and structures of which to be cognizant in order to take full advantage of all that Foundation Objects have to offer. Let's explore these terms and structures together.

6.1.1   Structures and Key Terms

On the surface, Foundation Objects are just structures for defining selection sets or listings of data values available to populate a given field—but they are more than that. Attached to each value is a list of properties that can be applied or inherited along with the value.

Location, for example, may have a sample value of World Headquarters Atlanta. However, when setting up this value we also included an address of 123 Main Street, Atlanta, Georgia, as one of its characteristics. When you select World Headquarters Atlanta as an employee's work location, you know not only the Location where an employee works, but also the specific address of the Location, all without having to enter in an address on the employee's record (see Figure 6.1). This is one powerful aspect of Foundation Objects.

Another key aspect of Foundation Objects is that they are *effective-dated*. This means that you store historical records and document changes to items as an organization changes. If a department name changes or a restructuring occurs, you do not lose any previous records. Instead, you can end date one record and place the new record on top. You can also delimit records no longer in use so that they cannot be selected and assigned to employees.

Figure 6.1 Location Foundation Object

We sometimes throw around terms interchangeably when working with Foundation Objects. A Foundation Object is the type of data listing you want to define, such as Location in the previous example. *Foundation Data* refers to the customer-specific values that populate your Foundation Object.

Looking back to the previous example, World Headquarters Atlanta would be an example of Foundation Data because it is a specific master data entry listed for a specific customer.

You store Foundation Data in Employee Central in *Foundation Tables*. Although each of these three terms—Foundation Object, Foundation Data, and Foundation Tables—refer to different and unique things, they are often used interchangeably. It's up to us to determine whether a colleague or document is referring to the definition of a structure (Foundation Object) or the customer-specific master data populating the structure (Foundation Data).

For those of you interested in technical or system jargon, Foundation Objects are defined in the Employee Central system as *HRIS elements*. These HRIS elements are effective-dated, meaning you store a start date and end date for records related to these objects. If our World Headquarters in Atlanta moved buildings, the new address could be recorded with a particular start date and the previous address saved for historical purposes. You do not need to overwrite entries in order to support current data.

Each Foundation Object or HRIS element can have multiple characteristic data fields or properties that help define the object. These fields are known technically in the system as *HRIS fields*. The address state of Georgia in the preceding Location scenario is an example of an HRIS field. Each Foundation Object or HRIS element has a CODE field, a NAME field, and a START DATE field.

6.1.2   Foundation Objects versus MDF Foundation Objects

There is an in-process plan to migrate existing Foundation Objects from their current platform, defined in XML data models, to being defined on the Metadata Framework (MDF). The MDF provides customers more options and flexibility in their Object Definitions and gives the option to skilled customer admins to make configuration changes as needed, because the MDF is accessed in the graphical user interface (GUI) found within the Admin Center. These MDF Foundation Objects are sometimes also referred to as *Generic Objects* (the term given to objects defined within the MDF). At the time of publication (December 2015), the following Foundation Objects have been successfully moved to the MDF:

▸ Legal Entity and Legal Entity Local   ▸ Job Classification

▸ Business Unit   ▸ Job Function

▸ Division   ▸ Pay Calender

▸ Department   ▸ Pay Group

▸ Cost Center

This means that configuration and associations for these objects occurs in the MDF portion of the Admin Center and not in the XML data models that traditionally define these objects. Permission settings and picklist definitions vary slightly as well.

Now that we've provided a basic overview of the structure of Foundation Objects and some important keys terms and discussed the differences between regular and MDF Foundation Objects, let's turn our attention in the next section to the different categorizations of Foundation Objects.

6.2   Categories

There are three key categories that nearly all Foundation Objects can be sorted into: organizational, job, and pay. Other or miscellaneous Foundation Objects are those that do not fit into these major categories. Table 6.1 provides a complete listing of these objects. The key categories are defined as follows:

▶ **Organizational**
These objects help create a company organizational structure and identify where in the structure an employee is found.

▶ **Job**
These objects help keep a consistent job catalog and are used to classify an employee's work assignment and job-related characteristics.

▶ **Pay**
These objects allow you to store tables of pay-related data, including payment types, groupings, and information related to payroll calendars.

Organizational	Job	Pay	Miscellaneous
▶ Company/Legal Entity*	▶ Job Classification	▶ Pay Component	▶ Event Reasons
▶ Business Unit*	▶ Job Function	▶ Pay Component Group	▶ Workflow Configuration
▶ Division*		▶ Pay Group	▶ Workflow Contributor
▶ Department*		▶ Pay Calendar	▶ CC Role
▶ Location		▶ Pay Grade	▶ Dynamic Role
▶ Location Group		▶ Pay Range	
▶ Cost Center*			
▶ Geozone			

*Available as a MDF Foundation Object.

Table 6.1 Foundation Object Categories

Let's take a look at the Foundation Objects shown in Table 6.1 and briefly discuss their use.

6.2.1 Organizational

Organizational objects provide the organizational structure of a company and align each employee within that structure. The components used are as follows:

▸ **Company/Legal Entity**
The terms *Company* and *Legal Entity* can be used interchangeably. This is the highest-level building block for an organizational structure and is a required field on an employee's record. As true legal entities are established and registered in a single country, so too are Legal Entity objects. Each instance of a Legal Entity (Company) object must be tied to one and only one country. This country assignment helps drive which country-specific fields to display on an individual employee's record. It also helps determine local currency, language, and standard working hours (optional for this object) for employees assigned to the company.

▸ **Business Unit**
A *Business Unit* represents a breakout of operating functions within an organization. It is the second level building block in an organizational structure and can span across multiple companies and countries.

▸ **Division**
A *Division* is the third level of an organizational structure and usually starts to narrow down an employee's position within a company. Depending on an organization's structure, we often see Division tied to either a Company or a Business Unit as a further defining point.

▸ **Department**
A *Department* is the fourth and most specific level of an organizational structure. It usually narrows down the group or team that an employee reports to and is often headed by the employee's manager. We often see Department fall directly subordinate to a Division.

> **Don't Have Four Levels to Your Organizational Structure?**
>
> Don't worry if you don't have four levels to your organizational structure. These four objects reflect commonly used organizational structures, but your organization may have more or fewer than four levels. Within Employee Central, you can remove and reorganize these four levels and even add additional levels if warranted.

If a level needs to be removed, we recommend removing the Business Unit. Legal Entity is a required level, and Division and Department are key filters for other SAP Success-Factors modules. Therefore, if you need to remove one level, Business Unit's absence will have the least impact across the entire system suite.

▸ **Location**

A *Location* is a specific physical work place for an employee. Each location can have a country-specific address.

▸ **Location Group**

A *Location Group* is a combination of multiple Locations for reporting or filtering purposes. This value does not display directly on an employee's record, but is derived by the system to assist administrators. An example of a Location Group is an entry called "Europe" that groups together all of the specific Locations within Europe. When running a report for that region, an HR manager would not need to select each individual Location but could instead select the Location Group.

▸ **Cost Center**

A *Cost Center* is usually a budget unit defined by your organization's financial system. It is not a direct part of an organizational structure but rather part of a financial or budget structure. Many companies align Cost Centers to Departments. If such a relationship exists, then you can utilize this information to help streamline data entry using associations, as discussed in Section 6.3.1.

▸ **Geozone**

A *Geozone* is a grouping of Locations that typically fall within the same cost-of-living spans. Use Geozone to help offset higher- and lower-than-average costs of livings and their impact to the salary range. A high-cost-of-living area may have a special premium or adjustment percentage allotted to it, whereas a low-cost-of-living area may have a reduced range. Geozone contains a field called ADJUSTMENT FACTOR to help indicate the offset amount when reviewing salary ranges.

6.2.2   Job

Job objects allow for a consistent and consolidated job catalog and have the advantage of sharing their characteristics with employees through inheritance.

▸ **Job Classification**

A *Job Classification*, sometimes referred to as *Job Class*, *Job Code*, or simply *Job*, is a specific job or role within an organization. It helps identify what work an employee does and how that work is classified. Job Classification is a key element in the system. You can derive many characteristics from a Job and apply them directly to the employee. Characteristics such as Employee Type, Regular/ Temporary, and Employee Class are just a few examples.

▸ **Job Function**

A *Job Function* helps you sort jobs based on functional work performed. This is a field that allows HR managers to grab groups of employees who perform similar work or functions. Job Functions can be very broad (i.e., Information Technology Group) or very specific (i.e., Accountants). Try to find a balance between being too general and too specific based on the reporting needs of your company and the generalness/specificity used in determining your Job Classifications and/or Business Units. You don't want to recreate data just for the sake of having it here.

6.2.3 Pay

Pay objects are used to handle pay- and compensation-related data. They include information about not only payments and deductions, but also frequency and pay periods. These objects include the following:

▸ **Pay Component**

A *Pay Component* is a specific payment or deduction assigned to an employee. Each specific type is denoted through a separate Pay Component. Pay Components can be one-time (such as a retention bonus) or recurring (such as annual salary). Pay Components are ideally defined globally, but on occasion some country-specific listings may be required. Modifications to the standard-delivered Pay Component setup can render Pay Components country-specific. If you do not provide a currency when creating an instance of a Pay Component, then the system will default to the employee's local currency.

Wage Types

Pay Components in SAP SuccessFactors are typically called *Wage Types* in on-premise SAP ERP Human Capital Management (HCM).

▸ **Pay Component Group**

A *Pay Component Group* is a grouping together of various Pay Components. This is helpful when looking for summations, totals, and annualizations, for example. A great example of a simple Pay Component Group is *Total Annual Compensation*, which can be a sum of annual salary and annual bonus. Pay Component Groups are able to convert various frequencies and currencies and display an annualized amount.

Technical Wage Types

Pay Component Groups in SAP SuccessFactors are typically called *Technical Wage Types* in on-premise SAP ERP HCM.

▸ **Pay Group**

A *Pay Group* is a grouping together of employees with the same payroll run information. These groupings are typically determined by your payroll system.

▸ **Pay Calendar**

For each Pay Group, there is the option to use a *Pay Calendar*. A Pay Calendar holds information about a Pay Group's pay periods, including work period, pay dates, and check dates.

▸ **Pay Grade**

A *Pay Grade* is a grade or a level on a pay scale that indicates where in a fixed structure of pay ranges an employee falls. This field is typically tied directly to a Job Code. A Pay Grade will typically point to a Pay Range or another type of pay structure.

▸ **Pay Range**

A *Pay Range* is a span of pay that is typically awarded for a particular Pay Grade. Because Pay Grade is typically tied to Job Code, another way to interpret Pay Range is that it is a span of pay typically applied to a Job. An employee holding a specific Job would likely or should likely have a salary or hourly wage found within the Pay Range. A Pay Range is used to help compute Compa Ratio and Range Penetration. These values indicate how well an employee's pay fits into the Pay Range guidelines.

▸ **Event Reason**

An *Event Reason* is a code assigned to an event or transaction on the employee record side to indicate why a particular change has taken place. This helps with reporting because you can tell not only how many new hires or terminations you've processed in a given period but also why these actions have taken place. Turnover reports are much more meaningful if you can designate not only the number of departures but also why employees terminated their employment. Event Reasons are typically defined globally to allow for global standardization and reporting. Modifications can be made to the standard configuration to permit for country-specific Event Reasons, if needed. In this scenario, you may sacrifice some global reporting capabilities.

▶ **Workflow Configuration**
The *Workflow Configuration* object allows you to define workflow routings and approvers. Types of participants available are Approvers, Contributors, and CC Participants. More information about workflows can be found in Chapter 4, Section 4.3.

▶ **Workflow Contributor**
A *Workflow Contributor* is a person who contributes to a workflow. This Foundation Object is somewhat misleading, because the various types of Contributors (Role, Dynamic Role, Person, Dynamic Group) are defined outside of this object and merely referenced within this object for importing purposes. The actual assignment of a Contributor to a workflow can also happen within the workflow definition itself if defined within the Admin Center.

▶ **CC Role**
A *CC Role* is a person or persons (Role, Dynamic Role, Person, Dynamic Group, External Email Address) that receive notice of a completed workflow. This Foundation Object is somewhat misleading, because the various types of CC Participants (Role, Dynamic Role, Person, Dynamic Group, External Email Address) are defined outside of this object and merely referenced within this object for importing purposes. The actual assignment of a Contributor to a workflow can also happen within the workflow definition itself if defined within the Admin Center.

▶ **Dynamic Role**
A *Dynamic Role* is a workflow participant that varies based on data criteria at the employee level. If the intention is to send the workflow to the head of an employee's faction, then the system can determine this recipient based on the employee's faction assignment. The recipient therefore varies based on the employee involved in the workflow.

6.3 Associations and Propagation

Now that you've learned a little about each Foundation Object, let's explore how they work together and enrich the system. Two key means of doing so are through *associations* and *propagation*.

6.3.1 Associations

Foundation Objects can be tied together using relationships known as associations. We put associations in place to help with data entry and validation. If your organization rolls Departments up into Divisions, then you have a relationship between the Department and Division objects. When you hire a new employee into a certain Division, you don't want to have to sort through all Departments to find the correct assignment. You only want to see the Departments that roll into that Division. An association assignment will help you do just that.

An association identifies which two Foundation Objects are related, in which direction the relationship flows, and the degree of the relationship. In the previous example, the related objects are Division and Department. The relationship flows up from Department to Division and allows for multiple Departments to flow into a single Division. This is known as a one-to-many association. If each Division only contained one Department, then you could set up a one-to-one association. This is the case with Pay Grades and Pay Ranges. Each Pay Range can be assigned to only one Pay Grade.

Associations help with data accuracy because data entry persons do not need to scroll through irrelevant values or impossible data combinations. Only relevant and possible values are presented. Associations are assigned for Foundation Objects directly in the Corporate Data Model or directly in the MDF Foundation Object Definition.

6.3.2 Propagation

Propagation is a tricky principle to master, but it yields huge benefits when working with employee records. The concept of propagation is that you can assign a Foundation Object to an employee's record and use that assignment to auto-populate values of related fields on the employee's record. This is possible as long as the related field has a corresponding entry on the Foundation Object side.

Let's look at an example. Say you have a Foundation Object called Location (see Figure 6.2). This Location has a characteristic field called TIMEZONE. This makes sense because each Location can have a specific time zone attached to it. For this example, say your LOCATION value is ATLANTA, GEORGIA and the corresponding TIMEZONE is EASTERN STANDARD TIME (EST). When you assign an employee to the Atlanta location, you don't want to search through a list of time zones to find the correct one. You've already stored the matching time zone in the Foundation Tables and want the system to pull that value for you. Propagation will populate the TIMEZONE field on the employee record with EASTERN STANDARD TIME (EST) if you have propagation set up properly. No entry is needed.

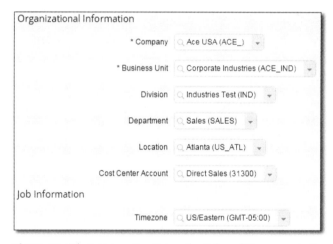

Figure 6.2 Selecting Location Drives the Value of Timezone via Propagation

Propagation is beneficial when trying to populate job attributes on an employee record. Many data fields are already stored as characteristics of a Job Code and can be defaulted in using propagation. This will help save time and help with data accuracy. Data entry people don't need to search for values; the values are presented for them instead. If there happens to be a deviation from a standard assignment, the value can always be overwritten at the time of entry directly on the employee's record.

All propagations are configured in the *Propagation Data Model*. An implementer can retrieve a best practices copy of the XML data model from the SAP Service Marketplace. That copy contains several commonly used propagations and can be edited to tailor existing scenarios to a company's needs and to add additional propagations. Once modifications are made, the revised Propagation Data Model should be imported into the company's system by the implementer, as shown in Figure 6.3.

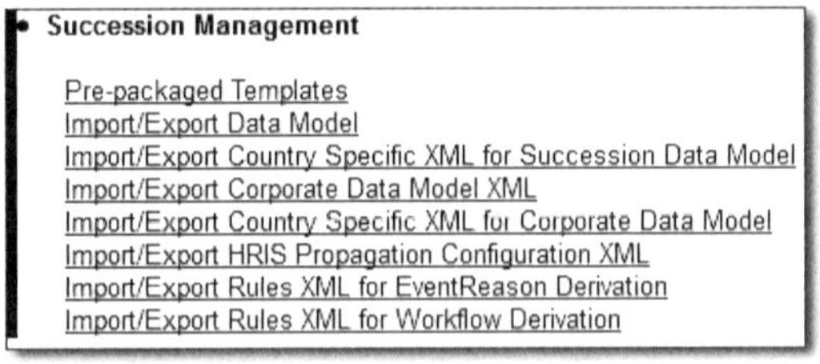

```
• Succession Management

  Pre-packaged Templates
  Import/Export Data Model
  Import/Export Country Specific XML for Succession Data Model
  Import/Export Corporate Data Model XML
  Import/Export Country Specific XML for Corporate Data Model
  Import/Export HRIS Propagation Configuration XML
  Import/Export Rules XML for EventReason Derivation
  Import/Export Rules XML for Workflow Derivation
```

Figure 6.3 Provisioning Import Path for the Propagation Data Model

Now that we've looked at how associations and propagations help Foundation Objects work together, we'll walk through the basic configuration of Foundation Objects.

6.4 Configuration

Foundation Object configuration takes place after requirements gathering and is fine-tuned during the project iterations. Configuration involves taking the customer requirements and building out the foundational structures to support these requirements. With the migration process from traditionally configured Foundation Objects to MDF Foundation Objects currently ongoing, we must explore two different configuration methods: configuration via a data model and configuration within the MDF.

Take Care during Requirements Gathering

Take care during requirements gathering to discuss the concepts of propagation and association. These two characteristics of Foundation Objects highlight the benefits of using Foundation Objects as opposed to elaborate picklists throughout the system. Please be sure to compare Foundation Object fields with employee data fields and build in additional fields where applicable on the Foundation Object side to help support propagation. The use of custom fields can be beneficial here.

6.4.1 Corporate Data Models

The traditional (and eventual legacy) method of configuring Foundation Objects is by using XML data models. This is the only method to configure non-MDF Foundation Objects. The data models used to configure Foundation Objects are referred to as the Corporate Data Model and the Country-Specific Corporate Data

Model because they help us define our company structures. The Corporate Data Model is used to define global object definitions, whereas the Country-Specific Corporate Data Model is used to define country-specific or local object requirements. These two data models work together almost in a parent–child manner.

XML Data Models

An *XML data model* is a technical design that allows you to structure your data for storage and transmission within Employee Central. Using data models, you can structure which data elements and fields to define in your system. SAP SuccessFactors uses a series of best practices or commonly used setups in its data models. An implementer will work to personalize these data models according to each customer's business requirements. These models can be downloaded from the SAP Service Marketplace by permitted implementers.

Structure of Corporate Data Models

Each Foundation Object is defined by an HRIS element, which has a technical name and is referred to by this technical name in the data model. One example is Location Group, shown in Figure 6.4, which has an HRIS element name of `locationGroup`. Each HRIS element has a series of properties that help define it (see Figure 6.4).

```
<hris-element id="locationGroup">
  <label>Location Group</label>
  <label xml:lang="ar-SA">مجموعة المواقع</label>
  <label xml:lang="bg-BG">Група на местоположение</label>
  <label xml:lang="bs-BS">Kumpulan Lokasi</label>
  <label xml:lang="bs-ID">Kelompok Lokasi</label>
  <label xml:lang="cs-CZ">Skupina umístění</label>
  <label xml:lang="cy-GB">Grŵp Lleoliad</label>
  <label xml:lang="da-DK">Stedgruppe</label>
```

Figure 6.4 HRIS Element locationGroup

Each HRIS element has a series of HRIS fields that store data relating to the HRIS element. Figure 6.5 shows an example of how these fields are defined within the data model. Each field has a series of properties that help define it:

▸ `label`
A label that can be translated into supported languages. This label becomes the field name on the Foundation Object screen. A separate label line is included for each label translation needed.

- ▶ **visibility**
  A visibility setting that indicates whether a field should be turned off, read-only (for system-calculated fields), or editable. The field's values are `none`, `read`, and `both`.

- ▶ **required**
  A required setting that indicates whether a field is mandatory or not. Its values are `true` and `false`.

- ▶ **max-length**
  A field length indicating how many characters the field should support.

- ▶ **id**
  An ID representing the field's technical field name. If a standard field is being used, then the `id` value is supplied by SAP SuccessFactors. If a custom field is being created, then a custom field `id` should be used.

- ▶ **maximumFractionDigits**
  A setting that indicates how many decimal places are supported for numeric fields (not shown in Figure 6.5).

- ▶ **showTrailingZeros**
  Defines whether trailing zeroes are shown after the decimal place. Its values are `true` and `false`.

- ▶ **pii**
  A Personally Identifiable Information (PII) setting that indicates if the field contains sensitive data that should be masked from regular view. Its values are `true` and `false`.

```
<hris-field max-length="128" id="description" visibility="both" required="false" pii="false" showTrailingZeros="false">
  <label>Description</label>
  <label xml:lang="ar-SA">الوصف</label>
  <label xml:lang="bg-BG">Описание</label>
  <label xml:lang="bs-BS">Perihalan</label>
  <label xml:lang="bs-ID">Deskripsi</label>
  <label xml:lang="cs-CZ">Popis</label>
```

Figure 6.5 HRIS Fields

If the field is a selection set that should reference a picklist, then the picklist is assigned at the bottom of the HRIS field definition using a picklist assignment statement, as shown in Figure 6.6.

```
<hris-field max-length="32" id="jobLevel" visibility="both"
  <label>Job Level</label>
  <label xml:lang="ar-SA">مستوى الوظيفة</label>
  <label xml:lang="bg-BG">Ниво на длъжност</label>
  <label xml:lang="bs-BS">Peringkat Kerja</label>
  <label xml:lang="bs-ID">Tingkat Pekerjaan</label>
  <picklist id="jobLevel" />
</hris-field>
```

Figure 6.6 HRIS Field Definition with Picklist Assignment at the End

Custom Fields

Custom fields are fully supported in both data models. Custom strings and numerous dates, longs, and doubles are available for use.

Associations

Associations between Foundation Objects are configured directly within the Corporate Data Model at the end of the configuration of all HRIS fields. The association statement links together the Foundation Object with its associated Foundation Object. Figure 6.7 shows an example of an association between Location and Geozone specifying that each Location can have one and only one Geozone.

```
<!-- Begin Location Associations -->
<hris-associations>
  <association id="id" multiplicity="ONE_TO_ONE" destination-entity="geozone" required="false" />
</hris-associations>
<!-- End Location Associations -->
```

Figure 6.7 Association between Location and Geozone Defined within the Corporate Data Model

Country-Specific Corporate Data Model

The Country-Specific Corporate Data Model functions in the same manner but is organized first by country and then by HRIS element. Each supported and configured country has a separate segment within the file. Note that not all HRIS elements/Foundation Objects are able to support a country-specific setup. Within the traditional XML-defined setup, the following areas have standard-delivered country-specific setups for various countries:

- Corporate Address for Location
- Job Classification

Custom fields are also supported in this data model. All properties for an individual custom field, except for Label, must be defined the same way across all the countries for which they are used.

> **Company**
>
> Company/Legal Entity also supports country-specific requirements; however, this object has been migrated to be an MDF Foundation Object. Therefore, its country-specific settings are handled within the MDF.

> **Caution**
>
> Please review basic XML protocol carefully if attempting to modify these data models. Be warned that several different fields may have the same labels and/or technical field names. For Employee Central, we work with the HRIS fields defined within HRIS elements. Standard elements are used elsewhere in SAP SuccessFactors, but not directly in Employee Central.

After tailoring the data models for a customer, we can import them in to the system using Provisioning. After selecting the COMPANY NAME from your Provisioning main screen you are able to find import links for uploading and downloading data models.

6.4.2 Configuring MDF Foundation Objects and Object Definitions

Configuration for MDF Foundation Objects takes place directly within SAP SuccessFactors via the CONFIGURE OBJECT DEFINITIONS area of the Admin Center. Navigate as follows: ADMIN CENTER • COMPANY SETTINGS • CONFIGURE OBJECT DEFINITIONS.

An Employee Central-provisioned SAP SuccessFactors system will come delivered with best practices definitions for all MDF Foundation Objects. The job is just to modify as needed to meet your company requirements.

Once you have navigated to the CONFIGURE OBJECT DEFINITIONS section of the Admin Center, you should see the screen shown in Figure 6.8. In the top-right corner, you'll see the option to CREATE NEW objects. In the top-left corner, you'll see the option to SEARCH for existing objects and picklists. Your MDF Foundation Objects are already defined, so select OBJECT DEFINITION in the first dropdown next to SEARCH and then the MDF Foundation Object you wish to modify in the second dropdown box.

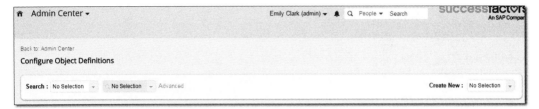

Figure 6.8 Entry Screen for Configure Object Definitions

Figure 6.9 shows the basic definition for our Division MDF Foundation Object. The basic properties are set at the top (Figure 6.9), and the FIELDS are shown at the bottom (Figure 6.10).

Configure Object Definitions

Search : Object Definition ▾   Division ▾   Advanced

Object Definition: Division (Division)

* Code	Division
* Effective Dating	Basic
API Visibility	Not Visible
* Status	Active
MDF Version History	Delete History
defaultScreen	
Label	Division
Subject User Field	
Workflow Routing	
Pending Data	Yes
Todo Category	Generic Object Change Requests

Fields

Name	Database Field Name	Maximum Length	Data Type	(16) More
effectiveStartDate	effectiveStartDate	255	Date	Details

Figure 6.9 Division MDF Foundation Object

Fields				
Name	Database Field Name	Maximum Length	Data Type	(16) M
effectiveStartDate	effectiveStartDate	255	Date	Details
mdfSystemEntityId	entityId	255	String	Details
mdfSystemRecordId	recordId	255	String	Details
mdfSystemObjectType	objectType	255	String	Details
mdfSystemProxyUser	proxyUser	255	String	Details
mdfSystemRecordStatus	recordStatusStr	255	Enum	Details
mdfSystemTransactionSequence	transactionSequence	255	Number	Details
mdfSystemVersionId	versionId	255	Number	Details
externalCode	externalCode	32	String	Details
name	externalName	32	Translatable	Details
description	sfFields.sfField1	128	Translatable	Details
effectiveStatus	effectiveStatusStr	255	Enum	Details
effectiveEndDate	effectiveEndDate	255	Date	Details
headOfUnit	sfFields.sfField2	255	User	Details
parentDivision	sfFields.sfField3	255	Generic Object	Details
createdDate	createdDate	255	DateTime	Details
createdBy	createdBy	255	String	Details
lastModifiedDate	lastModifiedDate	255	DateTime	Details
lastModifiedBy	lastModifiedBy	255	String	Details
rowId	id	255	Number	Details
internalId	internalCode	255	Number	Details

Associations				
Name	Multiplicity	Destination Object	Type	(9) More
cust_toBusinessUnit	One To Many	Business Unit	Valid When	Details

Figure 6.10 Division Fields

Associations tying together MDF Foundation Objects are made directly within the MDF Object Definition. Notice the ASSOCIATIONS area at the bottom of Figure 6.10.

Modifying MDF Object Definitions

Instructions on how to edit and modify MDF Foundation Objects can be found in Chapter 5, Section 5.1.

MDF Picklists

An important distinction must be made between picklists and MDF Picklists. MDF objects read from MDF Picklists and not the traditional picklist listing. To create a new MDF Picklist, go to CONFIGURE OBJECT DEFINITIONS and choose CREATE A NEW PICKLIST.

Propagation Data Model

Propagations are defined within an XML data model known as the Propagations Data Model. Propagations help you to default in data values on the employee data side based on the properties of a selected Foundation Object.

There are two key parts to defining a propagation scenario:

▸ Propagation statement

▸ Mapping statement

A *propagation statement* identifies the triggering Foundation Object, the referential Foundation Object field, and the destination employee data field. Figure 6.11 shows an example Propagation Data Model statement in which the selection of a job in the employee data record triggers a lookup of the Job Foundation Object and returns the assigned Pay Grade to the Pay Grade field on the Employee Record.

```
<propagate foundation-element-id="jobCode">
    <field id="grade">
        <destination hris-element-id="jobInfo" field-id="pay-grade"/>
    </field>
</propagate>
```

Figure 6.11 Propagation Data Model

A mapping statement identifies the lookup key between the Foundation Object code/ID and the triggering employee data field. This statement permits the lookup on the Foundation Object side. Figure 6.12 shows an example.

```
<propagation-mapping foundation-field="jobCode.externalCode" hris-field="jobInfo.job-code" />
```

Figure 6.12 Propagation Data Model Mapping

6.5   Creating Foundation Object Data

There are two methods used when creating *Foundation Object data*: importing templates and manual creation within the system. Each administrator will likely develop a preferred method. We recommend using the import templates for initial populations to save time and effort. Ongoing maintenance can be accomplished using either method, but it's often easier for small changes or additions to be made in a manual or direct fashion. We will walk through both methods in this section.

6.5.1 Importing Templates

The process for creating Foundation Objects in Employee Central using load templates is an excellent way to add multiple entries at one time. Each Foundation Object has its own load template. Templates are generated by the system and are specific to your configuration. Load templates can also be used to purge or overwrite existing entries in the system or to make mass updates, as may be needed for Company Reorganization Exercises (ReOrgs).

Load templates are accessed in the Admin Center. They can be found using the following path: ADMIN CENTER • EMPLOYEE FILES • IMPORT FOUNDATION DATA. At the top of the IMPORT screen, you can download a blank but properly formatted Foundation Object-specific template by clicking on the DOWNLOAD A BLANK CSV TEMPLATE link (see Figure 6.13). You will see a dropdown list of all relevant Foundation Objects and can choose the one you want to use.

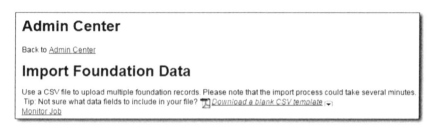

Admin Center

Back to Admin Center

Import Foundation Data

Use a CSV file to upload multiple foundation records. Please note that the import process could take several minutes.
Tip: Not sure what data fields to include in your file? 📄 Download a blank CSV template 🔽
Monitor Job

Figure 6.13 Import Foundation Data Screen

Load Template

Each load template is a comma-separated values (CSV) file containing two header rows, as shown in Figure 6.14. The first header row contains the technical name of each HRIS field, and the second row contains the field's label. It is important to keep the file in CSV format and to leave the header rows untouched.

	A	B	C	D	E	F
1	start-date	externalCode	name	description	status	Division.externalCode
2	Effective as of	Code	Name	Description	Status	Division

Figure 6.14 Simplified Load Template with Two Header Rows

Almost all load templates will contain columns for externalCode, start-date, name, and status (see Figure 6.14). A Foundation Object joined to another by association will also have a column to enter in the associated object's external code (Column F of Figure 6.14).

When populating a template with data, keep the following helpful tips in mind:

▶ Each object's external code must be unique.

▶ The start date value will determine the date on which each object can be assigned to an employee. Be sure to date it back far enough to be used on employee records.

▶ Choices for STATUS are ACTIVE or INACTIVE.

▶ When referring to a picklist value, use the picklist label or direct value, not its external code.

▶ When referring to other Foundation Objects, use the object's code, not its name or label.

Recommendation

Do not delay the data-gathering process for Foundation Objects. Spend time identifying all of the objects needed to support your organization's business, but try to avoid waiting until the last minute to do so. Foundation Object data must be imported prior to importing any employee data, so it is best to do so in a timely manner in alignment with your project plan.

Importing the Load Template

Once you finish populating a load template with your entries, import it into the system. To do so, return to ADMIN CENTER • EMPLOYEE FILES • IMPORT FOUNDATION DATA. This time, instead of downloading a blank template, scroll down to the bottom portion of the IMPORT FOUNDATION DATA screen (see Figure 6.15).

Follow these steps to import a file:

1. Select the type of Foundation Object you want to import from the radio button list.

2. Choose whether you're performing a FULL PURGE (overwrite objects existing on the file with the new data contained in the file) or an INCREMENTAL LOAD (adds these values as new records in an object's history).

3. Select the file for import.

4. Choose the corresponding file format. If there is any doubt about which format to use, choose UNICODE (UTF-8) so as not to lose any multi-character set formatting.

5. Click the VALIDATE IMPORT FILE DATA button. The system then reviews a subset of the file to ensure that the proper header rows have been used and that appropriate field values have been selected.

6. Once the file passes validation, go back through and click the IMPORT button to complete the load process.

7. Depending on the size of your file, it may be loaded directly and a results message displayed right on the screen. With larger files, the import job may process in the background and an email message will be sent to confirm the import. You can also actively monitor the import job's progress by clicking on the MONITOR JOB button at the top-left side of the screen or by selecting MONITOR JOB from the Admin Center.

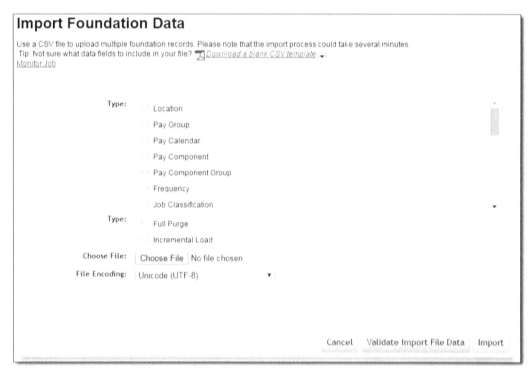

Figure 6.15 Import Foundation Data Screen with Key Areas Highlighted

> **Note**
>
> At the time of writing (December 2015), all Foundation Objects, even MDF Foundation Objects, can be loaded via template in this manner and from this screen. In addition, MDF Foundation Objects can also be loaded into the system using the IMPORT AND EXPORT DATA portion of the Admin Center. This process can be a little more involved, however.

6.5.2 Manual Creation

Manual additions to the Foundation Data and regular updates also can be made manually within the system. This is a task usually carried out by global administrators, because Foundation Objects are for the most part global in nature. Manual admin updates is a method preferred by many to update Locations, add a new Division or Cost Center, or update the Job Classification listing. The location within the Admin Center for making changes varies slightly based on whether you're modifying a regular Foundation Object or an MDF Foundation Object. Let's take a look at each scenario.

Managing Traditional Foundation Object Data

Manually add and edit non-MDF Foundation Objects in an area of the Admin Center known as MANAGE ORGANIZATION, PAY AND JOB STRUCTURES. Navigate to this area via ADMIN CENTER • EMPLOYEE FILES • MANAGE ORGANIZATION, PAY AND JOB STRUCTURES. The resulting screen allows you to search for existing Foundation Data in order to view, edit, update, and delete entries and to create new values (Figure 6.16).

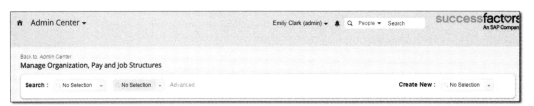

Figure 6.16 Manage Organization, Pay and Job Structures Area

Creating a New Entry

To create a new entry, select the Foundation Object type from the dropdown list next to the CREATE NEW header, shown in Figure 6.16. A blank entry screen for that Foundation Object will appear and will show each field that is defined as an

HRIS field for this particular HRIS element. Complete the entries and click SAVE at the bottom of the screen (see Figure 6.17).

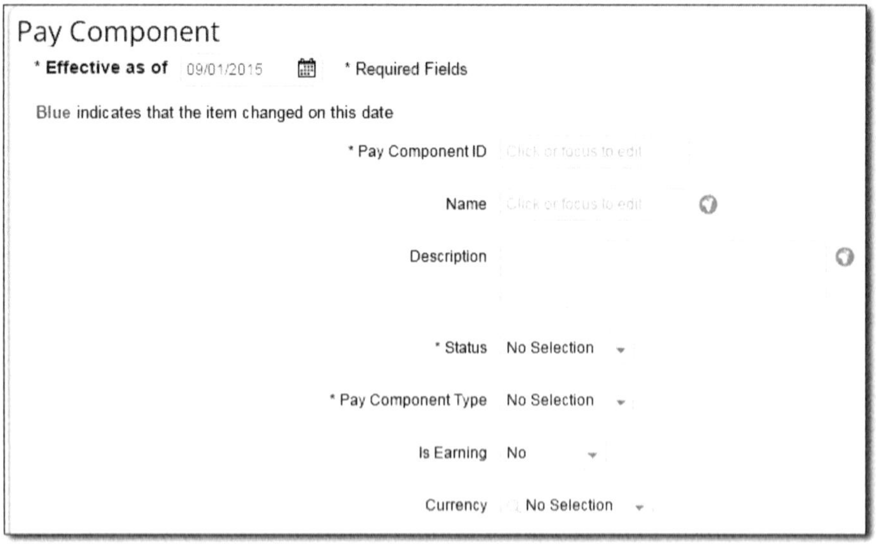

Pay Component

* Effective as of   09/01/2015   📅   * Required Fields

Blue indicates that the item changed on this date

* Pay Component ID   Click or focus to edit

Name   Click or focus to edit   🔘

Description   🔘

* Status   No Selection ▾

* Pay Component Type   No Selection ▾

Is Earning   No ▾

Currency   No Selection ▾

Figure 6.17 Blank Foundation Object Screen for a Pay Component Object

Effective As Of

Pay particular attention to the EFFECTIVE AS OF date at the top of the entry. This represents the entry's start date. It must be set back far enough that the object is in existence for an employee record it needs to be added to. If an employee needs to be assigned a Pay Component as of July 1, 2000, then the Pay Component start date must be on or before this date. This is a common oversight new administrators sometimes make when creating new entries.

Modifying an Existing Entry

To modify an existing entry, select the Foundation Object type from the dropdown list next to the SEARCH header, shown in Figure 6.17. From the second dropdown, select the specific entry you wish to view or edit. You can type in the name or code of this entry. Once selected, the entry should display in the center of the screen, as shown in Figure 6.18. Notice that because this is an effective-dated entity, there is an object history on the left-hand side of the screen. This allows you to track changes over time.

Back to: Admin Center
Manage Organization, Pay and Job Structures

Search : Location ▼   Beijing (CN_BJS) ▼   Advanced

History	
01/01/1990	Take Action ▼
Location: Record created	

Location: Beijing (CN_BJS)

Effective as of 01/01/1990

Blue indicates that the item changed on this date

Code	CN_BJS
Standard Hours	40
Name	Beijing 🌐
Description	Beijing, China 🌐
Status	Active
Location Group	APAC (APAC)
Timezone	Asia/Hong_Kong (GMT+08:00)
Geo Zone	Asia Pacific (APAC)

Legal Entity

Ace China (ACE_)

Figure 6.18 Left-Hand Side of Existing Location Entry, Ready for Viewing/Editing

If you need to make a correction to the data shown, click on the TAKE ACTION dropdown shown in the HISTORY section. Then, select MAKE CORRECTION or PERMANENTLY DELETE RECORD (see Figure 6.19). A correction should only be made if data is erroneous and needs to be fixed as of the already shown effective date (or if an effective date needs to be corrected).

Figure 6.19 Take Action Options: Make Correction or Permanently Delete Record

An update to existing data is needed if there has been a change to the existing record. This happens in the case of a new Department name, a new Division head, a new Location address, and so on. In these cases, you do not want to overwrite existing data but rather want to keep it in HISTORY while you make a new entry in the record. Accomplish this by clicking the INSERT NEW RECORD button in the top-right corner of the screen (see Figure 6.20). This allows you to add a new record without erasing previous information.

Figure 6.20 Location Record Showing Insert New Record Button

Managing MDF Foundation Object Data

The general process for creating and modifying an MDF Foundation Object Data entry is similar to the non-MDF Foundation Object process, but the area of the system for accessing this data is different.

From the MANAGE ORGANIZATION, PAY AND JOB STRUCTURE screen, choose to create or edit an MDF Foundation Object entry. When you do so, you are notified via a popup that the location for performing these tasks has changed. Click on the MDF FOUNDATION OBJECTS link (Figure 6.21) to be rerouted to the new location. Once there, the process of adding or editing an MDF Foundation Object entry is the same as the process for adding and editing non-MDF Foundation Objects described in the previous section.

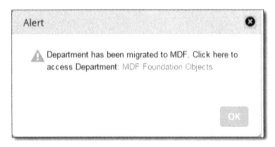

Figure 6.21 Popup Alert Rerouting to the Manage Data Area

Alternately, directly access the area for adding and editing MDF Foundation Object Data, the MANAGE DATA area, from the Admin Center, via ADMIN CENTER • EMPLOYEE FILES • MANAGE DATA. As you can see in Figure 6.22, the view and menu options are identical to what you saw in the MANAGE ORGANIZATION, PAY AND JOB STRUCTURES area.

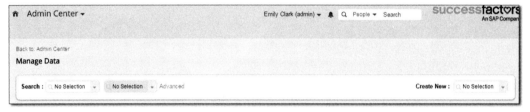

Figure 6.22 Manage Data Area of the Admin Center

6.6 Extending Foundation Objects

With the addition of the MDF to Employee Central, there are now several different options in terms of flexibility and customer-specific configuration. These options are seen directly with the use of Foundation Objects. Traditional data models are defined independently, but the MDF allows for universal consistency and reuse of existing Object Definitions. It also allows you to build your own custom objects (foundation or otherwise) and to insert and connect them to already existing structures as needed.

The greatest benefit of the MDF for Foundation Objects is the ability to create new and custom Foundation Objects for customers. This means that if the basic existing four-level organizational structure (Company, Business Unit, Division, Department) doesn't meet the needs of an organization, you can build new objects to help augment the existing structure. For example, you might add a Subfunction or Project Team object.

You can also build non-organizational-related Foundation Objects to assist companies with managing their employee data or characterizing their organization and employees. Items such as Buildings (to further breakout campus- or plant-style Locations) and Job Market Category are common examples.

These custom MDF objects can be used in the same manner as their traditional counterparts. They can be inserted into an existing structure using associations, used as filters when sorting through long data lists, and brought into parent–child relationships. In addition, they provide some extra functionality in the form of using business rules and workflows during their creation and use processes. For more information on the MDF, see Chapter 5.

6.7 Summary

In this chapter, you learned about Foundation Objects and their role in the Employee Central module. We introduced propagation and associations as well as the Foundation Object creation and maintenance processes. We ended the chapter by looking at how we can extend Foundation Objects further.

In the next chapter, we will take a deep dive into data imports and data migration. These two topics are important to master not only for initial system population, but also to assist with ongoing maintenance.

Migrating your existing HR data into your new Employee Central system is a necessary and critical activity. Employee data may also need to be imported into the system from time to time.

7   Data Imports and Data Migration

Whether performing a one-time migration, introducing a set of new employees into the system, or updating a number of Foundation Objects, data imports are a quick and reliable method of bringing data into Employee Central. Although the OData API is a robust and effective way of importing data into the system, the API requires a greater amount of technical skill and additional technology to use.

It goes without saying that importing data can be challenging. Ensuring that you meet file dependencies and use correct column formats can be a headache, and understanding the entire dataset can be difficult for even the most accomplished and knowledgeable business experts. Significant time should be put aside for data migration, particularly for larger organizations. Leveraging common extract-transform-load (ETL) tools can be a great help to ensure that you get your data in the right format and in the right files so that system validations are met.

Another factor is determining your current data freeze and the cutover date for your data, which may also coincide with the first transmission data for your system integration. If you're migrating historical data to Employee Central, then the number of years of history to migrate needs to be determined. If you're using SAP SuccessFactors Workforce Analytics (WFA), then we recommend migrating at least two years of data. If you're migrating data from SAP ERP HCM and will integrate data back to SAP ERP HCM from Employee Central, then you may consider only migrating data from your cutover date.

Most commonly, data migration is performed via data imports. Section 7.1 and Section 7.2 will discuss the requirements and processes that meet the needs for most customers importing and exporting data. SAP ERP HCM customers who are migrating to Employee Central will find tools and methodologies available to accelerate or facilitate data migration (see Section 7.3).

In this chapter, we'll look at the methodology and common elements for all data import methods and go through each type of import one by one. We'll also look at some of the more advanced import errors and how to solve them. Once we've looked at data imports, we'll move onto data exports before looking at the data migration tools available to facilitate the one-time movement of data into Employee Central.

7.1 Importing Data

SAP SuccessFactors accepts data imports in the comma-separated values (CSV) file format. The structure of the CSV import templates depends on the configuration of the system. You can export CSV import templates from the system to be filled with the data to be imported.

There are three types of data imports for importing Employee Central data:

- Foundation Object data
- Generic Object data
- User account and employee data

Each of these has its own nuances and individual characteristics, but luckily, they share certain attributes with each other. We'll cover each type throughout this section.

Prior to filling in data import files, you must understand the Employee Central data model, which we covered in Chapter 1, Section 1.2. Before we look at the import templates and data import types, we will first walk through the critical processes and considerations that you should review before beginning a data import.

7.1.1 Processes and Considerations

You should perform data imports after the system has been configured, although during the configuration iterations you should load a small subset of employee data to ensure testing and demonstration of the system according to the needs of the customer team. Typically, importing a subset of data makes it easier for a customer to understand how the system looks in a real-world scenario and enables the customer to better judge the configurations that have been made.

In this section, we will look at standard data import processes, key fields, settings, and other important considerations to keep in mind when performing a data import.

Data Import Order

You import data via various transactions in OneAdmin, depending on which type of import you're performing, and you should import the CSV import files in a specific order based on the type of import.

When importing data for the first time, you should import Foundation Object and Generic Object data before employee data. It's also important that you've imported picklists, especially those referenced in the CSV import templates. For the standard configuration, import object data in the following order:

1. Frequency
2. Pay Group
3. Location Group
4. Legal Entity
5. Legal Entity Local objects (e.g., United States, France, Germany, etc.)
6. Geozone
7. Location
8. Cost Center
9. Business Unit
10. Division
11. Department
12. Division-Business Unit
13. Department-Division
14. Pay Grade
15. Job Function
16. Job Classification
17. Job Classification Local (e.g., United States, France, Germany, etc.)
18. Pay Component

19. Pay Component Group

20. Pay Range

21. Pay Calendar

22. Event Reason

23. Position

24. Time Off objects (Time Profile, Work Schedule, Holiday Calendar, etc.)

25. Time Sheet objects (Time Recording Profile, Time Recording Admissibility, etc.)

26. Employee data

27. Dynamic Role

28. Workflow Configuration

29. Workflow Contributors

30. Workflow CC Roles

31. Other employee Generic Object data (e.g., Advances, Alternative Cost Distribution, Deductions, Payment Information, Time Accounts, custom Generic Objects data, etc.)

Depending on the system configuration, the order of objects imported may differ, and some objects may not need to be imported (e.g., Position, Time Off, or Time Sheet objects). Employee data files have a specific order that must be followed (see Section 7.1.3). There are some caveats about imports that are important to note:

▶ Business Unit, Division, Job Classification, and Position objects must be imported without parent objects filled and then reimported with the parent objects filled, because the system needs the objects to exist before they can be referenced.

▶ Business Unit and Division objects must be imported without the `headOfUnit` field filled and then reimported once employee data has been loaded, because this field references employees' user IDs.

▶ Likewise, Cost Center must be imported without the `costCenterManager` field filled and then reimported once employee data has been loaded, because this field references employees' user IDs.

▶ Any percentage-based Pay Component objects must be imported without the `basePayComponentGroup` field filled and then reimported with this required value filled after the Pay Component Groups have been imported.

The system performs validation on all Foundation Object and employee data imported, including checking the data against system logic and running any business rules that have been configured, should the settings be enabled. A sanity check is performed on the first ten records in Foundation Objects and employee data imports at the point of upload; this check lists any errors that are discovered. These errors must be resolved to pass the sanity check. See Section 7.1.5 for an example of this validation.

Several file encoding formats are available for import files:

▶ Western European (Windows/ISO)

▶ Unicode (UTF-8)

▶ Korean (EUC-KR)

▶ Chinese Simplified (GB2312)

▶ Chinese Traditional (Big5)

▶ Chinese Traditional (EUC-TW)

▶ Japanese (EUC)

▶ Japanese (Shift-JS)

Real-Time Synchronous and Asynchronous Loading

SAP SuccessFactors supports both *real-time (synchronous)* and *asynchronous* loading of data for Foundation Object and employee data imports. Real-time imports are performed if the number of records is below the threshold, which varies for each type of import. The threshold can be lowered so that an import file can trigger an asynchronous import instead of a real-time import. Generic Object imports are always asynchronous loads. All real-time loads should complete within five minutes.

Download the results of asynchronous jobs (imports and exports) from the MONITOR JOBS screen, located in OneAdmin in EMPLOYEE FILES • MONITOR JOB (see Figure 7.1).

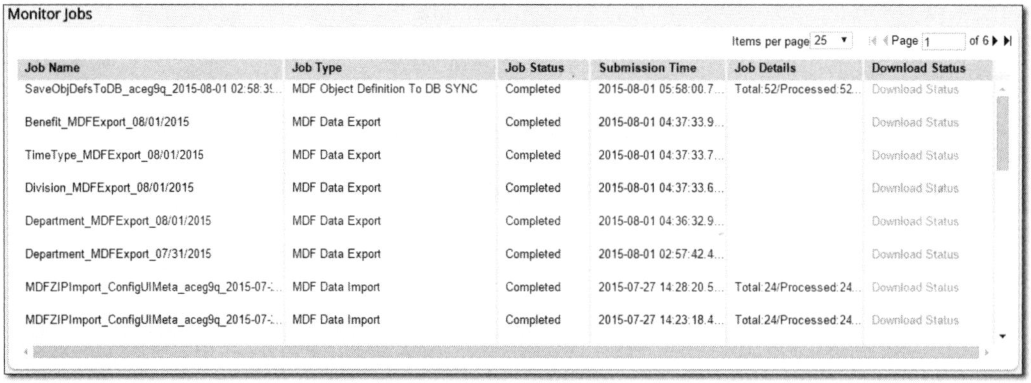

Monitor Jobs					
				Items per page 25 ▼ ◄ ◄ Page 1 of 6 ► ►|	
Job Name	**Job Type**	**Job Status**	**Submission Time**	**Job Details**	**Download Status**
SaveObjDefsToDB_aceg9q_2015-08-01 02:58:3! ...	MDF Object Definition To DB SYNC	Completed	2015-08-01 05:58:00.7...	Total:52/Processed:52...	Download Status
Benefit_MDFExport_08/01/2015	MDF Data Export	Completed	2015-08-01 04:37:33.9...		Download Status
TimeType_MDFExport_08/01/2015	MDF Data Export	Completed	2015-08-01 04:37:33.7...		Download Status
Division_MDFExport_08/01/2015	MDF Data Export	Completed	2015-08-01 04:37:33.6...		Download Status
Department_MDFExport_08/01/2015	MDF Data Export	Completed	2015-08-01 04:36:32.9...		Download Status
Department_MDFExport_07/31/2015	MDF Data Export	Completed	2015-08-01 02:57:42.4...		Download Status
MDFZIPImport_ConfigUIMeta_aceg9q_2015-07-:...	MDF Data Import	Completed	2015-07-27 14:28:20.5...	Total:24/Processed:24...	Download Status
MDFZIPImport_ConfigUIMeta_aceg9q_2015-07-:...	MDF Data Import	Completed	2015-07-27 14:23:18.4...	Total:24/Processed:24...	Download Status

Figure 7.1 Monitor Jobs Screen

If an import fails for any reason, the download includes the records and errors for each record that failed. If an import or export job was successful, the download contains a summary of the number of records processed. Access this information by clicking the DOWNLOAD STATUS hyperlink in the DOWNLOAD STATUS column.

Any asynchronously loaded job will trigger an email upon completion of the job.

Full Purge or Incremental Load

Data being imported can be either a full purge or an incremental load. *Full purge* means that all existing records in the system are wiped for each object/employee in the CSV import template and are replaced with the records in the CSV import template. *Incremental load* means that the records within the CSV import template are imported in addition to the existing records in the system. When using an incremental load, existing records in the system remain unaffected.

When performing an incremental load, it's possible to perform a *partial load*, in which only certain values are changed and others remain unchanged. Do so by using the value &&NO_OVERWRITE&& in the field(s) to be retained. This is useful if only certain changes need to be made during a bulk import, such as changing a Department or Pay Grade only.

There are certain limitations when using &&NO_OVERWRITE&&. The following fields do not support &&NO_OVERWRITE&& in any import file:

▶ user-id
▶ person-id-external

- `externalCode`
- `start-date`
- `end-date`
- `seq-number`
- `operation`
- `address fields`

In addition, the business key fields for each object must always be defined and cannot use `&&NO_OVERWRITE&&`, because they identify the object. Most business key fields are contained in the preceding list, but some additional fields can also define the business key for the following objects:

- Job Classification Local FO: `country`
- National ID Information: `country` and `card-type`
- Address Information: `start-date` and `address-type`
- Email Information: `email-type`
- Phone Information: `phone-type`
- Social Account Information: `domain`
- Emergency Contact: `name` and `relationship`
- Pay Components Recurring: `pay-component`
- Pay Components Non-Recurring: `pay-component-code` and `pay-date`

The following imports do not support the `&&NO_OVERWRITE&&` value:

- Pay Calendar Foundation Object
- Dynamic Role Foundation Object
- Workflow Foundation Objects (Workflow Configuration, Contributor, and CC Roles Foundation Objects)
- Personal Documents Information (Work Permit Information)
- Job Relationships

Note that the `&&NO_OVERWRITE&&` value cannot be used in the Job Information import for records that have an Event Reason for Hire or Rehire events.

The system treats blank fields differently depending on whether the file is imported as a full purge or incremental load. When imported as a full purge load, blank values are treated as blank. When imported as an incremental load, blank values are retained if the field supports `&&NO_OVERWRITE&&`; otherwise they are treated as blank.

Key Fields and Settings

There are several system settings that can be set in OneAdmin in Company Set-tings • Company System and Logo Settings. The following settings are all Bool-ean checkboxes:

- ▶ Enable rules execution during Job Information import
  Enables execution of business rules when importing Job Information data. Dis-abling this setting will speed up the data import, because executing business rules occurs for every record and increases the processing time. This setting should be disabled if you use Event Derivation with business rules; otherwise, it will cause an internal system error when importing data. This setting does not affect business rules that propagate data from the position to the employee.

- ▶ Enable Forward Propagation of Job Information Data for Inserts in Incremental Imports
  Enables forward propagation of Job Information data to future-dated records when loaded in an incremental load.

- ▶ Attach data with email for Import/Export jobs
  Enables job result data to be attached to the job completion notification email.

- ▶ Suppress update of identical records during Employee Central import for supported entities
  Enables duplicate records to remain as is if there is no change to them for both full purge and incremental load imports of Personal Information, Person Info, Job Information, and Employment Information data.

- ▶ Execute Business Rules and Propagation Against NO_OVERWRITE
  Enables business rules to be executed when importing Job Information data that uses the `&&NO_OVERWRITE&&` value for one or more fields.

The following settings enable inputting a batch size as an integer:

- ▶ Maximum threadpool size for Employee Central and Foundation Data imports
  Sets the number of batches processed at a single time; the default is five.

- ▸ BATCH SIZE FOR EMPLOYEE CENTRAL AND FOUNDATION DATA IMPORTS
  Sets the number of records for each batch; the default is 500.

The following Position Management settings (found in OneAdmin in EMPLOYEE FILES • POSITION MANAGEMENT SETTINGS) also can impact data imports:

- ▸ DO NOT ADAPT THE POSITION 'TO BE HIRED' STATUS DURING JOB HISTORY IMPORT
  Defines whether the TO BE HIRED field on a position should be changed if the position becomes filled as part of a Job Information import.

- ▸ VALIDATE POSITION ASSIGNMENT DURING JOB INFORMATION IMPORT
  Defines whether position assignments should be validated during a Job Information import (i.e., whether the position is already assigned to an employee when it is not a shared position).

- ▸ DO NOT ADAPT REPORTING HIERARCHY DURING POSITION IMPORT
  Defines whether the Reporting Hierarchy should be adapted to match the Position Hierarchy during a position import.

- ▸ DO NOT ADAPT HIERARCHY DURING IMPORT OF LEAVE OF ABSENCE RECORDS
  Defines whether the current hierarchy should be adapted based on a leave of absence when the Right to Return feature is used (i.e., employees should be reassigned to the holder of the parent position of their manager's position if their manager is on a leave of absence).

Special Characters

Special characters (e.g., &, #, or ~) are supported, except for caret (^), which is not supported. Keep the following caveats in mind when using some special characters:

- ▸ Any text fields that contain a comma (,) must be enclosed in quotation marks ("").

- ▸ Pipe (|) should not be used in the `externalCode` field of a Foundation Object if that object will be used in a field defining associations for another Foundation Object.

Date Formats

The format of dates used in date fields is dependent on the login locale of the user. For example, if the user's locale is `en_US`, then the date format will be MM/

DD/YYYY, whereas if the user's locale is en_GB, then the date format will be DD/MM/YYYY.

Let's go over some of the basics for import templates before looking at the three data import types.

7.1.2   Import Templates

All import templates consist of two header rows and multiple columns. The top row of the template is the technical fieldname, and the second row is the description of the field. Figure 7.2 shows an example of a filled CSV import file for the Legal Entity Foundation Object in Microsoft Excel.

Figure 7.2 CSV Import Template for Legal Entity

The import templates will look familiar to anyone that understands the data model of the configured Employee Central system. Most fields will be listed with their technical field names. However, there are two main caveats:

▸ **Object references and associations**
Fields that reference another object (e.g., a Foundation Object or Generic Object) or have an association with another object are always in the format <object>.externalCode, where <object> is the object code. For example, the DEPARTMENT field in the Job Information import template will be called department.externalCode in the first row.

▸ **Translatable Generic Object fields**
Translatable fields for Generic Objects appear once for each language in the system, along with one instance for the default value to be used. Each field uses the format <field name>.<locale>, where <field name> is the technical name

of the field and `<local>` represents the language. The format for the default value is `<field name>.defaultValue`. For example, if the system had American English, British English, and French enabled, then the NAME field would exist three times as `name.en_US`, `name.en_GB`, and `name.fr_FR`. In addition, the field would also appear as `name.defaultValue`.

Some common fields in all CSV import templates must be filled in the same way. The name of the fields may vary template by template, but the format is the same. These fields include the following:

- `start-date`
  The start date of a record, usually in format MM/DD/YYYY; we recommend using 01/01/1980 for Foundation Object records and for Generic Object records that represent Foundation Objects and related objects (e.g., position).

    - `effectiveStartDate`: Same as the `start-date`

    - `startDate`: Same as the `start-date`

- `end-date`
  Used for date delimitation; if blank, defaults to 12/31/9999.

- `status`
  The status of the object; ACTIVE or INACTIVE for Foundation Objects and employee data and A or I for Generic Objects.

    - `effectiveStatus`: Same as `status`

- `externalCode`
  The code (ID) of an object.

- `name`
  The name of an object.

- `user-id`
  The user ID of an employee.

    - `person-id-external`: Same as `user-id`

- `event-reason`
  The `externalCode` of the Event Reason used to define the reason for an event in the Job Information, Compensation Information, or Termination templates; we covered Event Reasons in Chapter 4.

- `seq-number`
  The sequence number used when multiple records exist on the same date.

- **Operation**
  Used to determine a delimitation or delete operation in certain import templates.

Some other common rules in place are valid for all templates when referencing objects or associated objects. When referencing a Foundation Object or Generic Object, the `externalCode` of the object is always used. For picklists, the type of picklist determines which value you enter into the import template:

- **Legacy picklists (used for Foundation Objects and employee data)**
  The value in the picklist (e.g., Full Time).

- **Metadata Framework (MDF) Picklists**
  The code of the value in the picklist (e.g., FT).

When referencing an employee, you should use the user ID of the employee.

Boolean fields have two sets of valid entries, depending on whether they are Foundation Objects or employee data, or Generic Objects:

- **Foundation Objects and employee data**
  Y, Yes; T, True; 1 for Yes; N, No; F, False; or 0 for No.

- **Generic Objects**
  TRUE for Yes and FALSE for No.

One challenge you may face when filling in CSV import templates is that you cannot tell which fields are required or what the field lengths are. Fields can be checked in the data model or in the system, but all required fields must be filled in order to import the CSV import template.

Read-only fields (i.e., those that have VISIBILITY set to VIEW) must have ALLOW IMPORT set to YES in order for the fields to be available in the CSV import template and for the CSV import template to be importable. Figure 7.3 shows the POSITION field as read-only and the ALLOW IMPORT field set to YES.

Due to limitations with some spreadsheet software, when filling CSV import templates, often you must use an apostrophe in front of leading zeroes (e.g., '00001234) and use quotation marks when a value includes a comma (e.g., "Director, HR Operations").

The order of the columns in the CSV import templates does not matter, although all fields need to exist as columns even if they are blank.

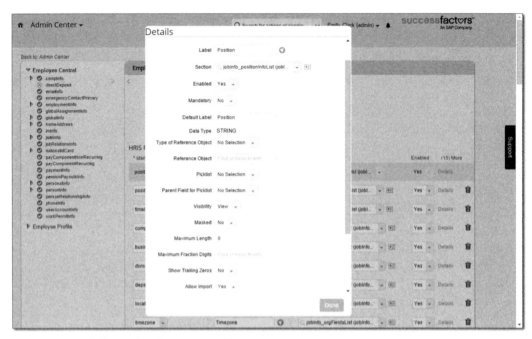

Figure 7.3 Details for Read-Only Position Field

Important!

If the data model in the system changes, then you may not be able to import any existing CSV import templates. You will need to download new CSV import templates again or modify existing CSV import templates to match the new configuration.

7.1.3   Types

As previously stated, there are three types of data imports: Foundation Object data imports, Generic Object data imports, and user and employee data imports. In this section, we will discuss these three types in detail.

Foundation Object Data Imports

At the time of writing, many of the Foundation Objects in Employee Central have been moved to the MDF. However, some of the objects remain on the legacy Foundation Object framework and therefore have their own characteristics. Until these remaining Foundation Objects have been moved to the MDF, the legacy method must be used to import them. In order to understand which objects are on the legacy framework and which are on the MDF, you should consult the latest *Migrating to Metadata Framework (MDF) Foundation Objects* implementation handbook at *http://help.sap.com/hr_ec/* under the heading MIGRATION GUIDES.

CSV Import Templates

CSV import templates can be downloaded from OneAdmin in EMPLOYEE FILES • IMPORT FOUNDATION DATA. This is also where you load filled-in import files. Figure 7.4 shows the IMPORT FOUNDATION DATA screen.

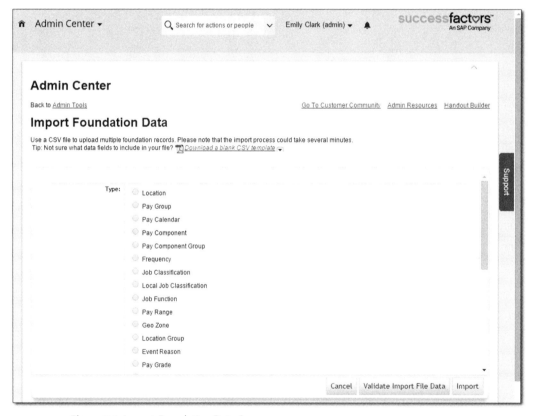

Figure 7.4 Import Foundation Data Screen

CSV import templates can be downloaded by clicking the DOWNLOAD A BLANK CSV TEMPLATE hyperlink and selecting the appropriate template.

> **Important!**
>
> The IMPORT FOUNDATION DATA screen shows all Foundation Objects, including Foundation Objects that have moved to the MDF. As a result, it's possible to download a CSV template that cannot be used to import data. For Foundation Objects that have been moved to the MDF, treat them as any other Generic Object data imports.

SAP SuccessFactors provides some Foundation Object data in the system as standard. The system provides Frequency objects along with the Pay Component Group object AnnualizedSalary. Based on this, no Frequency objects may need to be imported. Unless you need more than one Pay Component Group, no Pay Component Group objects need to be imported.

SAP SuccessFactors also provides a prefilled import template of around 180 Event Reason objects. Although many of these may not be needed and additional Event Reasons may be required, the file can be used as the basis for your CSV import template for Event Reason objects.

Translatable fields—such as NAME or DESCRIPTION—require a different process once all of the Foundation Object data has been imported. We'll cover that process shortly.

Template Rules

The CSV import templates should be completed using the basic rules and methods discussed in the previous section. Keep the following tips in mind (in addition to those mentioned in Section 7.1.2):

- Use a common start date for the first record of all objects (01/01/1980 is a good date to use).
- When filling in associated objects or references, remember to use the externalCode of the target object.
- Ensure that the dates of associated objects do not conflict (i.e., associated objects must exist in the timeframe of the current object).

Import Completed CSV Templates

Once your CSV import templates are filled with data, it's time to import them. The order in which the CSV templates should be imported depends on any associations between objects. Objects without associations should be imported first. Objects with associations should be imported after their parent objects have been loaded. For example, Location Group objects should be loaded before Location objects, because Location objects reference Location Group objects.

To import the completed CSV import templates, navigate to EMPLOYEE FILES • IMPORT FOUNDATION DATA in OneAdmin and follow these steps:

1. Select the Foundation Object to import.
2. Select the LOAD TYPE (FULL PURGE or INCREMENTAL LOAD).
3. Change the threshold value in the REAL-TIME THRESHOLD field if you want an asynchronous import to trigger.
4. Choose the file to import by clicking the CHOOSE FILE button.
5. Change the file encoding in the FILE ENCODING dropdown if required.
6. Click VALIDATE IMPORT FILE DATA to validate the file or click IMPORT to import the data.

We always recommend validating the import file prior to importing it to ensure that it is error free. If there are any errors after validation or after attempting to import the file, correct the errors and then try again. Refer to Section 7.1.5 to see some advance errors and their remedies, as well as an example screenshot.

Once the data loads, navigate to EMPLOYEE FILES • MANAGE ORGANIZATION, PAY AND JOB STRUCTURES in OneAdmin to validate that your data has loaded. If there are any mistakes, you can modify the import file and perform a full purge import. Alternatively, you can modify individual records directly in the MANAGE ORGANIZATION, PAY AND JOB STRUCTURES screen.

As mentioned previously in this section, translatable fields for Foundation Objects have a different process. Prior to beginning this activity, Foundation Object translations must be enabled in Provisioning by selecting the option ENABLE TRANSLATION OF EMPLOYEE CENTRAL FOUNDATION OBJECTS.

Once the Provisioning setting has been enabled and all of the Foundation Object data has been imported, then the steps in Section 7.2.1 should be followed to export Generic Object data for the FoTranslation Generic Object. This will contain the information for all translatable Foundation Object fields.

> **Important!**
>
> It may take several hours for Foundation Object data in the system to completely process for translations after you enable the Provisioning setting. If the downloaded FoTranslation CSV file only has the two header rows, then the processing is not yet complete.

Once you've downloaded the FoTranslation CSV file, you can complete it. Figure 7.5 shows an example of the downloaded FoTranslation CSV file with values for the loaded Foundation Objects. As you can see in the Figure 7.5, the columns for German (column H), British English (column I), and Spanish (column J) do not contain translations. These must be added to the CSV file and then uploaded.

	A	B	C	D	E	F	G	H	I	
1	[OPERATOR]	externalCode	foObjectID	foType	foField	value.defaultValue	value.en_US	value.de_DE	value.en_GB	value.es
2	Supported o	externalCode	foObjectID	foType	foField	defaultValue	US English	Deutsch (German)	English UK (English UK)	Español
3		company_name_182	182	company	name	ACE Argentina	ACE Argentina			
4		division_name_105	105	division	name	GCS Europe, Middle East	GCS Europe, Middle East			
5		division_name_106	106	division	name	GCS Asia, Pacific & Japan	GCS Asia, Pacific & Japan			
6		company_name_188	188	company	name	ACE Portugal	ACE Portugal			
7		costCenter_name_244	244	costCenter	name	GCS Netherlands	GCS Netherlands			
8		costCenter_name_246	246	costCenter	name	GCS New Zealand	GCS New Zealand			
9		location_name_246	246	location	name	Porto, Portugal	Porto, Portugal			
10		costCenter_name_248	248	costCenter	name	GCS France	GCS France			
11		company_name_45	45	company	name	Ace Germany	Ace Germany			
12		company_description_45	45	company	description	Ace Germany Corporaiton	Ace Germany Corporaiton			
13		company_name_55	55	company	name	Ace USA	Ace USA			
14		wfConfig_name_87	87	wfConfig	name	One Time Bonus	One Time Bonus			
15		wfConfig_description_87	87	wfConfig	description	Manager's Manager, Finance	Manager's Manager, Finance			
16		wfConfig_name_81	81	wfConfig	name	Pay Rate Change	Pay Rate Change			
17		wfConfig_description_81	81	wfConfig	description	Manager's Manager, HR Rep	Manager's Manager, HR Rep			
18		wfConfig_name_241	241	wfConfig	name	Position Change	Position Change			

Figure 7.5 FoTranslation CSV File with Translations to Be Added

The FoTranslation CSV file contains a series of headings that can be used to identify the objects. Internal system object IDs are used, so even with a knowledge of the loaded Foundation Objects, which objects are listed might not be immediately clear. The headings are as follows:

- **externalCode**
  The system-generated external code for a Foundation Object that is created specifically to load translations.

- **foObjectID**
  The system-generated internal code for the Foundation Object, which will differ from the externalCode seen in the CSV import templates that were loaded and in the system.

- **foType**
  The Foundation Object type, such as location or payGrade.

▶ `foField`
The translatable field name, typically `name` or `description`.

▶ `value.defaultValue`
The current value in the system.

▶ `value.<locale>`
The column that represents each enabled language in the instance, with `<locale>` representing the language (e.g., `en_US` for US English or `fr_FR` for French). This field will exist for the default language of the system and will contain the same value as the `value.defaultValue` field.

▶ `mdfSystemStatus`
The status of the record (A for active or I for inactive).

Once you have entered the necessary translations, the file should be uploaded to the system like any other Generic Object data, which we will cover in the following section.

Generic Object Data Imports

Generic Objects—including Foundation Objects moved onto the MDF—have their own process. Perform all imports and exports of Generic Object data and download CSV import templates in OneAdmin in EMPLOYEE FILES • IMPORT AND EXPORT DATA. Being able to export data can significantly reduce the time required to make changes to data. The options available for downloading templates, importing data, and exporting data are more substantial and represent the ability to leverage both simple and more complex object structures.

On the IMPORT AND EXPORT DATA screen, you can download templates and import and export data of the following types:

▶ Generic Object definitions (Object Definition object and Dependent objects)
▶ Generic Object data
▶ MDF Picklist data (MDF Picklist object and dependent Values object)
▶ Business rules (Rule object and Dependent objects)
▶ Configuration UIs (ConfigUIMeta object and dependent objects)

This includes Foundation Objects that have been migrated to the MDF.

Data imports and exports are processed asynchronously, and you can download the results of imports and exports from the MONITOR JOBS screen.

> **Important!**
>
> For Generic Objects that have security enabled, the import/export permission for each Generic Object must be provided to the user downloading the CSV import templates.

CSV Import Templates

Download CSV import templates by selecting DOWNLOAD TEMPLATE in the SELECT THE ACTION TO PERFORM dropdown. When downloading templates, there are four options available to the user. All options are mandatory, although the latter three are Boolean options. These options are as follows:

- SELECT GENERIC OBJECT
  The Generic Object template to download.

- INCLUDE DEPENDENCIES
  Indicates whether to include CSV import templates for dependent objects, such as associated objects, picklists, and business rules.

- INCLUDE IMMUTABLE IDs
  Indicates whether to include immutable (unchangeable) IDs, which are mainly used for MDF picklist objects.

- EXCLUDE REFERENCE OBJECTS
  Indicates whether to exclude related, nondependent objects (e.g., picklists or business rules).

Once these settings have been entered, the user clicks DOWNLOAD to download the CSV import template. Note that although a CSV import template exists for a Generic Object, a separate CSV import template exists for each association between the object and another Generic Object. This CSV import template simply defines the associations; a separate CSV import template exists for the associated objects. For example, for the Division object there is a CSV import template for Division objects, a CSV import template for Division-Business Unit associations, and a CSV import template for Business Units.

Templates typically contain the fields found below, plus any other standard or custom fields. Translatable fields also will appear, as we discussed in Section 7.1.2.

- [OPERATOR]
  An optional operator for either delimiting an existing record (DELIMIT) or clearing the data from existing record and all subsequent records (CLEAR) of an associated child record (cannot be used for top-level Generic Objects).

▶ `externalCode`
The code of the record or object.

▶ `effectiveStatus` or `mdfSystemStatus`
The status of the record (A for Active or I for Inactive).

Effective-dated objects usually contain an `effectiveStartDate` field to enter the start date of the record, but do not include an end date field, because the system can derive the end date of a record based on the start date of the previous record. The latest record will always have an end date of 12/31/9999. If an effective-dated object can have multiple changes per day, then it will also have the `transaction-Sequence` field to define the sequence of records that occur on the same day.

Template Rules

The CSV import templates should be completed using the basic rules and methods discussed in Section 7.1.2, although there are some unique rules for Generic Objects that are listed here:

▶ When filling in associated objects or references, remember to use the `externalCode` of the target object.

▶ Picklists used for fields on Generic Objects are MDF Picklists and not legacy picklists, so use the `externalCode` of the value.

▶ For Foundation Objects and the Position object, use a common start date for the first record of all objects (01/01/1980 is a good date to use).

▶ For Employee Time objects (leave requests), it's important only to include a maximum of five hundred records in the CSV import template and to only use an incremental load. In addition, the `fractionQuantity` field should be entered as a decimal up to ten decimal places (for example, two hours and thirty minutes should be entered as 2.5, whereas three hours and forty minutes should be entered as 3.6666666667).

▶ Ensure that the dates of associated objects do not conflict (i.e., associated objects must exist in the timeframe of the current object).

Attachments

Attachments can be included in a data import for Generic Objects that have one or more fields with the data type Attachment. Attachments can only be uploaded as ZIP files, and all attachments must be placed in a folder called ATTACHMENTS within the ZIP file. The file names must be referenced in the relevant attachment columns.

Import Completed CSV Templates

Completed CSV import templates are imported into the system by selecting IMPORT DATA in the SELECT THE ACTION TO PERFORM dropdown of the IMPORT AND EXPORT DATA screen. Choose from three options for which type of import to use:

- ▸ CSV FILE
  Import a single CSV import template of data.

- ▸ ZIP FILE
  Used to import a ZIP file containing multiple files, which is typically used for complex datasets.

- ▸ SUCCESS STORE
  This option allows you to import content provided by SAP SuccessFactors.

Figure 7.6 CSV File Import Options

Both the CSV FILE option and the ZIP FILE option are straightforward to use. For the CSV FILE option—shown in Figure 7.6—you must configure four additional options:

- ▸ SELECT GENERIC OBJECT
  The Generic Object for which you're uploading data.

- ▸ FILE
  The file to upload.

▶ FILE ENCODING
The file encoding, as listed in Section 7.1.

▶ PURGE TYPE
Either FULL PURGE or INCREMENTAL LOAD.

For the ZIP FILE option, you only have to select the ZIP file to import; the system can derive the remaining information from the ZIP file itself. For both the CSV and ZIP options, you can choose to validate the import file using the VALIDATE button or import the data without validation using the IMPORT button. The results of the validation and import are available in the MONITOR JOBS screen, as described in Section 7.1.

The SUCCESS STORE option is different than the other two options, as shown in Figure 7.7. Here, you will see a list of content to choose from, including the following, for example:

▶ Deductions user interface

▶ Global benefits user interfaces

▶ Income tax declaration content for India

▶ Name format content

▶ Payroll configuration picklists

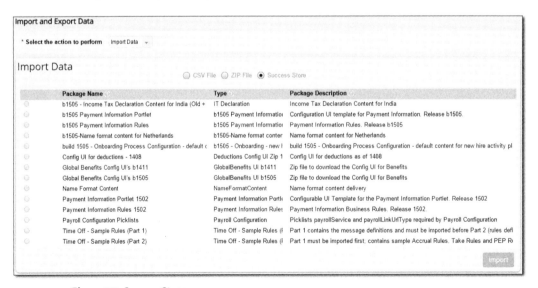

Figure 7.7 Success Store

To download a piece of content, select the radio button next to that content and click the IMPORT button. You can track the status of the import on the MONITOR JOBS screen. Once the import is complete, the content will be available in the system.

When importing Foundation Objects, you are most likely to use the CSV FILE option. For other imports, the best option depends entirely on the dataset. Sometimes, complex objects may have multiple files and require a ZIP file. This is the case for Generic Object definitions, because there are many components. The Success Store will always be used for specialist, optional content that isn't delivered in the standard system.

User and Employee Data Imports

Employee master data imports are performed by HRIS element, which typically are visualized as portlets on the PERSONAL INFORMATION and EMPLOYMENT INFORMATION screens. Some employee master data found on these screens and in other EMPLOYEE FILES screens are stored in Generic Objects, such as the following:

▶ Advances
▶ Alternative Cost Distribution
▶ Deductions
▶ Payment Information
▶ Time Off data
▶ Time Sheet data

These are imported like any other Generic Objects and are not covered in this section. Refer to the previous section to review how to import Generic Object data.

Employee master data—including user accounts—is loaded in OneAdmin in UPDATE USER INFORMATION • IMPORT EMPLOYEE DATA. Blank CSV templates can be downloaded in a similar way as Foundation Objects, by clicking the DOWNLOAD A BLANK CSV TEMPLATE hyperlink at the top of the screen and selecting the template.

The screen shown in Figure 7.8 will feel familiar to users who have used the IMPORT FOUNDATION DATA screen. It lists all of the imports, although there are a few minor differences. First, the FULL PURGE and INCREMENTAL LOAD options are found directly below the template that is selected for import, rather than at the bottom of the screen. Second, further options for BASIC IMPORT and EMPLOYMENT DETAILS ARE ADDED, as well as some additional options for importing consolidated datasets. The following list goes over each of the imports and any additional options:

▶ BASIC IMPORT

For importing the User Data File (UDF) that creates the user accounts and forms the basis of the employee record. There are several options provided for this import, although many of them are not Employee Central-specific, so we will not cover them here (however, even when implementing Employee Central, the settings may be relevant if a larger population is being used for talent than is being used in Employee Central). There are three relevant options:

  ▷ SEND WELCOME MESSAGE: Sends a welcome message to the user with his or her logon credentials.

  ▷ PROCESS INACTIVE EMPLOYEES: Select this option if you are importing inactive employees into Employee Central.

  ▷ VALIDATE MANAGER AND HR FIELDS: Validates whether the MANAGER and HR fields have an active user in them; used when EFFECTIVE DATED FIELDS IN BASIC IMPORT is enabled in Provisioning.

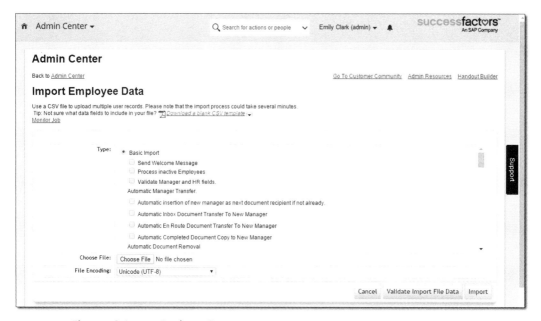

Figure 7.8 Import Employee Data

▶ EXTENDED IMPORT
Used to import Employee Profile extended data.

▶ BACKGROUND IMPORT
Used to import Employee Profile background data.

▶ BIOGRAPHICAL INFORMATION
Imports the data that is displayed in the BIOGRAPHICAL INFORMATION portlet on the PERSONAL INFORMATION screen. A full purge is always performed for this type of import.

▶ PERSON RELATIONSHIP
Imports dependents' relationship data that is displayed in the DEPENDENTS portlet on the PERSONAL INFORMATION screen. Note that the Personal Information and Addresses imports are required to import personal information about the related dependents. Alternatively, the Consolidated Dependents import can be used to import all dependents' data.

▶ EMPLOYMENT DETAILS
Imports dependents' data that is displayed in the EMPLOYMENT DETAILS portlet on the EMPLOYMENT INFORMATION screen. Three additional options are available here:

▹ GLOBAL ASSIGNMENTS: Imports global assignment(s) data.

▹ PENSION PAYOUTS: Imports pension payout data.

▹ BENEFICIARIES: Imports pension payout beneficiaries data.

A full purge is always performed for this type of import.

▶ PERSONAL INFORMATION
Imports data that is displayed in the PERSONAL INFORMATION portlet on the PERSONAL INFORMATION screen.

▶ GLOBAL INFORMATION
Imports country-specific personal data that is displayed in the PERSONAL INFORMATION portlet on the PERSONAL INFORMATION screen.

▶ TERMINATION DETAILS
Imports details of a terminated employee's termination. This information will be displayed in the EMPLOYMENT DETAILS portlet on the EMPLOYMENT INFORMATION screen. A full purge is always performed for this type of import.

▶ JOB HISTORY
Imports data that is displayed in the JOB INFORMATION portlet on the EMPLOYMENT

INFORMATION screen. Please note although both full purge and incremental load options are available, incremental load cannot be used for records with an Event Reason that uses either the Hire or Rehire events.

▶ COMPENSATION INFO
Imports data that is displayed in the COMPENSATION INFORMATION portlet on the EMPLOYMENT INFORMATION screen.

▶ PHONE INFORMATION
Imports phone data that is displayed in the CONTACT INFORMATION portlet on the PERSONAL INFORMATION screen.

▶ EMAIL INFORMATION
Imports email data that is displayed in the CONTACT INFORMATION portlet on the PERSONAL INFORMATION screen.

▶ SOCIAL ACCOUNTS INFORMATION
Imports social account data that is displayed in theCONTACT INFORMATION portlet on the PERSONAL INFORMATION screen.

▶ NATIONAL ID INFORMATION
Imports data that is displayed in theNATIONAL ID INFORMATION portlet on the PERSONAL INFORMATION screen.

▶ ADDRESSES
Imports addresses data that is displayed in the HOME ADDRESS portlet on the PERSONAL INFORMATION screen.

▶ EMERGENCY CONTACT
Imports email data that is displayed in the PRIMARY EMERGENCY CONTACT INFORMATION portlet on the PERSONAL INFORMATION screen.

▶ PERSONAL DOCUMENTS INFORMATION
Imports Work Permit data and—if required—document attachments that are displayed in the WORK PERMIT INFO portlet on the PERSONAL INFORMATION screen. There are further steps required if you wish to import documents as attachments, which are covered a little later in this section. A full purge is always performed for this type of import.

▶ PAY COMPONENT RECURRING
Imports compensation and pay target data that is displayed in the COMPENSATION INFORMATION portlet on the EMPLOYMENT INFORMATION screen.

- Pay Component Non-Recurring
  Imports spot bonus data that is displayed in the Spot Bonus portlet on the Employment Information screen.

- Job Relationships
  Imports data that is displayed in the Job Relationships portlet on the Employment Information screen.

- Composite (Zip) Data Upload
  Enables uploading a ZIP file that contains multiple CSV import files. When uploading multiple files, we recommend using this option. The system processes the mandatory template files in the required order and then processes the remaining files. Each file within the ZIP file can be monitored in the Monitor Jobs screen and an email notification is sent for each file. For new employees, it must contain the Basic Import, Biographical Information, and Employment Details CSV import templates. For existing users, there is no requirement as to which import files are included. It's possible to schedule an import by creating a Composite Employee Data Import job in Provisioning. Because this is a composite ZIP containing multiple CSV import templates, this is the only import option that doesn't have a corresponding CSV import template available for the Download a blank CSV template hyperlink.

- Consolidated Dependents
  Imports dependents' relationship data and dependents' personal data that is displayed in the Dependents portlet on the Personal Information screen.

- Compound Non-Effective Dated Entities
  Enables a single CSV import template to be imported that covers fields from the Employment Details, Biographical Information, Email Information, Phone Information, and National ID Information CSV import templates.

- Compound Delete
  Deletes all data for a specific HRIS element (e.g., Job Information or National ID Information). A full purge is always performed for this type of import.

CSV Import Templates

Six CSV import templates must be imported to create a complete employee dataset and must be imported in the specific order listed ahead. The CSV import templates are as follows:

1. Basic Import

2. Biographical Information

3. Employment Details

4. Job History

5. Compensation Info

6. Personal Information

All other employee data imports are optional in order to create an employee in the system.

Template Rules

The CSV import templates should be completed using the basic rules and methods discussed in Section 7.1.1. You may find the following general tips to be useful:

▸ A maximum of 50,000 records should be inserted into a CSV import template.

▸ `user-id` is the user ID defined in the Basic Import or when created in SAP SuccessFactors directly.

▸ `person-id-external` is the same as `user-id`.

▸ For the first or only record for an employee, the date in the `start-date` field in all CSV import templates should match the date in the `start-date` field in the Employment Details CSV import template.

▸ The `end-date` column can be left blank for the latest record.

▸ When filling in columns for Foundation Objects or Generic Objects (e.g., Department or Frequency), use the `externalCode` of the target object.

▸ Effective-dated records should have no time gaps between records.

▸ For multiple effective-dated records occurring on the same dates, use the `seq-number` column to define the sequencing.

▸ The value of the `zip-code` field is not validated upon import (it is validated when entered in the user interface), so be careful to enter correct values.

Now, let's go over some template-specific rules that you should consider:

▸ **Basic Import**
If you are migrating from an existing HRIS, it is recommended to insert the existing user IDs or personal numbers into the `userid` column. If an employee

has no manager, the value "no_manager" should be inserted into the manager column. If an employee has no HR manager, the value "no_hr" should be inserted into the hr column. Your implementation partner can provide you with a list of time zones for the TIMEZONE field and locales for the default_locale column.

An additional user should be created for each global assignment, pension pay-out, beneficiary, and dependent. Insert this value into the appropriate CSV import template in the personal-id-external column (for dependents, this is the related-personal-id-external column). It's good practice to add a suffix to the user ID to identify the purpose of these user accounts, such as a number for global assignments or the letter D for dependents.

▶ **Biographical Information**
The values of the user-id and person-id-external columns should be the same.

▶ **Recurring Pay Component**
For every record in the Compensation Information CSV import template, a corresponding record should exist in the Recurring Pay Component CSV import template and vice versa. The dates of these two CSV import templates should be aligned, and no overlapping dates can occur. For example, the Compensation Information CSV import template contains two records: 1/1/2005–6/31/2009 and 7/1/2009–12/31/9999. During the entire period from January 1, 2005, two different recurring pay components exist: Base Salary and Car Allowance. In the Recurring Pay Component CSV import template, both of these recurring pay components must exist for both periods—that is, 1/1/2005–6/31/2009 and 7/1/2009–12/31/9999. This is the case whether the value of the pay components are the same in each period or not.

The value of the paycompvalue column should not include any commas (e.g., 1000.00, not 1,000.00).

▶ **Job Information**
For the first or only record in the Job Information CSV import template, the Event Reason entered into the event-reason column should for the Hire event. For other records, the Event Reason entered into the event-reason column should be one that has an employee status maintained.

If an employee has no manager, the value "no_manager" should be inserted into the manager-id field.

For terminated employees, the date in the `start-date` column of the record should be the termination date, and the Event Reason should be an Event Reason with an employee status of Terminated.

In order to speed up the import significantly when Time Off is enabled, any Time Type Profile objects assigned to employees in the `time-type-profile-code` column should have the associated Time Type object removed before the import and readded after the import. After the import is complete, the creation of time accounts, accruals, and eligibility status should be performed in OneAdmin in Employee Files • Manage Time Off Calendars.

▶ **Global Assignment, Pensions Payouts, and Beneficiaries**
The value in the `person-id-external` column should be the user ID of an existing user. However, the value of the `user-id` field should be a unique ID that can be freely defined. We advise using the same naming convention used by the system.

▶ **Employment Details (for Concurrent Employment)**
To import a Concurrent Employment record, use the Employment Details template. Like with the templates mentioned in the previous bullet, the value in the `person-id-external` column should be the user ID of an existing user. However, the value of the `user-id` field should be a unique ID that can be freely defined. We advise using the same naming convention used by the system.

Remember to consider leading zeroes in user IDs. In general, you can use leading zeroes, but they can be problematic to handle when working with CSV files (typically when used in Microsoft Excel) and not all files support leading zeroes. Traditionally, the `user-id` field can support leading zeroes, but the `person-id-external` field typically does not. Therefore, if you choose to use leading zeroes for your employee user IDs, be careful when working with files and note that the following import templates do not support leading zeroes (although the key field will still match with the equivalent field that contains leading zeroes):

▶ Personal Information

▶ Email Information

▶ Phone Information

▶ National ID Information

▶ Emergency Contact Information

- ▶ Address Information
- ▶ Termination Information

Please note that the UI will not display leading zeroes from the `user-id` field or `person-id-external` field.

Work Permit Documents

As we mentioned earlier, work permit documents can be uploaded with the Personal Documents Information CSV import template so that they can be accessed in the Work Permit Info portlet as attachments. Follow these steps in order to upload the documents:

1. In the PERSONAL DOCUMENTS INFORMATION import template, enter the filename of the attachment in the `attachment-id` column for the relevant records.

2. Create a text file called *import.properties*.

3. In the import.properties file, enter "importFileName=filename.csv" and replace "filename.csv" with the name of the CSV import template.

4. Create a ZIP file of the CSV import template, the import.properties file, and the documents to upload.

5. Import the ZIP file.

Figure 7.9 shows an example import.properties file. In this example, the CSV import template is called *WorkPermitInfoImportTemplate_aceins.csv*.

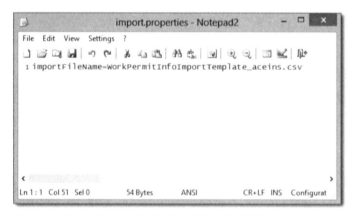

Figure 7.9 import.properties File Specifying the CSV Import Template

For incremental loads, you can delimit or delete records for the following HRIS elements:

- ▶ Addresses
- ▶ Phone Information
- ▶ Email Information
- ▶ Social Accounts Information
- ▶ National ID Information
- ▶ Emergency Contact
- ▶ Job Relationships
- ▶ Pay Component Recurring
- ▶ Pay Component Non-Recurring
- ▶ Direct Deposit

Do so by inserting the value "DELIMIT" or "DELETE" in the `Operation` column found in every CSV import template. DELIMIT delimits effective-dated records and enables partial deletion of data for non-effective-dated records. DELETE deletes the record from the system; note that the system looks for a record with the dates specified in the CSV import template. When the `Operation` column is left blank for any records, those records are treated as insert or update operations.

Once your CSV import templates are filled with data, it's time to import them.

> **Important!**
>
> Note that the setting ENABLE RULES EXECUTION DURING JOB INFORMATION IMPORT that we discussed towards the end of Section 7.1.1 should be disabled prior to importing Job Information data if an Event Derivation with business rules is used. Refer to Chapter 4, Section 4.2 for more details on Event Derivation with business rules.

Position Data Propagation

It is possible to force data propagation from a position to an employee's Job Information. This is performed by modifying and importing the position CSV import template after importing Job Information data. The steps to perform this as are as follows:

1. Open the Position CSV import template and add a new column called `technical-Parameters`.

2. For the positions that you wish to propagate data from, insert the word "SYNC" into the `technicalParameters` column for those records.

3. Import the position CSV import template.

Import Completed CSV Templates

Remember to load mandatory files in the correct order for new employees! To import the completed CSV import templates, navigate to UPDATE USER INFORMATION • IMPORT EMPLOYEE DATA in OneAdmin and follow these steps:

1. Select the import type.

2. Select the load type (FULL PURGE or INCREMENTAL LOAD), if available.

3. Change the threshold value in the REAL-TIME THRESHOLD field if you want an asynchronous import to trigger.

4. Choose the file to import by clicking the CHOOSE FILE button.

5. Change the file encoding in the FILE ENCODING dropdown if required.

6. Click VALIDATE IMPORT FILE DATA to validate the file or click IMPORT to import the data.

We always recommend validating the import file prior to importing it to ensure that it is error free. If there are any errors after validation or after attempting to import the file, correct the errors and then try again. Refer to Section 7.1.5 to see some common errors and their remedies.

The time to import data can vary significantly depending on each import. Table 7.1 gives a rough indication of the load times based on 10,000 records. For between ten thousand and 50,000 records, the processing time increases proportionally based on the number of records (e.g., 30,000 records takes three times longer than 10,000 records).

Import	Processing Time
Basic Import	60 minutes
Biographical Information	10 to 15 minutes
Employment Details	14 to 20 minutes
Job Information (without rules)	30 to 180 minutes
Compensation Information	10 minutes
Pay Component Recurring	10 minutes

Table 7.1 Import Processing Times

Import	Processing Time
Personal Information	45 to 60 minutes
Global Information	3 to 5 minutes
National ID Information	3 to 5 minutes
Address Information	5 to 10 minutes
Email Information	3 to 5 minutes
Phone Information	3 to 5 minutes
Social Accounts Information	3 to 5 minutes
Personal Documents Information	5 to 10 minutes
Emergency Contacts	15 to 20 minutes
Person Relationships	20 to 25 minutes
Termination	60 minutes
Pay Component Non-Recurring	10 minutes

Table 7.1 Import Processing Times (Cont.)

Note that for Job Information there are additional factors that can affect import, such as whether business rules are processed, how many business rules are processed, and what position management settings are enabled. The longest import time is usually around three hours without business rules, and three to five business rules can add around three to five seconds per record (around eight to fourteen hours). Typically, each business rule adds one-half to one second per record to the processing time.

Imports can be verified by viewing the portlet of the data that has just been loaded, with exception of the Basic Import.

7.1.4 Scheduling Imports

Data imports can be scheduled in Provisioning in the MANAGE SCHEDULED JOBS screen. The data import files should be placed onto the SAP SuccessFactors SFTP prior to running the jobs. A number of job types are available to schedule data imports:

▶ EMPLOYEE EXPORT AND EMPLOYEE IMPORT
Used to import the Basic User Import

- LIVE PROFILE IMPORT
  Used to import the Employee Profile data not part of the UDF

- FOUNDATION DATA IMPORT
  Used to import Foundation Object data

- EMPLOYEE DATA IMPORT (FOR EMPLOYEE CENTRAL ONLY)
  Used to import Employee Central data

- MDF DATA IMPORT (FTP)
  Used to import Generic Object data

Data Imports

No workflows are triggered based on data imports. Data propagation and HRIS Sync are both triggered upon data import.

7.1.5 Advanced Import Errors

Many common errors you may face when importing data are straightforward to interpret and resolve. However, a few advanced import errors can occur when importing data, depending on which type of object that is being imported. Errors for Foundation Objects and employee data will show the record and then provide the error message. Generic Object errors are always provided in a version of the CSV import template with just the record of that error and the error message. Figure 7.10 shows a sample general error.

Figure 7.10 Failure of the Sanity Check during Import of Employee Data

In the remainder of this section, values between angle brackets (<>) are used generically where an error message provides a specific value. For example, <FIELD> in an example error message would be replaced with the name of the message in the message received by the user. Therefore, a real-world example of the error message <FIELD> CONTAINS AN INVALID NUMBER FORMAT. is PAY-COMPVALUE CONTAINS AN INVALID NUMBER FORMAT.

The most common general errors found for Foundation Objects and employee data imports involve empty fields, blank fields, start dates greater than end dates, invalid date formats, and so on. In addition, you may encounter the following advanced errors:

▶ INTERNAL SYSTEM ERROR ENCOUNTERED WHILE IMPORTING RECORD.
Describes that the system has encountered an error that it cannot identify. This may be caused by Job Information rules being triggered on import (including event derivation rules), by no Event Reason or an invalid Event Reason being defined in the Job Information CSV import template, or by certain employee data not existing (i.e., an attempt was made to load data in an incorrect order); it can also be valid for Generic Object imports.

▶ THE SYSTEM HAS ENCOUNTERED AN UNKNOWN ERROR ON IMPORT. PLEASE CONTACT THE SYSTEM ADMINISTRATOR.
Typically occurs when the `externalCode` column is missing or the top header row is missing, but can also occur when other critical columns are missing; can also be valid for Generic Object imports.

▶ <VALUE> IS AN INVALID EXTERNAL CODE FOR <COLUMN>.
The `<VALUE>` value in the `<COLUMN>` column is not an `externalCode` of the referenced object in the system (the object is included in the column name).

▶ SECOND NATIONALITY HAS INVALID COUNTRY <COUNTRY>. and THIRD NATIONALITY HAS INVALID COUNTRY <COUNTRY>.
The value entered into the `second-nationality` field is not in the Country picklist; this error also occurs for the `third-nationality` field.

▶ INVALID START OF SEQUENCE NUMBER, IT SHOULD START WITH 1.
A value higher than 1 has been entered into the `seq-number` field for the first record of a sequence.

▶ THERE IS ALREADY ANOTHER RECORD WITH THE SAME START DATE.
Two records exist with the same start date for objects that are not effective-dated or there are overlapping records.

Generic Objects have a whole set of errors, with the more advanced errors as follows:

▶ IMPORT OF THIS RECORD FAILED DUE TO AN ERROR IN ONE OF THE RELATED RECORDS I.E. A FAILED RECORD WITH THE SAME EXTERNAL CODE OR ERROR IN EITHER A PARENT OR ANY COMPOSITE CHILD RECORD.
One or more records for the same object failed to import because an earlier record of the same object had an error.

▶ INVALID ENUMERATION FIELD VALUE (THE SUPPORTED VALUE: <VALUES> FOR <FIELD>).
An incorrect value has been used in a field that uses predefined enumeration values.

▶ <VALUE> IS AN INVALID VALUE FOR OBJECT: FO_<OBJECT>_T.
The value used for a field of type Foundation Object does not match the `externalCode` of any objects of the Foundation Object defined for the field.

▶ <VALUE> IS AN INVALID VALUE FOR OBJECT: <PICKLIST/OBJECT>.
The value `<VALUE>` defined for a field of type Generic Object or type Picklist does not match the `externalCode` of any objects of the Generic Object or picklist defined for the field.

▶ THIS OPERATOR IS NOT SUPPORTED ON TOP-LEVEL ENTITY.
A DELIMIT or CLEAR operator was defined for a record on a Generic Object that is a top-level object and not an associated child object.

▶ THIS OPERATOR IS NOT SUPPORTED IN FULL PURGE.
The DELIMIT or CLEAR operators cannot be used for a full purge load.

For Employment Details imports, the error PERSON-ID-EXTERNAL IS INVALID. will be received if the value of the `person-id-external` field does not match the value of the `user-id` field.

Several errors can be received during a Job Information import, such as the following:

▶ NO HIRE RECORD IS FOUND FOR USER <USERID>, IMPORT HIRE RECORD FIRST FOR INCREMENTAL IMPORT.
When performing an incremental import, an Event Reason for the Hire event wasn't loaded before or included in the CSV import template.

▸ HIRE RECORD ALREADY EXISTS FOR USER <USERID>, CANNOT IMPORT HIRE RECORD TWICE USING INCREMENTAL IMPORT.
Incremental load cannot be used for a Hire event if a record already exists.

▸ TERMINATION RECORD CANNOT BE IMPORTED FOR USER <USERID>, AS THIS WILL RESULT IN MORE THAN ONE TERMINATION RECORD IN THE SYSTEM.
Incremental load cannot be used for a Termination event if a record already exists.

▸ FAILED TO PERFORM COUNTRY-SPECIFIC VALIDATION. PLEASE ENSURE THIS RECORD IS ASSOCIATED WITH A VALID COMPANY RECORD FOR GIVEN DATES.
The `country-of-company` field was filled, but it should be left blank.

▸ <VALUE> FOR OBJECT <FOUNDATIONOBJECT> IS NOT A CONSISTENT VALUE WITH THE ASSOCIATED OBJECT <FOUNDATIONOBJECT> WITH VALUE <VALUE>.
A value was defined for a Foundation Object that is not valid for the associated Foundation Object (e.g., *Plastics* Division is not associated to the *Metal Operations* Business Unit).

For a Personal Info import, the error GENDER EXCEEDS THE MAXIMUM LENGTH ALLOWED OF 2 CHARACTERS. will be received if the value of the `gender` field exceeds two characters, whereas the error FIELD GENDER IS INVALID. FIELD GENDER TAKES "M" / "m" FOR MALE, "F" / "F" FOR FEMALE, "U" / "U" FOR UNKNOWN, "D" / "D" FOR UNDECLARED AND " " FOR NO GENDER. will be received if the value of the `gender` field is the valid length but is an incorrect value from the predefined list of values.

For Email Information and Phone Information imports, the error INVALID ISPRIMARY MENTIONED. ONLY T OR F ARE SUPPORTED. PLEASE SET ONE RECORD AS PRIMARY RECORD FOR <USERID>. will be received if a primary record is not set in the `isPrimary` field using the values t or f.

For National ID Information imports, you should be aware of two specific advanced errors:

▸ ISPRIMARY IS A REQUIRED FIELD FOR <COUNTRY> AND CANNOT BE BLANK. (COUNTRY IS DEDUCED FROM THE VALUE OF COLUMN COUNTRY.)
The `isPrimary` field has not been maintained.

▸ PLEASE ENTER A VALID NATIONAL ID OF THIS TYPE: <NATIONALIDTYPE> FOR <COUNTRY>.
The format of the number entered for the National ID matched the format defined in the Country-Specific Data Model but did not pass the country-spe-

cific validation (e.g., 123-45-6789 is in the correct format but is not a valid Social Security number in the United States).

For Emergency Contacts, the following errors may be received:

- ▶ PRIMARY_FLAG EXCEEDS THE MAXIMUM LENGTH ALLOWED OF 1 CHARACTERS.
  The value of the `primary_flag` column is two or more characters in length; only Y or N are supported values.

- ▶ INVALID PRIMARY FLAG MENTIONED. ONLY Y OR N ARE SUPPORTED.
  The value of the `primary_flag` column is one character in length but is an incorrect value (only Y or N are supported values).

- ▶ FIELD ZIP-CODE DOES NOT BELONG TO THIS COUNTRY. PLEASE REMOVE VALUE FOR THIS FIELD FROM THE INPUT FILE.
  The `zip-code` column is filled, but the COUNTRY column is not.

For Personal Documents (Work Permit Information), the following errors may be received:

- ▶ INVALID OR MISSING PROPERTY: {0} IN IMPORT.PROPERTIES FILE.
  When importing attachments, the content of the import.properties file is incorrect.

- ▶ CORRUPT OR NO ATTACHMENT EXISTS BY NAME <FILENAME> IN THE UPLOAD.
  When importing attachments, the system cannot find the attachment in the ZIP file or the file is corrupt.

For Person Relationships, the error FIELD ZIP-CODE DOES NOT BELONG TO THIS COUNTRY. PLEASE REMOVE VALUE FOR THIS FIELD FROM THE INPUT FILE. tells you that the `zip-code` column is filled, but the `country` column is not.

For Job Relationships, the error THE <USERID> IS AN INVALID USER. is received if no user exists for the user ID specified in the `rel-user-id` field.

For Global Assignment, Pensions Payouts, and Beneficiaries, the error YOU CANNOT IMPORT A RECORD WITH A USER-ID WHICH ALREADY EXISTS AND/OR BELONGS TO ANOTHER ASSIGNMENT TYPE. will be received if the value of the `person-id-external` field is:

- ▶ Blank
- ▶ The same as the value of the `user-id` field
- ▶ An existing employee

As previously stated, some of the errors you will encounter are relatively straight-forward, but the errors in this section identify those more complex issues that may not be interpretable from just the error message. The purpose of this section was to convey what these types of errors mean and how they can be resolved.

In the next section, we'll move on to the exporting options available in Employee Central.

7.2 Exporting Data

In addition to importing data, in some instances you can export data. The export options are far more limited than the import options, although as more and more objects move to the MDF, the export options become increasingly enhanced. In this section, we'll look at the four types/methods for exporting data in Employee Central and how to schedule data exporting.

7.2.1 Types

There are four main types/methods of exporting data from Employee Central: UDF, employee delta export, Generic Object data, and exporting data via reporting. Let's look at each of these options now.

User Data File

The UDF can be exported from OneAdmin via UPDATE USER INFORMATION • EMPLOYEE EXPORT. There are a number of options available, although only some of the options are relevant for Employee Central. Figure 7.11 shows the options. Under the SPECIFY EXPORT OPTIONS section, the VALID USERS ONLY option enables only active users to be included in the export file. Under the SPECIFY FILE LANGUAGE FORMAT AND BATCH/SCHEDULED PROCESSING OPTIONS section, select the file encoding and select the EXPORT AS A BATCH PROCESS option to process the export asynchronously.

Whichever options are selected, clicking the EXPORT USER FILE button will process the file download. If the EXPORT AS A BATCH PROCESS option is selected, then the file must be downloaded from the MONITOR JOBS screen.

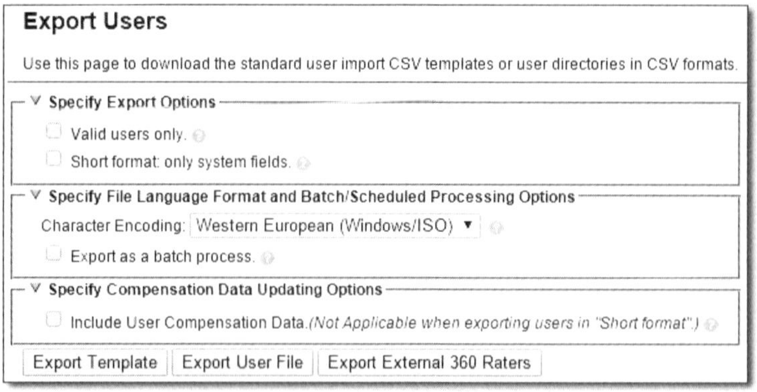

Export Users

Use this page to download the standard user import CSV templates or user directories in CSV formats.

┌─ ∨ **Specify Export Options** ───
│   ☐ Valid users only. ⓘ
│   ☐ Short format: only system fields. ⓘ
┌─ ∨ **Specify File Language Format and Batch/Scheduled Processing Options** ─
│   Character Encoding: Western European (Windows/ISO) ▼ ⓘ
│   ☐ Export as a batch process. ⓘ
┌─ ∨ **Specify Compensation Data Updating Options** ─────────────────────
│   ☐ Include User Compensation Data.*(Not Applicable when exporting users in "Short format".)* ⓘ

[Export Template] [Export User File] [Export External 360 Raters]

Figure 7.11 Export Users Screen

Employee Delta Export

The Employee Delta Export is used for exporting employee master data from Employee Central in the Microsoft Excel format so that it can be used in payroll systems. It provides a delta of employee data (i.e., it only provides data changes since the last run of the export) that considers both future-dated and retroactive changes of employee data and includes deleted data that must be actioned in the target system (e.g., deletion of a Pay Component).

The Employee Delta Export comprises an add-in for Microsoft Excel and two Microsoft Excel workbooks that provide the configuration and the layout of the data that is exported from Employee Central. These three components can be downloaded from OneAdmin in REPORTING • EMPLOYEE DELTA EXPORT. The Employee Delta Export leverages the Employee Central HRIS SOAP API in order to export the data from Employee Central into the workbooks.

We'll cover the Employee Delta Export in more detail in Chapter 19, Section 19.10.

Generic Object Data

As we discussed in Section 7.1.3, there are options to export Generic Object data from the system. This includes object definitions, object data, MDF Picklists, business rules, and Configuration UIs. Data is exported as a CSV file, although when dependencies are also exported the CSV file and dependent object CSV files are combined in a ZIP file.

263

Generic Object exports are performed in OneAdmin in Employee Files • Import and Export Data. Export data from the system by selecting Export Data in the Select the action to perform dropdown. There are five options available to select which type of import to use:

▸ Select Generic Object
The Generic Object for which to download data.

▸ Include dependencies
Indicates whether to export all associated objects and data—such as associated object definitions, data of associated objects, picklists, and business rules—with the CSV data file in a composite ZIP file.

▸ Include Immutable IDs
Indicates whether to include immutable (unchangeable) IDs; mainly used for MDF Picklist objects.

▸ Exclude reference objects
Indicates whether to exclude related, non-dependent objects (e.g., picklists or business rules).

▸ Select all data records
Indicates whether to select all records for the selected Generic Object, or only user-selected records (selecting No displays the Select objects dropdown from which to select records).

Once the appropriate settings have been made, clicking the Export button will process the data export asynchronously. Once processed, the export file will be available for download on the Monitor Jobs screen.

Exporting Data with Reporting

Another way of retrieving data from the system is through reporting. Either the Ad Hoc Reporting or Detailed Reporting option can be used to export data in an Excel file, which can then be uploaded to other systems. Both types of reporting are covered in detail in Chapter 17.

7.2.2   Scheduling Exports

Like with data imports, data exports can be scheduled in Provisioning from the Manage Scheduled Jobs screen. The data export files will be placed onto the

SAP SuccessFactors SFTP once the job has run successfully. There are a number of job types available to schedule data imports:

- EMPLOYEE EXPORT AND EMPLOYEE IMPORT
  Used to export the Basic User Import

- LIVE PROFILE EXPORT
  Used to export Employee Profile data not part of the UDF

- EXPORT EMPLOYEE DATA
  Used to export employee data via ad hoc reports

At present, Generic Object data cannot be scheduled for export. Employee Central data exports can only be viewed in Provisioning and cannot be viewed on the MONITOR JOBS screen in OneAdmin.

7.3   Data Migration from SAP ERP HCM

Data migration tools and methodologies are available for SAP ERP HCM customers migrating to Employee Central. At the time of writing (December 2015), the main methods of migrating data are as follows:

- SAP ERP to SAP SuccessFactors Employee Central Data Migration Rapid-Deployment Solution (RDS)

- Integration add-on for SAP ERP and SAP SuccessFactors Employee Central

These methods provide accelerated content and tools to migrate data from your SAP ERP HCM system into Employee Central quickly and painlessly.

Additional Resources

You can read more about data migration between SAP ERP HCM and SAP SuccessFactors in Chapter 11 of *Integrating SuccessFactors with SAP* by Vishnu Kandi, Venki Krishnamoorthy, Donna Leong-Cohen, Prashanth Padmanabhan, and Chinni Reddygari (SAP PRESS, 2015).

Let's go over both of these data migration options next.

7.3.1 SAP ERP to Employee Central Data Migration Rapid-Deployment Solution

The *SAP ERP to SuccessFactors Employee Central Data Migration Rapid-Deployment Solution* (RDS) is a rapid-deployment package built on SAP Data Services technology that provides an end-to-end solution to analyze, extract, clean, transform, and validate data from SAP ERP HCM and then load and reconcile that data directly into Employee Central. Figure 7.12 shows field mappings between Infotype 0006 and HRIS element `homeAddress` in SAP Data Services.

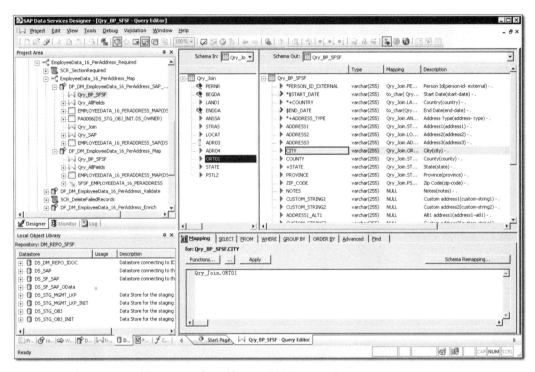

Figure 7.12 Field Mappings for Address in SAP Data Services

The package is available at no cost to SAP ERP HCM customers, although customers who do not use SAP Data Services need to license and implement this solution to use the package. Despite the name of the package, the data source for the migration doesn't actually have to be SAP ERP HCM; you can migrate data from any source and can include a mix of SAP and non-SAP data.

The package features full mappings between SAP ERP HCM infotypes and Employee Central HRIS elements and fields. These can be modified as required to cater for custom, specific use cases in both SAP ERP HCM and Employee Central. In addition, the package also features a project methodology, business process documents, and test plans for each object. The following objects are covered:

- All Foundation Objects, except for Workflow Configurations
- Positions
- Profiles and User accounts
- PERSONAL INFORMATION screen portlets:
  - National ID Information
  - Personal Information (including country-specific data)
  - Biographical Information
  - Address Information
  - Contact Information (Email, Phone, and Social Accounts)
  - Emergency Contact Information
  - Direct Deposit information
- EMPLOYMENT INFORMATION screen portlets:
  - Employment Details (including Termination Information)
  - Job Information
  - Job Relationships
  - Compensation Information (including Recurring Pay Components)
  - Spot Bonus
- Time Off data:
  - Time Types and Time Type Profiles
  - Time Account configuration
  - Employee Time

Employee Central Payroll migration is also available for the following infotypes:

- Residence Tax Area (IT0207)
- Work Tax Area (IT0208)
- Unemployment State (IT0209)
- Withholding Information W4/W5 US (IT0210)
- Additional Withholding Information (IT0234)

▸ Other Taxes US (IT0235)

▸ Payroll Results (T558B, T558C, and T5U8C)

▸ Garnishment Document (IT0194)

▸ Garnishment Order (IT0195)

▸ Contract Elements (IT0016)

▸ Loans (IT0045)

▸ Loan Repayments (IT0078)

Figure 7.13 shows the process architecture.

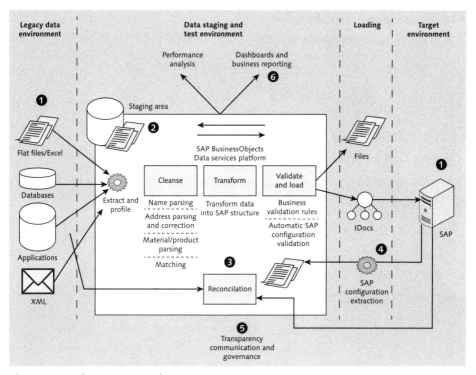

Figure 7.13 Package Process Architecture

Each number in Figure 7.13 represents a step in the methodology of the package. Let's walk through these steps:

❶ Analysis

In this step, the source and target systems are analyzed and the SAP Data Services environment is prepared. The data can be profiled on the source side to learn more about the source structure and understand the legacy data model, such as patterns of zip/postal codes and the different values for states and countries. The delivered mappings can be modified based on any specific requirements.

❷ Extract and clean

After the analysis is complete, data is extracted from the source system (e.g., SAP ERP HCM) into the SAP Data Services staging area, where it is profiled, analyzed for consistency (e.g., checking for country name variations, such as Germany, DE, or Deutschland for Germany, or for correct postcode formats), and prepared for cleansing, parsing, and transformation. This means ensuring that names, addresses, cost centers, and so on are in the correct format, that data follows the correct patterns, that target data types are matched, and validation of data integrity. Data can be reformatted and manipulated as necessary, such as concatenating fields, breaking them into two or more fields, or performing a search and replace on certain values to update them as necessary.

❸ Transform

Once the data is cleaned, reformatted, and prepared, it is transformed into the target Employee Central format using the mappings.

❹ Validate and load

After transformation, the Employee Central metadata (object structures, HRIS elements configuration, countries, languages, lookup values, etc. for validations) is extracted into SAP Data Services, and by using business rules defined by the metadata the transformed data can be validated to ensure that it matches the target Employee Central system. Once successful validation is complete, the data is loaded into Employee Central.

❺ Reconcile

Reconciliation of the loaded Employee Central data is performed to compare that what was actually loaded matches what was expected to be loaded.

❻ Report

Reports can be produced to help validate and reconcile the data using SAP Data Services dashboards and SAP BusinessObjects Web Intelligence reports in the SAP BusinessObjects Business Intelligence (BI) platform.

Further details—including the link to download the package—can be found at *http://service.sap.com/rds-dm2cloud*.

7.3.2 Integration Add-On for SAP ERP and Employee Central

SAP provides the option for SAP ERP customers to migrate data using the Integration add-on for SAP ERP and Employee Central, which integrates the two systems and replicates data on a permanent basis. This method uses IMG steps and programs in SAP to configure mappings and extract the data from SAP to CSV files. Data is then uploaded into Employee Central as we discussed in Section 7.1.

Once the migration is complete, the setup can be used for regular replication of data using the Dell Boomi AtomSphere middleware or SAP HANA Cloud Integration middleware.

When using the Integration Add-on for SAP ERP and Employee Central, you follow a five-step methodology:

1. **Preparation**
   In this step, the Employee Central data model is imported into SAP so that SAP ERP HCM fields can be mapped to Employee Central fields. This occurs by extracting the CSV import templates from Employee Central that we discussed in Section 7.1 and importing them using an SAP program.

2. **Mapping**
   This step involves defining value mappings and defining the field mappings between SAP ERP HCM and Employee Central fields.

   Value mapping involves mapping individual values in IMG Customizing activities, such as mapping actions in SAP ERP HCM with Event Reasons in Employee Central or mapping Personnel Areas in SAP ERP HCM with Locations in Employee Central. Values in Employee Central can be mapped to personnel actions in SAP ERP HCM, such as mapping a reorganization Event Reason to personnel action 02 (Organizational Reassignment). Standard value mappings are provided that cannot be changed because they map standard values between both systems; however, you can make custom value mappings.

   Field mapping involves mapping SAP ERP HCM fields to Employee Central fields.

3. **Extraction from SAP ERP HCM**
   The next step is to extract the data from SAP ERP HCM to CSV files or replicate it directly into Employee Central using the Dell Boomi AtomSphere middleware. First, you extract organization object data and then extract employee data. This process needs to be performed without parent fields maintained and then again with the parent fields maintained, because parent relationships cannot be imported before those objects have been imported.

If organizational data is being migrated, then additional mapping of Organizational Unit objects in SAP ERP HCM to the organization structure objects in Employee Central (i.e., Business Units, Divisions, Departments, and, if applicable, custom objects) needs to be performed.

4. **Import into Employee Central**
   After the data has been extracted from SAP ERP HCM into CSV files, it can be imported into Employee Central as we discussed in Section 7.1.

5. **Preparation of replication**
   After data has been migrated to Employee Central, then final steps can be taken to prepare for the regular replication of data from Employee Central back to the SAP ERP HCM infotypes for use in other processes. This includes setting up key mappings of extracted data to prevent data inconsistencies and creation of false or inaccurate data in the regular replication. Once the replication begins, the the key mappings tables are updated with each replication. We will discuss integration in more detail in Chapter 19. In addition, migration can be validated by analyzing the application via Transaction SLG1 in SAP ERP.

A number of steps and configurations and potential Business Add-In (BAdI) programming needs to be undertaken to ensure that the data migration and subsequent regular replication can take place.

Additional Resources

For more information on the overall process, the preparation, and each of these steps—along with step-by-step information about performing the activities of each of these steps—please refer to the *Migrating Data from SAP ERP to Employee Central* handbook found at *http://service.sap.com/ec-ondemand*.

7.4   Summary

In this chapter, we covered the various methods for importing data and how data imports work. We looked at some of the important processes and key nuances of data imports. We also looked at how this ties into data migration and some of the other options available when migrating data from another HRIS into Employee Central.

In the next chapter, we'll take a deep dive into the flexible and powerful Position Management module.

PART II
Features and Functionality

Implicit Position Management deals with positions only when there is no incumbent to manage, thus delivering the back office through self-services. This means that a structured organization can be built independent of employees. Position Management can provide benefits for budgeting, reporting, relationships, and more.

8   Position Management

Position Management creates an organizational structure independent of incumbents. A *position* is a Foundation Object and a transaction object at the same time in that it shares the properties of both. A position exists independent of its incumbent (individual who holds the job), and by that definition, it's a Foundation Object. On the other hand, the attributes that make up a position are the same as those inherited by the incumbent, so it also behaves like a transaction object.

The benefits of Position Management ironically occur when there is no incumbent in the position. It's possible to have processes run seamlessly when a position is vacant. Without positions, the termination of a manager creates broken processes that need to be explicitly handled. With positions, the termination of a manager automatically rolls up the processes to the next available incumbent in the hierarchy.

Positions can be very effective in driving processes such as recruiting, goals, learning, succession management, budgeting, and authorizations across the IT ecosystem, and herein lies their complexity. Almost all the benefits of having positions go to the teams or organizations that do not have the responsibility to maintain them. You can operate an HRIS system without positions, but downstream processes aren't as smooth.

Background

As a matter of academic interest, Position Management was the first feature built on the Metadata Framework (MDF). As a result, it's now a mature solution that leverages many of the features of the MDF, especially through the powerful Rules Engine.

In this chapter, we'll cover the use cases and reasoning behind using Position Management and how to define positions. We'll also review positions in other functionality, including the Position Org Chart, Succession Planning, Recruiting, and Job Profile Builder.

Following this, we'll start defining attributes of a position, security, synchronization of positions, position transfers and reclassifications, hierarchies, performing mass changes, and the right to return to a position.

Additional Resources

For more information on setting up and configuring positions, refer to the *Position Management (Implementation Guide)* handbook found at *http://service.sap.com/ec-ondemand*.

8.1 Implicit Position Management

Position Management and its downstream effects are at odds with self-service, in that it requires the user to do things distinct from the transaction for the system to work correctly. Implicit Position Management removes that need and enables transactions to be completed as business processes occur while automatically adjusting positions through a series of configurable rules and settings.

Most modern organizations are too dynamic to have a rigid set of structures define how they are organized. Business events such as mergers and acquisitions, reorganizations, and business transformations occur at a frequency that makes it difficult to determine what should come first: Do people structures determine the organization structures? Or vice versa? In short, Organization Management and Position Management, as implemented by most HRIS systems, are not flexible enough in structural and transactional senses to support the needs of the modern organization.

This is where implicit Position Management is useful. From the outset, Position Management, as implemented in SAP SuccessFactors and Employee Central, has been designed to keep the administrative effort of maintaining positions to a minimum. There are groups of users who work with positions and others who do not. The ideal solution would enable some users to work with positions and others to be completely oblivious, and to have these two approaches work together.

The premise is that Position Management as a process does not work with the self-services that have been the grail of HRIS systems for the past decade. We must have a solution that does not force the casual user to understand and interact with positions in any way. There are naturally times when everyone has to work with positions, such as when addressing vacancies.

The following guiding principles apply when dealing with implicit Position Management:

▶ Exceptions need to be handled. No organization stays static enough to be exempt from every situation.

▶ For each transaction, use either positions or incumbents. Never require a user to do both.

▶ Positions are optional; if a part of the business does not require positions, do not use them.

▶ Transactions can be configured to run off either positions or incumbents (e.g., the Approval Workflow hierarchy definition).

▶ Allow configurable overrides at the incumbent level.

Now that we've reviewed the concepts behind implicit Position Management, let's look at an overview of positions within Employee Central.

8.2 Positions Overview

In an HRIS system, positions are useful. They establish a framework to manage organizational processes. Processes such as budgeting and headcount planning, SAP SuccessFactors Succession Management, requisitions for SAP Success Factors Recruiting, Power of Expenditure policy, and IT workflow approval design are significantly simpler if positions are used. These processes have to operate in the absence of incumbents, and positions serve as placeholders when there is no incumbent or serve as the anchor to find the next incumbent up in the hierarchy when a particular incumbent is absent.

The problem is that the value created by having positions is not commensurate to the cost of maintaining positions; that is, cost outweighs value. The cost most often falls on the HRIS system, whereas the benefits of maintaining costs goes to the downstream processes that the HRIS system supports. Once allowances for exceptions and flexibility are made, the positions become a roadblock to efficiency rather than an enabler.

By enabling positions to be managed implicitly in transactions, you can meet the demands of a fast-paced organization while providing the structure needed for downstream processes.

To make this possible, you must treat positions and their hierarchies as distinct from incumbents and their hierarchies. Synchronizing them provides the flexibility needed to manage the organization by either position or incumbent. Indeed, when there are no vacant positions, the position hierarchy is the same as the employee–supervisor hierarchy. When there are vacant positions, the employee–supervisor hierarchy represents the effective hierarchy (using the next available incumbent). This also allows the incumbent to be assigned to a different set of attributes (e.g., location or grade) than defined by the position. The degree to which the incumbent can be different from a position is configurable using rules and permissions. This provides control to the customer not only over the level of variance, but also over which users are allowed to override.

The Position Object Definition is maintained just as any other object definition in OneAdmin in COMPANY SETTINGS • CONFIGURE OBJECT DEFINITIONS. The Position object—like every Generic Object—is comprised of the following types of attributes:

▶ **Framework attributes**
Mandatory for the SAP SuccessFactors system to work. Attributes such as External Code, Name, Effective-Date, and Status belong to this category.

▶ **Business attributes**
Define the position and are usually common to incumbents and positions. These are attributes such as Legal Entity, Business Unit, Department, Job Classification, Position Title, FTE, Standard Hours, and so on. Custom attributes can be assigned for these purposes.

▶ **Position Management attributes**
Delivered attributes that have defined behaviors in the context of Position Management. Depending on the features used, these attributes may be mandatory. Attributes that fall into this category are Capacity Controlled, Position Type, Target Capacity, Multiple Incumbents Allowed, To-Be-Hired, Parent Position, and Right to Return.

▶ **Relationships**
Used to define relationships between positions and they translate into incumbent relationships on Job Relationships. These define HR Manager, Matrix Manager, and so on.

▶ **System attributes**
Part of all MDF objects, but maintained by the system. Internal Code, Last Updated User, and Date are examples of these attributes. In some cases, these attributes are displayed.

▶ **Custom attributes**
Custom attributes may be added to a Position object in either business attributes or relationships.

▶ **Country-specific behavior**
There are no delivered country-specific behaviors, but country-specific fields and country-specific values can be assigned to a position. Define custom fields for these purposes where necessary. You can define country-specific behavior in two different ways:

  ▷ Use a *conditional association* to restrict the fields to countries.

  ▷ Define a position country child object and add the country-specific fields. This is the ideal method to use country-specific values, such as local title.

In this section, we will look at the different elements and important functions of positions within the Position Management context. We'll begin by looking at the structure of positions and explore the various types. Then, we'll look at the position org chart, time in positions, and position security. We'll round out the section by looking at what full-time equivalent (FTE) implies for positions and the use of mass positions.

8.2.1 Structure

The position structure is created using the parent position attribute. Each position can have a parent; however, at the time of writing, multiple parents for a single position are not supported. The parent position hierarchy creates the organization structure.

The position structure fits in to the organizational structure as defined by the organizational Foundation Objects and their associations. Use associations on

Foundation Objects to create an organizational hierarchy. While creating the positions, the associations defined between the objects are respected. If there is an association between locations and legal entities (a logical association given that a legal entity always belongs to a country), the list of locations that the position can belong to is restricted to the list of locations valid for the legal entity.

Matrix Relationships

Matrix relationships can also be defined between positions. Matrix relationships, by definition, can support multiple relationships and enable, say, an HR Manager or Matrix Manager to be defined on an employee based on their position. In addition, custom relationships may also be defined.

8.2.2 Types

Position types are used to define system behavior for positions. The standard behaviors that can be defined by position type are as follows:

▸ Triggering a workflow on Job Information if position changes have been synchronized to incumbents. The default behavior is not to trigger the workflow.

▸ Reassigning direct reports if the manager vacates the current position. By default, the system reassigns the direct reports to the next available manager.

▸ Adapting the reporting line after the position hierarchy has been changed.

By default, the system creates regular positions and shared positions as position types. Shared positions are positions with more than one incumbent. Additional position types may be defined as needed and they may be used to create the nuanced behaviors defined previously.

8.2.3 Position Org Chart

The *Position Org Chart* is the primary tool through which users interact with positions. The Position Org Chart is accessed via the COMPANY INFO screen by selecting the POSITION ORG CHART option. The basic organization chart is also accessed from the COMPANY INFO screen. Figure 8.1 shows the position organization chart.

The Position Org Chart provides a hierarchical representation of positions and a menu of actions. You can search by position or incumbent and can configure the list of attributes to search for a position. The position org chart is effective-dated; that is, you can view the hierarchy as of any particular date.

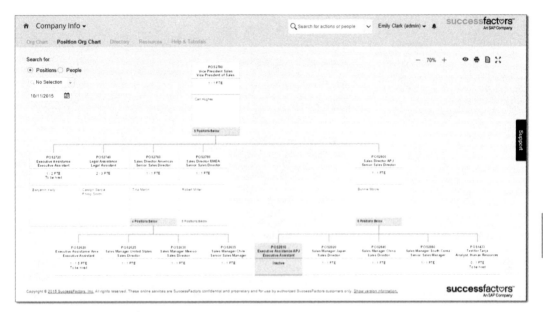

Figure 8.1 Position Org Chart

The Position Org Chart is distinct from the *basic organization chart*. The basic organization chart represents the supervisor relationship as defined by the incumbent, whereas the Position Org Chart represents the position hierarchy. In most cases, the hierarchies will be the same or very similar. However, when there are temporary overrides or if a position is vacant, the basic organization chart will differ from the Position Org Chart (e.g., vacant positions will be shown in the Position Org Chart but no equivalents will be shown in the basic organization chart).

By default, the organization chart opens with the logged in user's position at the top of the hierarchy. This is consistent with self-service, as most managers would be transacting on positions in their organization hierarchy. The last position searched for is maintained in the search history so that users do not have to search again for recently or regularly searched positions.

Figure 8.2 shows the position menu, which contains several options.

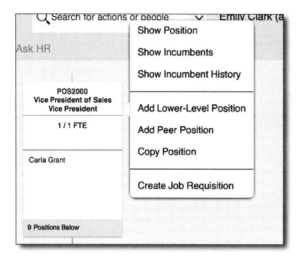

Figure 8.2 Position Menu in Position Org Chart

Because the object model of SAP SuccessFactors associates positions with incumbents, the SHOW INCUMBENT HISTORY option in the POSITION menu provides the reverse view: you can select a position and see the historical view of the incumbents of that position (see Figure 8.3).

Figure 8.3 Incumbent History

8.2.4   Position Entry Date and Time in Position

POSITION ENTRY DATE and TIME IN POSITION are delivered fields that track when the incumbent enters the position and for how long the incumbent has been in the position. These fields are found in the JOB INFORMATION portlet on the EMPLOYMENT INFORMATION screen of an employee.

POSITION ENTRY DATE is set to the effective start date on which the incumbent first entered the position. The POSITION ENTRY DATE is carried forward in all effective-dated rows until a different position is assigned to the incumbent. In that row, the POSITION ENTRY DATE is reset.

TIME IN POSITION is the length of time that the incumbent has been occupying the position. In the current row, it represents the difference between today and the POSITION ENTRY DATE. In historical rows, the time in position is stored for the record, whereas in the current row it's a calculated transient value.

8.2.5   Security

Positions are secured using Role-Based Permissions (RBPs). On the position org chart, each action can be controlled. In addition, when viewing or maintaining a position, each attribute can be controlled, as well as whether the user has the ability to edit the position that they are viewing.

The position org chart is effective-dated, and the permission to change the display date controls whether a user can view historical or future transactions. If a user does not have permission to view historical records, then he or she can only see the current information regarding positions. This permission does not control the ability to view the history of the position.

Figure 8.4 illustrates the global actions on the position that can be controlled by permissions. These permissions are not dependent on the target population.

The OPTION TO MOVE POSITION TO NEW SUPERVISOR ON JOB INFO CHANGE permission enables granular control over whether the position can be moved to a different reporting line altogether.

Positions can be used within Dynamic Groups so that they can determine the approver, notifier, or CC user of a workflow. Dynamic Groups represent both *granted users* and *target users*.

Specify what permissions users in this role should have.

	Manage Position	†= Target needs to be defined.
Manage Mass Changes	☑ Select All	
Employee Central API	☑ Access Position Organization Chart	
Manage Foundation Objects	☑ Change Display Date of Position Organization Chart	
Manage Foundation Objects Types	☑ Mass Copy of Position in Position Organization Chart	
Metadata Framework	☑ View Job Requisition in Position Organization Chart	
Manage Data Purge	☑ Create Job Requisition in Position Organization Chart	
Manage Instance Synchronization	☑ Select Job Requisition Template in Position Organization Chart	
Manage Position	☑ Option to move Position to New Supervisor on Job Info Change	
	☑ Access Position Management Settings in Admin Tools	

Figure 8.4 Position Permissions

Administering positions requires a professional user in many cases. When the distributed administration of positions is required, a list of positions that a user has access to can be configured. In this case, access can be restricted by Legal Entity, Business Unit, Location, or any other foundational relationship.

Security on positions can also be provided for managers and for HR business partners. Managers can have access to manage positions in their hierarchy. Similarly, access can be provided based on matrix relationships or HR relationships. In this case, however, the LEVEL(S) DOWN features, when available, are not of much use (see Figure 8.5).

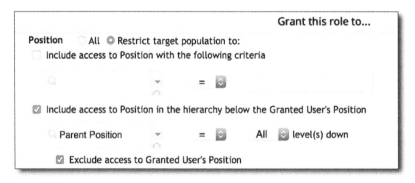

Figure 8.5 Controlling Access to Positions

8.2.6   Full-Time Equivalent

The *FTE* of an incumbent is calculated based on the standard hours that a person is scheduled to work. There is a progression of standard hours:

▶ Legal Entity

▶ Location

▶ Job Classification

▶ Position

Only the standard hours for the Legal Entity are necessary. The other three are optional, and if the standard hours are defined for a position, then that definition overrides the standard hours of the other objects. The calculation is standard, but the sequence of derivation can be modified if needed.

The standard hours functionality determines the FTE, and the FTE in turn is used in the calculation of Compa Ratio and Range Penetration. An optional setting bypasses the FTE normalization; it assumes that the FTE is one to calculate the Compa Ratio and Range Penetration if the standard hours functionality is not used.

If a position is subject to *position control*, the FTE of all incumbents assigned to the position should not exceed the target FTE. This check occurs when an incumbent is hired or the standard hours of an incumbent or position are changed.

8.2.7 Mass Positions

Mass positions, by definition, have an FTE and headcount that is more than one (for more information on headcount, see Section 8.3.6). Mass positions are typically used when there are a large number of positions that are in the same location, belong to the same department, and share the same title and grade. It's rare that the incumbents of these positions have off-cycle changes.

There are limitations to using mass positions; Succession Management cannot be performed on mass positions. This limitation is not material, as mass positions are typically used for scenarios in which the positions are not key positions, and Succession Planning is not performed for these types of positions.

Even with the limitation of mass positions, they serve as a useful configuration for those scenarios in which a single position with multiple incumbents shares the same attributes, thus simplifying position administration. However, the implicit position option must be reviewed to determine if the rule-based synchronization of positions and incumbents sufficiently reduces the administrative burden and use of 1:1 positions.

Now that we've looked at an overview of positions, let's dive into the settings that can be configured in Position Management in the next section.

8.3   Setting Up Position Management

Position Management settings are an administrative functionality that controls the behaviors of positions in the system. Implicit Position Management relies on these rules and settings to drive the behavior of positions and position assignments. These behaviors are constantly enhanced to provide more nuanced processing behavior. The Position Management settings are maintained in OneAdmin in EMPLOYEE FILES • POSITION MANAGEMENT SETTINGS. Figure 8.6 shows the POSITION MANAGEMENT SETTINGS screen.

Understanding the impact of the settings is a prerequisite for using the Position Management functionality. Position Management settings encompass a wide range of settings, including managing the TO BE HIRED status on the position based on incumbent changes to complex right to return transactions. Figure 8.6 shows an example of a setting. The VALIDATE POSITION ASSIGNMENT DURING JOB INFORMATION IMPORT setting checks against the target FTE and against the MULTIPLE INCUMBENTS flag on the Position object.

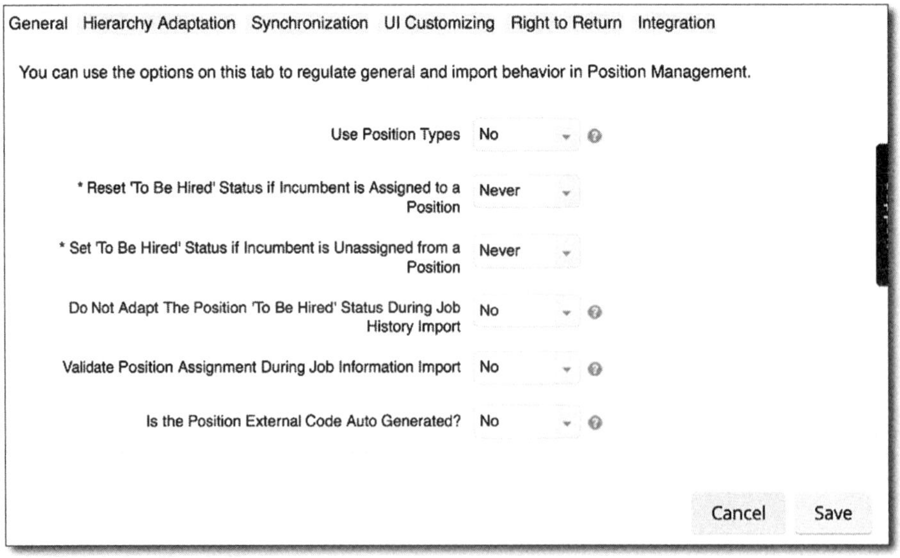

Figure 8.6 Position Management Settings

In this section, we'll cover some of the important features and settings that can be made within Position Management. Let's begin by looking at the filter functionality.

8.3.1   Filtering Positions

Selecting positions while transacting on incumbents could lead to a large result set. To reduce the risk of selecting the wrong position, there are two options to filter positions:

▶ **Supervisor**
   Provides an option to filter all the positions reporting to the incumbent of the parent position

▶ **Company**
   Allows you to filter all the positions belonging to a company

You can also define which fields are copied over to a new position when it's copied from an existing position. These settings are available the POSITION MANAGEMENT SETTINGS screen (covered in Section 8.3) under the UI CUSTOMIZING tab, as shown in Figure 8.7.

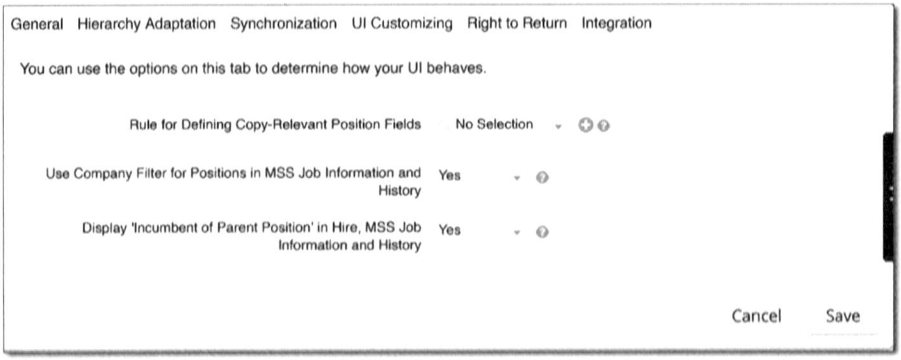

Figure 8.7 Configuring Filters and Copy Settings

8.3.2   Synchronizing Positions and Incumbents

Because positions and incumbents have separate structures, there is a configurable relationship between the two. Changes made to one have an impact on the other, and the extent of that impact is controlled using settings and rules.

Rules define common fields between the Position object and the employee's Job Information; synchronization triggers when changes are made to the Position object. This rule triggers for backend synchronization whenever a position with incumbents changes from the Position Org Chart and the user wants to update the incumbents' Job Information with the data from position fields defined for synchronization.

Position propagation updates the incumbent information based on the position, and position sync is the reverse of position propagation. The synchronization between the position and the incumbent data is controlled through a rule. This rule is triggered for backend synchronization whenever a position with incumbents is changed from the Position Org Chart and the user wants to update the incumbents' Job Information with the data from the position. This situation can occur in the following ways:

▸ The position attributes change and the incumbents need to be updated.

▸ The position of the incumbent changes to a different one.

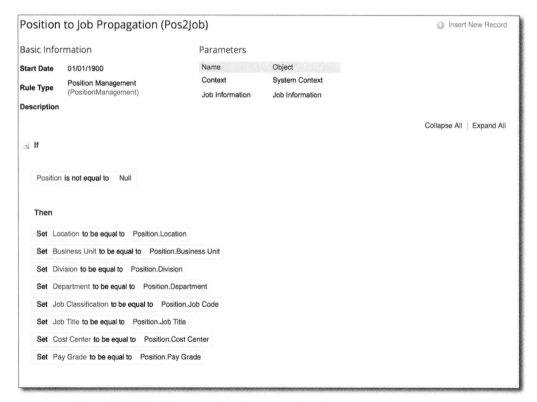

Figure 8.8 Rule to Propagate from Position to Job Information

Figure 8.8 shows a sample rule to propagate attributes from a position to the Job Information of the incumbent. This rule is attached as an `onChange` rule to the POSITION field in JOB INFORMATION. If the fields that are propagated to Job Information are defined as VIEW (and not EDITABLE) in JOB INFORMATION (i.e., they cannot be changed by the user irrespective of permission settings), then the system is configured to be completely controlled by position. In such cases, no overrides of incumbents are possible. Although this configuration is supported, it is inflexible and not recommended unless the organization using it is particularly static.

8.3.3   Transferring and Reclassifying Positions

A *transfer* occurs when an incumbent moves from one position to another. A *reclassification* occurs when an incumbent stays in the same position but the position attributes change. This important distinction forms the basis of implicit Position Management.

When a change is made to a position, the transaction is a reclassification. The decision must be made about whether the change needs to be cascaded to the incumbents.

Positions and incumbents are synchronized via rules, and there is a rule for each direction. However, positions and incumbents are usually the inverse of each other. Table 8.1 describes the differences among actions.

Action	Behavior
POSITION ORGANIZATIONAL CHART SYNCHRONIZATION	The following options are available for updating incumbents when a change is made to a position: ▶ USER DECISION: The user is prompted to make a decision about whether the incumbents should be updated. ▶ USER DECISION IF REQUIRED: Only if synchronization-relevant fields are modified, the user is prompted to make a decision about whether the incumbents should be updated. ▶ AUTOMATIC: The incumbents are always synchronized. ▶ NEVER: Incumbents are never synchronized.

Table 8.1 Position Transfer and Reclassification Actions and Behaviors

Action	Behavior
RULE FOR SYNCHRONIZING POSITION TO JOB INFORMATION	Refer to Figure 8.8, which defines the fields that will copied from the position to Job Information.
RULE FOR SYNCHRONIZING JOB TO POSITION INFORMATION	Defines which fields are copied from Job Information to the position when a change is made to the incumbent.
SEARCH FOR POSITION IN POSITION RECLASSIFICATION	The system first searches for available To Be Hired positions that match the attributes before changing the existing position. This is the recommended option.
SEARCH FOR POSITION IN POSITION TRANSFER	The system first searches for available TBH positions that match the attributes before creating a new position. This is the recommended option.

Table 8.1 Position Transfer and Reclassification Actions and Behaviors (Cont.)

Figure 8.9 shows the options available for configuring this behavior. These settings are maintained on the POSITION MANAGEMENT SETTINGS screen under the SYNCHRONIZATION tab.

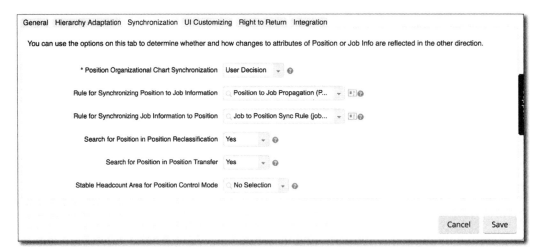

Figure 8.9 Position Synchronization Settings

8.3.4 Making Mass Changes on Positions

Mass changes have the ability to change the attributes of a group of positions in one transaction. Because positions are built on the MDF, the mass change functionality for positions is a general-purpose mass change that will be used for all Generic

Objects in the future. At present, only positions are supported using the Manage Mass Changes functionality, so the object type to be changed is vestigial for now.

A mass change for positions is performed in OneAdmin in EMPLOYEE FILES • MANAGE MASS CHANGES FOR METADATA OBJECTS. Figure 8.10 shows the MASS CHANGE RUN screen.

The mass change date represents the effective date of the mass change run. It is the date based on which the transaction is effective and thereby the date on which the records are selected.

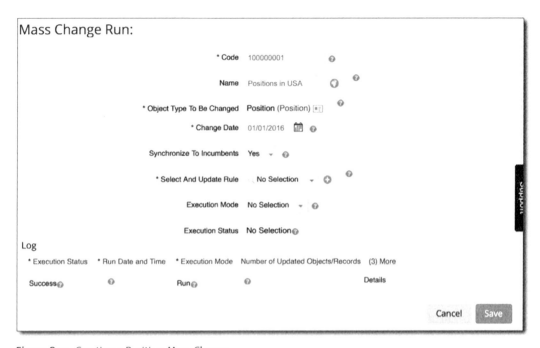

Figure 8.10 Creating a Position Mass Change

Changes made to positions can be synchronized with incumbents. The rule that is configured to synchronize incumbents is invoked to propagate the changes. Only fields defined in rule registered for the RULE FOR SYNCHRONIZING POSITION TO JOB INFORMATION setting in Position Management settings will be synchronized.

You must create a rule that will specify the selection and update of data. Effectively, the IF and THEN conditions of the rule specify what data is selected and what data is updated.

The mass change run can be executed in simulation mode for test purposes before it is executed in run mode. The status of mass changes are tracked using the following delivered statuses:

▸ SCHEDULED means the Mass Change Run is scheduled and will run soon.

▸ INPROGRESS means the Mass Change Run is being executed.

▸ EXECUTED means the Mass Change Run was successful.

▸ FAILED means there have been errors; check the log for information.

8.3.5 Maintaining Hierarchies

There are two hierarchies in the SAP SuccessFactors system: the position hierarchy and the reporting hierarchy. Tools and rules keep these two hierarchies synchronized. The *position hierarchy* represents the position-to-position relationship, whereas the *reporting hierarchy* represents the person-to-person relationship. You can view these hierarchies in the Position Org Chart and basic organization chart, respectively.

Defining the leading hierarchy significantly reduces the effort involved in keeping the position hierarchy and reporting line hierarchy synchronized.

Keeping the hierarchies synchronized is optional. In rare scenarios, if the position hierarchy and reporting hierarchies are used for different purposes altogether and you must keep them separate, the system should be configured to have no leading hierarchy. In common scenarios, picking one or the other as the leading hierarchy is the recommended approach.

If positions are chosen as the leading hierarchy, the system finds the next available incumbent in the position hierarchy and assigns it as the supervisor. The reporting line hierarchy acts just as it would if positions were not used at all.

If the supervisor is changed in the incumbent record and the change does not lead to a new position being created, the position is unaffected by the change.

Figure 8.11 shows the list of settings available to define how the hierarchies should be adopted. These settings are maintained on the POSITION MANAGEMENT SETTINGS screen under the HIERARCHY ADAPTATION tab.

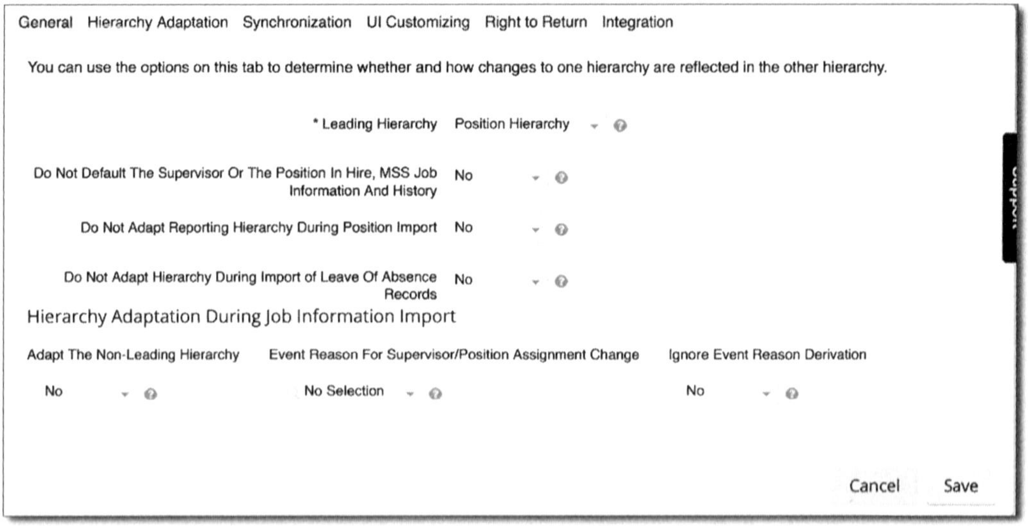

General   Hierarchy Adaptation   Synchronization   UI Customizing   Right to Return   Integration

You can use the options on this tab to determine whether and how changes to one hierarchy are reflected in the other hierarchy.

* Leading Hierarchy   Position Hierarchy

Do Not Default The Supervisor Or The Position In Hire, MSS Job   No
Information And History

Do Not Adapt Reporting Hierarchy During Position Import   No

Do Not Adapt Hierarchy During Import of Leave Of Absence   No
Records

Hierarchy Adaptation During Job Information Import

Adapt The Non-Leading Hierarchy   Event Reason For Supervisor/Position Assignment Change   Ignore Event Reason Derivation

No   No Selection   No

Cancel   Save

Figure 8.11 Hierarchy Adaptation Settings

Additional Resources

The *Position Management* implementation handbook provides a detailed list of the behaviors involved when selecting a leading hierarchy. To access this guide, go to *http://help.sap.com/hr_ec* and find POSITION MANAGEMENT under the IMPLEMENTATION GUIDES heading.

8.3.6   Maintaining the Stable Headcount Area

Implicit Position Management is designed to support the needs of the flexible and modern organization, but it also supports the need for position control. Position control and the stable headcount area are used when a transaction occurs on an incumbent and the change has to be synchronized to the position. These settings provide the guardrails of financial and operational control while decentralizing transactions.

Historically, all transactions were centralized to enforce such controls. However, when the transaction occurs within the guidelines of a budget, it's desirable for the process to be decentralized so that it can be completed quickly. Thus, as long as the transaction occurs within the controlled area, the headcount is not lowered.

When a transaction occurs within the stable headcount area, the controls are enforced and the synchronization processes update it. Headcount areas may be defined on the elements. When a headcount area is selected, control behaviors are executed.

8.3.7 Using Right to Return

Right to return is an employment practice that guarantees an existing position for an incumbent after a defined period away (see Figure 8.12). In some countries, this is a legal right for the employee, and it may be a practice to provide this as a benefit or a term of employment. By definition, the right to return is associated with leave of absence or temporary reassignment.

In Employee Central, right to return supports two scenarios:

▶ **Global assignments**
For a global assignment, the assignee may have the right to return to his or her position in his or her home country at the end of the global assignment. When creating a global assignment, the system automatically transacts on the home record as well as creating a right to return tag.

▶ **Leave of absence**
On return from certain leaves of absence, the employee may have a right to return to his or her original position. As part of the leave of absence transaction, the position is unassigned and a right to return tag is created. On returning from work, the employee returns to the original position for which the right to return tag was created. Usually, the right to return is created only for longer-term absences that require a substitute to be assigned to the position for business continuity. For short-term absences or vacations, right to return transactions are not created because work is temporarily assigned to others for business continuity.

Right to return is configured in the Position Management settings under the RIGHT TO RETURN tab (see Figure 8.12).

Now that we've walked through some of the important settings that can be found in Position Management, you should have a better understanding of the configurations that can be made. In the next section, we'll look at the use of Position Management with other SAP SuccessFactors applications.

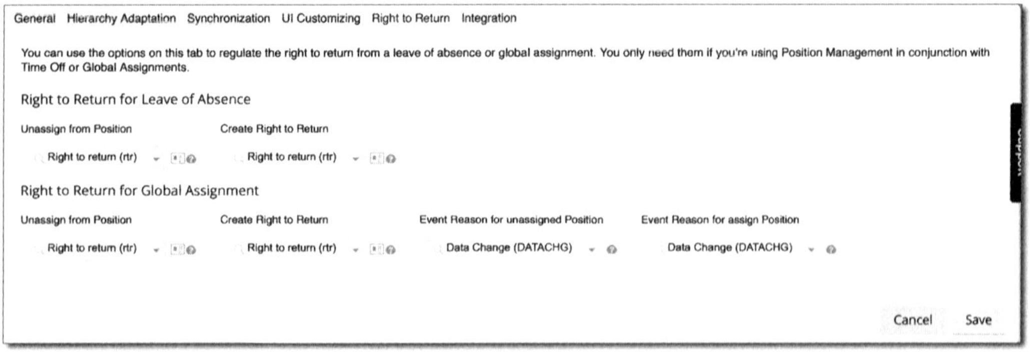

Figure 8.12 Right to Return Settings

8.4 Position Management in Other SAP SuccessFactors Applications

Position Management also extends into other SAP SuccessFactors modules. SAP SuccessFactors Succession & Development, SAP SuccessFactors Recruiting Management, and the Job Profile Builder all leverage the Position object when Position Management is used. We'll examine some of these use cases and integration points within this section.

8.4.1 Using Positions in SAP SuccessFactors Succession & Development

SAP SuccessFactors Succession & Development can be used with or without positions, but using positions provides the most complete succession functionality. Using positions is one of the methods to manage succession processes, and using positions enables Succession Planning and management of vacant positions—one of the key benefits of using positions. Position Management enables succession based on a target organization structure rather than the current organization.

By using RBPs, you can define the target positions to plan a succession for, thus decentralizing the administration of the succession process.

Additional Resources

For more information on setting up and configuring Succession Management using Positions, refer to the *Succession (Implementation Guide)* handbook found at *http://service.sap.com/ec-ondemand*.

8.4.2 Creating Requisitions from Positions

The talent acquisition process is initiated from the position organization chart (see Section 8.2.3). The mapping to create a requisition is configurable; both the requisition template to be used and the fields to be mapped into the requisition are configured with a rule. This provides the best mix of flexibility and automation.

Linking positions and requisitions is performed at both the start and end of the talent acquisition process. Approvals for initiating the requisition are made on the position so that once the requisition is created, the talent acquisition process moves as quickly as possible. If there are any changes made to the requisition, then the approvals for those changes are contained in the requisition and data changes do not flow back to the position. The position is then updated based on the attributes of the incumbent when the new hire is processed. The updating of the position is based on configurable rules. This design provides the optimum mix of speed and control.

Additional Resources

For more information on setting up and configuring the requisition integration, refer to the *Position Management (Implementation Guide)* handbook found at *http://service. sap.com/ec-ondemand*.

8.4.3 Job Profiles and Positions

Job profiles can be created using Family, Roles, and Job Classifications. When positions are enabled, a Job Profile can be created with a position-level granularity. This is especially useful when there are global job classifications but the requirements for a position are decided by local factors.

A common example is language proficiency. Although a sales job classification would have common competencies and skills globally, language proficiencies tend to be local. Positions therefore can help to define Job Profiles.

Figure 8.13 illustrates how the relationship between families, roles, and positions are mapped.

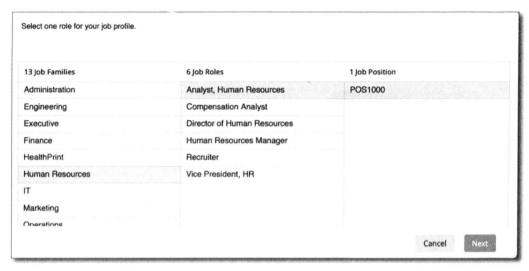

Select one role for your job profile.

13 Job Families	6 Job Roles	1 Job Position
Administration	Analyst, Human Resources	POS1000
Engineering	Compensation Analyst	
Executive	Director of Human Resources	
Finance	Human Resources Manager	
HealthPrint	Recruiter	
Human Resources	Vice President, HR	
IT		
Marketing		
Operations		

Cancel | Next

Figure 8.13 Selecting Positions for Creating a Job Profile

Additional Resources

For more information on setting up and configuring Job Profile Builder, refer to the *Job Profile Builder (Implementation Guide)* handbook found at *http://service.sap.com/sfsf* under FOUNDATION (INCLUDING APIs).

8.5 Summary

In this chapter, we discussed the key concepts of Position Management. We looked at position structures and types and dove into other position overview topics. We then looked at the different Position Management settings before discussing the use of Position Management in other SAP SuccessFactors applications.

Position Management in SAP SuccessFactors can be configured in such a way that the system can be tightly controlled in one part of the organization while being loosely controlled in another. Using positions can provide richer talent processes.

In the next chapter, we'll discuss managing employee data.

Employee Central can store and manage a complete set of data history for an employee, essentially documenting the employee's relationship with an organization. With self-service functionalities, employees and managers can actively participate in keeping their information up-to-date.

9   Employee Data

Managing employee data requires tools that can stretch across geographic boundaries and down to all levels of an organization. Employee Central is a global HRIS solution offering the ability to store a complete set of employee workforce data and deliver self-service functionality all in a single system of record. It offers opportunities for global standards and processes while meeting localized needs for compliance and reporting. It's flexible enough to support the needs of small organizations and robust enough to support large enterprises.

In this chapter, we'll look at how Employee Central manages employee data throughout an employee's complete lifecycle. We'll examine the basics of employee data and we'll explore transactions and self-service functionality.

User Interface and Figures

With the Q3 2015 release, we now have the ability to use the People Profile in lieu of the traditional Employee Profile. The People Profile format is a new user interface offering views to the same content of the traditional Employee Profile placed together on one screen. A second level of navigation is provided to allow users to jump from section to section. ESS and MSS are also both supported.

In the book, and specifically this chapter, we have provided updated UI screenshots where relevant to reflect new menu/navigation paths and on-screen elements.

9.1   Views

Employee Central enables users to store a myriad of data in an organized and easily accessible manner. Employee data is divided into different views. The two main views are *Personal Information* and *Employment Information*. Each of these categories has its own employee view, or record page, within Employee Central. Other important views include the Public Profile and others, such as those shown in Figure 9.1.

Views are accessed under EMPLOYEE FILES of the Public Profile (see Figure 9.1). Each item listed under EMPLOYEE RECORDS is referred to as a view.

Figure 9.1 Employee File Views

Each view is composed of several various squares or tiles known as *portlets*. Each portlet has a title and contains several data fields all related to each other and the portlet title. Figure 9.2 shows the top of the PERSONAL INFORMATION view, which contains the NATIONAL ID INFORMATION and ADDRESS INFORMATION portlets.

Within these portlets are portlet-specific fields, such as COUNTRY listed under HOME ADDRESS. Each portlet comes standard, delivered with a selection of configured fields. Fields that are not needed can be removed, and additional custom fields can be added when needed. Table 9.1 lists standard portlets within Employee Central.

Portlet	Effective-Dated	Supports Country-Specific Fields
National ID Card	No	Yes
Addresses	Yes	Yes
Personal Information	Yes	Yes
Person (Biographical) Info	No	No
Work Permit Info	No	No
Contact Information	No	No
Personal Contacts	No	No

Table 9.1 Employee Central Portlets

Portlet	Effective-Dated	Supports Country-Specific Fields
Dependents	Configuration-specific setting	Configuration-specific setting
Payment Information	Configuration-specific setting	Configuration-specific setting
Job Information	Yes	Yes
Employment Details	No	Yes
Job Relationships	Yes	No
Compensation Information	Yes	Yes
Spot Bonus	No	No

Table 9.1 Employee Central Portlets (Cont.)

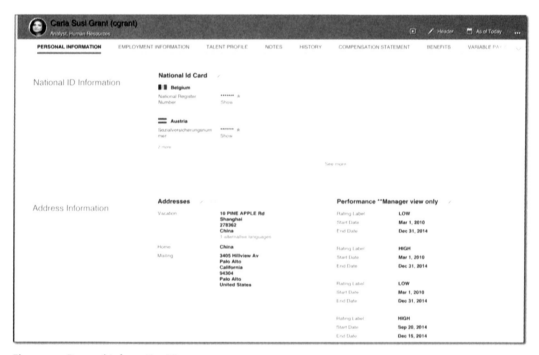

Figure 9.2 Personal Information View

To navigate from view to view, click on the section headers along the top of the People Profile to select a new view. In Figure 9.2, we've selected the PERSONAL INFORMATION view.

Certain portlets within Employment Information and Personal Information have special qualities associated with them. Many of the portlets are *effective-dated*, meaning you store historical records for the portlet and track changes made on certain dates. Each record within the history will have a start date and an end date. The list in Table 9.1 indicates which portlets are effective-dated. Figure 9.3 shows an example of some effective-dated records being kept in history.

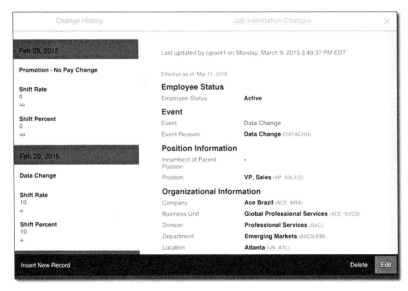

Figure 9.3 Effective-Dated Job History

In addition to some portlets being effective-dated, some portlets have country-specific fields, or fields that only display when an employee lives or works within a specific country. Country-specific fields allow you to use a global data template as the basis for your employee records and to augment with local data fields as needed to meet local requirements. This combination of a global standard combined with accommodating local needs makes Employee Central a complete solution. Numerous country-specific fields for several countries come standard delivered. Additional custom fields can be created as needed.

In this section, we will look at the different views provided in Employee Central. First, we'll explore the Public Profile, which is the default view for all employees. Next, we'll dive into the two main views in Section 9.1.2 and Section 9.1.3 for Personal Information and Employment Information. Finally, in Section 9.1.4, we'll round out our discussion by looking at some other, smaller views available for employee data.

9.1.1 Public Profile

The Public Profile is the primary employee view within SAP SuccessFactors. It is the default view that displays when you select EMPLOYEE FILES from the main navigation menu shown in Figure 9.4. The Public Profile is available to all customers regardless of whether they use Employee Central or not.

Figure 9.4 Main Navigation Menu

The general purpose of the Public Profile is to convey basic contact information about one employee to other employees in the system. You can think of the Public Profile as an electronic business card.

The Public Profile contains basic contact information (see Figure 9.5) as well as some organizational information, badges for recognition, and tags for collaboration (see Figure 9.6).

Figure 9.5 Public Profile Business Card

Figure 9.6 Organizational Chart, Tags, and Badges

Let's look at how to set up an employee's Public Profile in Employee Central.

You can select options for the Public Profile in the Admin Center under EMPLOYEE FILES • CONFIGURE EMPLOYEE FILES • PUBLIC PROFILE. Here, you can determine which portlets display in a view and whether to use auxiliary items such as the organizational chart, tags, and badges (see Figure 9.7).

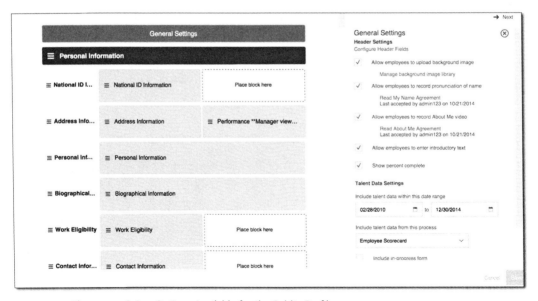

Figure 9.7 Setup Options Available for the Public Profile

9.1.2 Personal Information

As previously mentioned, employee data is stored within two main views: Personal Information and Employment Information. The first of these views, PERSONAL INFORMATION (Figure 9.8), contains information that is specific to an employee regardless of his or her role at an organization. This is information that the employee brought with him or her to the organization and will take with him or her upon departure. We typically see many of these data fields managed by employees using ESS, as discussed in Section 9.3.1.

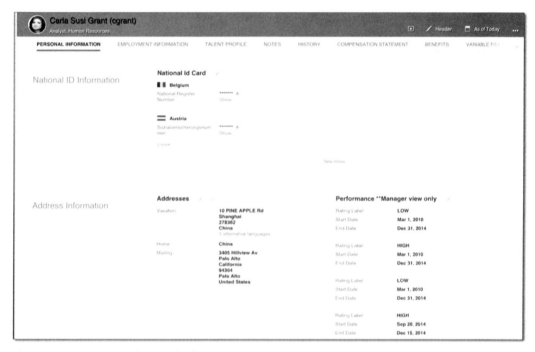

Figure 9.8 Top Sections of Personal Information

Employee Central views contain portlets. In this section, we will explore the different portlets in Personal Information.

National ID Information

The NATIONAL ID INFORMATION portlet is used to store an employee's national ID. It is a non-effective-dated portlet. Multiple values can be stored, and a mix of countries can be used per employee, if needed. Each ID provides a sample format and is validated for compliance upon entry. This portlet is an excellent example of localized country-specific capabilities.

Given that national IDs often fall under Personally Identifiable Information (PII), you have the option to mask the ID number from general view. The masked setting on the ID number is replaced with a series of asterisks (***). It can be viewed in full by clicking on the Show link (see Figure 9.9).

Figure 9.9 National ID Card Portlet with PII Masking

> **PII Masking**
>
> If you attempt to pull a national ID into an interface file and it does not seem to be populating, you may want to consider removing the PII masking.

Personal Information

The Personal Information portlet is effective-dated and divided into two main areas—global Personal Information and country-specific Personal Information. Personal Information is an ideal portlet for ESS access.

The Global section of the portlet contains basic demographic information, including First Name, Last Name, Gender, and Marital Status, as shown in Figure 9.10. Alternate Name fields are available for storing names in different character sets (not shown in figure).

On the country-specific side, fields related to disability/challenged status, veteran status, family information, and religion are maintained according to country-specific requirements (see Figure 9.11).

Views | **9.1**

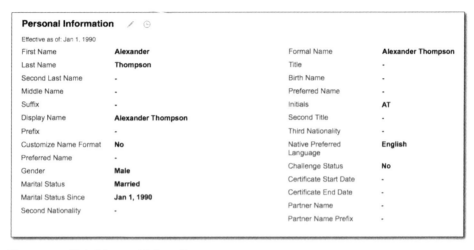

Figure 9.10 Global Personal Information

Figure 9.11 Country-Specific Personal Information

Addresses

Multiple addresses can be stored for an employee in the effective-dated
ADDRESSES portlet (see Figure 9.12). HOME ADDRESS is the most basic entry made

307

here, but other address types, such as VACATION, MAILING, EMERGENCY, and so on, can be maintained here as well. Country-specific formatting is evident in this portlet because address formats are configured to be country-specific. Making a country selection in this portlet brings up the country-specific format and state/region fields. A set of ALTERNATE ADDRESS fields are available in this portlet for storing addresses in an additional character set. Addresses are a popular area for ESS actions.

Figure 9.12 Addresses Portlet

Person Info

PERSON INFO is a non-effective-dated portlet that is also referred to as BIOGRAPHICAL INFORMATION because it contains relevant biographical information about each employee. The two most notable fields in this portlet are PERSON ID and DATE OF BIRTH. PERSON ID is the employee's unique employee ID, which can be manually entered at hire, or a system-generated value can be automatically assigned by the system. DATE OF BIRTH helps to further identify an employee (see Figure 9.13).

Figure 9.13 Person Info Portlet

Work Permit Info

The non-effective-dated WORK PERMIT Info portlet allows the storage of work permit–related documentation (see Figure 9.14). Two interesting fields here are

EXPIRATION DATE and ATTACHMENTS. EXPIRATION DATE is extremely useful for tracking when documents expire or need to be renewed. A job can be scheduled to provide reports on upcoming expirations. ATTACHMENTS allows for the verification and storage of relevant work permit documents. It's convenient to have copies of permits available directly in the portlet for verification and compliance purposes.

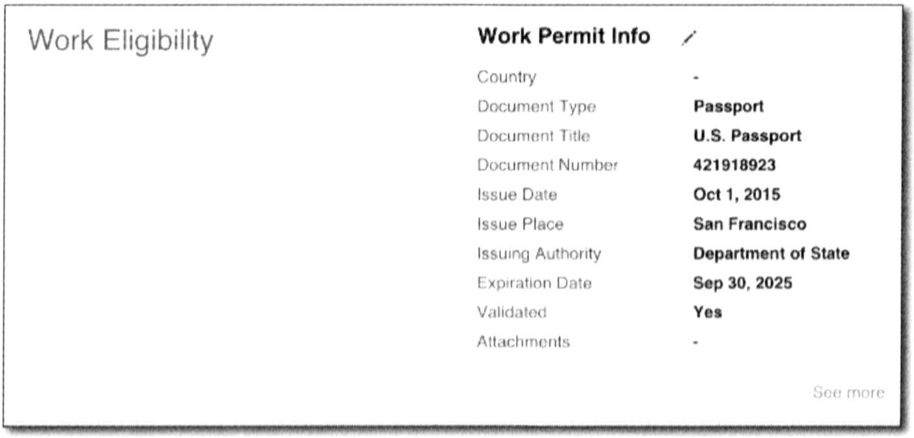

Figure 9.14 Work Permit Info Portlet

Contact Information

The CONTACT INFORMATION portlet is a non-effective-dated portlet with three key sections of contact information: email, phone, and social accounts (see Figure 9.15). Multiple values can be stored in each section, which is useful if an employee has both a personal and a business email address or phone number. ESS access can be granted for this portlet.

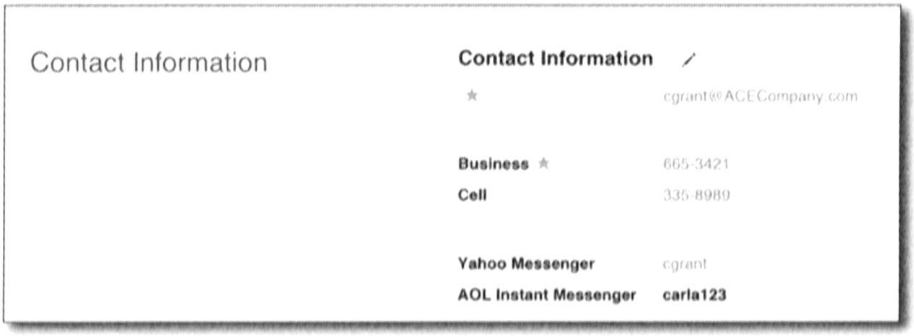

Figure 9.15 Contact Information Portlet

Personal Contacts

The Personal Contacts portlet is sometimes referred to as the Emergency Contacts portlet. It is a non-effective-dated portlet ideal for ESS maintenance. This portlet (shown in Figure 9.16) stores basic contact information for persons related to the employee. In some system configurations, this portlet may also indicate if this person is a dependent. If the person is a dependent, then several dependent-related fields can be maintained here as well.

Figure 9.16 Personal Contacts Portlet in the Personal Information View

Dependents

The Dependents portlet is effective-dated and allows for the storage of multiple dependents. This interesting portlet combines small snapshots of other portlets together in order to store information related to the following categories for each dependent:

▶ Person Relationship

▶ Personal Information

▶ Biographical Information

▶ National ID Information

▶ Addresses

In short, a mini, employee-like record is created in the system for each dependent, as shown in Figure 9.17. This record can then be shared with auxiliary systems, such as a benefits solution or a payroll processor.

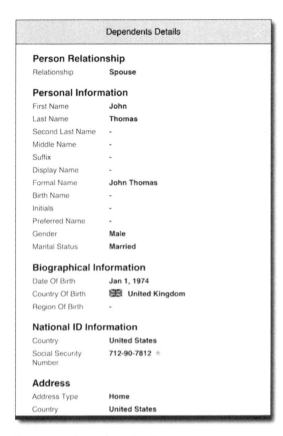

Figure 9.17 Dependents Portlet

Payment Information

The PAYMENT INFORMATION portlet allows you to choose a PAYMENT METHOD and enter in related bank information if the method is DIRECT DEPOSIT or BANK TRANSFER (see Figure 9.18). Multiple bank accounts can be entered and payments can be split using percentages and flat amounts. Different types of payments (payroll, bonuses, expenses, etc.) can be separated out to different accounts as well.

Other commonly used payment methods include CHECKS and CASH. These values can be customized to meet your specific methods of pay. This portlet has great value and is a pertinent piece of ESS.

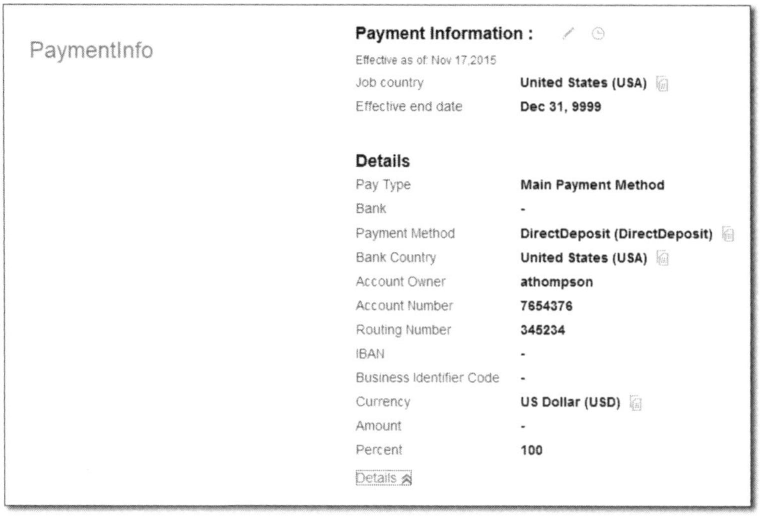

Figure 9.18 Payment Information Portlet

> **Versions**
>
> Other versions of the Payment Information portlet do exist. Earlier versions involved direct deposit on its own or combined with a separate Payment Method portlet. These portlets are not effective-dated but are still valid and in use.

Next, we'll look at the second main view for employee data: Employment Information.

9.1.3 Employment Information

The second key view within Employee Central is Employment Information. This view contains information that is specific to an employee and his or her position and role within an organization (see Figure 9.19). This is information that changes as the employee moves through the organization, changes jobs and managers, or has pay changes. We frequently see much of this data available for editing by managers using MSS, as discussed in Section 9.3.2.

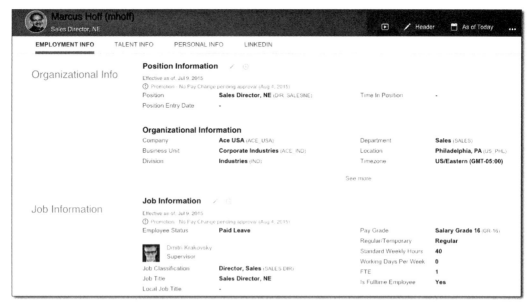

Figure 9.19 Top Section of Employment Information View

Let's explore the different data portlets available in the Employment Information view.

Job Information

The JOB INFORMATION portlet, shown in Figure 9.20, is likely the largest data portlet you'll encounter working with Employee Central.

Figure 9.20 Job Information Portlet

There are numerous employee job-related pieces of data to be stored, and this portlet houses most of these fields. The portlet is effective-dated and offers country-specific fields as well.

There are five main sections within the JOB INFORMATION portlet:

▶ POSITION INFORMATION
Contains information about the employee's current position.

▶ ORGANIZATIONAL INFORMATION
Contains the employee's organizational assignments, including COMPANY, BUSINESS UNIT, DIVISION, DEPARTMENT, and COST CENTER. The COMPANY field is an extremely important as it drives the portlet's country-specific fields. See Chapter 6, Section 6.2 for more information about Foundation Objects and the role Company plays in country-specific settings.

▶ JOB INFORMATION
Allows you to classify an employee with a JOB TITLE, PAY GRADE, and EMPLOYEE TYPE, and assign a SUPERVISOR. Several different employee and job classification fields are found in this area. Consult your system or workbook for a complete listing. At the bottom of this section, we often see several country-specific classification fields, including information about probationary periods, contract types, and pay scale information.

There are two key fields in this section:

▹ EMPLOYEE STATUS: Displays an employee's status and is driven by the most recent Event and Event Reason assigned to this portlet. For more information about events and Event Reasons, see Chapter 4, Section 4.2.

▹ FTE: FTE stands for full-time equivalent and is automatically calculated based on the populated number of standard working hours and the anticipated number of hours defined in the Foundation Tables.

▶ TIME INFORMATION
If the system is configured for any Time Management-related fields, then they will be found here in the TIME INFORMATION section. Common fields include TIME TYPE PROFILE, HOLIDAY CALENDAR, and WORK SCHEDULE.

▶ EEO INFORMATION (United States only)
Although not a major segment, the EEO INFORMATION section will appear for

employees working for a company tied to the United States. The EEO JOB GROUP and EEO CATEGORY fields are found here.

Employment Details

The EMPLOYMENT DETAILS portlet is non-effective-dated and stores date and eligibility information for employees. The portlet is broken into the following two sections:

▶ HIRE DETAILS
  HIRE DETAILS allows you to record information about an employee's hire date, original hire date, seniority date, and other key dates traditionally determined at the employee's time of hire or rehire (see Figure 9.21). When an employee is rehired, the HIRE DATE field resets with the rehire date and the original start date remains the same. Numerous standard-delivered date fields are included in this area to help support payroll, time, benefits, and stock granting. Some are even redundant. You likely will not need to use each one, and they can be turned off during configuration.

▶ TERMINATION DETAILS
  TERMINATION DETAILS allows you to record not only the employee's TERMINATION DATE but also other key supporting pieces of data such as a TERMINATION REASON, OK TO REHIRE, PAYROLL END DATE, REGRET TERMINATION, and a series of other end-of-service dates (see Figure 9.22). This section of EMPLOYMENT DETAILS only displays when an employee has gone through the termination process.

Employment Details			
Is Contingent Worker	No	Service Date	Jan 1, 2001
Hire Date	Jan 1, 2001	Initial Stock Grant	30,000
Original Start Date	Jan 1, 2001	Professional Service Date	Jan 1, 2001
First Date Worked	-	Initial Option Grant	300
Seniority Start Date	Jan 1, 2001	Years of Service	12
Eligible for Stock	No	Update Hire Date?	-
Updated Hire Date	Feb 20, 2015		

See less

Figure 9.21 Employee Details Portlet

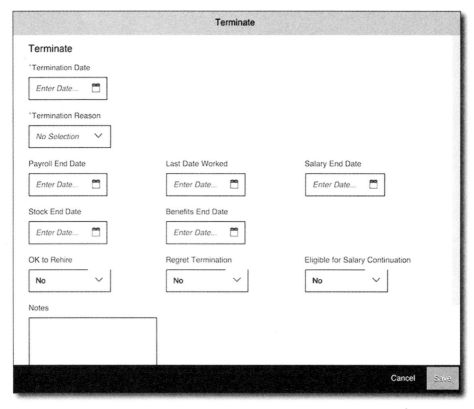

Figure 9.22 Terminate/Rehire

Job Relationships

The effective-dated Job Relationships portlet allows you to manage relationships between an employee and other employees in the system (see Figure 9.23). With the exception of the manager assignment (which is made in Job Information), all other relationships are defined here, including the following:

▶ HR Manager
▶ Matrix Manager
▶ Additional Manager
▶ Custom Manager
▶ Second Manager

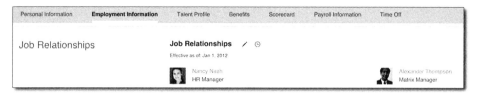

Figure 9.23 Job Relationships Portlet

Compensation Information

The COMPENSATION INFORMATION portlet is effective-dated and allows for country-specific fields. It is broken into a few different sections to help organize the data it contains (see Figure 9.24). This area is highly utilized through MSS because managers are able to propose pay changes for their team members.

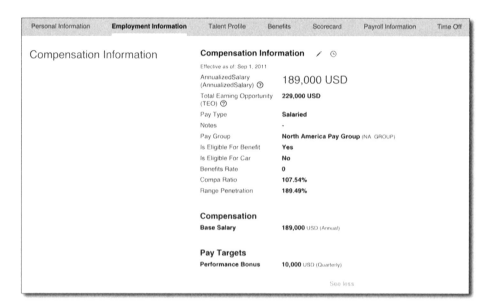

Figure 9.24 Compensation Information Portlet

Additional Fields

Please note that your Compensation Information portlet may have different or additional areas based on your business requirements. For example, an organization that uses Deduction Management may have an additional section.

The major areas of the COMPENSATION INFORMATION portlet are as follows:

► COMPENSATION INFORMATION

The COMPENSATION INFORMATION section of the COMPENSATION INFORMATION portlet houses basic compensation characteristics to help classify employees in terms of pay. You can designate what PAY GROUP an employee belongs to as well as the PAY TYPE. This is also where the calculated Pay Component Groups, COMPA RATIO and RANGE PENETRATION will appear. See Chapter 6, Section 6.2.3 for more information on Pay Component Groups.

Compa Ratio and Range Penetration

COMPA RATIO and RANGE PENETRATION will only calculate and display if the employee is assigned to a Pay Grade in Job Information and if the Pay Grade ID is assigned to a Pay Range in the Foundation Tables.

► COMPENSATION

This section of an employee's record lists the payment that the employee receives each pay period. These payments are known as Recurring Pay Components and generally include a BASE SALARY or HOURLY WAGE as well as any recurring supplements such as a HOUSING ALLOWANCE or CAR ALLOWANCE. Numerous frequencies and a full listing of currencies are standard delivered, and mixing different types is fully supported.

► PAY TARGETS

PAY TARGETS are awards that an employee is eligible to receive assuming some sort of criteria is met: company performance, individual performance, objective performance, and so on, or a combination of criteria. This value can be entered and maintained as an amount or as a percent. We typically see ANNUAL PERFORMANCE BONUSES entered in this area. These values are added to the compensation values listed previously and shown as a possible Total Earning Opportunity Pay Component Group.

Advances and Deductions

More information about advances and deductions can be found in Chapter 14.

Spot Bonus

The SPOT BONUS portlet is non-effective-dated and used to store one-time payments made to an employee (see Figure 9.25). Assign each payment an ISSUE

DATE to indicate when it should be or was paid to the employee. This is another popular area for MSS because managers can request recognition rewards or additional payments for their team members.

Figure 9.25 Spot Bonus Portlet

9.1.4 Other Views

Four additional employee data views—Pending Requests and Manage Time Off—help augment the employee data arrangement within Employee Central. We discuss employee benefits and Chapter 10 and payroll in Chapter 15. In the next two subsections we will look at the Pending Requests view and Manage Time Off.

Pending Requests

The PENDING REQUESTS view (Figure 9.26) organizes and displays Employee Central–related workflows for an individual user. This view is comprised of four portlets:

▶ REQUESTS WAITING FOR MY APPROVAL
Workflows for which the user is the current approver and the workflow is pending with him or her.

▶ MY REQUESTS WAITING FOR APPROVAL
Workflows initiated by the user that are pending approval with another user.

▶ REQUESTS STILL IN PROGRESS THAT I APPROVED
Workflows approved by the user but which haven't finished the approval process.

▶ MY NOTIFICATIONS
Notices received by the user providing information about completed transactions.

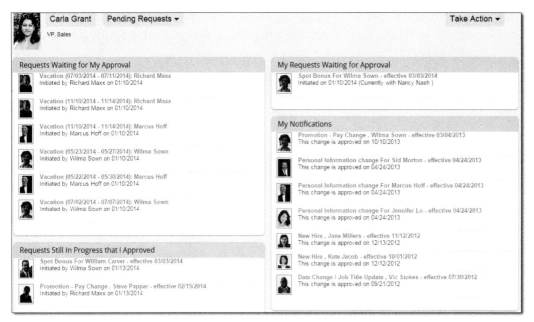

Figure 9.26 Pending Requests View

Manage Time Off

The MANAGE TIME OFF view displays all time-related data in a series of three portlets (see Figure 9.27). This view allows employees to actively manage their time-related activities via the following three portlets:

▶ TIME ACCOUNTS
Shows an employee what types of Time Off they qualify for, as well as how many days have been accrued and taken.

▶ TIME OFF OVERVIEW
Gives an overview of the Time Off requests made by an employee and approval information. A REQUEST TIME OFF link is included to facilitate requesting additional time off.

▶ TIME ACCOUNT POSTINGS
Lists actual posted or taken Time Off. Adjustments can be made to posted time and details about actual time off can be viewed.

Figure 9.27 Manage Time Off View

These additional views offer further functionality for employee data. In the next section, we'll take a look at Employee Central's ability to store and maintain employee data information.

9.2 History and Audit Trail

At the beginning of this chapter, we discussed how certain portlets are effective-dated, thereby allowing us to not only store current information about employees, but also to store and maintain previous information as well. The inherent nature of an effective-dated system is its ability to store and maintain history. Let's take a look at how this works in Employee Central and what additional options are available. We'll then discuss what audit capabilities are in place for different types of users.

9.2.1 History within Employee Central

Portlets that are effective-dated will store and display historical records, which means that all transactions (such as those listed in Section 9.4) are documented and basic changes do not overwrite each other in history. Figure 9.28 shows an example of a test employee's Job Information history. Different users can access history views according to their role-based permission settings.

One of the most useful visual aspects of Employee Central is the color-coding of changed data. As you can see in Figure 9.28, the new values are shown in a distinct text and the old changes are shown crossed out in gray on the side. In your system, the new values will either display with blue (older UI) or green (newer UI) text. It's easy to see what data has been changed and the previous value of the field, which makes jumping through an employee's record easy and streamlined. You can always tell what change was made from record to record. See Figure 9.29 for an alternate view.

Figure 9.28 Job History Changes in Job Information History View

Figure 9.29 Job Information Changes

As previously mentioned, a user must have the appropriate Role-Based Permissions (RBPs) to access the History views of a certain portlet. Each effective-dated portlet will have a CLOCK icon (see Figure 9.30) next to the portlet name. Clicking this button will open an employee's full record for that data set, including one's history.

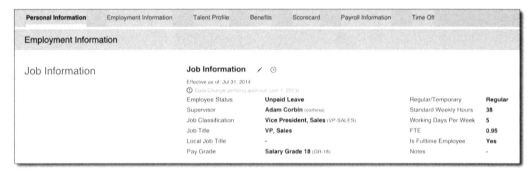

Figure 9.30 Note the History Button in the Top-Right Corner

You may be asking how historical changes are stored and recorded within the system. In the next section, we will discuss the audit trail feature, which records the chronological changes to a record.

9.2.2   Audit Trail

An *audit trail* records the chronological changes to a record, including detailed transactional data. In Employee Central, the audit trail is an electronic change log tracking data changes and corrections within an employee's effective-dated records.

There are two key ways in Employee Central to review who has made changes to an employee's effective-dated record and when those changes were made. The first method is to view the history of an employee's portlet. At the bottom of each record is a dated time stamp that records when a data change was last made for that specific entry and by whom the change was made (see Figure 9.31). This method is good for reviewing who made the most recent changes and what changes were made.

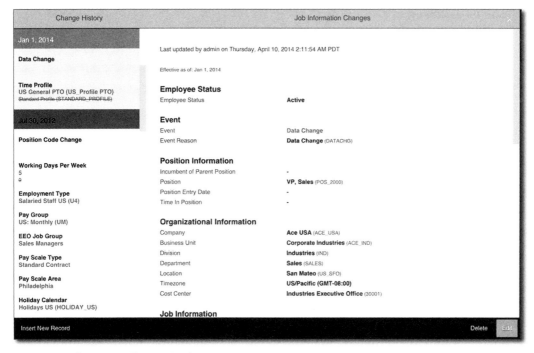

Figure 9.31 Changes Made

The second method is to run an audit report. An audit report is more detailed and more accurate, because it will capture not only the top-of-stack change information for a record but also the previous changes that were made to that same record. This method gives administrators the greatest oversight and review capabilities. Reports can be set up in the Reporting area of SAP SuccessFactors. More information on setting up reports can be found in Chapter 16. There is a separate domain for audit purposes called *Person and Employment Audit*.

9.3 Self-Services

Employee Central's self-service functionality is the hallmark of a true partnership between an organization's HR department and its employees. It allows for the entry and exchange of data and empowers both employees and managers to be owners of their own HR-related data. By having the owner of the data enter it directly into the system, you can cut down on errors and increase accuracy.

Whether it is an employee supplying a new home address or a manager requesting employee job changes, the data owner is always the most knowledgeable about the proposed change. It makes sense to have these owners input and maintain this data with HR overview and approval as needed. In turn, HR professionals can shift away from performing transaction-based tasks and into more strategic roles.

Employee Central can be tailored to provide ESS and MSS for any and all fields and transactions in the system. However, because employees typically shouldn't have access to adjust their own Compensation Information and managers don't usually need access to an employee's Personal Information, it's important to follow best practice guidelines for setup and to make customer-specific adjustments as needed to accommodate business processes. The features and functions made available to users depend a lot on an organization's view of employees' capabilities and willingness to embrace a new medium. At some levels, the choices boil down to the organization's culture and willingness to accept possible change. In the next sections, we'll look at both ESS and MSS in greater detail.

> **Self-Service Configuration**
>
> The actual setup and configuration of self-services functionality is contained within RBPs (see Chapter 3). You create user roles that allow employees and managers to have view/edit/action permissions for certain fields and portlets.

9.3.1 Employee Self-Services

ESS allows employees to view and update selected portions of their own employee records. We typically see ESS edit/update transactions limited to data contained within the Personal Information view and view-only access to the data contained in the Employment Information view. The thought behind this methodology is that employees know their own personal information better than anyone else. Giving them access to update their own personal information allows them to play an active role in keeping record data current and correct. As with all self-service functionality, you have the option to incorporate workflow approvals and notifications as needed.

To make changes to Personal Information, employees click the pencil icon next to the portlet name wherever an employee has edit capability (see Figure 9.32). If a portlet is effective-dated, then the employee will be prompted to enter a change date.

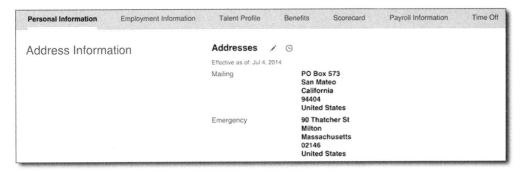

Figure 9.32 ESS Changes

The following are common areas in which employees edit/update their information:

▸ Personal Information
A lot of debate takes place during requirements gathering as to which fields within Personal Information an employee should be allowed to update. The biggest concern is that changes to Name, Gender, and Marital Status fields often require supporting documentation to help verify the new values. Keep in mind that all changes here can be routed through a workflow process (as covered in Chapter 4, Section 4.3) and verified by HR prior to approval. Depending on your location and company requirements, you may allow for all fields within Personal Information to be updated or none at all. At a minimum, consider allowing updates to the Nickname and Preferred Language fields.

▸ Home Address
Home Address is a slightly misleading term, because many different addresses may be stored here. Normally, all types of addresses are allowed to be added and maintained here using ESS.

▸ Work Permit Information
This is another popular area for ESS. The Attachment field makes this portlet ideal for employees to maintain and include supporting documentation all at the same time.

▸ Contact Information
This portlet contains the three key contact mediums: Email, Phone, and Social Accounts. These are ideal areas to be maintained by an employee. Using RBPs, you have the option to lock down changes to the Business Email Address. This is helpful if this value is assigned externally and should not be modified.

▶ PERSONAL CONTACTS

This includes EMERGENCY CONTACTS. It may not always be necessary to have an approval workflow for changes made in this portlet.

▶ DEPENDENTS

This portlet allows for listing and updating dependent information. Dependent information is useful for benefits enrollments.

▶ PAYMENT INFORMATION

This portlet includes a selection of preferred payment methods (e.g., direct deposit or check). If direct deposit is chosen, then bank details are maintained here as well.

▶ LEAVE OF ABSENCE

Although not contained within the PERSONAL INFORMATION view, LEAVE OF ABSENCE is sometimes used by employees. This is one transaction for which employees use the TAKE ACTION button in the top-right-hand corner of the screen to make an entry.

9.3.2 Manager Self-Services

MSS allows managers to view and update select portions of records that belong to their team members. The exact fields that a manager can view or edit are selected when setting up RBPs. Depending on the role assignment, managers can manage data for employees rolling up to their chain of command in the reporting structure.

We typically see MSS edit/update transactions limited to data contained within the Employment Information view and view-only access to limited data contained in the Personal Information view. Managers do not need full access to a team member's complete Personal Information record, as much of that information is sensitive. The thought is that managers know their team's employment information better than anyone else. Giving them access to update this information allows them to play an active role in keeping record data current and correct. As with all self-service functionality, you can incorporate workflow approvals and notifications as needed.

An additional feature of MSS that is sometimes employed is access to the Reporting or Analytics sections of SAP SuccessFactors. Empowering managers to run their own reports for their chains of command is also a useful tool. This is also controlled and assigned using RBPs. MSS data changes are typically made through the TAKE ACTION button, as shown in Figure 9.33.

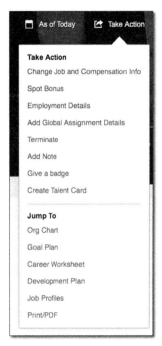

Figure 9.33 Take Action Dropdown in MSS

Here are some of the areas for which managers have self-service edit/update access (see Figure 9.34):

▶ JOB INFORMATION
This is the most common portlet for MSS to be employed in, because it contains the most data fields and the nature of the fields makes them prime for change. Fields are individually permissioned in this portlet and a manager can have access to update one, some, or all of them depending on business requirements. To make an update, managers click the TAKE ACTION dropdown (Figure 9.33) and then select JOB INFORMATION from the MSS change screen shown in Figure 9.34. Once the manager completes the proposed changes, he or she can scroll to the bottom and click SUBMIT to finish the entry and initiate the workflow.

▶ JOB RELATIONSHIPS
This portlet is updated to show changes to HR manager assignments or other managers, such as matrix managers. When an employee changes locations or jobs, updates to JOB RELATIONSHIPS may also be required.

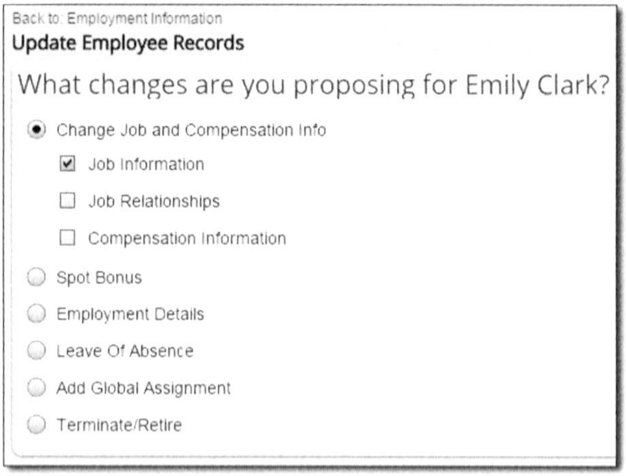

Figure 9.34 Update Employe Records

▶ COMPENSATION INFORMATION
This is the second-most commonly utilized portlet in MSS. Fields here are individually permissioned, and a manager can be assigned access to update one, several, or all fields depending on company requirements. A manager can request pay increases for team members using this portlet. To make an update, managers click the TAKE ACTION dropdown and then select COMPENSATION INFORMATION from the MSS change screen shown in Figure 9.34.

▶ SPOT BONUS
As described in Section 9.1.3, the SPOT BONUS portlet provides an area to designate recognition and rewards.

▶ EMPLOYMENT DETAILS
Also described in Section 9.1.3, this portlet provides information such as hiring and termination details.

▶ LEAVE OF ABSENCE
This is not a portlet itself, but updates are made to the JOB INFORMATION portlet when changes are confirmed using this link. LEAVE OF ABSENCE is managed through the TAKE ACTION dropdown.

▶ TERMINATE/RETIRE
Managers can initiate a Termination action using the option from the TAKE ACTION menu. Once the transaction is entered and the workflow is approved, updates will be reflected in both JOB INFORMATION and EMPLOYEE DETAILS.

Now that we've explored areas in which managers and employees make data changes through self-services, let's dive deeper into the types and classifications of changes that may be made.

9.4 Transactions

Transactions form the basis for organizing an employee's job history as well as keeping track of major career changes. A transaction is recorded each time there is a change to an employee's current role or classification. You may also hear the shortened term action being used in the same manner. Transactions are tied to events, and more information can be found in Chapter 4, Section 4.2.

Let's take a look at the major transactions used in Employee Central.

9.4.1 New Hire

A New Hire transaction is the first event recorded in an employee's history. The date and reason for the hire are recorded as well as the employee's first job classification and organizational assignment. This transaction is usually initiated and completed by an HR representative.

There are two main ways to access this transaction. First, if you have access to the Admin Center, you can go to ADMIN CENTER • MANAGE EMPLOYEES • UPDATE USER INFORMATION • ADD NEW HIRE or click ADD NEW EMPLOYEE in the action search box. Second, for those without access to the Admin Center, but with access to hire new employees, an ADD NEW EMPLOYEE button can be found at COMPANY INFO • ORGANIZATIONAL CHART view (see Figure 9.35).

Figure 9.35 Add New Employee

Rehire

The Rehire transaction can be processed in the same manner as the New Hire action, or an HR representative can use the Rehire functionality under the same navigational path in the Admin Center.

Manage Pending Hire

For those organizations integrating with SAP SuccessFactors Recruiting, approved candidates can be hired into the system by using the MANAGE PENDING HIRE functionality under the same navigational path in the Admin Center or by clicking on the link on the admin's homepage under ADMIN ALERTS.

9.4.2 Transfers

Transfer is a somewhat open-ended term because this transaction can be applied in a few different scenarios. This is where Event Reasons (see Chapter 4, Section 4.2) come into play. Event Reasons allow you to classify specific types of Transfers. Typically, Transfers are initiated by managers using self-service functionality. A common trend is that an employee's job and compensation typically remain the same. Some common Transfer examples include the following:

▸ Change in Location

▸ Change in Department

▸ Change in Manager/Team

9.4.3 Promotions

A *Promotion* typically involves a positive change in pay as well as a change in Job Code and/or Job Title. It is usually considered to be a vertical movement up both the organizational structure and the pay structure. Promotions are typically initiated by a manager using self-services.

9.4.4 Reclassification

A *Reclassification* occurs when the duties of a job or position are reevaluated and determined to be at a different level than currently stated. Pay is possibly regraded as well. Often, a new job or position title is given. We usually see this transaction being used during the course of a Job Responsibility Review, a Global

Job Catalog Exercise, or a Global Job Grading Review. These changes are typically initiated by an HR representative.

9.4.5 Job Changes

A *Job Change* is a change in job, job title, or classification that is typically not considered a Promotion. It may be a lateral move within the same department or to a different business area. It may also be the movement from part-time to full-time employment. These transactions are typically initiated by a manager using self-services.

9.4.6 Compensation Changes

Compensation Changes typically occur independent of a Job Change or a Pay Grade Change (otherwise, you could include Promotion or Demotion transactions). Compensation Change involves a positive or negative change in pay and can be applied universally to changes such as the following:

▸ Annual Merit Increases

▸ Cost of Living Adjustments

▸ Time in Role Adjustments

The use of a meaningful Event Reason can help classify and clarify the reason behind the change. Depending on the type of change being proposed, a manager or an HR representative may initiate this request.

9.4.7 Leave of Absence

The Leave of Absence transaction allows for thorough logging and tracking of leaves as well as the ability to incorporate an approval process by using workflows. You can track both PAID LEAVES and UNPAID LEAVES and specify exactly which LEAVE TYPE is being used. EXPECTED DATE OF RETURN can also be entered. If you are utilizing certain components of the Time Management functionality, then you can track proposed days of leave versus allocated time for the specified leave type.

The person or persons who can initiate a Leave of Absence request varies from company to company. One or more of the following people traditionally initiate Leaves: employees, managers, and HR representatives. Although the system can be configured to allow permissions for any or all of these users to initiate leaves, it comes down to a few factors when making a decision during requirements gathering:

- Types of leaves being tracked
- Availability of computers to employees
- Employee population and level of comfort with computers
- The confidential nature of certain types of leaves

There is not a right or wrong choice when setting up this permission. Spend some time during requirements gathering discussing which user scenario is right for your organization.

9.4.8 Terminations/Retire

Terminations is another broadly applied transaction in the Employee Central space. It is used to denote an employee's departure from the organization for a number of reasons, including the following:

- Voluntary Termination
- Involuntary Termination
- Retirement
- Resignation
- Death

It's the specific Event Reason used that helps you understand the reason for departure.

Although an HR representative can insert a new record into an employee's Job Information history portlet, the only way to bring up the full Termination/Retire portlet for completion is to use the TAKE ACTION button.

Modifying data and executing transactions requires a firmly defined set of data fields. These fields are configured in the system to have certain properties and characteristics that make them available for use and maintenance. Let's discuss how to configure employee data fields in the next section.

9.5 Configuration

There are two main ways to set up and configure employee data within Employee Central. The traditional manner is by configuring and importing XML data models through Provisioning. This option is only available for implementers. The second option allows customers access to make basic configuration changes. MANAGE BUSINESS CONFIGURATION is available in the Admin Center for system administrators. In this section, we will discuss both options for configuration so as to provide a complete understanding of the setup and maintenance process of employee data fields.

9.5.1   XML Data Models

An *XML data model* is a technical design that allows users to structure data for storage and transmission within Employee Central. Using this data model, you structure which data elements and fields you want to define in your system. SuccessFactors uses a series of best practices or commonly used setups in its data models. An implementer will work to personalize these data models according to each customer's business requirements. They can be downloaded from the SAP Service Marketplace by permitted implementers. This is the most direct method of beginning configuration for a system.

> **Preconfiguration**
>
> You will need to use data models for initial configuration unless you are working with a system that is preloaded with an Employee Central configuration or helping to support a system that already has a configuration in place.

There are two complementary XML data models used to set up employee data: the Succession Data Model and the Country-Specific Succession Data Model. In the Succession Data Model, you globally define your elements and fields. These fields will be available for all employees in the system regardless of their location. You define country-specific fields in the Country-Specific Succession Data Model. This configuration is broken out in sections by country, and the specified fields only display for the country for which the system is configured. The basic structure of each data model is the same. We'll look more closely at the structure of a data model in the next section.

9.5.2   Data Model Structure

Each Employee Central data portlet is defined by an HRIS element. An HRIS element is equivalent to an employee data object or portlet, as defined in Section 9.1 and covered in the beginning of this section. It has a technical name and is referred to by this technical name in the data model. One example is

Employment Details, which has an HRIS element name of `employmentInfo`, as shown in Figure 9.36.

Each HRIS element has a series of properties that help us define it. For more information on HRIS elements and their structure, see Chapter 6, Section 6.4.1.

```
<hris-element id="employmentInfo">
  <label>Employment Details</label>
  <label xml:lang="ar-SA">تفاصيل الموظف</label>
  <label xml:lang="bg-BG">Подробни данни за заетост</label>
  <label xml:lang="bs-BS">Butiran Pekerjaan</label>
  <label xml:lang="bs-ID">Detail Pekerjaan</label>
  <label xml:lang="cs-CZ">Podrobnosti o zaměstnání</label>
  <label xml:lang="cy-GB">Manylion Cyflogaeth</label>
  <label xml:lang="da-DK">Ansættelsesdetaljer</label>
  <label xml:lang="de-CH">Beschäftigungsdetails</label>
  <label xml:lang="de-DE">Beschäftigungsdetails</label>
```

Figure 9.36 HRIS Element

> **Caution!**
>
> Carefully review basic XML protocol if attempting to modify these Data Models. Be warned that several different fields may have the same labels and/or technical field names. For Employee Central, you work with the HRIS fields defined within HRIS elements. Standard elements are used elsewhere in SAP SuccessFactors, but not directly in Employee Central.

After tailoring the data models for a customer, import them in to the system using Provisioning. After selecting the COMPANY NAME from your Provisioning main screen, you will see import links for uploading and downloading data models (see Figure 9.37).

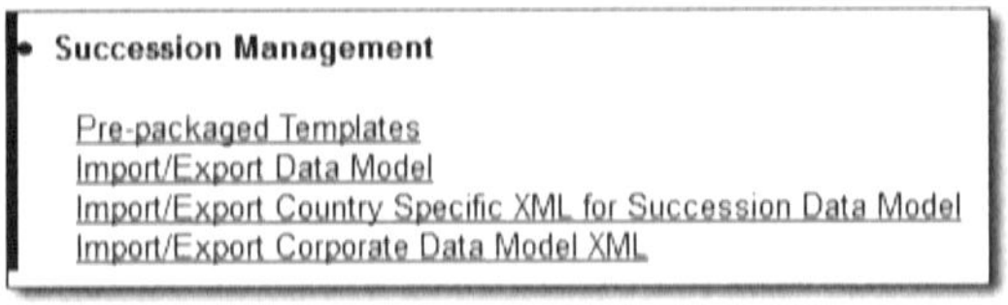

Succession Management

Pre-packaged Templates
Import/Export Data Model
Import/Export Country Specific XML for Succession Data Model
Import/Export Corporate Data Model XML

Figure 9.37 Menu Options in Provisioning for Import and Export of Data Models

As you can see, the data model configuration method is very cumbersome and intricate. The Manage Business Configuration method provides the same options and functionality, but it's contained within a web-based GUI that resides directly in the system.

9.5.3   Manage Business Configuration

Once you have an initial baseline of configuration in place, you can make modifications using functionality within the Admin Center. This functionality can be permissioned to administrators in order to allow them to make post-go-live configuration changes. These changes may include changing labels, adding new fields, and reordering fields.

Access Manage Business Configuration through Admin Center • Company Settings • Manage Business Configuration Settings.

Once inside this admin feature, you will see a listing of technical HRIS elements on the left-hand side of the screen, as shown in Figure 9.38. This menu will allow you to navigate back and forth between existing configurations for each element. As you click on each element, the associated HRIS fields will display in the center of the screen along with their current assigned properties.

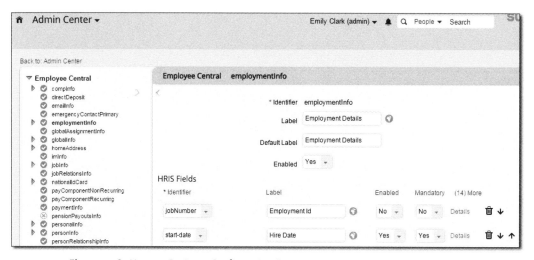

Figure 9.38 Manage Business Configuration Screen

Within this screen, you can turn fields on and off by changing the value in the Enabled dropdown and can set a field to be Required by changing the value in the Mandatory dropdown. You can also reorder the arrangement of the fields by using the up and down arrows on the far right-hand side of the screen. Fields that have an Enabled = No setting are turned off for this system.

The Manage Business Configuration area of the Admin Center provides a convenient way to enter label translations into the system. Figure 9.38 shows a language translation icon shaped like a globe next to each label. Clicking on the icon will open a language translation entry screen, as shown in Figure 9.39.

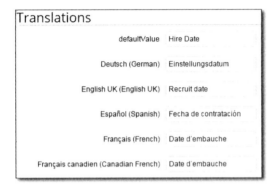

Figure 9.39 Translations

To view or set more details about a field, click on the DETAILS hyperlink in blue next to the field name. A popup window (Figure 9.40) will open and display additional parameters that you can set for each field.

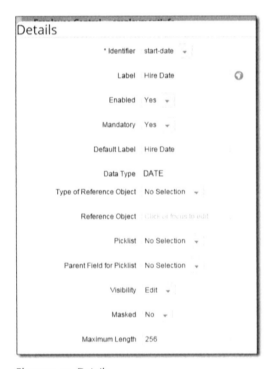

Figure 9.40 Details

9.5.4 Best Practices and Considerations

Here are a few tips and tricks we have found to be effective when working with different customers:

▶ **Consider required fields applicable to all employees.**
Be judicious when marking a field as REQUIRED. A required field must always be populated at a global level in mandatory portlets. Make sure that you're considering global requirements when setting a field to be required. A New Hire or Transfer cannot be submitted with required fields not completed. Always be sure to mark system-required fields as REQUIRED, or the system will do it for you.

Required Fields Exception

There is a special scenario to be aware of with REQUIRED fields and the New Hire action. A required field will only trigger as required in a required portlet or if a non-required portlet is being used for an employee. A required portlet is a portlet that contains a system-required field. All required fields in a system-required portlet will be absolutely required.

In a portlet without system-required fields, the portlet is considered to be a non-required portlet. The validation checker will skip over these portlets unless an entry has been started. In the National ID Information portlet, for example, there are no system-required fields. We are able to skip this portlet entirely for contractors and for employees who reside in data-sensitive locations. However, if we begin to make an entry for National ID Information and skip a required field, then the validation checker will prompt us to finish completing the required fields.

▶ **Make proper use of field labels and translations.**
Changing the label on a field will only change the one language value entered in to the system. Be sure to translate label changes into all applicable languages and enter the translations into the system.

▶ **Check your character set.**
Be sure to use Unicode (UTF-8) or appropriate local character coding formats when importing files, including Foundation Objects, employee data, and picklists. Failure to do so may corrupt or rescind local character sets.

▶ **Don't delete unneeded fields.**
Standard fields that are not needed for your implementation do not need to be deleted. They can be set to be not used during configuration. Deleting them entirely will make it a little tougher to add them back in later if you should

decide you need them. It will also wipe out standard-delivered translations, and those are always nice to have if needed.

▶ **Don't repurpose standard fields.**
Try and avoid repurposing standard-delivered fields whenever possible. There are numerous custom fields available for use, and these should be used first in most scenarios. If a standard field is repurposed, you will likely lose the ability to use it later on. With new functionality being introduced quarterly, you may find that some fields have added appeal in the future. Also, standard-delivered reports will use these fields in their originally intended form, so you may be configuring yourself out of being able to use some reports.

9.6   Summary

In this chapter, we explored employee data and how it is stored and maintained. We learned about views and portlets, effective-dated and country-specific capabilities, and transactions made by HR persons and through self-services.

In the next chapter, we will expand upon the basic concepts of employee data and learn how the Payroll Time Sheets, Time Off, Global Benefits features help to augment an employee's record within the system.

Time off from the workplace and employee benefits are two ways outside of salary that an organization can compensate its employees. A Time Off system allows employees to keep track of their requested and actual time off and empowers managers to plan an adequate resource schedule.

10   Employee Time, Absences, and Benefits

Receiving time off and benefits has become a common occurrence in the workplace. More and more companies are offering various time off policies and additional and alternate benefits to employees. Companies need a way to successfully determine eligibility and track what has been received. In addition, time recording goes hand in hand with time off to form a complete time management process and they create many synergies when implemented together.

Employee Central's Payroll Time Sheet, Time Off, and Global Benefits features have the capability to determine eligibility, display account details, and record redemptions and payouts. Time Off and Global Benefits can function independently or in conjunction with other features. Payroll Time Sheet can be used in addition to Time Off because it reuses many of the base objects defined within Time Off.

Payroll Time Sheet, Time Off, and Global Benefits are all built on the Metadata Framework (MDF), which we looked at in Chapter 5. As such, the setup structures and configuration steps for each feature are very similar. You will also see some similarity between the terminologies used when discussing each feature.

In this chapter, we will review common Time Management terminology before we look at the Payroll Time Sheet and its capabilities. We will then move onto Time Off and look at the different views and functions provided for each user type. Finally, we will look at Global Benefits and its common use cases.

10.1   Time Management Overview

Payroll Time Sheet and Time Off combine to create the Time Management offering in Employee Central. They are both self-service driven features designed to make it easy for employees to enter time worked and to book time off. Before we deep dive into each feature, we should first look at some of the common terminology used for both Payroll Time Sheet and Time Off, as well as examine where Time Management profiles are assigned to employees. These profiles determine the behavior of various aspects of Payroll Time Sheet and Time Off for an employee, specifically around making time bookings.

10.1.1 Objects

In order to fully understand Payroll Time Sheet and Time Off, you must understand the different objects used within the Time Management modules. Knowing these terms will come in handy when reviewing the functionality and setup of each feature and they should be fully understood prior to completing any requirements gathering or configuration for Time Off (including Leave of Absence) and Payroll Timesheet. The following are common Time Management objects:

▶ TIME TYPE

TIME TYPE is a specific category of time to be worked or not worked against which hours are recorded. Examples include REGULAR WORKING HOURS, OVERTIME HOURS, MATERNITY LEAVE, SICK LEAVE, and so on. When working with the Payroll Time Sheet, the TIME TYPE can represent both worked time (known as *attendance*) and leave. When working with just Time Off, the TIME TYPE correspond to leaves only. Figure 10.1 displays a sample SICK LEAVE Time Type.

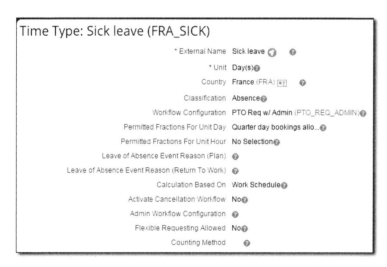

Figure 10.1 Time Type for Sick Leave for France

► TIME ACCOUNTS

TIME ACCOUNTS store the amount of time currently available to use for their respective TIME TYPE. They function similarly to bank accounts in that you can add and withdraw time. Depending on system setup, you may also be able to overdraw on certain TIME ACCOUNTS. A TIME ACCOUNTS view is available in ESS. This is helpful because employees can see exactly how many vacation or sick days they have available for use. If these days accrue based on days worked, then the balance of the TIME ACCOUNTS will continue to increase each period until a withdrawal occurs. Employees can have multiple TIME ACCOUNTS (e.g., VACATION, PTO, SICKNESS, etc.). Figure 10.2 shows how TIME ACCOUNTS are displayed to end users in the system. In this example, two TIME ACCOUNTS are shown: SICKNESS and VACATION.

Time Accounts							
Account Details as of: Today 📅							
Time Account	Account Valid From	Account Valid Until	Earned	Taken	Balance	Planned	Bookable Until
Sickness Current Year	01/01/2001	12/31/9999	10 days	0 days	10 days	0 days	12/31/9999
Vacation Current Year	01/01/2001	12/31/9999	25 days	4 days	21 days	0 days	12/31/9999

Figure 10.2 Time Accounts

► TIME ACCOUNT TYPE

Any TIME TYPE that needs TIME ACCOUNTS must have a TIME ACCOUNT TYPE tied to it. This indicator lets the system know that Time Accounts should be created (see Figure 10.3).

Time Account Type: Sickness Current Year (SICKNESS_CURRENT)

Payout Eligibility	No Selection❓
Interim Account Update Rule	❓
Country	United States (USA) ❓
Accrual Frequency Period	No Selection❓
Balance Cannot Fall Below	❓
* External Code	SICKNESS_CURRENT❓
* External Name	Sickness Current Year 🔵 ❓
Unit	Day(s)❓
* Account Creation Type	Permanent❓
Start Day Of Accrual Period	❓
Start Month Of Accrual Period	❓

Figure 10.3 Time Account Type

343

A business rule can be created and assigned to a TIME ACCOUNT TYPE to have accruals automatically created for employees. When creating a TIME ACCOUNT TYPE, you must specify whether it is a permanent account (one per employee that continually accrues) or a recurring account, which has a set life span of one year and renews each year (rollovers can be set for certain time periods). Figure 10.3 shows a TIME ACCOUNT TYPE for SICKNESS CURRENT YEAR.

▶ HOLIDAY CALENDAR
HOLIDAY CALENDAR is a local calendar populated with public holidays and other days of significance that should be taken into account when an employee requests time off. An employee can only be assigned to one Holiday Calendar, even though multiple calendars can be supported for a particular location. Figure 10.4 shows the configured HOLIDAY CALENDAR for the United Kingdom and the year 2013.

Figure 10.4 Holiday Calendar for the United Kingdom, 2013

▶ WORK SCHEDULE
WORK SCHEDULE represents an employee's typical work pattern, as shown in Figure 10.5. When you merge a WORK SCHEDULE with a HOLIDAY CALENDAR, you can accurately predict planned working time, account for overtime or holiday pay, and appropriately withdraw from TIME ACCOUNTS when time off is scheduled.

```
Display Work Schedule: Mon-Fri 8 Hour Days

  Schedule Details      Preview

                                  Name   Mon-Fri 8 Hour Days

                          Starting Date  Sunday, 01/01/2006

  Day        Category                           Duration

   1         Planned Hours                       0:00

   2         Planned Hours                       8:00

   3         Planned Hours                       8:00

   4         Planned Hours                       8:00

   5         Planned Hours                       8:00

   6         Planned Hours                       8:00

   7         Planned Hours                       0:00
```

Figure 10.5 Typical Monday through Friday, Eight-Hour Work Schedule

Payroll Time Sheet Objects

Payroll Time Sheet uses some objects that are specific to it alone:

▶ TIME TYPE GROUP
A TIME TYPE GROUP contains all of the Time Types that should be taken into account during time validation.

▶ TIME PAY TYPE
TIME PAY TYPE is an indicator that characterizes a TIME TYPE GROUP as relevant for payroll purposes.

▶ TIME RECORDING PROFILE
TIME RECORDING PROFILE is a listing of all recording time types that an employee will have access to on the time sheet. Figure 10.6 shows an example.

▶ TIME RECORDING ADMISSIBILITY
TIME RECORDING ADMISSIBILITY indicates how far in the past an employee can amend time sheets that have already been submitted.

▶ TIME VALUATIONS
TIME VALUATIONS are used to calculate working time and to transfer the results, in the form of hours, to payroll. Time account deductions are taken into account.

▶ EMPLOYEE TIME VALUATION RESULT (ETVR)

EMPLOYEE TIME VALUATION RESULT (ETVR) is a single, calculated time evaluation based on the sums of all TIME PAY TYPES. This value is sent to payroll for processing.

Time Recording Profile: Overtime Recording weekly (OT_WEEK_CALC)

* External Name	Overtime Recording weekly
* Time Recording Method	Overtime
Workflow Configuration	Time Sheet Approval (TimeSheet)
* External Code	OT_WEEK_CALC

Time Valuation

Split Weekly Overtime for Overtime recorder (OT_WEEK_OT_CALC_SPLIT) 📄

Calc Overtime weekly salaried (Calc overt weekly salaried) 📄

Figure 10.6 Time Recording Profile for Weekly Overtime Recording

Time Off Objects

Like Payroll Time Sheet, Time Off has its own object: the TIME TYPE PROFILE.

A TIME TYPE PROFILE is a determined collection of Time Types assigned to employees based on their location, type, and employment classification. If all of the salaried, full-time employees in Canada receive the same time off allotments for VACATION, SICK TIME, and TRAINING DAYS, then it would make sense to have a set time profile to assign to all of those employees that gives them all those allotments. Figure 10.7 shows an example of a configured TIME TYPE PROFILE.

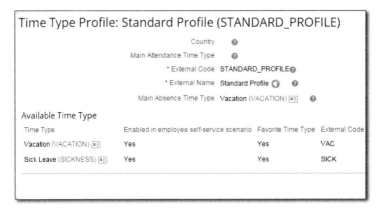

Figure 10.7 Time Profile for Standard Absences and Time Off

346

10.1.2 Profiles

TIME PROFILE, HOLIDAY CALENDAR, WORK SCHEDULE, and TIME RECORDING PROFILE are the four fields in an employee's JOB INFORMATION portlet that make up the Time Management profile. They are found in the TIME INFORMATION section in the JOB INFORMATION portlet of an employee, seen in Figure 10.8.

▼ Time Information	
Holiday Calendar	US Holidays (HOLIDAY_US)
Work Schedule	Mon-Fri 8 Hour Days (5DAY8HOUR) More
Time Profile	Standard Profile (STANDARD_PROFILE)
Time Recording Profile	Positive - Daily Overtime & Weekly Split (POS_DAY_WEEK_OT)
Time Recording Admissibility	6W (6 Weeks)

Figure 10.8 Time Information Section of Job Information

Now, let's look at the Payroll Time Sheet feature.

10.2 Payroll Time Sheet

The Payroll Time Sheet feature allows employees to enter their time for payroll purposes. The timesheet is structured in a weekly format. Numerous time entries can be made, cost center assigned, and an approval process put in place for weekly submission. As entries are made, employees can view their recorded time and the time valuation results immediately, including overtime amounts. Once entries are approved, they are consolidated into one time result that can be sent to payroll if required. The Payroll Time Sheet has two distinct use cases:

▸ **Positive time recording**
With *positive time recording*, all worked time is recorded by each (hourly) employee in the Payroll Time Sheet. The system takes those entries and compares them to the employee's planned work time to help determine base pay, any overtime, or any holiday pay.

▸ **Overtime recording**
Overtime recording involves a (salaried) employee entering hours worked beyond the typical work schedule into the Payroll Time Sheet. Overtime hours are then tallied and alternate business rules can be applied to help determine whether premium overtime with augmented pay rates is applicable.

Both scenarios support the recording of allowances and on-call duty.

Although the type of recording may vary based on business practices and setup, the structure of the time sheet remains the same. In this section, we will look at the composition of the time sheet.

10.2.1 Composition

The Payroll Time Sheet is composed of four key areas that allow for the entry and monitoring of hours:

▶ DATA ENTRY
The DATA ENTRY area is the main entry point for data. A series of columns represent each day of the week. The selected day is highlighted in blue and is ready for input. Make entries here using the input fields.

▶ WEEKLY SUMMARY
WEEKLY SUMMARY is to the right of the weekly calendar and displays the current week, month, and year. Also displayed is a total of recorded hours and the breakout of time valuation results for the week shown. The status of the time sheet is also displayed. Options for status include the following:

  ▸ TO BE SUBMITTED

  ▸ TO BE APPROVED

  ▸ APPROVED

  ▸ DRAFT AMENDMENT (for changes after approval)

  ▸ AMENDMENT TO BE APPROVED (changes submitted for reapproval)

  ▸ CANCELLED

If on-call entries or allowances are recorded, an indicator will be shown here as well.

▶ DETAILS
The DETAILS area is directly below the DATA ENTRY area. It can be expanded and collapsed to save space. In this area, you will see the amount of time entered in the DATA ENTRY area assigned to the default time type. Using the additional rows and columns in the DETAILS area, a user can add additional time worked, view requested time off, and break out and assign initial time worked to different time types as needed. Different cost centers can also be used to distribute worked hours. On-call time and allowances are recorded here as well.

▶ TIME SHEET BUTTONS
The final area of the Payroll Time Sheet contains the TIME SHEET BUTTONS, which are used to confirm and save data entries, save as a draft, or cancel and wipe out partially entered values.

Figure 10.9 shows an example Payroll Time Sheet, including the DATA ENTRY and WEEKLY SUMMARY areas.

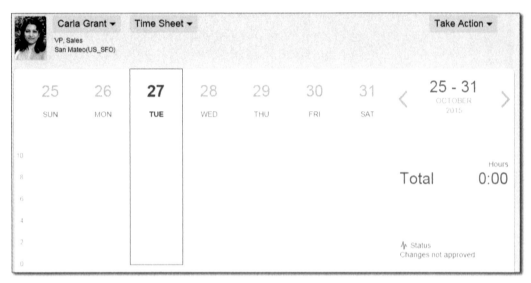

Figure 10.9 Payroll Time Sheet Showing the Data Entry Area and Weekly Summary

Now that you are familiar with the different areas on Payroll Time Sheet, let's move on to steps for setup.

10.2.2 Setup

Configuring the Payroll Time Sheet is a multistep process. Once the feature has been enabled in Provisioning, the remaining setup steps can be completed within Employee Central itself by accessing OneAdmin.

Configuration Steps

For more information on enabling Payroll Time Sheet in Provisioning as well as the other configuration steps covered in this section, refer to the *Payroll Time Sheet* implementation guide found at *http://help.sap.com/hr_ec* under the IMPLEMENTATION GUIDES heading.

Any user that has been permissioned can perform these tasks. Ideally, most of them will be completed during initial implementation, and customers will only need to maintain preexisting entries.

The following three tasks fall into the initial setup category:

1. Turn on the Payroll Time Sheet view by selecting the SHOW checkbox next to TIME SHEET in OneAdmin via EMPLOYEE FILES • CONFIGURE EMPLOYEE FILES.

2. Set the appropriate permissions for employees, managers, and HR administrators who need access to the TIME SHEET view and/or need to maintain the TIME OFF fields in the JOB INFORMATION portlet.

3. Set up an approval workflow for the Time Sheet submission, as covered in Chapter 4.

The remaining configuration tasks involve setting up the appropriate Time Types, Time Profiles, and other time-related objects. These are created in OneAdmin in EMPLOYEE FILES • MANAGE DATA. The following list contains the remaining setup tasks in the order in which they should be handled:

1. Create Time Types for attendance and overtime recording as well as on-call scenarios and allowances.

2. Attach the Time Types to Time Profiles. These profiles may already be in existence from your Time Off setup activities.

3. Define the Time Type Groups and Time Valuations.

4. Define the Time Recording Profiles.

5. Define the Time Recording Admissibility Rules.

Once these steps have been completed, a TIME RECORDING PROFILE and a TIME RECORD ADMISSIBILITY RULE need to be assigned to employees that will maintain time in Payroll Time Sheet. These are assigned in the Job Information portlet, which you saw in Section 10.1.2.

Once you've completed the setup, employees and managers can begin to use Payroll Time Sheet. In the next section, we'll discuss how this is done.

10.2.3 Using Payroll Time Sheet

Two main user groups use Payroll Time Sheet: employees and managers. Each user group has a different experience, which plays a different part in the overall time entry and approval process. We will look at both of these user groups in this section.

Employees

The process begins with employees. Employees are the primary users of the Time Sheet feature, as they must enter in their day-to-day regular worked time or overtime as applicable. Figure 10.10 shows a complete Time Sheet view for an employee who enters in overtime only. Notice that the WEEKLY SUMMARY shows an assumed forty hours of regular worked time. The time sheet entries are picked up as overtime beyond the initial forty hours.

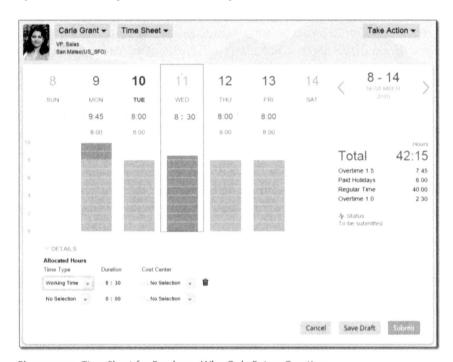

Figure 10.10 Time Sheet for Employee Who Only Enters Overtime

Employees should enter time in DATA ENTRY and refine entries in the DETAILS area. As entries are made, the recorded values and time valuation results are updated in the WEEKLY SUMMARY. Entries can be saved in draft mode and edited over the course of the week.

While this is taking place, the time sheet is in the TO BE SUBMITTED status. When an employee has completed his or her time sheet, he or she can click the SUBMIT button to save the time sheet and send it for workflow approval by a manager. The time sheet is now in the SUBMITTED status. The employee will receive an email notice when the time sheet is approved. This final step moves the time sheet to the APPROVED status once the time sheet is approved.

Depending on system configuration options, if an error was made or an addition needs to be inserted after the time sheet has been submitted, the employee can make adjustments. These times of changes and additions are known as *retroactive changes*.

If the time sheet has not yet been approved, then the employee can return to the time sheet and click the WITHDRAW button. This sets the time sheet back to the TO BE SUBMITTED status and allows for updates and corrections. The time sheet can then be resubmitted in the same way in which it was originally submitted.

If the time sheet has already been approved, then the employee must return to the time sheet and click the MAKE AMENDMENT button. This sets the time sheet to the DRAFT AMENDMENT status and allows for adjustments and resubmission. The originally approved workflow would remain intact, and a second draft amendment time sheet is started. When the second time sheet is submitted to a manager for approval, the manager can compare the two time sheets. If the manager decides to approve the amended version, then the initially approved time sheet is set to the CANCELED status.

Managers

Managers have the responsibility to approve time sheets. Once a time sheet has been submitted for review, a pending task will display in the manager's TO DO portlet as in workflows. The workflow can be selected to access the time sheet directly for review. The time sheet workflow, shown in Figure 10.11, resembles and functions like all other Employee Central workflows. The data to be approved is displayed in the middle, and the approver has the option to APPROVE or DECLINE, or make comments and POST them to the workflow.

If a manager has to approve an amended time sheet that was previously approved, he or she can compare the two time sheets and choose to either keep the initially approved version or approve the amended version.

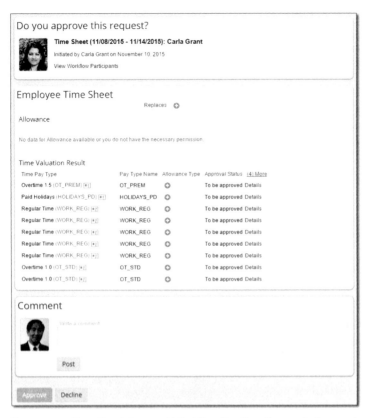

Figure 10.11 Time Sheet Approval Workflow Pending Manager's Approval

Submitting for Others

Depending on permissions, managers and HR administrators may have the ability to submit time sheets on behalf of their team members. In such a case, the manager can submit the time sheet by going directly to the employee's time sheet and entering in the correct values. If the manager is also the time sheet approver, then the approval step is bypassed.

Additional Resources

For more information on Payroll Time Sheet—including setup, configuration, and usage—refer to the *Payroll Time Sheet* implementation guide found at *http://help.sap.com/hr_ec* under the IMPLEMENTATION GUIDES heading.

Moving on, in the next section we'll look at the Time Off feature.

10.3 Time Off

The Time Off feature provides a direct means for monitoring employee absences from the work environment. This functionality includes a means for reporting absences, an integrated workflow approval process, and a method for keeping track of allotted leave time. These attributes provide different benefits to the three major user groups who utilize Time Off: employees, managers, and HR administrators.

On the employee side, employees can enter their own requests for time off and monitor their leave balances. Managers can view a Team Absence Calendar to ensure proper staffing prior to approving leave request workflows. HR administrators can review, maintain, and manually amend leave awards and balances.

In this section, we will look Time Off setup, features, using Leave of Absence, and user groups.

10.3.1 Setup

Prior to working with Time Off, you must enable its functionality. First, Time Off must be enabled in Provisioning. Then, follow these steps in order to enable Time Off:

1. Log in to Provisioning and navigate to the appropriate company instance. Open up COMPANY SETTINGS and check the boxes for ENABLE TIME OFF and ENABLE GENERIC OBJECTS. Save your changes.

2. Verify that your Succession Data Model contains the following three supporting fields under JOB INFORMATION:
   ▸ HOLIDAY CALENDAR (`holiday-calendar-code`)
   ▸ WORK SCHEDULE (`workschedule-code`)
   ▸ TIME PROFILE (`time-type-profile-code`)

3. Verify that your Succession Data Model contains the following HRIS tabs:
   ▸ TIME OFF (`tab-element id="timeOffTab"`)
   ▸ MANAGE TIME OFF (`tab-element id="timeOffAdminTab"`)

The remaining setup steps can be completed within Employee Central itself by accessing key areas of OneAdmin. Any user that has been permissioned can perform these tasks. Ideally, most of them will be completed during initial implementation and customers will only need to maintain already existing entries.

The following three tasks fall into the initial setup category:

1. Turn on the TIME OFF and MANAGE TIME OFF views by checking the SHOW checkboxes next to TIME OFF and MANAGE TIME OFF in OneAdmin via EMPLOYEE FILES • CONFIGURE EMPLOYEE FILES.

2. Set appropriate RBPs for employees, managers, and HR administrators who need access to the TIME OFF view, MANAGE TIME OFF view, and/or to maintain the TIME OFF fields in JOB INFORMATION.

3. Set up an approval workflow for Time Off request submission and approval, as covered in Chapter 4.

The remaining configuration tasks involve setting up the appropriate Time Types, Time Profiles, and other time-related objects. These are created in OneAdmin in EMPLOYEE FILES • MANAGE TIME OFF STRUCTURES.

Using Objects

In Section 10.1, we reviewed several key objects that are used in Time Off. They come together like a perfect puzzle to provide the foundation for recording leaves and absences. These data entries can be made in OneAdmin via EMPLOYEE FILES • MANAGE TIME STRUCTURES by using the CREATE NEW dropdown and selecting the appropriate object. Now, let's look at how to create and use these objects in a Time Off context.

Time Type

Time Types are the cornerstone of Time Off. A time type must be created for each absence or leave that will be taken. When creating the Time Type, be sure to include characteristics that help define it, including the following:

▶ Whether time will be recorded in hours or in full or partial days.

▶ If a workflow should be triggered when this type of absence is requested.

▶ If a Time Account Type is relevant for this particular time type. In order to make that assignment, you must have Time Account Types defined.

Time Account Types

Create Time Account Types as needed to support any Time Types kept in an account or with a balance. Vacation and Sick Days are two examples of Time Types that usually require a Time Account Type. When setting up Time Account types, be sure to indicate the following:

- The unit of measure or tracking as days or hours; this value must align with the value defined for the Time Type.
- If the Time Account Type is marked as permanent or recurring.
- A start date for when the days or hours should start accruing; common choices include Hire Date and the first of the year.

Once you have created the Time Account Types, be sure to assign them to the Time Type that you created earlier.

Time Profile

With the catalog of Time Types defined, you can combine them together into commonly assigned groupings that are called *Time Profiles*. You can create as many different Time Profiles you need to support different scenarios of time off eligibility. It's normal to have multiple Time Profiles for various locations, because employee composition and leave strategies can vary from location to location. An employee can only have one Time Profile assigned.

When defining Time Profiles, we have the ability to indicate up to three favorite (or most commonly used) Time Types. These time types will display as quick select buttons for employees when using the Time Off view to request time off (shown in Figure 10.12 in the Section "Leave of Absence"). You also can indicate whether a particular Time Type can be maintained by employees via self-services or if it should be tracked and maintained by HR administrators only.

Holiday Calendar

A Holiday Calendar must be defined for each country so that the system will know which days are nonworking days. The first step when creating a Holiday Calendar is to create a series of holidays. Holidays can be applied globally and across multiple years, so each instance only needs to be created once and can then be reused. They can also be full or half days. For example, December 25 is a holiday every year on the same date for all locations that celebrate Christmas. This holiday can be created and used for multiple countries and years.

The second step when creating a Holiday Calendar is to assign holidays to the calendar definition. In the Holiday Calendar, a year must be assigned to the generic holiday date. An employee can only be assigned one Holiday Calendar.

Work Schedule

Various combinations of Work Schedules must be created to support Time Off. The system needs to know when an employee is expected to work so that it can properly deduct leaves and absences from Time Accounts. Work Schedules can be used globally or defined locally depending on business requirements. Here are the steps for determining and setting up Work Schedules:

1. Identify different work patterns or schedules that your employees are assigned to. Each scenario should have its own Work Schedule.

2. Determine how many days are in each patterns before the pattern repeats. This is typically seven days (one week), but some common alternative schedules involve five, fourteen, or twenty-eight days.

3. Of your pattern days, identify which are work on days and which are work off days. Record the work off days as zero hours in the Work Schedule.

4. For the work on days, enter the number of planned hours per day.

5. Set a start date so that the system knows when to start the pattern.

An employee can only have one Work Schedule assigned.

> **Tip**
>
> When configuring a Work Schedule, the numbers represent the days of the week, with 1 representing the day of the week on which the date defined in the STARTDATE field starts. For example, if the date entered in the STARTDATE field is 4 January 2016, then day 1 would be a Monday, day 2 would be a Tuesday, and so on. However, if the date

entered in the STARTDATE field is 1 January 2016 then day 1 would be a Friday, day 2 would be a Saturday, and so on.

Assigning Time Values to Employees

The next step to set up Time Off is to assign a Time Profile, Holiday Calendar, and Work Schedule to each employee who will use Time Off.

When hiring a new employee, rules can be created to default values based on employee type, class, job, location, or any other attribute, should business requirements permit.

For existing employees who may start to use Time Off for the first time, these values can be assigned in one of the following ways:

▶ Use TAKE ACTION • CHANGE JOB AND COMPENSATION INFO for each employee (employee actions are covered in Chapter 9).

▶ Use mass changes to assign values across groups of employees (mass changes are covered in Chapter 13).

▶ Perform a data import (data imports are covered in Chapter 7).

With the initial setup now complete, let's move onto the features and functions of Time Off.

10.3.2 Features and Functions

In Time Off, you can use a number of different features, such as calendars, accruals, period-end processing, and leave of absence. We'll look at each of these functions within this section.

Calendars

Calendars are used in Time Off to process mass jobs or changes in Time Accounts. This allows for processes such as accruals to run on their own. Calendars are typically used to automate the following:

▶ Process accruals

▶ Period-end processing

▶ Creation of accounts

▶ Interim Time Account updates

Calendars can be scheduled to run automatically through a scheduled job. They can be scheduled to reoccur automatically based on a given time and can be scheduled in the future. Calendars can also be manually processed or run.

Period-End Processing

Period-end processing is the term given to activities that take place at the end of the year for time accounts. It is called "period-end" processing and not "year-end" processing because this same concept can be applied to time accounts whose ends correspond to a fiscal year or to an employee's anniversary of hire date. Period-end processing finalizes recurring time accounts.

There are three main options for period-end processing:

▶ The Time Account balance is zeroed out and is no longer available for use.

▶ The Time Account balance rolls forward into the new Time Account and is therefore not lost, but rather applied in addition to the new Time Account.

▶ A portion of the Time Account balance is carried forward into the new Time Account balance. Any balance beyond this carryover amount is lost and not available for use.

Accruals

Accruals are regular additions of time to a Time Account. Keeping with the previous analogy of a Time Account being like a bank, accruals are similar to regular fixed-amount deposits. An *accrual rule* is used to determine how much time should be posted to the Time Account and when it should be posted. Once the time is posted, it can be used by an employee.

Accrual rules are configured in the Rules Engine. An accrual rule should contain the following parameters:

▶ AMOUNT POSTED
The amount of unit time to be added to the Time Account.

▶ EXTERNAL CODE
A unique code will be generated automatically by selecting GENERATE EXTERNAL CODE FOR TIME OFF().

▶ POSTING DATE
The posting date, typically set to accruable start date (accrualRuleParameters, Accruable Start Date).

- ▶ POSTING TYPE
  Always set to ACCRUAL.

- ▶ POSTING UNIT
  This value must match the unit type found on the Time Account, so enter "TimeAccountType.Unit".

> **Additional Resources**
>
> More information about accruals can be found in the *Time Off* implementation guide located at *http://help.sap.com/ec_hr* under the IMPLEMENTATION GUIDES heading.

Leave of Absence

A leave of absence is a period of time during which an employee is away from work but is still considered an employee. These absences are usually related to personal life events. Leaves of absence can be managed in Time Off like other types of Time Off. Time Off can also keep track of how much leave a person is permitted and how much has been requested or taken.

There are two events for leave of absence, one for taking the leave of absence (Leave of Absence) and one for returning from a leave of absence (Return to Work). Any number of Event Reasons can be defined for the Leave of Absence event, but at least one Event Reason must be defined for each event.

When defining an Event Reason for a Leave of Absence event, an employee's status can be set to PAID LEAVE or UNPAID LEAVE. Depending on system integrations, these individual statuses can feed payroll or benefit solutions and indicate if an employee's pay should continue during the leave time period or whether the employee can accrue benefits.

For a Return to Work event, the EMPLOYEE STATUS of an Event Reason should be set to ACTIVE. Figure 10.12 shows a typical Event Reason for a Leave of Absence event.

Because leaves of absence can vary by country, you have the option of using country-specific Event Reasons. Some consideration should be given to that approach for companies looking to apply a global template. An alternate solution is to create just one pair of generic Leave of Absence/Return to Work Event Reasons and create numerous Time Types that can be broken out at the country or location level.

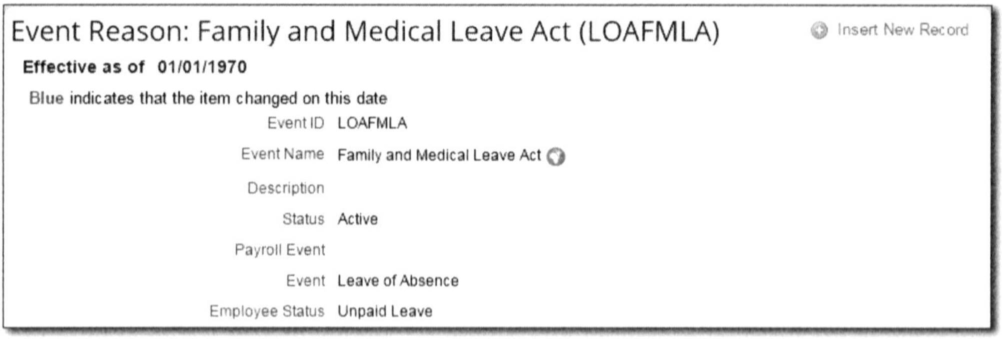

Event Reason: Family and Medical Leave Act (LOAFMLA)   ⊕ Insert New Record

Effective as of 01/01/1970

Blue indicates that the item changed on this date

Event ID LOAFMLA

Event Name Family and Medical Leave Act 🔵

Description

Status Active

Payroll Event

Event Leave of Absence

Employee Status Unpaid Leave

Figure 10.12 Basic Leave of Absence Event Reason

The next step in the setup process is to assign your Event Reasons to Time Types. Each Event Reason that was created needs to have a Time Type defined for it. Assign both a Leave of Absence Event Reason and a Return to Work Event Reason to each Time Type in the respective fields. Figure 10.13 shows an example of a completed TIME TYPE for a Leave of Absence event.

Time Type: Long-Term Family Leave (JPN_LTF)

* External Name Long-Term Family Leave 🔵   ❔

* Unit Day(s)❔

Country Japan (JPN) [▪]   ❔

Classification Absence❔

Workflow Configuration PTO_REQ_ADMIN (PTO_REQ_ADMIN)❔

Permitted Fractions For Unit Day Only full day bookings al...❔

Permitted Fractions For Unit Hour No Selection❔

Leave of Absence Event Reason (Plan) Family Leave Birth/Adoption (LOAFAMLY)❔

Leave of Absence Event Reason (Return To Work) Return From Leave (RETLEAVE)❔

Calculation Based On Calendar Days❔

Activate Cancellation Workflow No❔

Admin Workflow Configuration ❔

Flexible Requesting Allowed No❔

Counting Method ❔

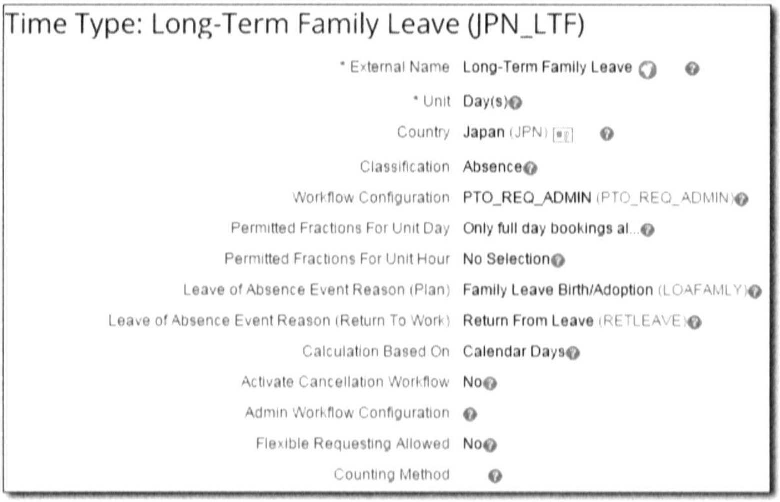

Figure 10.13 Time Type with Completed Event Reasons

Unlike other Time Types that you may define for Time Off, Leave of Absence Time Types can only be requested in full day bookings, and calculations must be based on calendar days. The next setup step is to incorporate the new Time Types into your existing Time Profiles.

10.3.3 User Groups

When we discuss putting Time Off into practice and using its functionality, we must remember that there are typically three groups of users that use Time Off: employees, managers, and administrators. Each group has a separate experience with Time Off. We'll look at each of these user groups within this section.

Time Off for Employees

Employees typically make up the largest population of users for Time Off. They use Time Off functionality for three main tasks:

- Manage Time Off requests
- Access the Team Absence Calendar
- View Time Off account details

Giving employees the ability to submit time off requests and view the team calendar helps place the focus on the employee and takes some burden off managers and HR administrators, who may have previously managed such tasks. Time Off plays a large role in offering a complete self-service solution for employees.

An employee manages time off requests, views details, and views the team absence calendar all in the same place. Employees access this area by navigating to MY EMPLOYEE FILES and then choosing TIME OFF in the menu. An alternative means of accessing Time Off is to select TIME OFF from the MY INFORMATION QUICK LINKS on the homepage. Regardless of the navigation path, the Time Off page (seen in Figure 10.14) is the same.

The main view contains a three-month calendar showing planned and/or taken time off for the different Time Types. The calendar displays planned working time in white and nonworking time in gray. Holidays from the Holiday Calendar that is assigned to the employee are also shown in gray, although these days contain an asterisk. Hovering over a holiday shows a popup that specifies what the holiday is (e.g., New Year's Day). Above the calendars are up to four buttons showing the available leave types, which are Time Types. Three can be set as favorites, and the fourth contains any other types of leave for which the employee is eligible. The planned and taken leave displayed on the calendar are color-coordinated with these buttons.

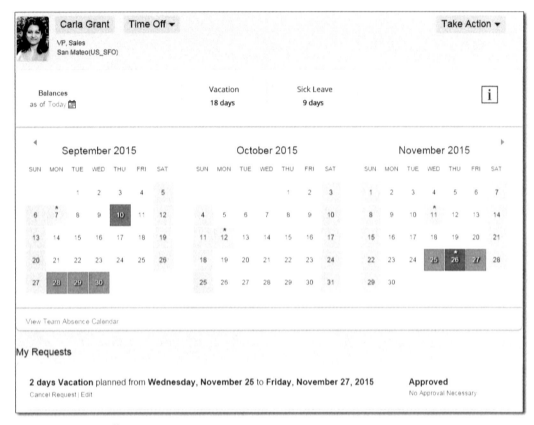

Figure 10.14 Time Off Page

Managing Time Off Requests

Within the Time Off solution, employees have the ability to request time off, edit existing time off requests, and cancel time off requests. This empowers employees to be key stakeholders in communicating their time away from work.

Employees request time off by first selecting the leave type button that corresponds to the type of leave they wish to take. The mouse cursor then changes to a paintbrush and employees can highlight the calendar day(s) for which they wish to request leave. At the same time, the LEAVE REQUEST form opens below the calendars, and the leave type and dates are populated in a draft form based on the calendar selection. Planned leave days display on the calendar in a striped format, whereas approved leaves have a solid format. The system also displays any over-lapping requests with other team members in a TEAM ABSENCES view that appears while planning (see Figure 10.15).

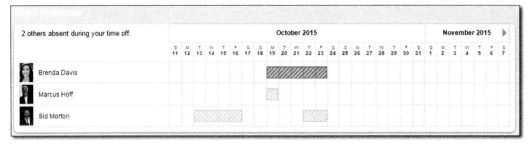

Figure 10.15 Team Absences View Showing Overlapping Leave Requests

When the employee is ready to submit the request, he or she clicks the SUBMIT button at the bottom of the request form to initiate the workflow approval pro-cess. The Time Off request process is shown in Figure 10.16.

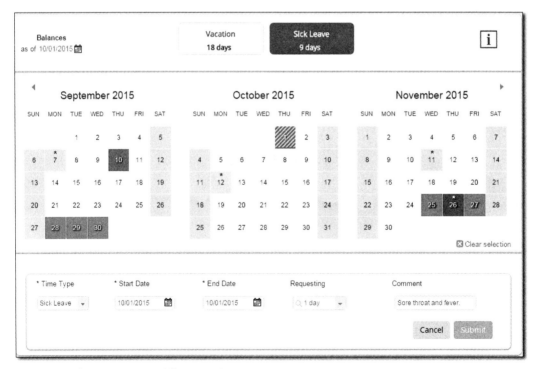

Figure 10.16 Time Off Request Process

Employees can view, edit, and cancel existing Time Off requests in the My Requests section just below the calendar display. This section lists all of the current and approved requests, their approval statuses, and links to cancel and edit a request. Figure 10.17 shows the My Requests section and the Cancel Request and Edit links.

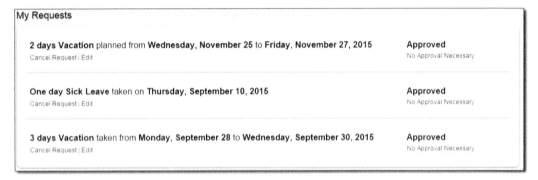

Figure 10.17 My Requests

If an employee chooses to cancel a request, he or she may do so by clicking the Cancel Request link. A window (see Figure 10.18) pops up asking the employee to confirm his or her choice.

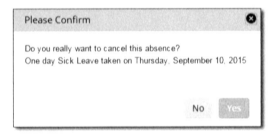

Figure 10.18 Cancel Request Confirmation Popup Window

To edit a request, an employee clicks the Edit link and the leave request opens for modifications. There is also a link to cancel the request from this view.

Accessing the Team Absence Calendar

Employees can access the Team Absence Calendar by clicking on the View Team Absence Calendar link located just below the Calendar view. This pops open a team calendar (seen in Figure 10.19), showing each team member's absences stacked on top of each other. The calendar is especially helpful for managers and considerate employees who are trying to ensure adequate staffing at all times.

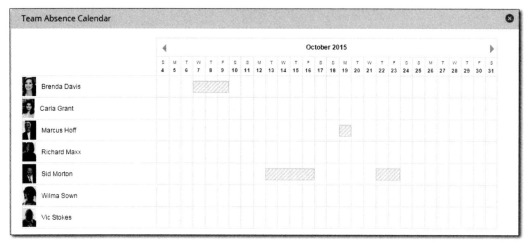

Figure 10.19 Team Absence Calendar

Viewing Time Off Account Details

Employees can view the account details of each Time Account by clicking on the giant "i" INFORMATION icon found in the top-right corner of the TIME OFF page. Doing so opens the TIME ACCOUNT SNAPSHOT window. Here, employees can view information about each Time Account that they have assigned in their Time Profile and how many days of each leave type are in the following categories:

► EARNED

► TAKEN

► PLANNED

► BALANCE

Figure 10.20 shows the TIME ACCOUNT SNAPSHOT window.

Any submitted time off requests or edits to existing requests can be routed through a workflow process and require approval from someone such as a manager. Managers play a vital role in Time Off because they are responsible for approving leaves in a manner that still leaves them and their teams with enough resources on a given day to be successful.

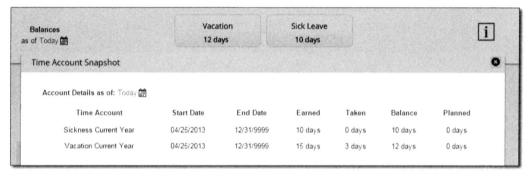

Figure 10.20 Time Account Snapshot

Time Off for Managers

Managers make up the second largest population of users for Time Off. They use Time Off functionality for two main tasks:

▸ Approving Time Off requests
▸ Accessing the Team Absence Calendar

Let's look at each of these activities.

Approving Time Off Requests

Managers can process Time Off-related workflows in the same manner in which all Employee Central workflows are processed. The workflow appears in the manager's To Do portlet on the homepage. When the manager clicks on the workflow link, he or she is taken to the workflow request. Figure 10.21 shows an example.

Here, the manager can review the request and choose to approve or reject it in the same way that he or she would approve or reject a standard workflow. Prior to taking one of these actions, the manager can also post comments for discussion, just as with a standard workflow.

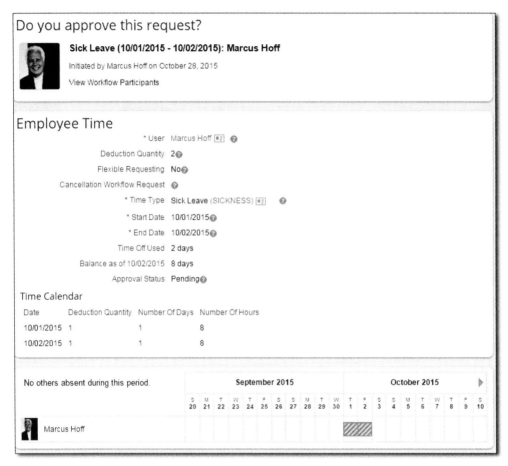

Figure 10.21 Manager Workflow Approval Screen for Time Off Request

Accessing the Team Absence Calendar

Managers can easily view their Team Absence Calendars by selecting the Show Team Absences dropdown under the My Team tile on the homepage, as shown in Figure 10.22. This opens a grid view of absences for their direct and indirect reports for the current period. Managers can scroll forward and backward to view different points in time.

Figure 10.22 My Team Tile with Option to View Team Absences

Time Off for HR Administrators

The last user group in Time Off is the HR administrator group. These individuals need oversight and control over employee time accounts and leaves. They also need the ability to intervene in the time off process by creating and editing time off requests on behalf of employees. An HR administrator's key tasks on the front end of Time Off are as follows:

- Monitor Time Off data for employees
- Submit Time Off requests on behalf of employees
- Manually adjust Time Account balances

> **HR Administrator Tasks**
>
> HR administrators engage in several other tasks behind the scenes for Time Off. Some of these tasks include creating accruals, changing work schedules, and assigning Time Off for new employees. More information about these tasks can be found in the *Time Off* implementation guide located at *http://help.sap.com/ec_hr* under the IMPLEMENTATION GUIDES heading.

HR administrators can monitor Time Off data for a specific employee by navigating to the employee's Public Profile in Employee Files and choosing the MANAGE TIME OFF view from menu. The MANAGE TIME OFF page can be seen in Figure 10.23.

This page gives HR administrators all of the access needed to review current Time Accounts, manually request time off on behalf of an employee, and adjust existing Time Account postings instantly.

Figure 10.23 Manage Time Off

This completes our look at time and absences with Time Off. In the next section, we will look at the Global Benefits feature in Employee Central.

10.4 Global Benefits

The Global Benefits feature in Employee Central allows organizations to track, maintain, and award payment and non-pay awards beyond regular salary or wage compensation and to manage benefits, benefit plans, and benefit enrollments.

This feature is a vital tool in keeping track of the ever-growing list of government-mandated benefits companies must provide, as well as the supplemental perks that companies provide to retain employees. Common examples of benefits include a company car, food allowance, and health insurance.

The Global Benefits feature supports both global benefits and local benefits. It supports a number of countries and benefit types, and the lists of both grow with each release. For the latest information, refer to the *Global Benefits* implementation guide found at *http://help.sap.com/hr_ec* under the IMPLEMENTATION GUIDES heading.

The following terms should be reviewed prior to completing any requirements gathering or configuration for Global Benefits:

▶ **Benefit types**
A *benefit type* is the classification of benefit being awarded. Common examples include Reimbursement, Allowance, Pension, and Insurance.

▶ **Benefit programs**
A *benefit program* is a grouping together of one or more benefit types. When an employee is assigned a benefit program, he or she receives all of the benefit types contained within the program.

Now that we've explored some basic terminology and presented some foundational knowledge, for the remainder of this section we will look at the different types of Employee Central benefits, how to set up different types of benefits, and finally how to use Global Benefits for benefit enrollment and claims.

10.4.1 Types of Benefits

There are four main types of benefits currently supported in Employee Central:

▶ **Reimbursements and allowances**
For example, home Internet reimbursements and gym membership allowances

▶ **Pensions**
Contributions to a pension fund

▶ **Benefits-in-kind**
For example, use of a company car and company cellphone

▶ **Insurance**
For example, life insurance and long-term disability coverage

Companies can create their own benefits within these benefit groups or they can take advantage of pre-delivered benefit entities such as the following:

- Service Anniversary
- Birthday Voucher
- Marriage Voucher
- Child Birth Voucher
- Company Housing
- Company Car
- Fuel Reimbursement
- Leave Travel Allowance (India)

With each quarterly release, additional pre-delivered benefit types are released and made available to customers.

10.4.2 Setup

Global Benefits is built on the MDF, so the process of enabling and configuring this feature is similar to the process that we looked at for Payroll Time Sheet and Time Off. First, Global Benefits must be enabled in Provisioning.

The remaining setup steps can be completed within Employee Central itself by accessing key areas in OneAdmin. Any user that has been permissioned can perform these tasks. Ideally, most of these tasks will be completed during initial implementation, and customers will only need to maintain already existing entries.

The following three tasks fall into the initial setup category:

1. Turn on the Global Benefits view by checking the SHOW checkboxes next to Global Benefits in OneAdmin via EMPLOYEE FILES • CONFIGURE EMPLOYEE FILES.
2. Set appropriate RBPs for employees, managers, and HR administrators who may need access to the Global Benefits view.
3. Set up an approval workflow for benefit enrollment and submission.
4. Set up an approval workflow for time sheet submission, as covered in Chapter 4.

The remaining configuration tasks involve setting up the appropriate benefit types, benefit profiles, and other benefit-related objects. These are created in OneAdmin by navigating to Employee Files • Benefits Admin Overview. Create new entries by clicking on the Create New dropdown and selecting a benefit object.

The first entries that you should make in the Benefits Admin Overview screen are the benefit entries. Create all benefits that should be awarded here. Figure 10.24 shows an example of the benefit object for Tuition Reimbursement.

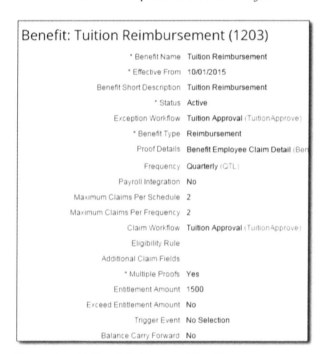

Figure 10.24 Tuition Reimbursement Benefit

Next, create all Allowances, Reimbursements, Pensions, and Insurances that may be needed. Once these items are created, they can be assigned to benefit programs. This process is very similar to the assignment of Time Types to Time Profiles.

10.4.3 Using Global Benefits

Employees can see and manage their benefits and enrollments using the EMPLOYEE OVERVIEW page shown in Figure 10.25. Access this screen from the Employee Files menu by selecting the EMPLOYEE BENEFITS option. This screen contains the following sections:

▶ CURRENT BENEFITS
Displays any benefits the employee is claiming and the available balance/amount.

▶ CLAIMS
Displays any claims made against any of the benefits, such as a dentist visit.

▶ ENROLLMENTS
Displays the benefit enrollments and benefit program enrollments that are available for the employee and those for which the employee has enrolled.

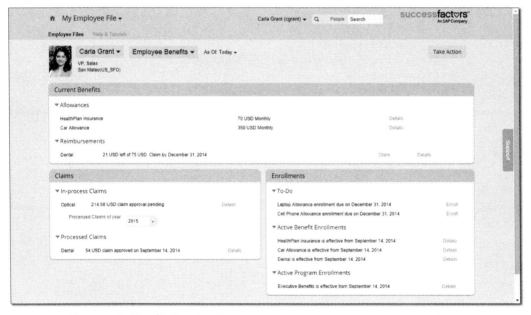

Figure 10.25 Benefits Overview Page

Employees who are eligible for benefits can perform two key functions in relation to those benefits:

- ▶ Benefits enrollment
- ▶ Benefits claims

Let's look at both of these.

Benefits Enrollment

The To-Do section in the Enrollments portlet displays which benefits and benefit programs are available for an employee for enrollment. To enroll in a benefit, the employee clicks on the Enroll link next to the benefit that he or she wishes to enroll for. To enroll in a benefits program, the employee clicks on the Enroll for Program link next to the benefits program that he or she wishes to enroll in. Both of these links are shown in Figure 10.26.

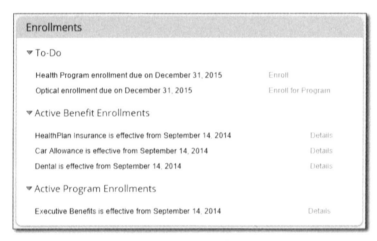

Figure 10.26 Enrollments Portlet Showing Different Enrollments Available

After clicking the Enroll or Enroll for Program button, the employee will be taken to a screen from which he or she can complete the enrollment. Figure 10.27 shows enrollment into a benefits program. Different benefits available under the program can be selected, and the employee can request an amount up to the eligible amount. Once the employee has entered the details for the enrollment, he or she clicks the Save button to save the enrollment. If configured, a workflow will trigger for a manager and/or HR administrator to approve the enrollment request.

Figure 10.27 Benefits Program Enrollment

Benefits Claim

The REIMBURSEMENTS section of the CURRENT BENEFITS portlet displays any claims that are available to the employee (see Figure 10.28). If the employee has a claim to make, then he or she can click on the CLAIM link and complete the CLAIM FORM (see Figure 10.29). An HR administrator or benefits coordinator typically approves claims, so workflows are typically configured to trigger once an employee submits a claim.

Figure 10.28 Current Benefits Portlet Showing Available Claims

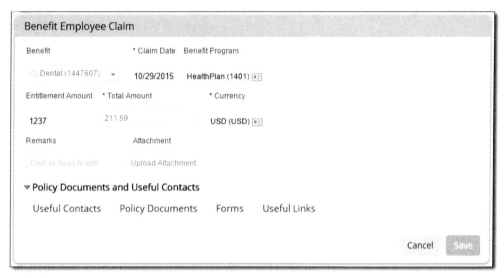

Figure 10.29 Benefits Claim Form

Any claims that are in process or have been processed can be seen in the CLAIMS portlet (see Figure 10.30).

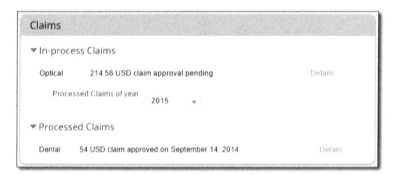

Figure 10.30 Claims Portlet

Additional Resources

For more information on Global Benefits—including setup, configuration, and usage— refer to the *Global Benefits* implementation guide found at *http://help.sap.com/hr_ec* under the IMPLEMENTATION GUIDES heading.

10.5 Summary

In this chapter, we examined the Employee Central functionality that covers Time Management and benefits: Payroll Time Sheet, Time Off, and Global Benefits. These features are optional additions that augment the overall Employee Central solution and allow for a more robust HRIS offering. By offering employees the ability to enter their time, book vacation, enter a leave of absence, and manage their benefits and enrollments, you provide a complete one-stop ESS shop within Employee Central.

We looked at how to set up each of these features, how to use them, and what capabilities they offer for each process. We also looked at high-level configuration steps that are common among each of the modules.

In the next chapter, we will learn about the Global Assignments feature and the management of global employees for both home and expatriate assignments.

In today's globalized world, sending employees on overseas assignments is becoming more common. Employee Central enables you to manage and track home and abroad assignments across companies with ease.

11 Global Assignments

Sending employees on an assignment to another company within the organization is a common activity for multinational and global organizations. HR and managers need to continue to manage these employees while away on assignment, as well as have the employees managed by their host companies.

The Global Assignments module in Employee Central enables employees to be sent on assignment to another company within the organization. It also enables both home and host HR professionals and managers to view either or both assignments, depending on the permissions setup.

In this chapter, we'll look at sending an employee on assignment, managing different assignments, employees returning from assignment, and how to setup the Global Assignments feature. We'll begin by discussing the steps necessary to set up a global assignment, and then we'll look at how to send an employee on assignment.

11.1 Setting Up Global Assignments

There are a number of areas to configure to setup the Global Assignments feature. Let's run through each of the steps.

Additional Resources

For more information on setting up and configuring the Global Assignments feature, refer to the *Global Assignments* implementation guide handbook found at *http://service.sap.com/ec-ondemand* under the IMPLEMENTION GUIDE heading.

11.1.1 Provisioning

Global Assignments must first be enabled in Provisioning. If you have Provisioning access, then you can enable the Global Assignments feature by selecting the ENABLE GLOBAL ASSIGNMENT MANAGEMENT option in COMPANY SETTINGS.

11.1.2 Picklist Values

Once enabled, there are a few actions that need to be taken before you can use the Global Assignments feature. First, check if your system has the required picklist values. When downloaded from OneAdmin, the picklist file should include values for Picklist ID `global_assignment_type` as well as the following events:

- ADD GLOBAL ASSIGNMENT
- END GLOBAL ASSIGNMENT
- AWAY ON GLOBAL ASSIGNMENT
- BACK FROM GLOBAL ASSIGNMENT
- OBSOLETE

The picklist file should also have two values in the `employee-status` picklist:

- DISCARDED
- DORMANT

11.1.3 Events and Event Reasons

Global Assignment uses specific events that may or may not be in your system. The following are picklist values for the *event* picklist:

- ADD GLOBAL ASSIGNMENT
- END GLOBAL ASSIGNMENT
- OBSOLETE
- AWAY ON GLOBAL ASSIGNMENT
- BACK FROM GLOBAL ASSIGNMENT

Even if the event values are in the system, you should also check if the Event Reasons needed are in the system. Typically, they follow a similar naming convention to the events. If they don't exist in the system, add them as per the *Global Assignments* implementation guide.

11.1.4 Global Assignments Configuration

The Global Assignment configuration is a record of the *Global Assignment Configuration* Generic Object. You can create or maintain this object in OneAdmin via Employee Files • Manage Data. The code of the Global Assignment Configuration record is always GACONFIG. There are several settings that you can make to define the behavior of the Global Assignment feature, all of which are shown in Figure 11.1.

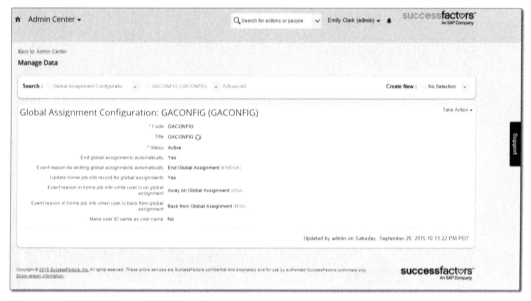

Figure 11.1 Global Assignment Configuration

Specifically, these settings enable the following:

▸ Automatic ending of global assignments and the Event Reason to use
▸ Whether the home employment should be updated when an employee goes on assignment and the Event Reason to use
▸ The Event Reason to use when an employee returns from assignment
▸ Whether to make the user ID the same as the username for the host employment

11.1.5 Role-Based Permissions

Global assignments have their own set of permissions located in the Employee Data category. This enables access to the Add Global Assignment Details and

381

MANAGE GLOBAL ASSIGNMENT DETAILS options in the TAKE ACTION menu, as well as the ability to edit the GLOBAL ASSIGNMENT DETAILS portlet directly and to permission individual fields within the portlet.

When choosing who to grant a role containing these permissions, there are four options available:

▸ HOME MANAGERS

▸ HOME HR MANAGERS

▸ HOST MANAGERS

▸ HOST HR MANAGERS

These roles enable permission to be granted to the direct reports of both home and host managers and HR managers assigned in Job Relationships. These options are shown in Figure 11.2.

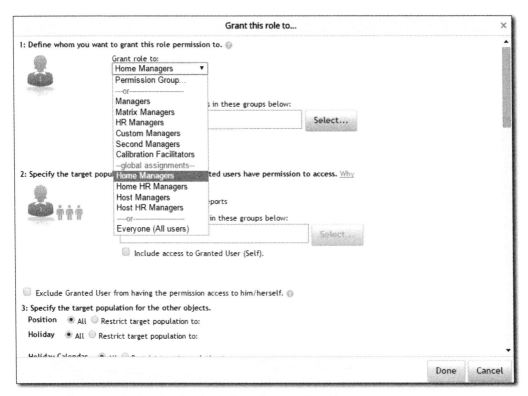

Figure 11.2 Options for Granting Roles to Home or Host Managers

11.1.6 Workflows, Alerts, and Notifications

Like other areas of Employee Central, workflows, alerts, and notifications can be used for global assignments. They are set up in a similar way as other modules. Workflows, alerts, and/or notifications can be triggered from the creation, editing, or ending of a global assignment. They can be triggered based on either the Global Assignment event or a specific Event Reason.

Now that we've reviewed the general setup of global assignments in Employee Central via the Global Assignments module, let's look at how to send an employee on an assignment.

11.2 Sending an Employee on a Global Assignment

When an employee is sent on assignment to another company, this is considered another employment in Employee Central. The Global Assignment employment is referred to as the *host employment*.

An employee is sent on global assignment by selecting the ADD GLOBAL ASSIGN-MENT DETAILS option in the TAKE ACTION menu in the PERSONAL INFORMATION or EMPLOYMENT INFORMATION screens in Employee Files or through the quickcard.

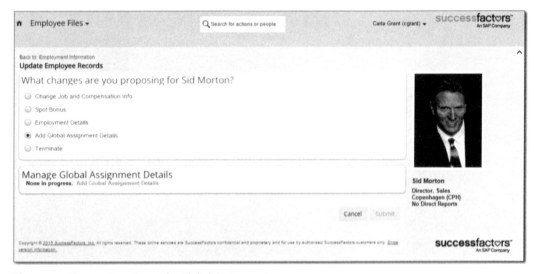

Figure 11.3 Transactions Screen for Global Assignment

> **Important!**
>
> An employee can only have one global assignment at any one time. An employee cannot have a global assignment and concurrent employment simultaneously.

You will be taken to the transaction screen. To begin the assignment process, click the ADD GLOBAL ASSIGNMENT DETAILS hyperlink, as shown in Figure 11.3.

You will see five fields in the MANAGE GLOBAL ASSIGNMENT DETAILS portlet (see Figure 11.4):

► EVENT REASON
The reason for the assignment.

► ASSIGNMENT TYPE
The type of assignment.

► START DATE
The start date of the assignment.

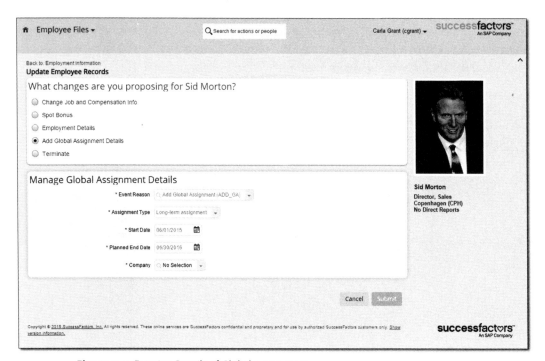

Figure 11.4 Entering Details of Global Assignment

▶ PLANNED END DATE

The planned end date of the assignment.

▶ COMPANY

The company to which the employee will be on assignment.

After selecting the company in the COMPANY field, you will see the following four portlets below the MANAGE GLOBAL ASSIGNMENT DETAILS portlet:

▶ JOB INFORMATION

▶ JOB RELATIONSHIPS

▶ WORK PERMIT INFO

▶ COMPENSATION INFORMATION (also includes fields from the SPOT BONUS portlet)

These four portlets are for the host employment and should be completed just as they are when an employee is hired into Employee Central. Figure 11.5 shows the JOB INFORMATION portlet being completed.

Figure 11.5 Completing Host Employment Details

Once the details of the host employment have been entered, click SUBMIT. If a workflow is used, then the request will be routed for approval; otherwise, it will become effective immediately.

The system can be configured so that the status of the home employment of an employee on global assignment can be set to DORMANT. This keeps the employment active as opposed to inactive.

When employees who are on global assignment log in to SAP SuccessFactors, they will see their global assignment listed under their names in the header panel next to a dropdown arrow. The arrow enables them to switch between assignments so that they can perform different processes for each assignment.

11.3 Managing Home and Expatriate Global Assignments

An employee's host assignment is accessed from his or her EMPLOYMENT INFORMATION screen. A button with the label of the home employment is displayed at the top of the screen and acts as a menu to toggle between the home and host employments. The home employment has a HOME icon next to it.

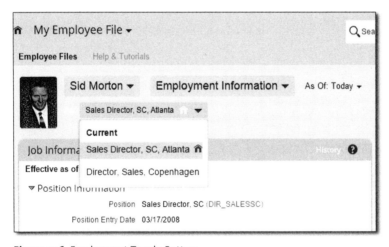

Figure 11.6 Employment Toggle Button

The menu is found just below the Employee Files menu, as shown in Figure 11.6. In this example, the employee's home employment—Sales Director, SC—and his host employment—Director, Sales, Copenhagen—are shown in the dropdown

menu. Selecting one of these employments will load the Employment Information screen for that employment. On this screen, actions can be performed for
the employee of that specific employment in the Take Action menu. On the
Employment Information screen, any action performed is for the employment
selected in the dropdown menu.

The employment toggle button will always remain visible if an employee is on
assignment, on assignment in the future, or has been on at least one global assignment in the past. In Figure 11.7, the dropdown for Sid Morton is shown after the
completion of the assignment shown in Figure 11.6.

Figure 11.7 Multiple Previous Global Assignments

The Employment Information screen for the host employment is the same as the
screen for a home employment. The only difference can be found in the Global
Assignment Details portlet, which replaces the Employment Details portlet. Figure 11.8 shows the Global Assignment Details portlet, along with other details
about the host employment.

This portlet shows details about the assignment that were entered during the creation of the assignment, such as Assignment Type, Start Date, Planned End Date,
and Company.

When the system is configured to end assignments automatically, the portlet also
displays the Actual End Date (for an active assignment, this is the same as the
value of the Planned End Date field; otherwise, it is the end date of the assign-

ment), the Event Reason for the end of the assignment (REASON FOR END), and the PAYROLL END DATE.

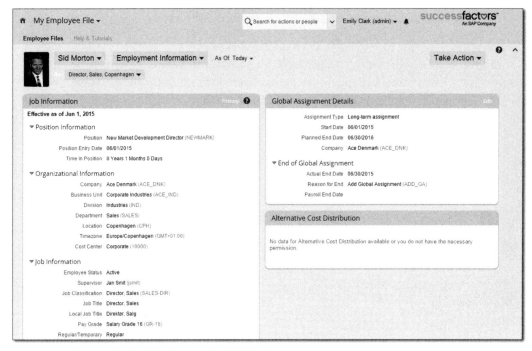

Figure 11.8 Host Employment for Sid Morton

To edit an active or past global assignment, click the TAKE ACTION button and then select the MANAGE GLOBAL ASSIGNMENT DETAILS option. This replaces the ADD GLOBAL ASSIGNMENT DETAILS option that is in the menu for an employee who is not on an active global assignment. Once on the transactions screen, the EDIT GLOBAL ASSIGNMENT DETAILS radio button should be preselected, as shown in Figure 11.9, but if not, select it. Now, you can edit details of the global assignment. Once your edits are complete, click SUBMIT. If a workflow is configured, it will be triggered at this point.

Details about the employment itself (e.g., a change of manager or change of employee class) can be edited using the CHANGE JOB AND COMPENSATION INFO in the TAKE ACTION menu, so long as you are on the EMPLOYMENT INFORMATION screen for the assignment that you wish to change.

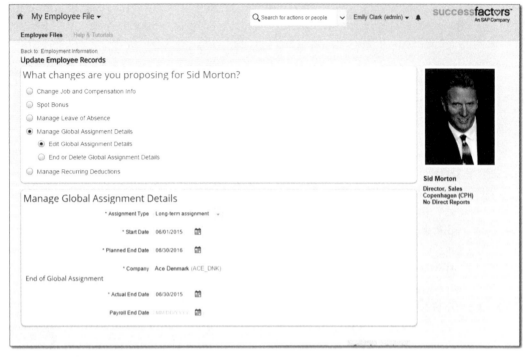

Figure 11.9 Editing an Assignment

Administrators who look at the user directory file will see a user account for the employee as well as a user account for each global assignment. User accounts for active global assignments are active, whereas user accounts for past assignments are inactive.

11.4 Ending a Global Assignment

There are two ways a global assignment can end:

▶ Automatically by the system, based on the planned end date defined during the creation of the assignment

▶ Manually

If configured, global assignments can be automatically ended in the system. This means that when the date is reached that is defined in the PLANNED END DATE field, the assignment ends. Set up this option during the creation of a global assignment by creating a future-dated Job Information record that ends the global assignment. Whenever someone edits the PLANNED END DATE field of a global assignment, the record is updated with this new date.

> **Alerts and Notifications**
>
> Alerts and notifications can be set up to alert certain employees about the expiration of global assignments. We cover these settings in Section 11.1.

To manually end a global assignment, navigate to the EMPLOYMENT INFORMATION screen of the host employment, click the TAKE ACTION button, and then select the MANAGE GLOBAL ASSIGNMENT DETAILS option. On the transactions screen, select the END OR DELETE GLOBAL ASSIGNMENT DETAILS radio button. Here, you can either end or delete the global assignment. When ending the global assignment, you can enter the ACTUAL END DATE, select an EVENT REASON, and then enter the PAYROLL END DATE before finishing (see Figure 11.10).

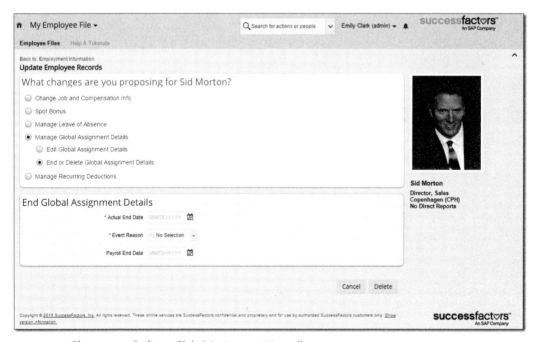

Figure 11.10 Ending a Global Assignment Manually

When deleting an assignment, simply click the DELETE button.

11.5   Using SAP SuccessFactors while on Global Assignment

Users who wish to use SAP SuccessFactors when on global assignment should continue to log in as they did before they went on assignment. Once on global assignment, a user will see a hyperlink below his or her name to access other assignments. This is similar to the button shown on the EMPLOYMENT INFORMATION screen (employee toggle button). By selecting between different employments, employees can perform different processes for each employment. Figure 11.11 shows the menu seen by employees.

Figure 11.11 Menu to Select Different Assignments

This menu appears on all screens in SAP SuccessFactors.

11.6   Summary

Global assignments are important for multinational and global organizations, and Employee Central helps you to manage employees in these organizations. The Global Assignments module gives HR administrators and managers the ability to manage home and host employments and to have employees return at the appropriate time. In this chapter, we looked at how to send employees on assignment, how to manage and view assignments, how to end an employee assignment, how employees on assignment use SAP SuccessFactors, and how to set up the Global Assignment feature.

In the next chapter, we'll take a look at the Contingent Workforce Management feature.

As the workforce becomes increasingly contingent, tracking contingent workers and their cost is a must-have. Employee Central provides native Contingent Workforce Management capability along with an integration with SAP Fieldglass to get the job done.

12 Contingent Workforce Management

A *contingent worker* is a person who has a work relationship with an organization tied to a work order. The work order has a definite end date.

Not all contingent workers are the same. The need to track a contingent worker can be divided into three categories:

- **Badging**
  For contingent workers who need access to facilities to provide services on campus but don't contribute to company processes.

- **Facilities and IT**
  Most IT and business contingent workers fall into this category. They need access to the facilities and need IT equipment.

- **Talent**
  Highly skilled resources in areas of talent shortage who can fill in for specific projects.

Contingent workers have been a part of the workforce for a long time now, but until recently they have not been part of the HRIS system. The reasons for this have to do with the risk associated with co-employment coupled with the lack of involvement from the HR function in the work lifecycle of Contingent Workforce Management. The hiring and management of a contingent workforce is decentralized in many organizations, and this lack of standardization creates disparate processes.

The good news is that standardization is integrated into Contingent Workforce Management. In this chapter, we'll highlight the use of Contingent Workforce

Management in Employee Central. We'll begin with the configuration steps to enable a contingent worker in the system, then examine the process of importing contingent workers, viewing contingent workers, and finally look at the SAP Fieldglass integration with Employee Central for Contingent Workforce Management.

12.1 Configuration

Contingent workers and employees are built on the same person model. However, to have a different set of attributes for a contingent worker, the contingent worker needs a subset of the attributes that an employee would have. The objects needed for a contingent worker include the following:

▶ Person Info

▶ Personal Information

▶ Employment Information

▶ Email Information

▶ Vendor Information

▶ Work Order

▶ Job Information

A business rule tied to the `onInit` trigger hides those fields not applicable to contingent workers. RBPs should be used to restrict the fields of the contingent worker for view and edit purposes.

A contingent worker can be assigned to a vacant position just as an employee can, and position vacancy processes include contingent workers. The contingent worker can also manage employees if such scenarios are present.

You can enable contingent workforce functionality through the Upgrade Center.

12.1.1 Vendor and Work Order

Vendor and Work Order are Foundation Objects associated with contingent workers, but not employees. Employee Central is typically not the system of record for these elements.

The vendor information is typically imported in from a vendor master. It may be also be maintained in the Employee Central system. Figure 12.1 illustrates the structure of the Vendor object. Custom fields can be added as necessary.

Figure 12.1 Vendor

Every contingent worker is tied to a work order. The work order contains the start and the end date of the contingent worker contract. The end date of the contingent worker in the Work Order object is the driver of the transaction. Figure 12.2 illustrates the structure of a Work Order object. Custom fields can be added to this object as necessary.

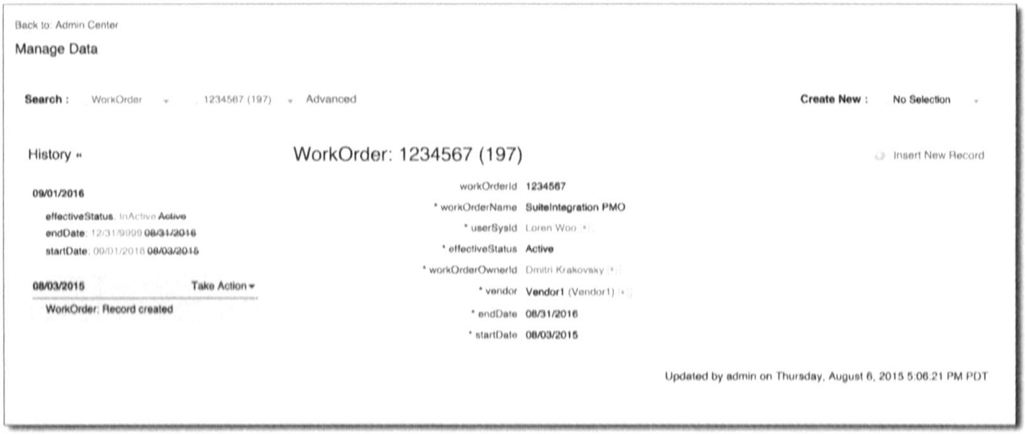

Figure 12.2 Work Order

Both the Vendor and the Work Order objects are built in the MDF, and the portlets are built on the Configuration UI framework.

12.1.2 Contingent Lifecycle

There are two delivered Event Reasons—*Start Contingent Worker (SCWK)* and *End Contingent Worker (ECWK)*—associated with contingent workers. These two events are used to initiate and terminate a contingent worker assignment. SCWK maps to an employee status of ACTIVE and ECWK maps to an employee status of TERMINATED.

When adding a contingent worker, the system automatically creates the end of the transaction based on the end date of the contract, as specified in the work order. The `endDate` is a required field when adding a contingent worker. The contract is automatically terminated when the end date is reached. To extend the contract, change the end date.

All the validations that are applicable to the Job Information portlet—Foundation Object validations and associations—will be enforced for the contingent workforce.

On the `employmentInfo` object, there is a delivered field called the `is_contingent_worker`. This field is used to distinguish an employee from a contingent worker for reports and interfaces. Figure 12.3 shows the field IS CONTINGENT WORKER in the EMPLOYEE INFORMATION portlet. This field is used to create groups and roles based on contingent workers.

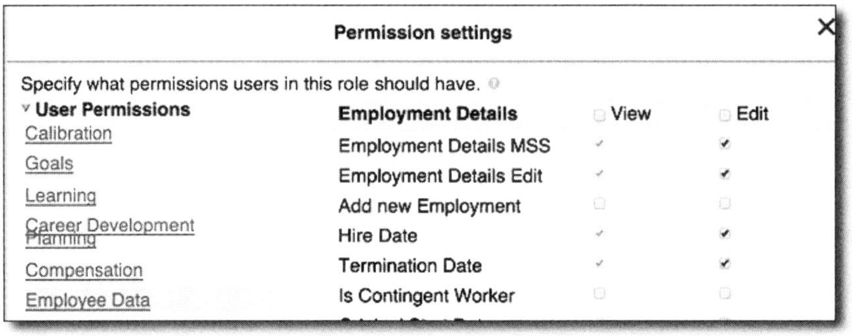

Figure 12.3 Contigent Worker Permissions

The permission to add a contingent worker is different than the permission to add an employee.

12.1.3 Importing Contingent Workforce Information

To import contingent workers into the system, the following employee data imports are necessary:

- ▶ Basic User Import
- ▶ Person Information
- ▶ Personal Information
- ▶ Employment Information
- ▶ Vendor (MDF Import)
- ▶ Work Order (MDF Import)
- ▶ Job Information

You can import these files via the steps and guidelines provided in Chapter 7.

12.2 Viewing a Contingent Worker

A viewer should be able to distinguish a contingent worker from an employee in the Org Chart. Accordingly, in both the Org Chart and in the People Profile, a CONTINGENT WORKER label appears next to a contingent worker's name (see Figure 12.4). This label is translated.

Figure 12.4 Contingent Worker on the Org Chart

From the ORG CHART, you can view a contingent worker's quickcard. The quick-card contains all the worker's permissioned actions, such as viewing the profile and making job and personal information changes.

The Contingent Worker Profile is similar to the Employee Profile, but the list of sections and the fields are different from those for employees. Figure 12.5 illustrates the People Profile of a contingent worker.

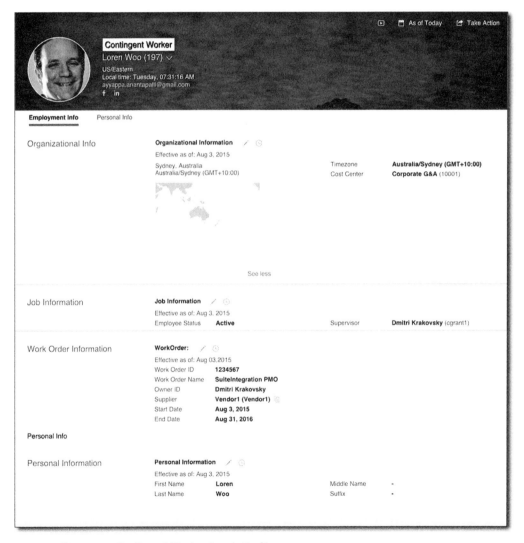

Figure 12.5 Contingent Worker People Profile

Now that you know how to configure a contingent worker in the system and how to view that contingent worker's information, in the next section, we'll look at the integration available with SAP Fieldglass.

12.3 SAP Fieldglass Integration

Although contingent workers can be managed directly in Employee Central, they are often managed through vendor management systems (VMSs). It can be valuable to integrate the data from such VMSs into Employee Central to provide a total workforce view.

SAP Fieldglass is a VMS to manage contingent workforce and services procurement programs. A delivered integration exists between SAP Fieldglass and Employee Central.

SAP Fieldglass is always the system of record for a contingent workforce. To provide the total workforce view, the contingent management capabilities of Employee Central provides a view of the contingent worker profile. The integration then updates the contingent profile at a defined frequency. The default data mapping between SAP Fieldglass and Employee Central can be modified in the SAP HANA Cloud Integration (HCI) platform.

Downstream processes, such as Workforce Analytics, will take advantage of the total workforce. For the integration, the following Foundation Objects must be kept in sync between SAP Fieldglass and Employee Central:

- Legal Entity
- Business Unit
- Location
- Cost Center
- Vendor

This represents the standard set of Foundation Objects; other Foundation Objects also may be used.

The following data objects will be loaded into Employee Central from SAP Fieldglass:

- ▸ Person Information
- ▸ Personal Information
- ▸ Employment Information
- ▸ Work Order
- ▸ Job Information

12.4   Summary

The contingent workforce segment of the workforce is increasing in both size and relevance. Employee Central provides contingent workforce capabilities that are distinct from employee management capabilities. Contingent workers can be selectively included or excluded in talent and learning processes. For customers using SAP Fieldglass, a delivered integration will bring in contingent worker information to provide a total workforce view.

In the next chapter, we'll look at the mass changes feature.

The Manage Mass Changes tool allows you to make changes related to Job Information and Job Relationships for groups of employees in a single update. This tool is a strong alternative to spreadsheet updates or manual entry.

13 Mass Changes

There are many times during normal business practices when a group or groups of employees are impacted by the same data change. The Manage Mass Changes tool in Employee Central allows you to make one or multiple Job Information or Job Relationships changes for employees en masse. This option eliminates the need for manual, one-by-one changes or the alternative data file import. It's a guided process typically reserved for HR managers or administrators who have a keen sense of how Employee Central functions. When used correctly, it can be a huge timesaver for HR managers and a means for standardizing data across organizational and functional areas. If you make a change using the Manage Mass Changes tool, you can ensure that all selected employees receive the same proposed data changes.

In this chapter, we'll explore the Manage Mass Changes tool and learn about its capabilities and limitations. We'll discuss when the Manage Mass Changes tool may be beneficial to use in lieu of other means of data entry. We'll also walk through the tool's guided change process and each step of its setup and execution. At the end of this chapter, you should have a thorough understanding of the tool and its processes and be comfortable using it to perform mass changes within Employee Central.

13.1 Employee Data Mass Changes

Employees move throughout an organization for various reasons: transfers, promotions, job changes, and more. MSS and HR manager screens provide the functionality to input this employee data into the system at the individual employee level. It is inevitable, however, that some of these changes will impact groups of employees rather than individuals. Such cases often arise from organizational realignment, department and location changes, job title or function reassignment, and other types of internal restructuring.

In all of these cases, multiple employees are selected for the same data change. For example, in terms of organizational reassignment, it may be that all members of a certain department are being realigned to a different department, or perhaps two existing departments are merging to form one new department. In either scenario, department changes must be made in the JOB INFORMATION section of each impacted employee's record. The Manage Mass Changes tool gives you the ability to make these changes at the group level instead of the individual employee level.

Manage Mass Changes is a favorite tool of many HR managers and administrators because of its powerful functionality and straightforward operation. It has many capabilities, but also some limitations with which users should be familiar.

13.1.1 Capabilities

The ability to make mass updates to groups of employee records without the use of a data import file is a key function of the Manage Mass Changes tool. Companies have the ability to declare their own relevant employee groupings for the transaction using basic group functionality similar to what is used with Workflow Group setup (see Chapter 4) and RBPs (see Chapter 3).

The Manage Mass Changes tool allows an organization to indicate an effective date on which it wants a change to take effect. This date can be the current day, in the past, or future-dated (helpful for organizational realignments). The tool also allows you to make multiple data changes in one single transaction—all with the same effective date and Event Reason code. Finally, mass change functionality can be permissioned out to selected users and administrators through RBPs. Once a transaction is executed, the initiator receives an email notification and a status log complete with results and error reporting.

13.1.2 Limitations

The Manage Mass Changes tool is not without some limitations. One of its greatest limitations is that only proposed Job Information and Job Relationships changes can be executed with the Manage Mass Changes tool. There is no current functionality for Compensation Information.

Compensation Information

For Compensation Information-related mass changes, we recommend using a data file import or exploring the Employee Central Pay Scale solution. This functionality is available through the MDF and allows for mass pay changes.

A second, albeit minor, limitation of the Manage Mass Changes tool is that it will not process or change employee records if the current employee record is missing prerequisite information or is in some other way incomplete (i.e., one or more required fields are blank). The tool performs a data validation run on all proposed record changes and will skip over employees whose records do not pass. We sometimes see examples of incomplete records when a field that was not previously marked as required has been changed to be required. Older employee records may be missing this field value and will not be processed during the mass change.

Although this limitation will prevent these employee records from being updated, it can also be viewed as somewhat positive because it helps identify incomplete employee data. Any failed record changes will be clearly logged in the transaction report so that corrections and updates may be made afterwards.

13.2   Performing Mass Changes

When faced with a mass change, you must first consider whether the Manage Mass Changes tool is an appropriate choice to make the change. Different variables will point you in the direction of using the tool or going a different route, which we will discuss in the next subsection. Once you've decided to use the Manage Mass Changes functionality, you must then make sure that you have the proper permissions assigned to execute the transaction.

13.2.1   When to Use Mass Changes

We know that the Manage Mass Change tool can be helpful for making various types of job data changes for groups of employees. Determining when to use this tool as opposed to manual entry or a data import file can require some thought. The first step is gathering together all of the information associated with the change. Specifically, you should make sure you know the following:

- ▸ Employees impacted
- ▸ Fields that are changing
- ▸ New data values
- ▸ Date of change
- ▸ Event Reason for change

Once you have all of that information gathered, you can review it to see if your change can and should be made using the Manage Mass Changes tool. There will be some changes that are not possible with the tool (see Section 13.1.2) and some scenarios that are better off initiated in a different manner.

Table 13.1 presents some scenarios and alternative approaches to consider when using the Manage Mass Changes tool.

Manage Mass Changes	Alternative Solution
The employee population impacted by the change must be large enough to warrant running a mass job.	If the population is small, changes can often be made faster through manual entry.
All of the impacted employees must have the same proposed data value, effective date, and Event Reason.	Consider a data import file if this is not the case.
Employees must be easily grouped together by a common characteristic, such as division, department, location, job, manager, etc.	Consider a data import file if this is not the case.
The proposed data change must impact only Job Information or Job Relationships in employee data.	Consider a data import file if this is not the case.

Table 13.1 Guidelines for when to Use Manage Mass Changes

If your proposed change meets the criteria in Table 13.1, then the Manage Mass Changes tool may be a good option to consider.

13.2.2 Preparing to Use Mass Changes

With all necessary data gathered, as described in Section 13.2.1, you can execute your mass change within Employee Central. Before you begin, ensure that you/

your initiator has the proper system security authorization to perform the mass change. Specifically, the initiator's RBP settings must include access to the MANAGE MASS CHANGES section of the Admin Center.

The permissions setting can be verified by checking that the initiator's role has access to MANAGE MASS CHANGES, located under ADMINISTRATOR PERMISSIONS, as shown in Figure 13.1.

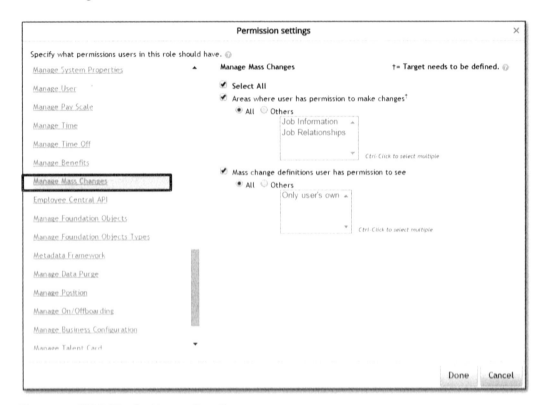

Figure 13.1 RBP Setting for Manage Mass Changes

In addition to having access to the MANAGE MASS CHANGES area of the Admin Center, the role must also designate if the user can make mass changes related to Job Information, Job Relationships, or both. In Figure 13.1, we chose SELECT ALL to indicate that the user has permission to make changes to all areas. Finally, the role must note whether or not the initiator has permission to view mass changes that have been made in Employee Central by users other than him- or herself. If ALL is selected under the MASS CHANGE DEFINITIONS USER HAS PERMISSION TO SEE setting, then the initiator can see all mass changes that have been made in the system and also copy them as starting points or templates during configuration steps. If OTHERS is selected, then the initiator will only be able to view his or her own mass change transactions.

A system security administrator can make changes or updates as needed to assign the appropriate access to the appropriate users. Manage Mass Changes access is typically reserved for HR managers or HR administrators who have a thorough knowledge of the system and Employee Central.

13.3 Using Manage Mass Changes

The Manage Mass Changes tool involves two phases: setup and execution. Once the setup is complete, it can be used multiple times for repeat actions or as a starting template for a new change definition. Let's look at the steps involved in the process.

13.3.1 Set Up Mass Change

Access the Manage Mass Changes tool in Admin Center under EMPLOYEE FILES • MANAGE MASS CHANGES. For HR administrators who perform regular mass data changes, it's a good idea to set this menu path as a FAVORITE.

Figure 13.2 Initial Change Template

The main screen of the tool lists any currently configured MASS CHANGE TEMPLATES and their statuses. This includes changes that have been run in the past as well as planned changes. Depending on authorizations, you may also see changes run/

planned by other users. Click on CREATE NEW in the top-left corner to bring up a blank *change template*. Figure 13.2 shows an example of the change template. Let's use the transfer of an HR team from Plant A to Plant B as an example exercise.

Start each change by filling out the DETAILS section. The following subsections walk through each setting.

Mass Change Name

The first step in setting up a change is to assign the change a MASS CHANGE NAME, as shown in Figure 13.3. It should be clear and meaningful and accurately describe the type of change that will be made. This is especially helpful when reusing existing change templates.

Figure 13.3 Initial Properties of Change Template: Name, Employee Group, and Effective Date

Employee Groups

The next step in the process is to designate the impacted group of employees — the EMPLOYEE GROUP — as shown in Figure 13.3. In our example, we want to group together all HR department employees located at Plant A. A dropdown list contains the previously defined employee groups for reuse.

If an existing group does not meet your needs, you can create a new one by clicking the CREATE link to the right of the EMPLOYEE GROUP setting. This link will open the standard GROUP DEFINITION popup (see Figure 13.4) used to create groups for RBPs, workflows, and recruitment. More information about creating groups can be found in Chapter 3.

> **Employee Groups**
>
> Employee groups created in one area of the system (RBPs, workflows, recruitment, mass changes) are not accessible in other areas of the system. An employee group created for use in RBPs will not be available for use in Manage Mass Changes.

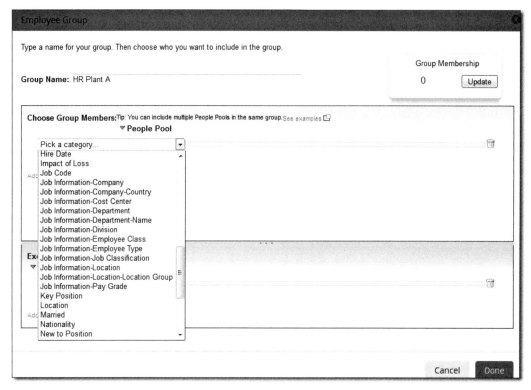

Figure 13.4 Employee Group Definition Popup

Effective Date

The EFFECTIVE DATE field is the date on which you want the change to begin. This is entered as the start date of the new record in each employee's history. In our example, the EFFECTIVE DATE is the date on which the HR team from Plant A moves to work at Plant B, as shown in Figure 13.3.

Now that the details are filled in, let's begin populating the data change information.

Mass Change Fields

In this section, we choose the field(s) to be affected by the mass change as well as assign the new value to these fields. Once a single field is selected for change, a new, blank row appears that can be used to designate another field to change. Multiple fields can be updated in a single mass change.

The following subsections look at the fields found under the MASS CHANGE section.

Area

In the AREA field, choose whether the change is to a JOB INFORMATION field or to a JOB RELATIONSHIP assignment. If the change relates to a JOB RELATIONSHIP, then choose the specific relationship you wish to modify. If the change relates to JOB INFORMATION, then a secondary line appears for you to select an Event Reason. This reason will be recorded in the history of each group member's employee file. In our example, we chose JOB INFORMATION and designated LOCATION CHANGE as the Event Reason (see Figure 13.5).

Figure 13.5 Completed Mass Change Section of the Change Template

Field Name

For the FIELD NAME, choose the field that is to be changed/updated. You will notice that country-specific fields are listed here as well with their three-character ISO country code as a prefix (see Figure 13.5). It's sometimes helpful to begin typing in the name of the field you wish to change in order to narrow down the listed options. In our example, the field we're changing is LOCATION, as shown in Figure 13.5.

New Value

In the NEW VALUE field, specify the new value to be assigned to all members of the designated EMPLOYEE GROUP. In our example, the NEW VALUE is PLANT B, shown in Figure 13.5.

13.3.2 Execute Mass Change

Once you've completed the change template, you're ready to save your work and execute the process. You have two options at this point: SAVE AND INITIATE and SAVE. SAVE allows you to save your setup and return to run the change at a later time. This is helpful if you're waiting on confirmation or approval of the changes. SAVE AND INITIATE will save your setup and run the changes immediately. You can monitor the progress of the job on the main page of the Manage Mass Changes tool. You'll receive an email notification when the job is complete. The email will provide a transaction report that includes any errors the process may have encountered. You can also view the transaction report, as shown in Figure 13.6, on the main page of the Manage Mass Changes tool by clicking directly on your change or on the status of your change.

Figure 13.6 Web Version of Mass Change Transaction Report

As a time saver for additional changes, you can click the COPY button on the main MANAGE MASS CHANGES page to copy an existing change template and reuse some or all of its settings. You can quickly swap out groups, change values, or insert a new effective date and have a new template without starting from scratch.

13.4 Summary

In this chapter, we looked at the benefits, capabilities, and limitations of the Manage Mass Changes tool. We explored when to use or not use the tool and how to set up and run a mass change. This functionality is extremely powerful and can greatly expedite data changes and maintenance, as well as help with accuracy.

In the next chapter, we'll dive into advances and deductions and how these features can augment the management of compensation and other pay-related activities.

Allowing employees to request an advance against their salary and set up a one-off or recurring deduction to recover the advance is a common practice in many companies. Employee Central provides functionality to manage these processes and integrate the process data with payroll systems.

14 Advances and Deductions

Many companies provide their employees with the ability to request advances and deduct these advances back either in a lump sum or with a number of payments over a period of time. Once given, the company will want to recover the deduction.

In Employee Central, two independent but related functionalities exist to enable you to manage both of these processes. Built on the MDF and therefore completely configurable from OneAdmin, the Advances and Deductions features provide ESS and MSS capabilities to view, request, and manage advances and deductions for employees.

In this chapter, we'll cover the ins and outs of each feature, their setup, and how their data is integrated with payroll systems. Let's start by taking a detailed look at the Advances feature.

14.1 Advances

The Advances functionality is designed to be used by employees to request advances. These can then be approved using workflow capabilities. Employees can request advances based on *eligibility*. Eligibilities are set up to determine the type of advance, amount, number of installments, type of recovery, and which groups of employees are eligible. Advances cannot be given to employees without setting up an eligibility. Therefore, let's begin by looking at this process.

14.1.1 Setting Up Eligibilities

Prior to requesting an advance, it's important that employees know what they are eligible for. Eligibilities in Employee Central are used to define what advances an employee is entitled to. There are three activities required to create an eligibility: creating a Pay Component, creating an eligibility, and creating eligibility rules.

Creating a Pay Component

Each advance type defined in an eligibility and selectable in the ADVANCES TYPE field when requesting an advance is a Pay Component Foundation Object. A Pay Component must be created for every advance type prior to setting up an eligibility, and they are created in OneAdmin under EMPLOYEE FILES • MANAGE ORGANIZATION, PAY AND JOB STRUCTURES. These Pay Components are non-recurring, defined by setting the value of both the RECURRING and TARGET fields to NO. Figure 14.1 shows a Non-Recurring Pay Component for a PERSONAL LOAN. Pay Components are covered in detail in Chapter 6, Section 6.2.3.

Figure 14.1 Non-Recurring Pay Component

Once a Pay Component is created, it must be permissioned to the appropriate users (for example, employees, managers, and HR professionals) so that they can access it when creating eligibilities and requesting advances.

Creating an Eligibility

Eligibilities for advances are created and maintained in OneAdmin in EMPLOYEE FILES • MANAGE ADVANCE OBJECTS. Accumulation for advances—which defines how many advances against an eligibility an employee has taken—can also be created and maintained here.

Creating and maintaining these objects follows the same process as creating and maintaining any Generic Object records on the MANAGE DATA screen. These processes are covered in Chapter 5, Section 5.1.6.

To create a new advance, select ELIGIBILITY FOR ADVANCES in the CREATE NEW dropdown. The following mandatory fields are available to define the details of the eligibility:

- ► ELIGIBILITY ID
  The ID of the eligibility.

- ► ENABLE AUTO RECOVERY
  This field will be displayed if the Deductions feature is enabled and is used to enable the automatic recovery of an advance in the form of a deduction; we'll cover this a little further on in this section.

- ► EFFECTIVE START DATE
  The date that the eligibility is active from.

- ► STATUS
  Whether the eligibility is ACTIVE or INACTIVE in the system.

- ► ADVANCE TYPE
  The Non-Recurring Pay Component.

- ► RECOVERY MODE
  The method used to recover the advance (BANK TRANSFER, CASH, or CHECK).

- ► NUMBER OF INSTALLMENTS
  The number of installments that will be used to recover the advance.

- ► INSTALLMENT FREQUENCY
  The frequency in which the installment will be deducted.

- INTEREST TYPE
  The type of interest to be applied (NO SELECTION, NOT APPLICABLE, SIMPLE, or COMPOUND).

- EMPLOYEE CAN EDIT NUMBER OF INSTALLMENTS
  Defines whether the employee can modify the value of the NUMBER OF INSTALLMENTS field.

- EMPLOYEE CAN EDIT RECOVERY MODE
  Defines whether the employee can modify the value of the RECOVERY MODE field.

The following optional fields can be used to further define eligibility details:

- DEFAULT WORKFLOW
  Defines the default workflow to approve a requested advance (optional).

- EXCEPTION FOR REQUESTED AMOUNT
  Defines if the employee can request the amount of an advance to be greater than the amount maintained in MAXIMUM ELIGIBILITY AMOUNT/PERCENTAGE field.

- EXCEPTION FOR NUMBER OF INSTALLMENTS
  Defines if the employee can request the number of installments of an advance to be greater than the amount maintained in NUMBER OF INSTALLMENTS field.

- EXCEPTION WORKFLOW
  Defines the default workflow to be triggered if an exception is made when requesting advance.

- ELIGIBILITY RULE NAME
  The name of the eligibility.

- LEGAL ENTITY
  The legal entity for which this eligibility applies.

- PAY GRADE
  The pay grade for which this eligibility applies.

- MAXIMUM ELIGIBILITY AMOUNT/PERCENTAGE
  The maximum amount that the employee is eligible for.

- CURRENCY
  The currency of the eligibility.

- MAXIMUM ELIGIBLE OCCURRENCES
  The maximum number of requests that an employee can make within the eligibility period.

- ► ELIGIBILITY VALID FOR (NUMBER)
  The value of the eligibility period.

- ► ELIGIBILITY VALID FOR (UNIT)
  The units (DAY(S), MONTH(S), or YEAR(S)) of the value of the eligibility period.

- ► FIRST OCCURRENCE DATE
  The date on which the first period of the MAXIMUM ELIGIBLE OCCURRENCES starts.

Figure 14.2 shows an example of an ELIGIBILITY FOR ADVANCES object for a personal loan for employees in the United States.

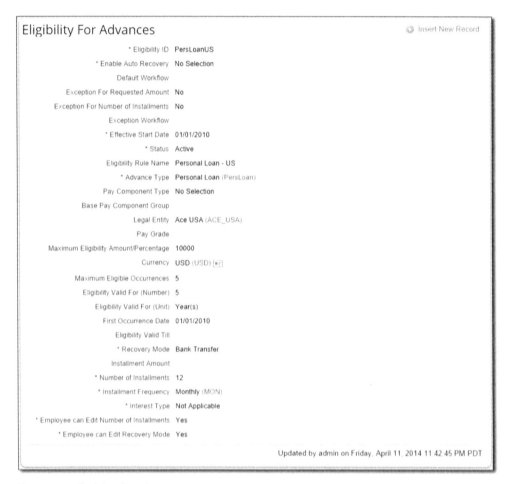

Figure 14.2 Eligibility for Advance

You will see some fields in the figure that were not listed previously. These fields are view only and are automatically filled based on the selection of other fields.

When the Deductions feature is enabled, the ENABLE AUTO RECOVERY field will be visible below the ELIGIBILITY ID field. To enable a deduction to be created automatically once an advance request is approved, the value of the ENABLE AUTO RECOVERY field should be set to YES.

When creating an advance, additional fields will be displayed if the value of the ENABLE AUTO RECOVERY field is YES. The additional fields that are displayed include the following:

▶ RECOVERY PAY COMPONENT (RECURRING)
Defines the Pay Component to be used for a recurring deduction.

▶ RECOVERY PAY COMPONENT (ONE TIME)
Defines the Pay Component to be used for a one-off deduction.

▶ RECOVERY FORMAT
Defines whether the deduction should be recovered on a specific date of each month (AS PER DATE) or on a specific day each month (AS PER DAY).

Depending on which option is selected for the RECOVERY FORMAT field, additional fields will display. When the value of the RECOVERY FORMAT field is set to AS PER DATE, then the MONTHLY RECOVERY DATE field is displayed, which enables a numerical value to be selected between 1 and 31. When the value of the RECOVERY FORMAT field is set to AS PER DAY, then the WEEK NUMBER and DAY OF WEEK fields are displayed. The WEEK NUMBER field enables you to select in which week of the month (FIRST, SECOND, THIRD, FOURTH, or LAST) and on which day of that week (MONDAY through SUNDAY) the deduction will be made.

Let's take a look at a couple of examples for each option. For the first example, let's say that you want the deduction to be made on the first of each month. In the RECOVERY FORMAT field, select AS PER DATE, and then in the MONTHLY RECOVERY DATE field, select 01. Likewise, for the deduction to be on the twenty-eighth of each month, you would select 28 in the MONTHLY RECOVERY DATE field.

For the second example, let's say that you want the deduction to be made on the Wednesday of the third week of each month. In the RECOVERY FORMAT field, select AS PER DAY; in the WEEK NUMBER field, select THIRD; and in the DAY OF WEEK field, select WEDNESDAY.

Creating the Eligibility Rule

A rule is used to determine who is eligible to access an eligibility. The rule is used to determine overall eligibility rules, such as Legal Entity or Pay Grade. Any field on the Job Information portlet can be used. The rule is executed for every employee that requests an advance. To set up the rule, navigate to the CONFIGURE BUSINESS RULES screen and click the CREATE NEW RULE button.

The RULE ID must be ADVANCESRULE and the BASE OBJECT must be ELIGIBILITY FOR ADVANCES, as shown in Figure 14.3. If the JOB INFORMATION fields are needed as part of the eligibility conditions, then add the Job Information object via the MANAGE PARAMETERS hyperlink. The RULE NAME, RULE TYPE, and START DATE fields can be entered as you see fit. A RULE DESCRIPTION is optional. No THEN conditions are required for this rule.

The IF condition(s) must be defined to determine which conditions allow an employee to be eligible. In the example in Figure 14.3, the employee's Legal Entity must match the Legal Entity of the eligibility.

Figure 14.3 Advances Rule Example

Specific conditions can be used, such as the employee's Legal Entity needing to be USA for this example.

14.1.2   Requesting an Advance

Once employees know what they are eligible for in terms of advances, they can begin the advance request process. Employees can request an advance by selecting the ADVANCES option from the TAKE ACTION menu on either the PERSONAL INFORMATION or the EMPLOYMENT INFORMATION screen.

If a manager or HR administrator wishes to set up an advance for or on behalf of an employee, he or she can use the same option, or can select the ADVANCES option under the TAKE ACTION section in the QUICKCARD menu. Figure 14.4 shows an advance being requested by an employee.

Figure 14.4 Requesting an Advance

The first step when requesting an advance is to select the ADVANCE TYPE. All advances that an employee is eligible for will be available in the ADVANCE TYPE field. Once selected, a number of fields will prefill. The employee enters the requested advance amount in the REQUESTED AMOUNT field and then selects the PAYMENT MODE. An optional description can be entered in the DESCRIPTION field.

Next, the employee should enter the method of recovering the advance in the RECOVERY MODE field and then enter the number of installments in the NUMBER OF INSTALLMENTS field. After entering the number of installments, the installment amount is automatically calculated. The number of installments cannot be higher than the amount defined in the eligibility.

Once the advance details are entered, clicking the SUBMIT button will submit the request and send it for approval if a workflow is assigned.

14.1.3 Viewing Advances

Once approved, an employee's advances can be viewed on the EMPLOYMENT INFORMATION screen in the SPOT BONUS portlet, listed under ADVANCE. Any eligibilities are displayed in the ELIGIBILITY FOR ADVANCES portlet, which also takes into account advances taken against an eligibility. Figure 14.5 shows these portlets.

Figure 14.5 Eligible and Requested Advances in Employment Information

If permissioned, a user can edit advances and eligibilities by selecting the EDIT button in the appropriate portlet.

Now, let's take a look at some of the Generic Objects used in the Advances feature.

14.1.4 Advances Objects

Several Generic Objects are used in the Advances feature:

▶ **Eligibility for Advances**

The Eligibility for Advances object stores the details of eligibilities that have been set up. We'll look more closely at this object in Section 14.1.5.

▶ **Accumulation for Advances**

The Accumulation for Advances object stores the details of an eligibility for an employee once an advance has been taken. There may be multiple records for each employee if multiple advances have been taken. It records such details as the amount taken against the eligibility, how much of the eligibility remains, how many requests have been made, how many requests remain, the accumulation period, and the currency in which the eligibilities are made.

The Accumulation for Advances object is associated with the Non-Recurring Payment object, with the Non-Recurring Payment object as the child. This association links all advances requested against the eligibility.

▶ **Non-Recurring Payment**

The Non-Recurring Payment object stores high-level details of an advance that has been requested. It is associated with the Advance object and AdvancesInstallments object, which are both child objects. They associate details of the advance and any recovery installments. When a record of the Non-Recurring Payment object is viewed in the MANAGE DATA screen, the complete details of an advance are displayed.

▶ **Advance**

The Advances object stores detailed information about an advance that has been requested. This information matches the fields shown when requesting an advance, as you saw in Figure 14.4.

▶ **AdvancesInstallments**

The AdvancesInstallments object stores the details of any recurring deductions that have been set up to recover an advance if the Deductions feature has been set up. We'll cover recurring deductions in Section 14.2.2.

14.1.5 Setting Up Advances

There are a number of steps required to enable and configure the Advances functionality. First, the Advances feature must be enabled in Provisioning. The remaining steps are performed in OneAdmin and we'll cover each of these steps now.

Permissions

Once the Advances feature is enabled, you should permission the ADVANCES ELIGIBILITY permission for any roles in which users will create and administer advances. The CREATE ADVANCE permission should be assigned to any roles in which the user can request an advance. Both options are found under the MANAGE ADVANCES section when assigning permissions to permission roles.

Workflow

Next up is creating an approval workflow for approving advance requests. The workflow is created in the usual method, which was covered in Chapter 4, Section 4.3.3. Once created, the workflow should be assigned to the Non-Recurring Payment object definition. Assigning workflows to Generic Objects is covered in Chapter 4, Section 4.3.4.

Payment Mode Picklist

The Payment Mode picklist needs to be created so that the user can select the appropriate payment method to receive the advance. This process is covered in Chapter 5, Section 5.1.4. The EXTERNAL CODE for the picklist should be PAYMENT-MODE.

Pay Component Group Rule

A rule must be created to autopopulate the PAY COMPONENT TYPE and BASE PAY COMPONENT GROUP fields when creating an Eligibility for Advance. These values are defaulted from the Pay Component selected in the ADVANCE TYPE field. Figure 14.6 shows an example of a rule. With the exception of the BASE OBJECT, the IF conditions, and the THEN conditions, the rest of the rule can be set up as you see fit.

Once defined, the rule should be assigned to the ADVANCESTYPE field in the Eligibility for Advances Object Definition.

Figure 14.6 Rule to Populate the Pay Component Type Field

Eligibility Criteria

Additional eligibility criteria can be defined by adding custom fields to the Eligibility for Advances object definition. For example, you may wish to use Division as an eligibility criterion. For each custom field, the value of the VALID VALUES SOURCE field should be the object field name that is the source of the values to be selected on the eligibility. In our example, this would be DEPARTMENT.

Decimal Precision

If required, the decimal precision used by advances can be set to be more or less than the default three decimal places by modifying specific fields in the object definition of the Eligibility for Advances, Accumulation for Advances, Advance, and Non-Recurring Payment objects. Specifically, the value of the DECIMAL PRECISION field for each of these fields should be changed to the number of decimal places required for the fields. The fields for each object are listed in Table 14.1.

Generic Object Definition	Field Name(s)
Eligibility for Advances	eligibilityAmount
Accumulation for Advances	accumulateAmount remainingEligibileAmount
Advance	accumulateAmount remainingEligibileAmount
Non-Recurring Payment	payCompValue

Table 14.1 Fields to Modify to Change Decimal Precision

Now that we've covered using and setting up advances, let's turn our attention to the Deductions feature.

14.2   Deductions

The *Deductions* feature enables one-time and recurring deductions to be made from an employee's salary, perhaps for a medical plan, pension, student loan repayment, or to recover an advance. Typically, deductions are classified as items deducted from gross income that reduce the taxable portion of an employee's income.

Deductions can be requested by employees or created on behalf of employees by managers or HR administrators. When an employee requests a deduction, it can trigger a workflow if the system is configured as such.

If defined on the eligibility for an advance, a deduction is created automatically to recover an advance. This means that you don't need to manually create a deduction to recover advances.

Pay Components that are part of a Pay Scale Structure and are percentage- or unit-based (e.g., hours or weeks) can also be handled by the Deductions feature.

14.2.1 One-Time Deductions

One-time deductions are requested by or created for an employee by selecting TAKE ACTION on the PERSONAL INFORMATION or EMPLOYMENT INFORMATION screen and selecting ONE TIME DEDUCTION. The details of the deduction are entered as shown in Figure 14.7.

The Pay Component selected in the PAY COMPONENT field is non-recurring. The value of the AMOUNT/PERCENTAGE/NUMBER OF UNITS and CURRENCY fields will be propagated from the selected Pay Component if they have been defined on the Pay Component. If the deduction is to recover an advance with only a single repayment, selecting the advance in the ADVANCE field autopopulates the AMOUNT/PERCENTAGE/NUMBER OF UNITS and CURRENCY fields.

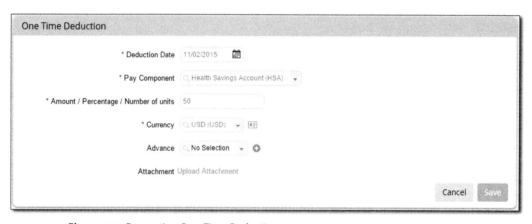

Figure 14.7 Requesting One-Time Deduction

After the details have been entered, clicking SAVE will complete the transaction. If a workflow is configured, then the workflow will trigger for approval; otherwise, the data will become immediately available.

One-time deductions are displayed in the ONE TIME DEDUCTION USER portlet on the EMPLOYMENT INFORMATION screen. Figure 14.8 shows the deduction that we just created in the ONE TIME DEDUCTION USER portlet.

If a user has the appropriate permissions, he or she can edit a one-time deduction by clicking the EDIT button on the ONE TIME DEDUCTION USER portlet. Likewise, if the user has permission, he or she can view the history of one-time deductions by clicking the HISTORY button.

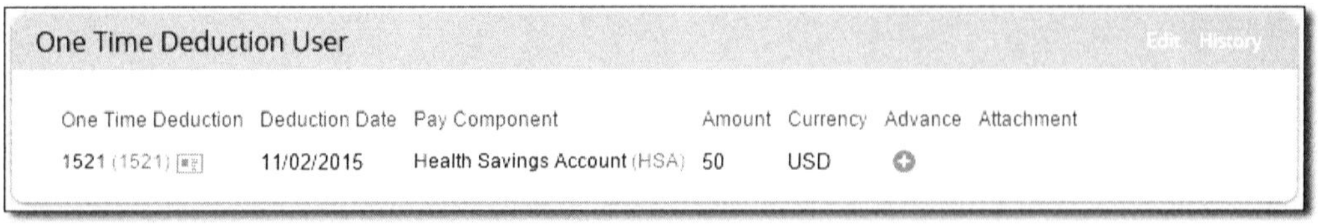

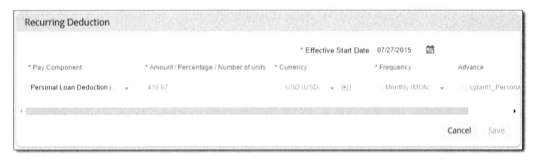

Figure 14.8 Deduction in the One Time Deduction User Portlet

14.2.2 Recurring Deductions

Recurring deductions are requested by or created for an employee by selecting Take Action on the Personal Information or Employment Information screen and selecting Manage Recurring Deductions. The details of the deduction are entered as per Figure 14.9. As you'll notice, the details are very similar to those entered for a one-time deduction, with the main difference being the inclusion of the Frequency field to determine how often the recurring deduction should be made.

Figure 14.9 Entering Recurring Deduction

Like with a one-time deduction, selecting the advance in the Advance dropdown auto-populates the Amount/Percentage, Currency, and Frequency fields. After the details have been entered, clicking Save will complete the transaction. If a workflow is configured, then the workflow will trigger for approval; otherwise, the data will become immediately available.

One-time deductions are displayed in the Recurring Deduction portlet on the Employment Information screen. Figure 14.10 shows the deduction that we just created in the Recurring Deduction portlet.

Figure 14.10 Recurring Deduction in Recurring Deduction Portlet

If a user has permission, he or she can edit a recurring deduction by clicking the EDIT button on the RECURRING DEDUCTION portlet. Likewise, if the user has permission, he or she can view the history of recurring deductions by clicking the HISTORY button.

14.2.3 Deductions Objects

Several Generic Objects are used in the Deductions feature:

▶ **Configure Deduction Screen IDs**
The Configure Deduction Screen IDs object is used to define which configuration UIs will be used for requesting and viewing a one-time deduction and for requesting a recurring deduction. We'll cover this in Section 14.2.4.

▶ **One Time Deduction**
The One Time Deduction object stores details of each one-time deduction requested by an employee.

▶ **One Time Deduction User**
The One Time Deduction User object stores a list of all of the one-time deductions requested by an employee (a list of One Time Deduction objects associated via the OneTimeDeductionItem object). This enables all One Time Deductions for a user to be viewed in the ONE TIME DEDUCTION USER portlet on the EMPLOYEE INFORMATION screen of an employee.

▶ **OneTimeDeductionItem**
The OneTimeDeductionItem object is used to list all of the One Time Deduction objects on the One Time Deduction User object.

▶ **OneTimeDeductionReplication**
The OneTimeDeductionReplication object stores details for replication of one-time deductions to external payroll systems.

▶ **Recurring Deduction**
The Recurring Deduction object stores a list of all of the recurring deductions

requested by an employee (a list of RecurringDeductionItem objects). This enables all recurring deductions for a user to be viewed in the RECURRING DEDUCTION portlet on the EMPLOYMENT INFORMATION screen of an employee.

► **RecurringDeductionItem**
The RecurringDeductionItem object stores details of a recurring deduction requested by an employee.

► **RecurringDeductionReplication**
The RecurringDeductionReplication object stores details for replication of Recurring Deductions to external payroll systems.

14.2.4 Setting Up Deductions

There are a number of steps required to enable and configure the Deductions functionality. First, the Advances feature must be enabled in Provisioning. The remaining steps are performed in OneAdmin and we'll cover each of these now.

User Interface

The Deduction Configuration UIs need to be imported into the system and assigned to the configuration. The Configuration UIs are imported from the Success Store in OneAdmin via EMPLOYEE FILES • IMPORT AND EXPORT DATA.

Once on the IMPORT AND EXPORT DATA screen, select IMPORT DATA in the SELECT THE ACTION TO PERFORM dropdown. At the top of the screen, there are three options: CSV FILE, ZIP FILE, and SUCCESS STORE. Select SUCCESS STORE and you will see a screen similar to the one shown in Figure 14.11.

Select the package for CONFIG UI FOR DEDUCTIONS (it may be titled slightly differently) and click IMPORT. You will be notified that the package is being imported. It should take no longer than five to ten minutes to import the package. You can monitor the import process in OneAdmin via EMPLOYEE FILES • MONITOR JOB.

Once the configuration UIs are imported, create a configuration to map them so they're read by the Employee Central UI. Do so in OneAdmin via EMPLOYEE FILES • MANAGE DATA. On this screen, select CONFIGURE DEDUCTION SCREEN IDS in the CREATE NEW dropdown. Select the appropriate Configuration UI in each dropdown, as shown in Figure 14.12, and click SAVE.

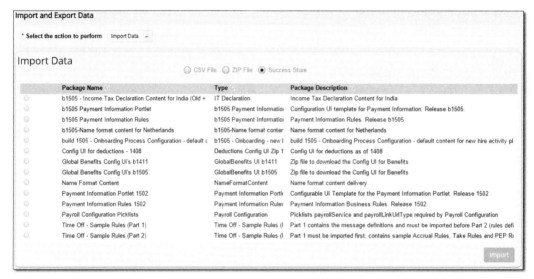

Figure 14.11 Importing Configurations from Success Store

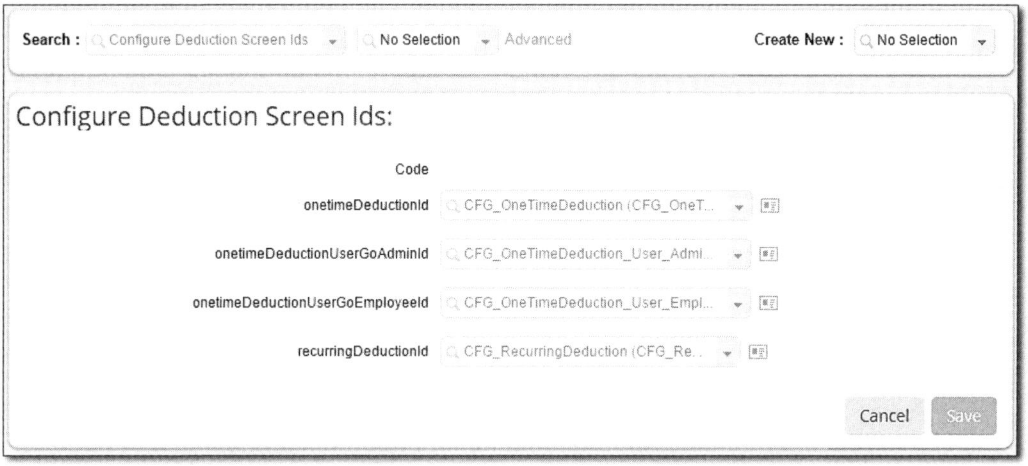

Figure 14.12 Assigning Configuration UIs for Deduction Screens

It's possible to make changes to the Deductions Generic Object and modify any of the Configuration UIs. Once a change has been made to the object definition, the appropriate Configuration UIs can be modified in OneAdmin in Employee Files • Manage Configuration UI.

As time goes on, you may need to create a new Configuration UI and change an existing mapped configuration UI. Do so by modifying the CONFIGURE DEDUCTION SCREEN IDs record that was created previously in the MANAGE DATA screen. CONFIGURE DEDUCTION SCREEN IDs is an object, and here we're editing the record of that object.

Permissions

There are three permissions available for one-time deductions that can be assigned to permission roles, all under the under the MANAGE DEDUCTIONS section:

▶ CREATE ONE TIME DEDUCTION

▶ EDIT ONE TIME DEDUCTION

▶ VIEW ONE TIME DEDUCTION

The appropriate permissions should be added for users who need to be able to create, edit, and/or view one-time deductions.

Recurring deductions are all controlled at the Generic Object level. Typically, the Recurring Deduction object has no permissions applied, so it can be accessed by all users. To apply security, modify the object definition and enable security. To permission the object, assign the appropriate permissions to the Generic Object under the permissions category that was assigned when the object was permissioned.

Workflow

Workflows can be assigned to both one-time and recurring deductions. Once the workflow configurations have been created, they are assigned to the One Time Deduction object definition or the Recurring Deduction Object Definition as required.

Pay Components

Pay Components need to be created for the one-time deductions and recurring deductions. For one-time deductions, they should be created as non-recurring, which is the same as creating Pay Components for advances. For recurring Pay Components, they should be created in the same way as standard Pay Components (i.e., set the value of the RECURRING field to YES and the TARGET field to NO when creating the Pay Component).

Pay Scale Structure

If a Pay Scale Structure is used in Employee Central, then it can be used to determine the amount for a Deduction if the Pay Component is a percentage- or unit-based Pay Component. Once a Pay Component has been created and permissioned, it should be assigned to a Pay Scale Level. The Pay Scale Structure is covered in Chapter 16, Section 16.1.

14.3   Summary

In this chapter, we covered the Advances and Deductions features in Employee Central. We discussed how these processes work, when they can be applied, what functionality is available, and how they are set up and maintained. We've looked at setting up eligibilities for advances, requesting advances, and recovering advances using deductions.

In the next chapter, we'll look at the payroll option for Employee Central: Employee Central Payroll.

When you run your core HR operations in the cloud, moving your payroll there may be a logical next step. Consolidation of existing payroll systems into a robust, global payroll system can offer a lot of value for your organization.

15 Employee Central Payroll

Employee Central Payroll combines the payroll capabilities of SAP ERP Payroll with the benefits and advantages of Employee Central. With integrations to third-party systems and UI capabilities in Employee Central, Employee Central Payroll is a viable option for Employee Central customers.

In this chapter, we'll cover how Employee Central Payroll fits in with Employee Central, which features are exclusive to this scenario, and how employees and managers can run self-service transactions in Employee Central Payroll via Employee Central.

Let's begin by explaining what Employee Central Payroll is.

15.1 Overview

Employee Central Payroll is a cloud-hosted payroll system that is only available for Employee Central customers and is built on the SAP ERP Payroll system. Employee Central Payroll is available for thirty countries at the time of writing (December 2015). SAP plans to eventually bring the number of Employee Central Payroll countries in line with SAP ERP Payroll. SAP can provide a current list of country versions for Employee Central Payroll, or you can review the list at *http://scn.sap.com/docs/DOC-45501*.

Like SaaS software, Employee Central Payroll has upgrades, patches, legal changes, and tax updates applied to the payroll engine as part of the hosted service. For data replication from Employee Central, a packaged integration is used, which we cover Chapter 19, Section 19.2.5. Packaged integrations are also available for BSI TaxFactory SaaS and BSI eFormsFactory, which we will cover in Chapter 19, Section 19.11.1. In addition, web services are provided in Employee Central Payroll, which we will cover in Chapter 19, Section 19.11.2.

Employee Central Payroll data is stored in infotypes, which will be familiar to any SAP ERP HCM or SAP ERP Payroll customer. *Infotypes* are tables that store related employee data. Many Employee Central Payroll infotypes can be updated by employees and managers in Employee Central. Payroll managers often make changes directly in the Employee Central Payroll system. These changes are known as *mash-ups* and are also available for SAP ERP Payroll customers who are on SAP ERP 6.0 or above.

Additional Resources

You can read more about SAP ERP Payroll in *Practical SAP US Payroll* by Satish Badgi (2nd edition, SAP PRESS, 2012).

Now that we've reviewed what Employee Central Payroll is, in the next section we'll discuss the key processes that can be performed within Employee Central Payroll.

15.2 Processes

Employee Central Payroll features a comprehensive set of payroll processes for managing and processing payrolls of all levels of complexity. These processes include the following:

▶ Gross pay calculation based on time entered in the Time Sheet or third-party time systems

▶ Gross-to-net calculation of paychecks

▶ Retroactive pay calculation

▶ Garnishment calculation

▶ Paychecks and deposit advices (viewable in Employee Central)

▶ Direct deposit of paychecks

▶ Payroll tax forms to be filed using a tax report

- Quarterly and year-end reports and forms
- End-to-end payroll process interfacing with SAP ERP FI-CO
- Advanced Reporting (discussed in Chapter 17, Section 17.6)

Let's now take a look at how employees access Employee Central Payroll.

15.3 Access

Access to Employee Central Payroll varies by user role. Employees and managers access payroll functionality in ESS and MSS, just like other self-service transactions. We'll take a look at these functionalities shortly.

Although HR administrators can access payroll functionality in a similar way, they can also log into the Employee Central Payroll system directly via the SAP GUI through a virtual private network (VPN) connection. This is how payroll managers access Employee Central Payroll, although payroll managers will have access to the development and test instances of Employee Central Payroll as well.

Figure 15.1 demonstrates the different access points for employees into Employee Central Payroll.

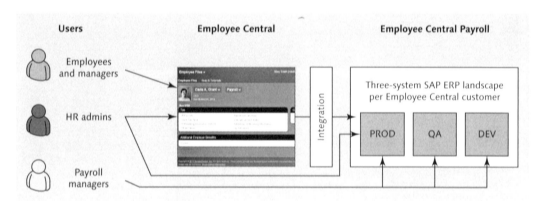

Figure 15.1 Access Points for Each User Role

Now, let's take a look at some of the payroll transactions accessed in self-service in Employee Central.

15.4 Self-Service Transactions

Employees and their managers access and maintain payroll information in EMPLOYEE FILES in the PAYROLL INFORMATION view. This functionality is also available for SAP ERP Payroll customers who integrate with Employee Central.

In this section, we'll briefly look at ESS and MSS in Employee Central Payroll.

15.4.1 Employee Self-Services

In PAYROLL INFORMATION, employees can view and maintain tax various tax data and documents, depending on their locations. They can also view their pay slips and other pay and benefits statements.

Figure 15.2 shows the screen for entering tax information for the United States federal W4 and W5 tax withholding forms. You can access this screen through WITHHOLDING INFORMATION W4/W5 in the TAX portlet. The screen inside the TAX portlet may be familiar to SAP ERP customers because it's a Web Dynpro screen shown directly from the Employee Central Payroll system.

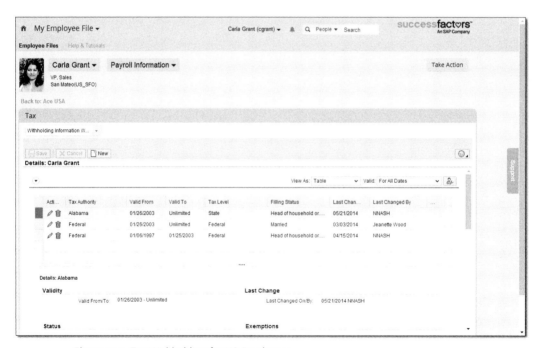

Figure 15.2 Tax Withholding for US Employees

Employees also can view their pay slips in Employee Central. They are generated and displayed directly from the Employee Central Payroll system, as shown in Figure 15.3.

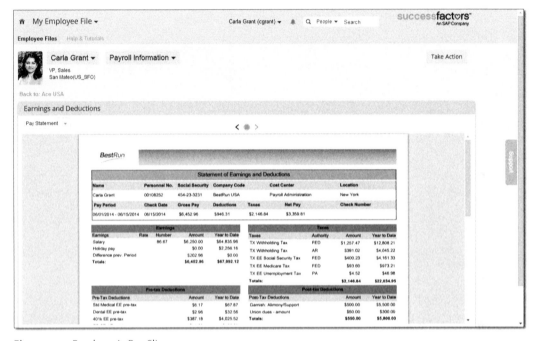

Figure 15.3 Employee's Pay Slip

15.4.2 Manager Self-Services

In PAYROLL INFORMATION, managers and HR administrators can view and maintain the following data for their reports, depending on their countries:

▶ Social Insurance and Social Security information

▶ Work and residence tax areas

▶ Working hours information

▶ Reduction of working hours

▶ Unemployment State

▶ Tax withholding information

▶ Garnishments information (in the United States)

- Additional employer benefits
- Pension and retirements information
- Earnings and deductions
- Pay and benefits statements
- Other tax and payments information

Figure 15.4 shows the PAYROLL INFORMATION screen that US-based managers can see for their employees.

Figure 15.4 Payroll Information View in Employee Files

Figure 15.5 shows the ADDITIONAL EMPLOYER BENEFITS screen, where managers and HR administrators can maintain any payroll-related benefits for employees. You can add new employer benefits by clicking the NEW button followed by one of the available options.

Additional Resources

For more information on integration, field mappings, and BAdIs for Employee Central Payroll, refer to the *Employee Central Payroll* handbook found at *http://help.sap.com/hr_integration* under the heading SUCCESSFACTORS AND SAP ERP: CORE HYBRID HCM.

Figure 15.5 Additional Employer Benefits

15.5 Payroll Control Center

In order to control, monitor, and take corrective action on payroll, the Payroll Control Center can be used with Employee Central Payroll. The Payroll Control Center enables payroll managers and admins to perform activities in a user-friendly, SAPUI5-based solution.

Payroll managers can view payroll processes in the PAYROLL PROCESS tile on the homepage and can enter the PAYROLL PROCESS screen in the Payroll Control Center by navigating to PAYROLL in the navigation menu. On the PAYROLL PROCESS screen, payroll managers can perform the following activities:

▸ Plan, execute, and monitor payroll processes and each process step

▸ Monitor the progress and status of each payroll process and confirm successful completion of each step

▸ Execute validation rules and route issues to payroll administrators for correction

▸ Enable audit processes using an automatically filled log file

Figure 15.6 shows the ONE-CLICK MONITORING screen used to monitor payroll processes.

Figure 15.6 One-Click Monitoring Screen

Payroll administrators can view payroll errors in the PAYROLL ERROR tile on the homepage as well. They access the Payroll Control Center by navigating to PAYROLL in the navigation menu and are taken to the PAYROLL ERROR screen. On the PAYROLL ERROR screen, payroll administrators can perform the following activities:

▸ Propose solutions for payroll errors

▸ Correct employee master data

▸ Validate data after applying solutions using the recheck function

▸ Forward errors to another payroll administrator

▸ View a list of unassigned errors and assign these errors to themselves for resolution

▸ View error KPIs

Figure 15.7 shows an example of unresolved errors. In this example, it is for gross pay with a variance of more than 10%.

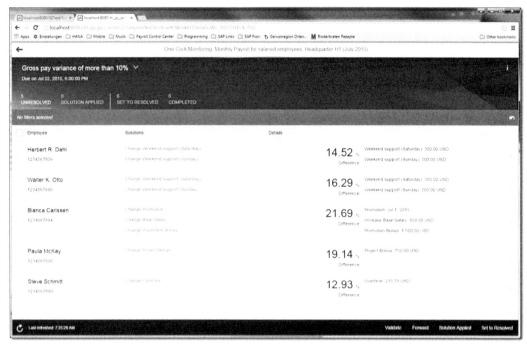

Figure 15.7 Unresolved Errors

Additional Resources

For more information about the Payroll Control Center and its implementation, refer to the *Employee Central Payroll* handbook found at *http://help.sap.com/hr_integration* under the heading SUCCESSFACTORS AND SAP ERP: CORE HYBRID HCM.

15.6 Summary

Employee Central Payroll is a world-class payroll engine that can process even the most complex payrolls across multiple countries. It supports ESS and MSS—as well as HR administrator access—through the Employee Central UI. Available for thirty countries, it's a comprehensive solution that can suit any organization.

In this chapter, we provided an overview of the solution, what processes it offers, how it's accessed, and what transactions are available. In the next chapter we'll look at other important features and functions in Employee Central.

In a mature and robust HR system, there is a wealth of functionality beyond employee administration. Some of these features can be large and complex, but some smaller and simpler features offer a lot of value for customers.

16   Other Features and Functionality

Employee Central contains numerous features and functionalities to cover a number of processes, activities, and functions required by HR administrators, managers, and employees, including the following:

- Pay Scale Structure
- Concurrent Employment
- Document Generation
- Pensions Payouts
- Alternative Cost Distribution

In this chapter, we'll take a look at each of these features, how they are used, and how they can be configured.

16.1   Pay Scale Structure

The *Pay Scale Structure* feature will be familiar to SAP customers as a standard feature in SAP ERP HCM. The Pay Scale Structure is a structure for determining salary scales, often used to implement collective agreements from unions or other works' councils. Because of this common customer need, SAP has also introduced this feature into Employee Central. It's also used in Employee Central Payroll and enables feature parity.

The Pay Scale Structure enables hourly-paid/nonexempt employees to be assigned to the correct pay scale tariff in the structure by entering the appropriate

Pay Scale Group and Pay Scale Level in an employee's Job Information portlet. The Pay Scale Area and Pay Scale Type are also used, but not mandatory in Employee Central. Pay Components for the employee's pay can be automatically assigned to the employee based on configurable rules. This is called indirect valuation. Employees' pay can also be updated when the elements of the Pay Structure are updated, such as when a collective agreement is modified or replaced.

The Pay Scale Structure is built on the MDF and uses four components:

▶ PAY SCALE AREA
Defines a geographical area in which to apply the Pay Scale Structure.

▶ PAY SCALE TYPE
Defines a type of industry in which to apply the Pay Scale Structure.

▶ PAY SCALE GROUPS
Defines groups of Pay Scale Levels in the Pay Scale Structure.

▶ PAY SCALE LEVELS
Defines each of the levels within the structure and defines the Pay Component amounts to be paid to employees assigned to a particular level.

These objects are configured in OneAdmin in PAY SCALE STRUCTURE • MANAGE PAY SCALE OBJECTS. They are then assigned to the JOB INFORMATION portlet during hire and can be updated via a transaction (see Figure 16.1).

Figure 16.1 Assignment of Pay Scale Structure to Employee

Mass changes to Pay Scale Structure values can be made automatically. These are configured in OneAdmin in PAY SCALE STRUCTURE • ADJUST EMPLOYEES' COMPENSATION TO TARIFF CHANGES. Mass changes to the Pay Scale Structure are effective-dated so that they can be future-dated and can be simulated prior to being run. Once changes have been made to the Pay Scale Structure objects, the mass change can be run to create records to apply the changes to the Pay Scale Structure.

16.2 Concurrent Employment

Concurrent Employment enables employees to have multiple employments within their company simultaneously. A concurrent employee will often have different jobs, compensation information, and other employment details.

The Concurrent Employment feature operates in a similar manner to the Global Assignment feature we looked at in Chapter 11. We recommend reviewing Chapter 11 before reading the rest of this section as it will provide a good overview of how this type of functionality works.

Important!

An employee with one or more concurrent employments cannot be sent on a global assignment. Likewise, an employee on global assignment cannot have multiple employments.

Add a Concurrent Employment by selecting ADD EMPLOYMENT DETAILS in either the TAKE ACTION menu in Employee Files or through the quickcard. On the transaction screen, click the ADD EMPLOYMENT DETAILS hyperlink in the ADD EMPLOYMENT DETAILS portlet, in the same way that you would add a global assignment. Several fields will appear in the ADD EMPLOYMENT DETAILS portlet to maintain (Figure 16.2).

Many of the fields in the ADD EMPLOYMENT DETAILS portlet are the same as the fields seen in the EMPLOYMENT DETAILS portlet in the EMPLOYMENT INFORMATION screen.

As with global assignments, once the COMPANY field is filled, a set of additional portlets are displayed. JOB INFORMATION, JOB RELATIONSHIPS, and COMPENSATION INFORMATION (which includes the fields from the SPOT BONUS portlet) are displayed and represent the details of the concurrent employment details. However, a portlet appears directly above these called SECONDARY EMPLOYMENT INFORMA-TION. In this portlet, the Boolean field SET AS SECONDARY EMPLOYMENT FOR ALL SUCCESSFACTORS PROCESSES? determines if this employment will be the primary or secondary employment of the employee.

Figure 16.2 Add Employment Details Portlet

Once all details of the concurrent employment have been entered and saved, then the concurrent employment is created (if a workflow is enabled for Concurrent Employment, then the concurrent employment will be created after the workflow is fully approved). As with a global assignment, view a concurrent employment by clicking the EMPLOYMENT button that appears at the top of the screen (see Figure 16.3).

When employees who are on concurrent employment log in to SAP SuccessFactors, they will see their main employment listed under their name in the header panel, just as with a global assignment. As with that functionality, this enables the employee to switch between each of their employments to perform the different processes for each employment. This dropdown also appears in the Public Profile.

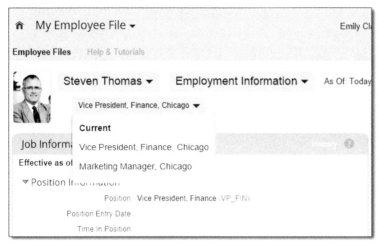

Figure 16.3 Employment Toggle Button

For more details, refer to the section *Working with Multiple Employments* in the *Employee Central Master* implementation guide found at *http://help.sap.com/hr_ec* under the heading IMPLEMENTATION GUIDES.

16.3   Document Generation

The Document Generation feature enables HR administrators and managers to generate documents for employees using predefined templates and Employee Central data. Document templates—and therefore documents generated from those templates—can contain images and dynamic "tags" that represent information about the target employee (called *dynamic content*).

Documents are generated from document templates, so a document template needs to be set up for each type of document that you want to generate. A document template can have dynamic content added to fill with employee data. Therefore, a template can be used to generate multiple documents that are identical except for the unique information about the subject employee. For example, a dynamic content field called [[LAST_NAME]] and mapped to the LAST NAME field from PERSONAL INFORMATION would be replaced with the last name of each employee the document is generated for.

Complete two steps to create a document template for generating documents:

1. Create the document template.

2. Map fields to the dynamic content added in the document template.

Let's look at these steps now.

16.3.1 Creating a Document Template

A document template is created in OneAdmin in EMPLOYEE FILES • DOCUMENT GENERATION - MANAGE DOCUMENT TEMPLATE.

To create a new document template, select DOCUMENT GENERATION TEMPLATE in the CREATE NEW dropdown that is located on the right-side of the screen. To view, maintain, or delete an existing document template, select DOCUMENT GENERATION TEMPLATE in the SEARCH dropdown and then select the document template to view in the adjacent dropdown box. Figure 16.4 shows the screen after selecting DOCUMENT GENERATION TEMPLATE in the CREATE NEW dropdown.

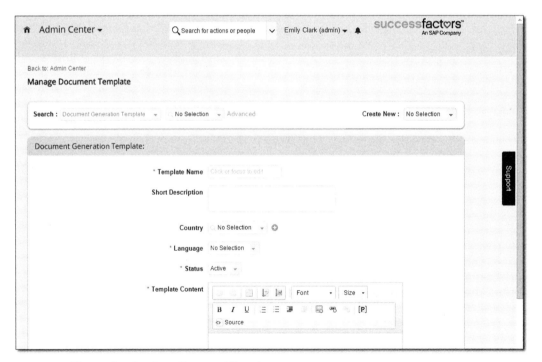

Figure 16.4 Creating a Document Template

Several fields define the behavior of the document template:

▶ TEMPLATE NAME
The name of the document template.

▶ SHORT DESCRIPTION
An optional description.

▶ COUNTRY
The country that the document template is available for.

▶ LANGUAGE
The language of the document template.

▶ STATUS
Whether the document template is active or inactive.

▶ TEMPLATE CONTENT
Enables the design of the document template using a rich text editor (RTE). The RTE enables the use of fonts, bullet points and lists, images, hyperlinks, and dynamic content placeholders used to map Employee Central fields to the template (Figure 16.5).

Figure 16.5 Document Template

An RTE allows you to create documents that look like they would in common word-processing software. This enables professional-looking documents to be created easily within Employee Central. Figure 16.5 shows an example of a letter designed in an RTE. Dynamic content can be seen in the document template. These are the words surrounded by double square brackets (e.g., [[FIRSTNAME]] or [[COMPANY]]). Insert dynamic content by using the P button while using the RTE. This dynamic content will be mapped to Employee Central fields after the document template is created.

Now that you've seen how a document template is created and walked through an example, let's see how we can map the dynamic content with Employee Central fields.

16.3.2 Mapping Fields

Once a document template is created, the dynamic content added in the document template needs to be mapped to Employee Central fields. Perform this process in OneAdmin via Employee Files • Document Generation - Generate Document. On the Manage Document Template Mapping screen, select the type of template in the Select a Template dropdown (the default option is All); otherwise, select the template in the adjacent dropdown.

Figure 16.6 shows the document template mapping for the document template you saw in Figure 16.5. There are six fields defined as dynamic content in the document template, which appear in the far-left column in bold.

The second column contains a dropdown to determine how the fields are mapped. There are two options here:

▶ Direct Mapping
Enables the field to be mapped directly to an Employee Central field.

▶ Calculated Mapping
Uses a business rule to define the field mapping.

The third and fourth columns are maintained when Direct Mapping is selected. The third column is the Employee Central object, and the fourth column is the field from the Employee Central object. The fifth column is used to select the business rule when Calculated Mapping is selected.

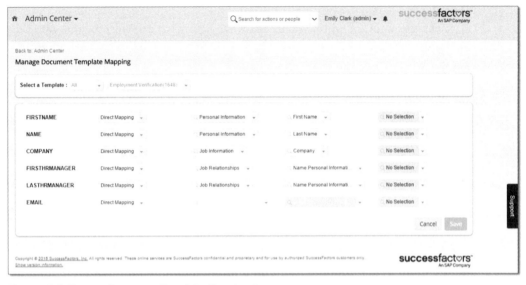

Figure 16.6 Manage Document Template Mapping Screen

Once all fields are mapped, click SAVE. You are now ready to generate a document from the document template.

16.3.3 Generating a Document

To generate a document from a document template, navigate to EMPLOYEE FILES • DOCUMENT GENERATION—MANAGE DOCUMENT TEMPLATE in OneAdmin. Here, you will see the GENERATE DOCUMENT screen (see Figure 16.7), where you can select the different options to generate the document. The following options are displayed:

▶ COUNTRY
The country that the document is for (optional).

▶ LANGUAGE
The language that the document is for (optional).

▶ TEMPLATE
The document template to use.

▶ USER
The employee to generate the document for.

▸ DOCUMENT TYPE
The output format of the document (PDF or Microsoft Word document).

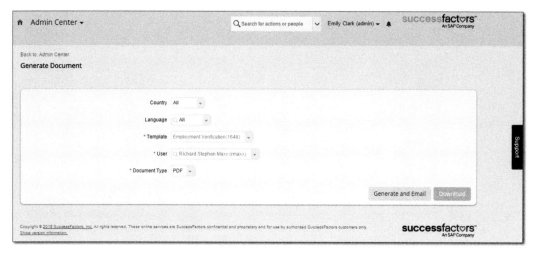

Figure 16.7 Document Generation Screen

Once the fields are set, choose from two options to generate the document:

▸ GENERATE AND EMAIL
Emails the created document to you.

▸ DOWNLOAD
Creates the file for download.

Figure 16.8 shows the PDF document generated from our document template for employee Richard Maxx, who we defined in the document generation fields shown in Figure 16.7. This PDF can be used as required by the generator of the document.

Additional Resources

For more details, refer to the *Document Generation* implementation guide located at *http://help.sap.com/hr_ec* under the heading IMPLEMENTATION GUIDES.

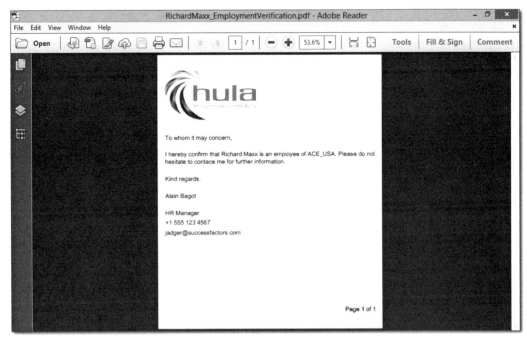

Figure 16.8 Generated Document

16.4 Alternative Cost Distribution

Alternative Cost Distribution is a simple feature to enable additional cost centers to be assigned to an employee to distribute their costs over multiple cost centers. Employees can have up to twelve cost centers assigned, each with a percentage of costs. The total percentage of the cost centers must add up to a maximum of 100%. Alterative cost centers are displayed in the ALTERNATIVE COST DISTRIBUTION portlet in the EMPLOYMENT INFORMATION screen (see Figure 16.9).

Add one or more alternative cost centers by selecting CHANGE JOB AND COMPENSATION INFO in the TAKE ACTION menu. Once on the transactions screen, select the ALTERNATIVE COST DISTRIBUTION checkbox under CHANGE JOB AND COMPENSATION INFO to open the ALTERNATIVE COST DISTRIBUTION portlet (see Figure 16.10).

Here, you can add, change, or remove one or more cost centers. The distribution only goes into effect on the date selected when adding the changes.

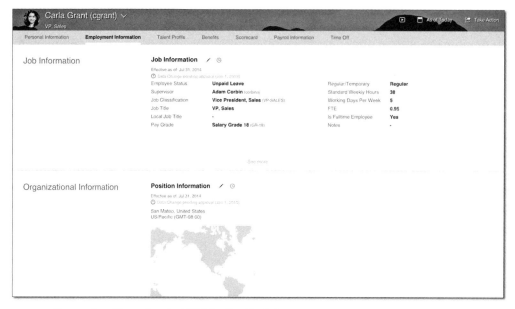

Figure 16.9 Alternative Cost Distribution Portlet

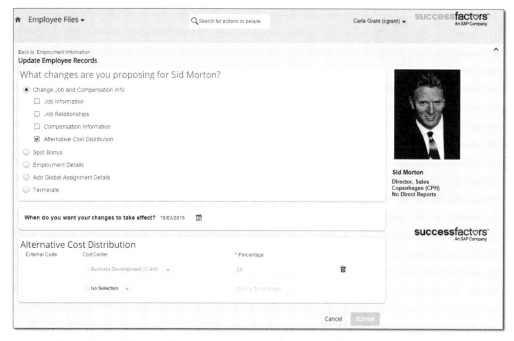

Figure 16.10 Adding an Alternative Cost Center for Cost Distribution

16.5   Pensions Payouts

The Pensions Payouts feature enables you to create a pensionable payout for an active or terminated employee. Typically, this payout begins when the employee leaves the company and his or her employee status in Employee Central is set to Retired (instead of Terminated). Pension payouts data can be integrated with payroll systems to pay pensioners.

Pension payouts are created by selecting Manage Pension Payout Details in either the Take Action menu or in the quickcard. Once on the transactions screen, click the Add Pension Payout Details hyperlink in the Manage Pension Payout Details portlet to begin entering a pension payout for an employee.

After clicking the Add Pension Payout Details hyperlink, you will see the following fields (see Figure 16.11):

Figure 16.11 Adding a Pension Payout

▸ EVENT REASON
The Event Reason for pensions payouts (must use the event Start Pensions Payout).

▸ START DATE
The date the pensions payout starts (typically the termination date).

▸ END DATE
The date the pensions payout will cease (optional field).

▸ PENSION PROVIDER
The company that will pay the pension.

Similar to selecting a value for the COMPANY field when adding a concurrent employment (see Section 16.2) or global assignment (see Chapter 11), selecting the PENSION PROVIDER field displays a number of portlets to complete:

▸ PENSION PAYOUT DETAILS INFORMATION
The Job Information portlet.

▸ RELATIONSHIPS
The Job Relationships portlet.

▸ COMPENSATION INFORMATION
The Compensation Information portlet, where the pay components for the pension can be assigned (these payments can be integrated with a payroll system).

▸ DEPENDENTS
Enables dependents to be entered if DEPENDENTS MANAGEMENT is used in Employee Central.

Once this data is saved, the Pension Payouts information can be viewed similarly to information in the Global Assignments and Concurrent Employment features, through the job toggle menu at the top of the EMPLOYMENT INFORMATION screen. You can toggle between the pre-pensions payouts record and the pensions payouts record.

Additional Resources

For more details, refer to the *Pensions Payouts* implementation guide located at *http://help.sap.com/hr_ec* under the heading IMPLEMENTATION GUIDES.

16.6   Summary

In this chapter, we looked at a variety of features that are important to a number of different organizations. The Pay Scale Structure functionality is critical to support collective pay and salary agreements, whereas concurrent employment is a trend across multiple industries. The Document Generation feature provides easy-to-manage functionality to produce custom-defined documents for employees. We also took a brief look at assigning multiple cost centers to employees and defining pension payouts for employees.

Next up is the all-important reporting functionality available in Employee Central. We'll take a look at the standard-delivered reports and the functionality provided to enable you to build your own reports.

The ability to quickly and easily extract useful and meaningful data from an HRIS system is an absolute business need. Employee Central offers robust reporting capabilities from both standard-delivered and custom reports.

17   Reporting

Access to accurate and current data is essential for running a business. Staffing decisions and organizational balance require employee data reports in formats that are meaningful and easy to read. Employee Central offers a complete reporting solution with multiple methods for extracting and analyzing data from the system.

In this chapter, we will review the available options for reporting. We will learn about the Online Report Designer and Advanced Reporting techniques, and how to create and schedule a report. After reading this chapter, you should have a thorough understanding of how reporting works, what reporting options are available, and how to create and schedule reports. Let's begin by reviewing what types of output are available.

17.1   Report Components

There are several different types of reporting outputs available. Depending on your data needs, you may find some forms more appealing than others. Outputs range from simple lists to fully developed graphical analysis charts. The process that creates these outputs is known as a *query*, and query outputs are called *components*. A *report* is a page composed of one or more components. Let's go through an explanation of each major component type:

▸ **Lists**
 A *list*, also called a query, is the most basic type of report. It gives a series of data results, each placed in a row and displayed line after line in a scroll or register

format. The list can have one or more columns of returned data. Lists can be sorted and filtered based on various criteria. They can also be used as building blocks for other reports. A list is often the quickest and easiest way to get data directly from Employee Central, and because of its simple setup, it's a preferred method of reporting for many HR representatives. Figure 17.1 shows an example of a list report.

Pay Grade Info							
start-date	**end-date**	**status**	**externalCode**	**name**	**description**	**paygradeLevel**	
01/01/1990	12/31/9999	A	GR-1	Salary Grade 1		1	
01/01/1990	12/31/9999	A	GR-10	Salary Grade 10		10	
01/01/1990	12/31/9999	A	GR-11	Salary Grade 11		11	
01/01/1990	12/31/9999	A	GR-12	Salary Grade 12		12	
01/01/1990	12/31/9999	A	GR-13	Salary Grade 13		13	
01/01/1990	12/31/9999	A	GR-14	Salary Grade 14		14	
01/01/1990	12/31/9999	A	GR-15	Salary Grade 15		15	
01/01/1990	12/31/9999	A	GR-16	Salary Grade 16		16	
01/01/1990	12/31/9999	A	GR-17	Salary Grade 17		17	
01/01/1990	12/31/9999	A	GR-18	Salary Grade 18		18	
01/01/1990	12/31/9999	A	GR-19	Salary Grade 19		19	
01/01/1990	12/31/9999	A	GR-2	Salary Grade 2		2	
01/01/1990	12/31/9999	A	GR-20	Salary Grade 20		20	
01/01/1990	12/31/9999	A	GR-3	Salary Grade 3		3	
01/01/1990	12/31/9999	A	GR-4	Salary Grade 4		4	
01/01/1990	12/31/9999	A	GR-5	Salary Grade 5		5	
01/01/1990	12/31/9999	A	GR-6	Salary Grade 6		6	
01/01/1990	12/31/9999	A	GR-7	Salary Grade 7		7	
01/01/1990	12/31/9999	A	GR-8	Salary Grade 8		8	
01/01/1990	12/31/9999	A	GR-9	Salary Grade 9		9	
01/01/1990	12/31/9999	A	H-1	Hourly Non-Exempt 1		1	
01/01/1990	12/31/9999	A	H-10	Hourly Non-Exempt 10		10	

Figure 17.1 List Report

▶ **Pivot tables**
   A *pivot table* is a summarized view of data formatted in rows and columns that are defined by the *pivot query*. You define the vertical and horizontal data types, and the system populates the data. In SAP SuccessFactors, we pivot a list report into a pivot table. Figure 17.2 shows a sample pivot table depicting retention rate per department broken out by gender.

	Corporate	Energy and Utilities	Government	Healthcare	Retail
Female	94.4%	89.2%	85.1%	72.3%	49.3%
Male	93.9%	93.9%	90.2%	82.9%	86.7%

Figure 17.2 Pivot Table

▶ **Pivot charts**
   A *pivot chart* is a view of summarized data in graphical form. We define the vertical and horizontal data types, and the system populates the data. In SAP

SuccessFactors, we can pivot a list report into a graphical pivot chart. Figure 17.3 shows the pivot chart view of a company's retention rate per department broken out by gender. This is the graphical chart form of the pivot table shown in Figure 17.2.

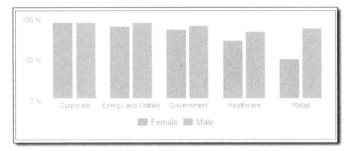

Figure 17.3 Pivot Chart

These components are the reporting outputs for Employee Central and SAP SuccessFactors. In the next section, we'll review the different reporting methods that will be covered in this chapter.

17.2 Reporting Methods

In terms of reporting, ad hoc reporting is the oldest form of reporting used in SAP SuccessFactors. There are two ways to create and run ad hoc reports for Employee Central:

▸ The legacy Ad Hoc Reporting tool

▸ Online Report Designer

The legacy tool known as *Ad Hoc Reporting* allows users to build and execute basic ad hoc reports. With the introduction of the second method for creating ad hoc reports, the Online Report Designer, the Ad Hoc Reporting tool is no longer considered the main reporting solution. It remains a powerful reporting option, however, and is the primary choice for many HR representatives due to its simplicity of use. Its basic output is reporting lists, although additional technology such as the open-source *Business Intelligence and Reporting Tool (BIRT)* can be used to render visualizations.

Ad hoc reporting in both mediums are driven by a collection of subdomain schemas. Each subdomain schema is a collection of views and fields, such as Person and Employment (As of Date) and Job Information (Date Range). Data transformations such as picklist labels or row-to-column conversion for objects with multiple rows are delivered. The list of delivered subdomain schemas can be found in the *Employee Central Master* implementation handbook available at *http://help.sap.com/ec_hr*.

Another method of reporting in Employee Central—specifically, Employee Central Advanced Reporting—involves the *Operational Data Store (ODS)*. Advanced Reporting delivers preconfigured reporting content. It's an enhanced toolkit available for transactional reporting in Employee Central.

In the sections that follow, we'll look at the legacy Ad Hoc Reporting Tool and the Online Report Designer for ad hoc reporting, and the ODS and Advanced Reporting tool.

17.3   Legacy Ad Hoc Reporting

In addition to being able to create custom reports, the legacy Ad Hoc Reporting tool also includes approximately fifteen standard-delivered reports for Employee Central that can be run as is or saved as templates for creating your own reports. Some SAP Jam reporting groups also contain repositories for downloading additional report templates.

Benefits of the legacy Ad Hoc Reporting tool include the following:

▶ An easy, simple-to-use guided process for creating reports leads to high rates of adoption.

▶ Export capability to CSV, Microsoft Excel, Microsoft PowerPoint, Microsoft Word, and PDF formats.

▶ One-click access for users to run reports.

▶ Report sharing is direct and straightforward.

▶ Reports can be scheduled via Provisioning.

▶ No additional configuration or setup is required; this tool works out of the box.

The Ad Hoc Reporting tool is accessed directly in SAP SuccessFactors via ANALYT-ICS • REPORTING • AD HOC REPORTS. Note that your system's menu path may vary slightly based on the naming convention used for your system's different reporting tools. Figure 17.4 shows an overview of what the AD HOC REPORTS section looks like. Run reports by clicking on their hyperlinked names. Create new reports by clicking on the CREATE NEW REPORT button.

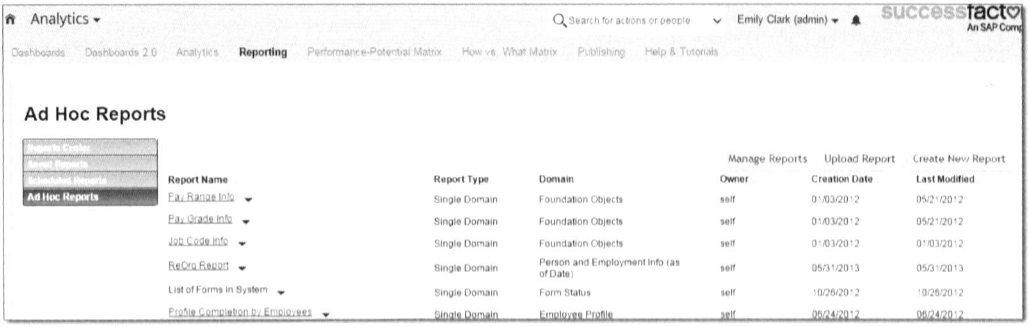

Figure 17.4 Ad Hoc Reports

The legacy Ad Hoc Reporting tool may no longer be the main area for reporting, but it continues to be a powerful option for those looking for quick and easy, albeit simple, reports. The functionality is not outdated, however. Reports created through the Ad Hoc Reporting tool can be used as building blocks by the Online Report Designer, and the value of having generic ad hoc reporting available also is not lost: The Online Report Designer supports the creation of ad hoc reports within its arena.

17.4   Online Report Designer

The *Online Report Designer (ORD)* is an integrated reporting solution that allows users to design, build, and execute reports. It is extremely versatile in nature as it permits users to select fields, layouts, and output mediums.

Here are some basic benefits the ORD provides:

▶ The ORD supports the creation of custom queries and reports. Users with access can build their own reports and share them with others.

- List queries, pivot queries, and complex pivot components are all supported.
- Cross-module reporting is supported, allowing users to pull data from multiple modules into a single report.
- The executed report can be downloaded in several file formats, such as:
  - PDF
  - Microsoft Excel
  - Microsoft PowerPoint
  - Microsoft Word
- Reports can be arranged to run on set schedules and on a recurring basis.
- Reports can be shared with other users, and results can be emailed to different recipients.
- The ORD supports the use of custom calculations and field formatting.
- IF/THEN/ELSE statements are supported, allowing for a tailored report output.
- Headers can be relabeled, making this an excellent tool for generating file extracts for import into auxiliary systems or for sharing with nontechnical users.

> **Online Report Designer System**
>
> The ORD is not an inherent part of your SAP SuccessFactors system. It's a separate system that must be linked to your Employee Central system. Single Sign-On (SSO) is enabled internally to connect the two systems together and to allow for seamless navigation back and forth.

Access the ORD by clicking on the ANALYTICS option under the main HOME navigational dropdown and then selecting the ANALYTICS link from the second level of navigation. Figure 17.5 shows an example of the ORD in action. The menus on the left-hand side of the figure represent the Report Designer portion of the ORD. The center of the screen shows live data.

> **Note**
>
> The ORD can be used by customers with and without Talent Insight or Workforce Analytics.

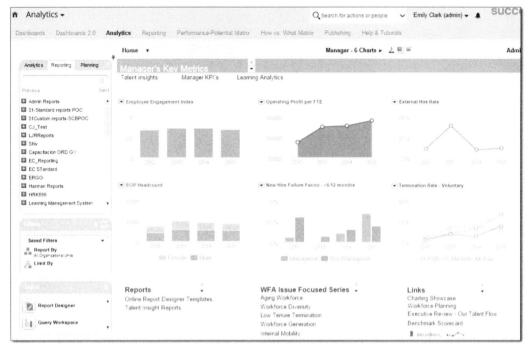

Figure 17.5 Main Screen of the Online Report Designer

At its base, the ORD offers ad hoc reporting. In its advanced form, pivot tables and charts can be produced and placed on compiled report pages.

17.4.1 Implementation

There are three main steps to implementing the ORD. These steps must be completed in the following order:

1. Configure the existing SAP SuccessFactors and Employee Central system in Provisioning to connect to the ORD instance.

2. Set the appropriate permissions within RBPs to allow a user or users to access the ORD.

3. Set up permissions within the ORD for ORD users.

Detailed instructions for each step can be found in the *Online Report Designer* implementation guide available at *http://help.sap.com/ec_hr.*

17.4.2 Running Reports

Reports can be executed directly from the main ORD screen. You'll see a listing of reports available to you based on your permissions in the top-left corner of the screen in a box titled REPORTING. Open and expand folders to find the report you are looking for (Figure 17.6). When you find the report, double-click its title to run it. The report will run, and results will be shown in the center of the screen. Quick buttons are available for you to save or download the report results.

Figure 17.6 Listing of Reports Available for Execution

17.5 Operational Data Store

The *Operational Data Store (ODS)* is an internal name used to reference Advanced Reporting and other pre-delivered reporting content for the ORD within SAP SuccessFactors. It refers to the source of the data, which has been transformed and optimized for reporting.

Although Advanced Reporting refers specifically to Employee Central, the ODS refers to delivered report content and data for all modules. It's often the term you hear when discussing integration with SAP HANA, because integration with all modules is possible and the sourcing of data is required.

We will discuss the ODS in terms of Employee Central by reviewing Employee Central Advanced Reporting and its available features and functionality.

17.6   Employee Central Advanced Reporting

Employee Central Advanced Reporting is an augmented toolkit available for transactional reporting in Employee Central. It's accessed through the ORD, and therefore the ORD is a prerequisite. It contains two main parts: standard-delivered reports, and grouped categories, columns, and tables that can be used for quick queries and for creating complex reports. It offers reporting on MDF objects and can be integrated with SAP HANA.

17.6.1   Standard-Delivered Reports

Advanced Reporting delivers preconfigured reports that include lists, pivot tables, and pivot charts.

There are more than seventy-five advanced reports available, including some that are country-specific to assist with compliance reporting. These reports can be executed as is or can be used as starting point templates and modified to meet your specific business needs. The output and share options available for all ORD reports are still available here. Most importantly, RBPs are respected within reports. The user executing the report will only have access to the data he or she is permissioned to see.

Country-Specific Advanced Reports

Country-specific reports are included with the delivered Advanced Reports. These reports have a country code filter included with them so that they only return results for the specified country. Depending on the composition of the report, the results can be used to help fulfill local compliance reporting needs. Some reports are specifically formatted to meet the structure of official compliance reports.

Categories of Advanced Reports

The delivered Advanced Reports can be broken into the following groups; an example report is listed for each group:

- Personal/Employee Information
  - Dependents

- ▶ Job/Employment Information

  - ▹ New Hires, Terminations

- ▶ Compensation Information

  - ▹ Alternative Cost Distribution

- ▶ Payment Information

  - ▹ Payment Information

- ▶ Payroll (replication information)

  - ▹ Payroll Results

- ▶ Position Management

  - ▹ Position Details

- ▶ Workflows

  - ▹ Workflow Audit Statistics

- ▶ Time-Off

  - ▹ Time Account Overview

- ▶ Global Assignments

  - ▹ Global Assignment Contract Details

- ▶ Pension Plans

  - ▹ Pension Overview

- ▶ Benefits

  - ▹ Benefits Enrollment

A complete list of delivered reports can be found in the Employee Central *Advanced Reporting: Standard Reports* handbook located at *http://help.sap.com/ec_hr*.

17.6.2 Custom Reports

Custom reports can also be created using Advanced Reporting, which offers pre-delivered data schematics that you can use to construct your own reports.

The Advanced Reporting data schematic is broken into three levels: categories, tables, and columns. These levels help you find the data you need to include in a report. Figure 17.7 shows an example.

▸ **Category**

A *category* is the highest breakout of data within the data schematic. It provides a top grouping that can be broken out and drilled down into to find data field. The four main categories used for Employee Central are as follows:

  ▹ *Employment*: Contains tables and columns related to Employment Information, such as job and pay history.

  ▹ *Person*: Contains tables and columns related to Personal Information, such as addresses and dependents.

  ▹ *Compensation*: Contains tables and columns related to compensation and pay.

  ▹ *Foundation Objects*: Contains tables and columns related to Foundation Objects and their values.

▸ **Table**

A *table* is the next level down, and it provides further divisions for sorting data. Tables usually correspond to employee data portlets (see Chapter 9) found in Employee Central. Examples include Job Information and Employment Details.

▸ **Column**

A *column* is the final level in the data schematic structure and represents individual data fields found within a table. These fields correspond to data fields found within Employee Central. Examples include First Name, Last Name, and Job Title.

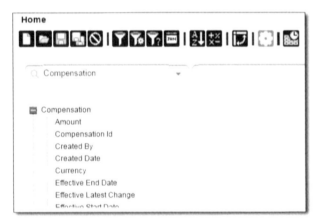

Figure 17.7 Advanced Reporting Showing the Compensation Category, Compensation Table, and Related Columns (Fields)

Categories and tables help us easily navigate the Advanced Reporting data schematic to find the data needed to create custom reports.

Now that we've looked at the different reporting options, let's turn our attention to the process of creating and scheduling reports in Employee Central.

17.7 Creating Reports

So far, we've discussed the ability to create reports using the legacy Ad Hoc Reporting tool, the ORD, and Advanced Reporting contained within the ORD. In this section, we'll look at how to create reports within the ORD. The principles discussed here can be applied down to the legacy Ad Hoc Reporting tool and applied up to Advanced Reporting.

As mentioned, a report is composed of one or more components. The simplest way to create a report is to add existing components to your report. However, let's assume that a component with the data you need does not exist and you need to create it. You can proceed in one of two ways:

▶ Create a report and add components to the report. When asked to select an existing component or to create a new one, choose CREATE NEW. This allows you to build the components directly in the report. Components built in this manner can still be utilized in other reports.

▶ Create the components first and then add them as existing components to a new or existing report.

In our example for this section, we'll choose the first method.

17.7.1 Creating a New Report

Begin on the main page of the ORD (see Section 17.4 for navigational instructions). Select REPORT DESIGNER from the TOOLS menu in the bottom-left corner (Figure 17.8).

Figure 17.8 Select Report Designer under Tools

The resulting screen brings up your existing reports menu structure and a new
MANAGE REPORT menu on the middle-left side. From here, you can create a new
folder, create a new file (report), or add a page to an existing report. Highlight an
existing folder in the main screen folder structure, or choose to create a new
folder. Then, select NEW REPORT by double-clicking the folder. Highlight the
report in the folder structure, and then select BLANK PAGE under the ADD PAGE
dropdown, as shown in Figure 17.9. A blank report page opens in the center of
the screen, and you can now add components, which we'll cover next.

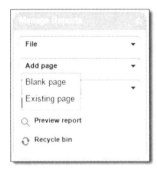

Figure 17.9 Blank Page Option

17.7.2 Adding a Component to a Report

The current screen is a blank canvas that can be populated with various reporting
components. To add a component to the report, choose the type of component you
wish to add from the ADD COMPONENT menu. Click on the component to expand
your selection options (Figure 17.10), and then drag and drop the component on to
the blank report screen. A generic component placeholder will display on the report.

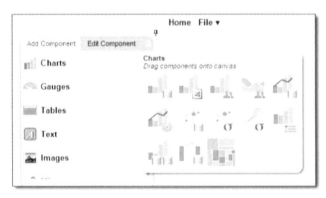

Figure 17.10 Adding a New Component

Next, select the specific component you want to appear. Highlight the placeholder, and under EDIT COMPONENT choose EDIT QUERY, as shown in Figure 17.11.

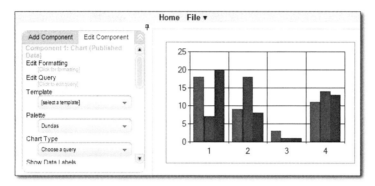

Figure 17.11 Highlight Placeholder and Click to Edit Query

The component selection screen appears and allows you to select a specific list, query, pivot table, or pivot chart. If the required component does not exist, click NEW QUERY on the right side of the screen, as shown in Figure 17.12.

Figure 17.12 Choose Existing Query or Pivot Item or Create a New One

17.7.3 Creating a Component

If you select an existing component, then it will appear on your report page. If you choose to create a new component, then you will need to add fields and build the new query.

If you selected a list component, you will be prompted to select data fields and add them to output columns. If you selected a pivot table or chart, you will be prompted to build out the pivot.

The steps for building a basic query are as follows:

1. Drag and drop the required fields into the query. Add the required fields to your list or query by dragging them from the data schematic and onto the blank query screen.

2. Define the PEOPLE SCOPE.

3. Add the appropriate filters so that the correct employees are included.

4. Set the appropriate PEOPLE view.

5. Set the DATE OPTIONS.

6. Sort the columns.

7. Include calculated columns.

8. Hide any duplicate rows.

9. Pivot the list (if applicable).

10. Save your work.

The next two sections look in depth at some of the preceding steps.

Defining the People Scope and Filters

People scope refers to the group of people who should be returned for each user when the report is run. Common scenarios include the *team view*, a default view that allows managers to view reports on their team members.

Set PEOPLE SCOPE by going to EDIT • PEOPLE SCOPE from the menu.

Filters allow us to exclude certain employee populations from reports. You can set filters by clicking the MANAGE FILTERS button in the bottom-left corner of the screen.

People Scope

The default people scope is the team view, which is popular for managers. If you are not a manager and create a report without adjusting PEOPLE SCOPE, you will not see any results when the query is executed.

Including Calculated Columns

Calculated columns can be entered to calculate amounts and values as well as to concatenate or otherwise alter field values. To insert a calculated field, choose CALCULATED COLUMN under the EDIT menu option, as shown in Figure 17.13.

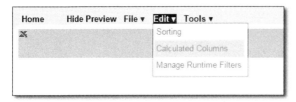

Figure 17.13 Calculated Columns Option in Edit Menu Dropdown

When the CALCULATED COLUMNS popup menu appears, you can use an already defined calculated column or define your own by clicking on the plus button in the top-right corner. Calculated columns can be shared with other users.

Calculated columns can include a wide array of calculations based on the DATA TYPE selected. Here are some examples:

▶ NUMBER
Supports mathematical calculations with numbers including sums and totals.

▶ TEXT
Supports the joining together of words and characters or the trimming of characters.

▶ DATE
Supports the addition and subtraction of dates.

▶ IF/THEN/ELSE
Statements supported for all data types.

Figure 17.14 shows a sample configuration of a calculated column. It shows two texts fields being concatenated together.

Once you've selected all of your data columns and set your filters, you're ready to execute and then share the list via a report. If you created a list report, you may decide to take it one step further and create a pivot table or chart that will offer greater insight. In the next section, we discuss how to set up a pivot query.

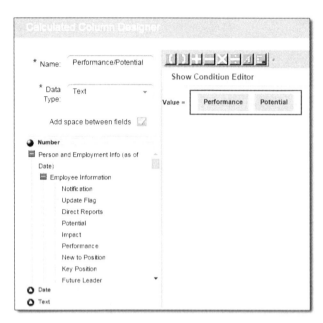

Figure 17.14 Concatenation

17.7.4 Setting Up a Pivot Query

A list report can form the basis of a pivot query that can then be turned into a pivot table or chart, because the list report can be pivoted for display. To create a pivot table or chart from an existing list, go to TOOLS • PRINT QUERY DESIGNER.

Complete three steps to set up a pivot query:

1. Place the data you want to measure into the center of the pivot setup screen using drag-and-drop functionality.

2. Determine the pivot function, such as average, sum, minimum, maximum, or so on.

3. Populate the pivot by adding in rows and columns of data.

Standard View

The standard view for creating a pivot component is the Show Design view. You can toggle back and forth between Design view and Table view to confirm visual layouts.

Once the pivot query is complete, you can add the query to both pivot tables and pivot groups within your report.

17.7.5 Completing a Report

Now that you've created the query and assigned it to the component, your report should contain the newly reported data. Be sure to save your work with the SAVE or SAVE AS option. You can continue adding additional lists and pivots onto the report page or create an additional page to support multiple components at once. The report is now ready for to run and share. You can also give your report a header and/or footer and set basic page properties such as sizes and borders. The PAGE PROPERTIES menu offers this functionality, as shown in Figure 17.15.

Figure 17.15 Page Properties Edit Screen

Once inside the EDIT PAGE PROPERTIES settings (Figure 17.16), you can set up headers and set border parameters.

Page Properties		
Name	RM_WOMEN_TERMINATION - Page #1	
Output Defaults		
Paper Size	LETTER	
Orientation	● Portrait ○ Landscape	
Top Margin	0.5	
Bottom Margin	0.5	○ Millimetres ● Inches
Left Margin	0.5	
Right Margin	0.5	
Canvas Size		
Constrain to Paper Size	☑	
Height	960	
Width	720	

Figure 17.16 Page Property Settings

Reports can be shared with users both with and without access to the Online Report Designer. The process is relatively straightforward assuming your desired recipient has access to different reporting folders.

17.7.6 Sharing a Report

There are two ways to share a report. The first is to share it with groups of users. To do so, share the report in a shared folder within the menu structure, as shown in Figure 17.6. Access to menu folders is controlled through permissioning in RBPs. Placing a report in a shared folder gives access to the report to anyone with permissions for that folder.

The second option is to share with selected users. Do so by choosing the REPORT SHARING option under MANAGE REPORTS, as shown in Figure 17.17.

Figure 17.17 Edit Ownership under Manage Reports

Users with access to the folder can run the report, but only the report creator/ owner and ORD admins can edit the report. The report owner can be reassigned by choosing the EDIT OWNERSHIP option, also under MANAGE REPORTS, as shown in Figure 17.17.

This complete the report creation process. In the next section, we will look at the report scheduling options in Employee Central.

17.8   Scheduling Reports

The ability to schedule reports is convenient. It not only saves you the time vs. having to run reports manually, but it also helps you keep on task. Scheduling a report may also be referred to as *distributing* a report.

The following steps take place in the ORD under TOOLS • REPORT DISTRIBUTOR, as shown in Figure 17.18.

Figure 17.18 Report Distributor under Tools

In the following sections, we'll walk through the process of scheduling a report.

17.8.1 Creating a Bundle

The first step in scheduling a report is to create a *bundle*. A bundle is one or more reports grouped together for the purpose of sending the results to recipients. Click on the NEW BUNDLE option under the menu. Give the bundle a name and choose an output format, such as PDF. A blank bundle page opens in the center of the screen. This is where you can place the report or reports you want to schedule.

17.8.2 Adding Items to a Bundle

Next, add items to your new bundle. Add a report to the bundle by clicking on the ADD ITEM button within the bundle screen. Choose the intended report, CSV table, or Microsoft Excel table. The selected item now will be listed underITEMS in the bundle, as shown in Figure 17.19. Tabs for DESTINATION, RECIPIENTS, and SCHEDULE are available to provide additional information about your bundle.

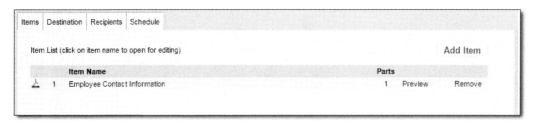

Figure 17.19 Standard Report Included in Bundle

Clicking on the Destination tab allows you to select where you want the file to be delivered. Our choices are as follows:

▸ Email

▸ Run Offline

▸ FTP (default server)

On the Recipients tab, indicate who should receive copies of the executed reports. Click on the Add Recipients button to add a new user to the delivery process.

17.8.3 Scheduling a Bundle

Clicking on the Schedule tab brings up the scheduling area. This is where you indicate how frequently the report(s) should be run and distributed, as shown in Figure 17.20.

Click on the Add button to set up a new schedule. Multiple schedules can be set up if the report needs to be received at multiple times—Monday mornings and Friday afternoons, for example.

Complete the following fields:

▸ Schedule Start
   The date on which the report(s) should begin running and sending.

▸ Time of Start
   The time the report(s) should execute.

▸ Frequency of Recurrence
   Options include One Time, Daily, Weekly, and Monthly.

▸ Recur Every
   Set how many times per frequency period (set in Frequency of Recurrence) the report should run.

▸ Days
   If Weekly is selected as the Frequency of Recurrence, then a day or days of the week on which to run the report must be selected.

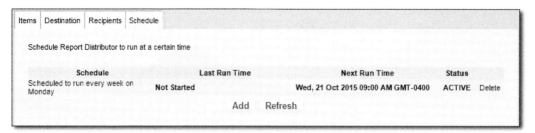

Figure 17.20 Options Set for Scheduling the Bundle

The scheduling operation is complete, and the report(s) will run and distribute at the selected time.

17.9 Summary

In this chapter, we learned about the different options available for Employee Central reporting, including legacy Ad Hoc Reporting, the Online Report Designer, and Advanced Reporting. These tools offer users a robust medium for creating, building, and executing reports.

In the next chapter, we'll discuss the mobile functionality available for Employee Central. Highlights include employee and manager interactions and Time Off capabilities.

For employees on the move, mobility is key. When off-site, employees need access to important administrative activities, such as approving requests or booking vacations. In this chapter, we discuss the features and functionality that make this access possible in Employee Central.

18 Mobile

Mobile access has become increasingly critical over the years. For field-based employees and those constantly on the move, it provides the ability to get work done without having to find a computer. Whether managers are approving requests from a direct report or employees are requesting time off, the ability to perform these activities while away from the office is crucial to optimal workflow. With this in mind, SAP SuccessFactors created the SAP SuccessFactors Mobile app, which is included in your SAP SuccessFactors subscription.

The SAP SuccessFactors Mobile app covers functionality across the SAP SuccessFactors HCM Suite, although in this chapter we will only look at the core functionality and features of Employee Central. For Employee Central, there are several features available in the SAP SuccessFactors Mobile app, including the following:

- **Employee Self-Services**
  - View your own profile
  - Change name
  - Change phone number
  - View Talent Information
  - View scorecard
  - View location in the Org Chart
  - View meetings
  - View touchbase items
  - View badges

- ▶ **Manager Self-Services**
  - ▷ View team
  - ▷ View profile of team members
  - ▷ Search for employees
  - ▷ Annotate notes for team
  - ▷ Approve workflow requests, such as job change or time off requests
- ▶ **Time Off**
  - ▷ View approved vacation requests
  - ▷ Request vacation
  - ▷ View team calendar
- ▶ **Additional features**
  - ▷ Home page
  - ▷ View Org Chart
  - ▷ View meetings from device calendar
  - ▷ Access Touchbase
  - ▷ Access SAP Jam

The SAP SuccessFactors Mobile app is available for Apple iOS devices (e.g., iPhone or iPad), Android devices (e.g., the Samsung Galaxy S6), and Blackberry devices. You can download the app from the app store of the respective device/operation system.

Important!

At the time of writing (December 2015), the Android version of the app is not at parity with the iOS version of the app in terms of user interface and range of features. However, SAP SuccessFactors is currently working to bring the Android version of the app in line with the iOS version of the app.

Further Resources

More details on SAP SuccessFactors Mobile across the enterprise can be found in *SuccessFactors with SAP ERP HCM: Business Processes and Use* by Amy Grubb and Luke Marson (2nd edition, SAP PRESS, 2015).

In this chapter, we'll look at how different Employee Central features are enabled, how users can be activated or self-activate their devices, how users are managed, and how the different Employee Central features of SAP SuccessFactors Mobile can be used by employees and managers.

We'll begin by exploring and enabling the different features.

18.1   Enabling Features

Different settings and features for SAP SuccessFactors Mobile can be enabled or disabled in OneAdmin via MOBILE • ENABLE MOBILE FEATURES (see Figure 18.1). This includes settings such as security and device management and enabling features for Employee Central and other applications, such as the Org Chart, SAP Jam, SAP SuccessFactors Recruiting, and more.

Figure 18.1 Enable Mobile Features Screen

The screen is split into two sections: MOBILE SPECIFIC and MODULES. The MOBILE SPECIFIC section covers enabling the following features:

▶ THEMING
Determines whether you wish to use a different theme for the app than you use in your SAP SuccessFactors system.

▶ ON DEVICE SUPPORT
Enables whether users can contact support from within the ABOUT section of the app.

▶ SF NOTIFICATIONS
Enables notifications to be sent to the app.

▶ MOBILE SECURITY
Contains two options: one to select whether to force users to create a PIN or password for each device, and one to enable secure storage of data on a device, which is recommended.

▶ MOBILE FEATURES
Enables the Org Chart and/or Touchbase feature.

▶ MOBILE DEVICE MANAGEMENT
Enables device activation to be managed using a unique key value that pairs managed devices with the system.

The MODULES section covers enabling application-specific features such Employee Central, Recruiting, Goals, Presentations, and Analytics. For Employee Central, you can enable or disable any of the three features we discussed at the beginning of this chapter by simply checking the checkbox next to the feature.

18.2 Activation and Deactivation

Users who wish to use the SAP SuccessFactors Mobile app should download the app and then activate it in SAP SuccessFactors. An administrator can send an email notification to users with instructions on how to install and activate the SAP SuccessFactors Mobile app. This is done in OneAdmin via MOBILE • MANAGE MOBILE USERS. Here, the user searches for the users to notify in the SEARCH PEOPLE box and then selects the SEND A NEW MOBILE ACTIVATION EMAIL button at the bottom of the screen to send the email notification.

User Permissions

For a user to be able to access SAP SuccessFactors via the SAP SuccessFactors Mobile app, he or she must have the MOBILE ACCESS permission assigned to one of the permission roles he or she is granted. This permission is located in the GENERAL USER PERMISSION category. A user's permissions in SAP SuccessFactors are respected within the SAP SuccessFactors Mobile app.

The email notification template is enabled and configured in OneAdmin viaMOBILE • EMAIL TEMPLATE NOTIFICATION or COMPANY SETTINGS • E-MAIL NOTIFICATION TEMPLATES SETTINGS. The email template is called MOBILE ACTIVATION NOTIFICATION.

After installing the SAP SuccessFactors Mobile app, activate your device in SAP SuccessFactors. After logging into the SAP SuccessFactors Mobile app for the first time, you'll see the activation screen, shown in Figure 18.2 on the iPad app.

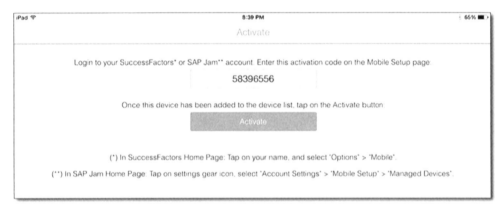

Figure 18.2 Activation Screen in SAP SuccessFactors Mobile App (iPad)

Log in to SAP SuccessFactors, navigate to OPTIONS in the user menu, and select the MOBILE option. Enter the activation code in the ACTIVATION CODE box and click SAVE. The device will then be registered and listed on the screen, as shown in Figure 18.3.

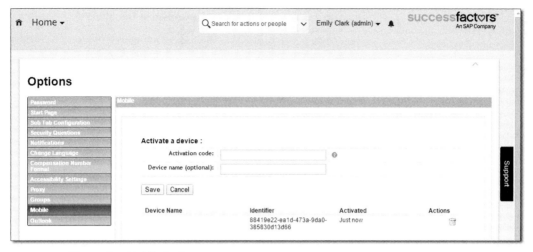

Figure 18.3 Mobile Options

Click the ACTIVATE button on the ACTIVATION screen in the SAP SuccessFactors Mobile app, as shown in Figure 18.2. You will see the user license terms, which you need to accept. Once you accept the user license terms, activation is complete, and you can use the app.

An administrator can view existing users and deactivate them if required in the MANAGE MOBILE USERS screen mentioned at the start of this section.

18.3   Using SAP SuccessFactors Mobile

Using the SAP SuccessFactors Mobile app is fairly straightforward and intuitive. After entering the app, you'll see with the home page, as shown in Figure 18.4. Here, users can see a number of tiles, based on the features enabled and their permissions. For example, you may see some analytics and a summary of your SAP Jam feeds.

In this section, we'll run through the features for ESS, MSS, Time Off, and Global Benefits, as well as other features that can be useful. Let's start with ESS features.

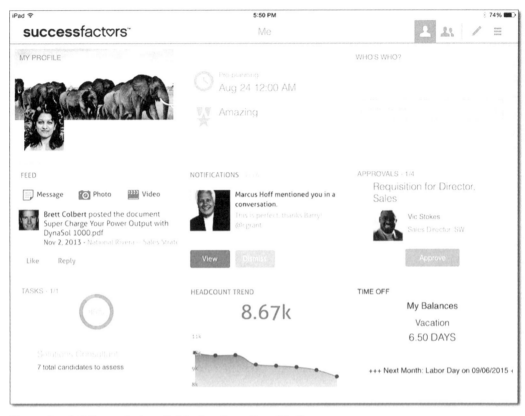

Figure 18.4 SAP SuccessFactors Mobile App Home Page (iPad)

18.3.1 Employee Self-Services

Depending on permissions, you can see several details about yourself and make some data changes. By clicking on the MY PROFILE tile on the home page (see Figure 18.4), you can view your profile, as shown in Figure 18.5. This is also the same screen that a manager sees when viewing the profiles of their reports.

There are several options available on the left side:

▶ DETAILS
  Allows you to view Talent Info, Personal Information, and Scorecard data; a dropdown menu lets you select different dates (see Figure 18.5).

▶ ORG CHART
  Navigate to your location in the Org Chart.

- ▶ MY MEETINGS
  View all meetings found in the device calendar.

- ▶ TOUCHBASE
  View any touchbase activities added.

- ▶ BADGES
  View your badges.

Figure 18.5 Employee's Profile and Expanded Dropdown Menu

Click the EDIT icon (seen for both the FIRST NAME and LAST NAME fields in Figure 18.5) to edit various fields based on your permissions. Clicking the ORG CHART option will take you to the ORG CHART, as shown in Figure 18.6.

The Touchbase functionality enables a manager to request a meeting with another employee. Select the TOUCHBASE option to see any Touchbase requests that have been made (see Figure 18.7).

Figure 18.6 Org Chart Showing a User's Details

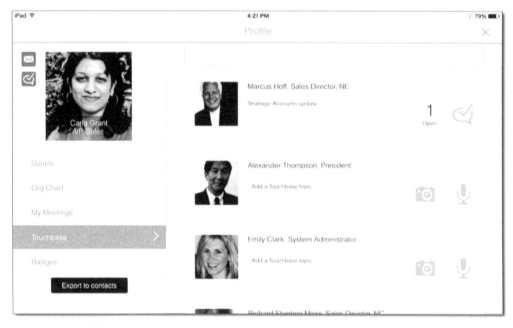

Figure 18.7 Touchbase

The BADGES option shows all of the badges assigned to you, as shown in Figure 18.8.

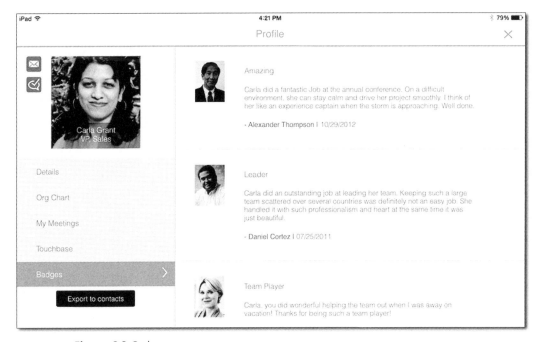

Figure 18.8 Badges

18.3.2 Manager Self-Services

Managers have a wide variety of functionality available. Managers can perform MSS transactions, such as:

- ▶ Change job and compensation info
- ▶ Grant spot bonus
- ▶ Change employment details
- ▶ Terminate/retire

Managers can also view their teams by clicking the TEAM button in the top-right corner. This button is highlighted in Figure 18.9. Each team member is shown as a tile on the screen, with matrix reports displaying a dotted border around their tiles. Figure 18.9 shows a matrix report—Thomas Clark. If you click a tile, you will be taken to the profile of that employee, where you can view the same sort of details and options as employees can view in their own profiles.

Figure 18.9 Viewing the Team

Click the ANNOTATE button next to the TEAM button to annotate notes on the screen (see Figure 18.10).

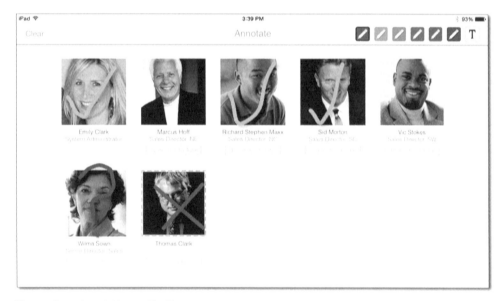

Figure 18.10 Annotating on the Team

Back on the home page, you can scroll through and select workflow requests. By clicking on a tile heading, you will be taken to the Requests screen, where you can view and respond to requests. Figure 18.11 shows a workflow request for a Spot Bonus. Like in SAP SuccessFactors, you can approve, decline, or delegate a request using the appropriate button.

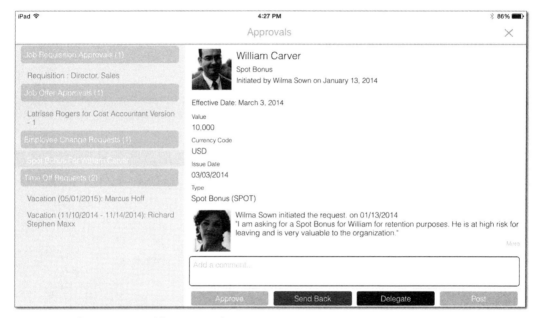

Figure 18.11 Workflow Approval Screen

18.3.3 Time Off

If Time Off is enabled in SAP SuccessFactors, then you'll have access to several features in the SAP SuccessFactors Mobile app. On the homepage, the Time Off tile (seen in the home page in Figure 18.4 and in detail in Figure 18.12) displays time accounts and available days. Each time account is shown one by one for a few seconds each, rather than all being shown. Any upcoming holidays (as defined in the Holiday Calendar) will scroll across the tile one by one. Figure 18.12 shows an employee's vacation time account balance and an upcoming holiday.

By selecting the Time Off tile, you will be taken to the Time Off screen, where you can request time off for any of your time accounts, view approved time off requests, and view the Team Absence Calendar. Figure 18.13 shows the calendar of the current month and any vacation in that month. You'll notice in Figure

18.13 that the employee has five days of vacation in the week of August 17. On the right side of the screen you can see all of the employee's time accounts and their current balances.

TIME OFF

My Balances

Vacation

6.50 DAYS

+++ Next Month: Labor Day on 09/06/2015 +

Figure 18.12 Time Off Tile on Homepage

| iPad 📶 | | | | 5:50 PM | | | | 74% 🔋 |

? Time Off ✕

◆ August 2015 ➡

My Balances as of Today

Sun	Mon	Tue	Wed	Thu	Fri	Sat
26	27	28	29	30	31	1
2	3	4	5	6	7	8
9	10	11	12	13	14	15
16	17	18	19	20	21	22
23	24	25	26	27	28	29
30	31	1	2	3	4	5

6.5 days

10 days
Sick Leave   >

My Requests   Public Holidays

2015

Vacation: 0.5 days   Approved
May 01

Vacation: 5 days   Pending
Jun 15 - Jun 19

Vacation: 5 days   Pending
Aug 17 - Aug 21

🗓 Team Absence Calendar   🔲 Before You Go

Figure 18.13 Time Off Screen

Figure 18.14 shows an employee requesting five days of vacation. This process is similar to the Time Off request in the SAP SuccessFactors application in that the user simply draws over the days required and selects the SUBMIT button (see Chapter 10, Section 10.3). The request will then go for approval.

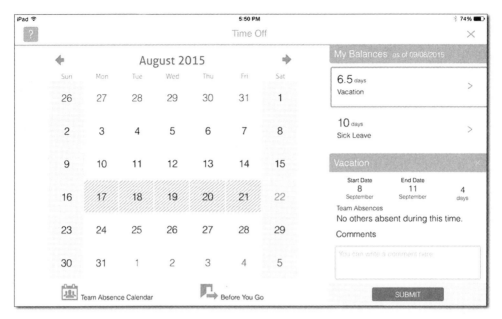

Figure 18.14 Requesting Time Off

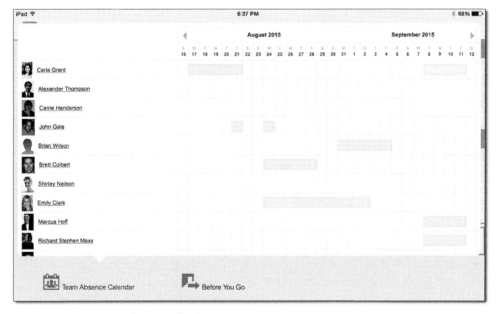

Figure 18.15 Team Absence Calendar

View the Team Absence Calendar by clicking TEAM ABSENCE CALENDAR at the bottom of the screen. This shows all of the absences in the employee's team and will usually look similar to Figure 18.15.

18.3.4 Other Features

There are a few other features that can be useful in the SAP SuccessFactors Mobile app. The search function on the homepage can be used to find other employees and can be used in both ESS and MSS. Figure 18.16 shows how this search works.

Figure 18.16 Employee Search

The analytics we saw back in Figure 18.4 can be powerful for managers to identify areas of concern.

SAP Jam can also be fully utilized through the SAP SuccessFactors Mobile app, enabling employees to stay on top of their collaborative activities.

18.4 Summary

In this chapter, we covered the ins and outs of the SAP SuccessFactors Mobile app and all of the Employee Central functionality it entails. We've specifically looked at what functionality is in the app, how to enable and disable functionality, what user permissions are required, where to download the app and how to activate it, and how to use the functionality within the app.

In the final chapter of our book, we'll review how Employee Central integrates with other SAP and non-SAP systems.

PART III

Integrating Employee Central with Other Systems

Given the many HR and other systems used by organizations outside of their core HR systems, integration is a critical component to ensure data can flow between the right systems at the right time. SAP provides a host of packaged integrations and API capabilities for Employee Central to make this possible.

19   Integration

You most likely use a number of different systems that require employee and/or other data from your core HR system. Ensuring that data can flow between these systems is critical for many business operations to function effectively, and Employee Central has a number of capabilities to make sure this happens. Currently, the Dell Boomi AtomSphere middleware is bundled into the Employee Central subscription. SAP has invested significantly in creating a wealth of packaged integrations for both Dell Boomi AtomSphere and its proprietary cloud-based middleware SAP HANA Cloud Integration. SAP also has created adapters for SAP Process Integration (PI) middleware as well as application programming interfaces (APIs) that can be used to integrate different systems inside and outside of the SAP family of applications.

Because it owns both SAP ERP and SAP SuccessFactors, SAP can deliver integrations between these systems in a way other vendors cannot. This means that there are technical and process advantages to leveraging SAP's packaged integrations. First, these packaged integrations are designed to work with both systems, and therefore both systems' logic can be used together. Second, SAP supports and maintains its packaged integrations. Third, the packaged integrations accelerate the effort required to integrate the systems.

Additional Resources

You can read more about integrations between Employee Central and other systems in Chapter 3 of *SuccessFactors with SAP ERP HCM: Business Processes and Use* by Amy Grubb and Luke Marson (2nd edition, SAP PRESS, 2015).

Further details and use cases for the Full Cloud HCM and Side-by-Side deployment models can be found in Chapter 3 and Chapter 5 of *Integrating SuccessFactors with SAP* by Vishnu Kandi, Venki Krishnamoorthy, Donna Leong-Cohen, Prashanth Padmanabhan, and Chinni Reddygari (SAP PRESS, 2015).

In this chapter, we'll look at various Employee Central integration topics. We'll start with the basics of an Employee Central integration that apply to any integration scenario. We'll then discuss the packaged integrations provided by SAP and how they can be leveraged to simplify the integration effort for common integrations.

We'll then look at integrating Employee Central with SAP, other applications in the SAP SuccessFactors HCM Suite, and by using a variety of tools that enable customer integrations to be built. These tools include the Event Bus, SAP SuccessFactors adapters, APIs, and Employee Delta Export.

19.1 Integration Overview

For many customers, integration is not a new topic. However, when implementing a HR system, new integration challenges must be overcome to ensure existing and new systems can talk to each other properly. Formulating an integration strategy is often influenced by the myriad of systems in the landscape and the integration technology options available, which in themselves can be influenced by the integration strategy of the vendor.

Figure 19.1 shows the different integration options and packaged integrations for Employee Central.

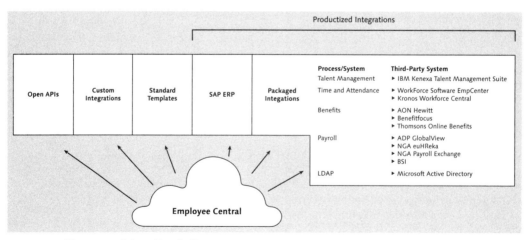

Figure 19.1 Integration Options

When defining integrations, you should always look to see which packaged integrations can be used to support your system integrations. If a packaged integration doesn't exist, then it will need to be built manually, either with middleware or through a CSV file. Depending on the middleware, a guided wizard or modeling interface can be used to quickly build integrations. SAP Process Integration (PI), SAP HANA Cloud Integration, and Dell Boomi AtomSphere enable this type of integration building. APIs also can be used by these middleware or other middleware platforms to create integrations (see Section 19.8).

In this section, we'll begin our integration journey by looking at the different packaged integrations available for Employee Central. Then, we'll discuss the various integration technologies.

19.1.1 Packaged Integrations

SAP's approach to integration has been to provide data, process, and user interface integration in the form of packaged integrations for the most common processes and third-party applications. A large number of these packaged integrations support master data, organizational data, and financial and payroll data integration between Employee Central and SAP ERP. This is largely because many SAP ERP customers want to move their core HR processes to the cloud but want to keep other functions—such as payroll, sales and distribution, or materials management—in their on-premise SAP ERP system. At the time of writing, packaged integrations area available to integrate Employee Central with SAP ERP for the following data and processes:

- Employee data
- Organizational data
- Cost center data
- SAP ERP Payroll and Employee Central Payroll
- SAP Governance, Risk, and Compliance (GRC)
- SAP Identity Management (IDM)

These packaged integrations cover both the Full Cloud HCM and Side-by-Side deployment models. We will cover integrating Employee Central with SAP and these deployment models in Section 19.2. With these packaged integrations for SAP ERP, SAP intends to support customers by providing support for:

- Custom fields and flexibility to map them to on-premise fields
- SAP ERP custom attributes and custom infotypes
- Initial transmission and delta loads of data
- Error resolution through a central data replication monitor in Employee Central
- Error analysis within the integration middleware
- Retaining historical data untouched in SAP ERP

Table 19.1 lists the packaged integrations available at the time of writing for integrating Employee Central with third-party systems.

Process/System	Third-Party System
Talent Management	▶ IBM Kenexa Talent Management Suite
Time and Attendance	▶ WorkForce Software EmpCenter
	▶ Kronos Workforce Central
Benefits	▶ AON Hewitt
	▶ Benefitfocus
	▶ Thomsons Online Benefits
Payroll	▶ ADP GlobalView
	▶ NGA euHReka
	▶ NGA Payroll Exchange
	▶ BSI
LDAP	▶ Microsoft Active Directory

Table 19.1 Packaged Integrations for Integrating Third-Party Systems

More information on the integrations between Employee Central and third-party systems can be found in Section 19.3.

What if the application you want to integrate doesn't have a packaged integration? For those applications, SAP provides standard integration templates and APIs. Adapters for SAP PI and SAP HANA Cloud Integration also are available. Figure 19.2 illustrates SAP's approach to third-party application integration, including standard integration templates and APIs.

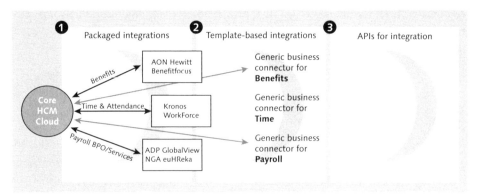

Figure 19.2 SAP's Integration Strategy for Employee Central

Specifically, Figure 19.3 shows SAP's strategy for each third-party integration.

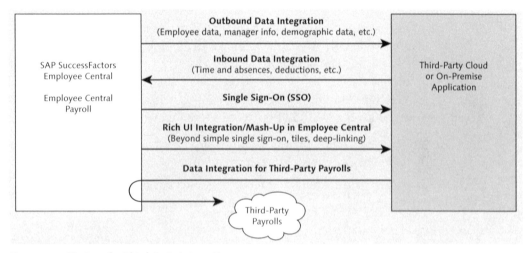

Figure 19.3 Strategy for Third-Party Integrations

For third-party applications, SAP provides wizard-based, prebuilt, configurable bidirectional processes with prominent partners for benefits, time and attendance, and payroll. These are built by SAP or the partner. In general, these processes cover close to or all requirements for these type of integrations.

For benefits, time and attendance, and payroll vendors that do not have a packaged integration, SAP provides standard integration templates that can reduce development effort by around 50–80%. These templates leverage HR-XML standards and best practice knowledge of integration patterns in each of these categories. Integrations built using these templates are maintained by the customer. We'll look at standard integration templates in Section 19.9.

For other types of integration, SAP provides a range of APIs and adapters for SAP middleware. We'll look at APIs in Section 19.8 and adapters in Section 19.7.

19.1.2 Integration Technology

Any integration middleware can be used to integrate Employee Central with other systems, including SAP ERP. The APIs provided in SAP SuccessFactors make it easy to use web services-based technology to integrate systems. CSV-based integration is possible also. SAP's packaged integrations are provided for two middleware technologies: SAP HANA Cloud Integration and Dell Boomi AtomSphere.

Dell Boomi AtomSphere

Dell Boomi AtomSphere is an Integration-Platform-as-a-Service (IPaaS) middleware integration platform designed to integrate on-premise and cloud-based systems without the need for additional coding, software, or technology. As an IPaaS solution, the platform benefits from many of the same advantages as SaaS solutions, such as subscription pricing, regular releases, scalability, and lower total cost of ownership (TCO). In addition, it offers the following benefits and abilities:

▸ An easy-to-use graphical interface with wizard-based designers that provide the ability to design workflows using drag and drop
▸ Create data transformations and model complex business logic
▸ Perform integrity checks and validate data, introduce decision handling
▸ Create event-based messages
▸ Build unique connectors

Dell Boomi AtomSphere is included as part of the Employee Central subscription.

SAP HANA Cloud Integration

Like Dell Boomi AtomSphere, SAP HANA Cloud Integration is also an IPaaS middleware integration platform designed to integrate on-premise and cloud-based systems without the need for additional coding, software, or technology. It's essentially the next-generation, cloud-based successor of SAP PI, and it's included as part of the Employee Central subscription.

SAP Process Integration

SAP PI—previously called SAP Exchange Infrastructure (SAP XI) until version 7.0—is SAP's reliable and high-performance, service-oriented architecture (SOA) middleware product for integrating and transferring message-based data between SAP systems and other internal or external systems. Approximately 35% of SAP ERP HCM customers currently use SAP PI to integrate SAP systems. The license for SAP PI is included in the SAP licenses that every SAP customer receives, which means that there are no licensing implications for using SAP PI as an integration middleware.

Comma-Separated Values

CSV files are a common method of integration. They're text-based, flat files that use commas to separate values. Typically, they're transferred between systems using an FTP, SFTP, or middleware platform. Although this method is fairly simple to create and maintain, it does have some disadvantages that might be undesirable for some customers, such as a lack of security or encryption, standards, or validation for data, and transformation and mapping capabilities. However, some tools are available that can validate or transform data in flat files. When using an SAP SuccessFactors FTP—which only supports SFTP protocol—*Pretty Good Privacy* (*PGP*) encryption can be used.

19.1.3   PI Pass Through

For customers who do not want to open up their SAP ERP system for calls from outside their firewalls, they can use SAP PI as a pass through; that is, a cloud-based middleware communicates with SAP PI, which then communicates with the SAP ERP system. Although called a pass through, SAP PI does not just forward the messages it receives; it also creates new messages to pass through to the SAP ERP system. This requires additional monitoring effort to monitor messages.

The pass through is available for replicating the following data:

- Employee data (bidirectional)
- Organizational data (Employee Central to SAP ERP)
- Time Off data (Employee Central to SAP ERP)
- Cost center data (SAP ERP to Employee Central)

19.2 Integration with SAP

There is a substantial amount of packaged integration content provided by SAP to integrate Employee Central with SAP ERP and other SAP systems, in order to enable the scenarios described in Section 19.1.1. Figure 19.4 shows the types of data and process integrations available. The integrations shown between Employee Central and SAP ERP in the diagram are grouped into three packaged integrations: employee data, organizational data, and cost center data. In addition to the diagram, there is an integration for the Side-by-Side deployment model that was described in Chapter 1, Section 1.12, and SAP Business ByDesign—both of which we'll cover in this section.

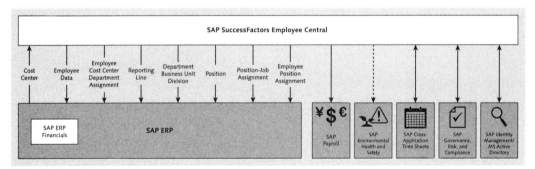

Figure 19.4 Integrations between Employee Central and SAP ERP

► At the time of writing, the following integrations are planned between Employee Central and the following:

► SAP GRC

► SAP Fieldglass

Before we run through all of the integrations one by one, let's take a quick look at some of the caveats and tips for integration between Employee Central and SAP ERP.

19.2.1 Integration Considerations

There are several things to consider when integrating two systems, particularly when one system is as flexible as Employee Central. For example:

▶ **Transmission date and data freeze date**
Setting the transmission date — also known as the *Full Transmission Start Date (FTSD)* — and data freeze date in the target system is important to ensure no duplication of data. This is especially important when replicating data to an existing payroll system.

▶ **Field lengths**
Employee Central field lengths are less restricted than those of many other systems, so it's important to ensure they are aligned. This is particularly important for SAP ERP integration; the standard character length of some Employee Central fields exceeds the character limitation of the inbound service in SAP ERP, and the default field lengths in Employee Central far exceed many of the object code fields, object name fields, and transparent table fields.

▶ **Data types**
Differing data types between systems may require conversion of data in the middleware or target system to ensure compatibility of data formats. This is critical for object IDs and numerical fields.

▶ **Interface and middleware limitations**
As mentioned previously, quite often the SAP ERP inbound interface has limitations that do not align with the source and/or target fields. In addition, the middleware may also have limitations. There may be different field lengths for the source field, middleware, inbound system interface, and target field.

▶ **Mapping tables**
Due to differences in data models, data consolidation, and/or data migration, it's necessary to maintain mapping tables.

▶ **Corresponding objects and fields**
Not all SAP ERP objects and fields exist in Employee Central and vice versa. For example, Personnel Area doesn't exist in Employee Central, and likewise, the org structure in Employee Central has objects that have no corresponding object in SAP. These details must be considered when designing Employee Central and the integration.

▶ **Testing**
Although integration testing is important, follow-on process testing can be critical. For example, payroll parallel testing is necessary to ensure that payroll output remains accurate.

▸ **Resource loading**

To avoid high resource usage and slow response times from Employee Central, we recommend scheduling middleware processes for execution at "odd" times (e.g., 1:07 a.m.), not just on the full hour (e.g., 1:00 a.m.). Different processes should be scheduled at different times so that multiple processes do not run simultaneously.

▸ **Picklist externalCode**

Some picklist values do not have an `externalCode` in the picklists file. These should be maintained for integration, because SAP ERP will map the `external-Code` with the code values in transparent tables. Typically, the `externalCode` of picklist values used in integration should be changed to map the values of the codes in SAP ERP.

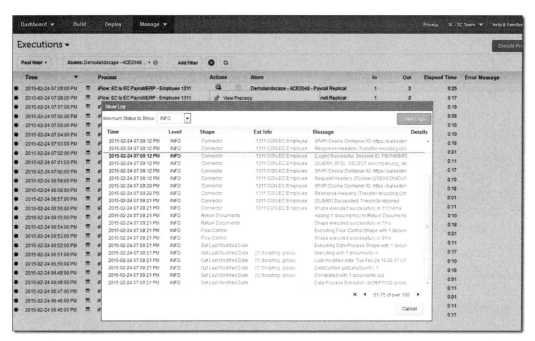

Figure 19.5 Dell Boomi AtomSphere Process Monitor

For the Dell Boomi AtomSphere middleware, there are a number of things to be aware of. Twelve connectors are provided for each customer, although this number can be increased free of charge. Likewise, each customer receives 1 GB of data volume per month, but using more than this amount does not incur an additional cost as of the time of writing. Request accounts for named users via a support ticket in the SAP ONE Support Portal. For monitoring, access the Boomi Process Monitor, shown in Figure 19.5, via *https://ondemand.boomi.com*.

Now that we've covered some important considerations when approaching the integration, let's explore the different integration scenarios with SAP.

19.2.2 Employee Data

As your system of record, Employee Central is where all employee master data is housed and the employee lifecycle is managed, as discussed in Chapter 9. When using processes in SAP ERP modules such as Payroll, Finance, SAP Employee Health and Safety Management (EHSM), or Cross-Application Time Sheet (CATS), it's important to ensure that employee data is available in SAP ERP so that it can be used in these processes.

A set of HR master data can be replicated from Employee Central to the Personnel Administration (PA) infotypes in SAP ERP using a packaged integration. This set of HR master data is often referred to as the mini-master. This same packaged integration is used for replicating data to Employee Central Payroll. Delta replication of employee data is supported.

Prerequisites

The following prerequisites must be met to fulfill this integration:
- Appropriate version of SAP NetWeaver
- SAP_APPL 600 SP 15 or higher
- PA_SE_IN 100 SP 8 or higher

Integration Process

Once Employee Central is set up, all configuration of the packaged integration (such as infotype mapping and assigning BAdIs) is performed in the middleware and in SAP ERP. Within SAP ERP, configuration is performed in the IMG via menu path PERSONNEL MANAGEMENT • INTEGRATION WITH SUCCESSFACTORS EMPLOYEE CENTRAL • REPLICATING DATA FROM EMPLOYEE CENTRAL TO SAP ERP.

The integration process is as follows:

1. The integration middleware calls SAP SuccessFactors APIs (see Section 19.8) to retrieve the data.

2. Data conversion and transformation is performed as necessary in the middle-ware.

3. The data is sent to SAP ERP, where it's processed by the inbound web service interface `EmployeeMasterDataReplicationRequest_In`.

4. The data is written to SAP ERP HCM infotypes. Records are created, edited, or delimited as required based on the data sent from Employee Central and the infotype framework in SAP ERP.

This data flow is represented in Figure 19.6.

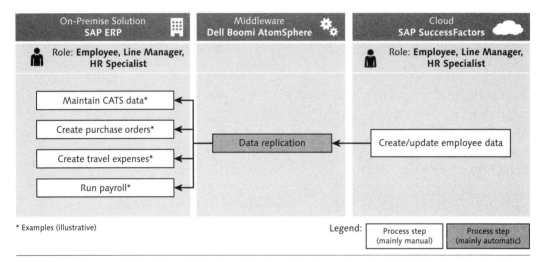

Figure 19.6 Data Flow of Employee Data from Employee Central to SAP ERP

Field Mapping

The employee data and corresponding fields shown in Table 19.2 are part of the standard employee data integration.

Employee Data	Fields
Biographical Information	▸ Person ID external
	▸ Birth Name (PA0002-NAME2)
	▸ Date of Birth (PA0002-GBDAT) *
	▸ Country of Birth (PA0002-GBLND)
	▸ Place of Birth (PA0002-GBORT)
	▸ Region of Birth (PA0002-GBDEP)

Table 19.2 Employee Data Fields

Employee Data	Fields
Personal Information	▶ First Name (PA0002-VORNA) * ▶ Middle Name (PA0002-MIDNM) ▶ Last Name (PA0002-NACHN) * ▶ Additional Family Name (PA0002-NACH2) ▶ Suffix (PA0002-NAMZU) ▶ Salutation (PA0002-ANRED) * ▶ Marital status (PA0002-FAMST) * ▶ Native preferred language (PA0002-SPRSL) * ▶ Gender (PA0002-GESCH) * ▶ Nationality (PA0002-NATIO) *
Address Information	▶ Address type (PA0006-ANSSA) * ▶ Start Date (PA0006-BEGDA) * ▶ End Date (PA0006-ENDDA) * ▶ Address1-8 (PA0006; *country dependent*) ▶ City (PA0006-ORT01) ▶ State/Province/County (PA0006-STATE) ▶ ZIP Code (PA0006-PSTLZ) ▶ Country (PA0006-LAND1) *
Email Address Information	▶ Email address (PA0105-USRID_LONG) * ▶ Email address type (PA0105) * ▶ Primary Indicator (PA0105)
Job Information	▶ Event (PA0000-MASSN) * ▶ Event Reason (PA0000-MASSG) ▶ Location (PA0001-BTRTL and PA0001-WERKS) * ▶ Company (PA0001-BUKRS) * ▶ Cost Center (PA0001-KOSTL) ▶ Employee Class (PA0001-PERSG) * ▶ Employment Type (PA0001-PERSK) * ▶ Is Full-Time Employee (PA0007-TEILK) ▶ Working Days per Week (PA0007-WKWDY) * ▶ Pay Scale Area (PA0008-TRFGB) * ▶ Pay Scale Type (PA0008-TRFAR) * ▶ Pay Scale Group (PA0008-TRFG)

Table 19.2 Employee Data Fields (Cont.)

509

Employee Data	Fields
Job Information (Cont.)	▸ Pay Scale Level (PA0008-TRFST) ▸ Work Schedule (PA0007-SCHKZ) ▸ FTE (PA0008-BSGRD)
Compensation Information	▸ Pay Group (PA0001-ABKRS) *
Pay Component Recurring	▸ Pay Component (PA0008-LGA01 to PA0008-LGA40 or PA0014-LGART) * ▸ Currency Code (PA0008-WAERS) * ▸ Amount (PA0008-BET01 to PA0008-BET40 or PA0014-BETRG) * ▸ Frequency (PA0014-ZEINZ and PA0014-ZANZL) * ▸ Unit of Measure (PA0014-ZEINZ)
Pay Component Non-Recurring	▸ Pay Component (PA0015-LGART) * ▸ Pay Date (PA0015-UWDAT) * ▸ Currency Code (PA0015-WAERS) * ▸ Amount (PA0015- BETRG) * ▸ Unit of Measure (PA0015-ZEINZ) ▸ Alternative Cost Center (PA0015-KOSTL)
Cost Distribution	▸ Start Date (PA0027-BEGDA) ▸ End Date (PA0027-ENDDA) ▸ Cost Center (PA0027-KST01 to PA0027-KST12) ▸ Percentage (PA0027-KPR01 to PA0027-KPR12)
Payment Information	▸ Payment Method (PA0009-ZLSCH) * ▸ Account Type (PA0009-BKONT) ▸ Account Number (PA0009-BANKN) ▸ Account Name (PA0009-EMFTX) ▸ Routing Number (PA0009-BANKL) ▸ IBAN (PA0009-IBAN) ▸ Bank Control Key (PA0009-BKONT) ▸ Bank Country (PA0009-BANKS) * ▸ Deposit Type (PA0009-BNKSA) ▸ Processing Type (PA0009-BNKSA) * ▸ Payment Type Code (PA0009-ZLSCH) ▸ Currency (PA0009-WAERS) ▸ Building Society Roll Number (PA0009-PSKTO)

Table 19.2 Employee Data Fields (Cont.)

Employee Data	Fields
National ID Card	▶ Country (PA0002) *
	▶ National ID (PA0002-PERID) *
* Indicates a required field. Please note that some fields not marked with * are required for certain countries.	

Table 19.2 Employee Data Fields (Cont.)

In addition to these fields, various dates are also replicated to SAP ERP into Infotype 0041. These include the following:

▶ Hire date

▶ Termination date

▶ Global Assignment planned start date

▶ Global Assignment planned end date

▶ Pension Payouts planned start date

▶ Pension Payouts planned end date

To ensure correct mapping, various mapping tables are provided to map values between Employee Central and SAP ERP. These include the following:

▶ Employee Central object codes to SAP ERP global data types (GDTs)

▶ Employee Central object codes to SAP ERP code value lists

▶ Employee Central codes to SAP ERP code value lists for country-dependent fields

▶ Employee Central date types to SAP ERP date types

▶ Employee Central company object codes to SAP ERP company keys

▶ Employee Central cost center object codes to SAP ERP cost center keys

▶ Employee Central location codes to SAP ERP place of work keys

▶ Employee Central pay component and country combinations to SAP ERP Infotype 0008 or Infotype 0014

▶ Employee Central custom fields to SAP ERP HCM infotypes

▶ Employee Central fields to custom fields in SAP ERP HCM infotypes

For the last two points, custom mappings can be made to Infotypes 0001, 0002, 0007, and 0008 in SAP ERP HCM.

Employee key mapping entities are stored in a special mapping table PAOCFEC_
EEKEYMAP. Table 19.3 shows the fields of this table.

Key Field	Field	Description	Source System
X	MANDT	Client	SAP ERP
X	EMPLOYEE_ID	User ID of employee (field *USE-RID* from UDF)	Employee Central
X	EMPLOYMENT_ID	The internal ID of an employee's employment record	Employee Central
X	WORK_AGR_ITEM_ID	The internal ID of an employee's Job Information record	Employee Central
	PERNR	Personnel number in SAP	SAP ERP
	BUKRS	Company code in SAP	SAP ERP
	EMPLOYEE_ID_EXT	External User ID of employee (field person-id-external)	Employee Central
	USER_ID	The internal ID of the employee's employment record (field USER_SYS_ID)	Employee Central

Table 19.3 Key Mapping Fields

Figure 19.7 shows the relationships among these entities.

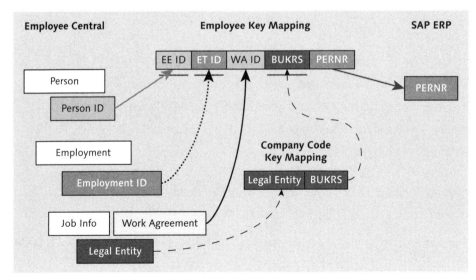

Figure 19.7 Key Mapping Table Entity Relationships

Certain fields need special consideration for value mappings, such as marital status or gender. For example, Table 19.4 shows the different mappings between Employee Central and SAP ERP for the different marital status values.

Marital Status	Employee Central Code	SAP Global Data Type Code	Technical Values in SAP ERP
Single	S	1	0
Married	M	2	1
Widowed	W	3	2
Divorced	D	4	3
Separated		5	4

Table 19.4 Marital Status Values in Employee Central and SAP ERP

Two BAdIs are provided to modify the logic and behavior of replicated fields. The first determines the Employee Central field to use for Personnel Number, and the second excludes infotype records from deletion for specific subtypes.

Other IMG configuration settings include allowing currencies to be assigned to wage types (so that currencies with more than two decimal places can be used without rounding to two decimal places) and restricting and filtering which infotypes are replicated for certain countries.

Additional Resources

For more information on the details of the integration, field mappings, BAdIs, and minimum requirements and prerequisites, refer to the *Replicating Employee Master Data from Employee Central to SAP ERP* integration guide found at *http://help.sap.com/hr_integration* under the heading SUCCESSFACTORS AND SAP ERP: CORE HYBRID HCM.

19.2.3 Organizational Data

Although not required by all processes, in some processes—particularly workflows—SAP ERP needs organizational Foundation Objects and those assigned to employees. We discussed Foundation Objects in Chapter 6 and covered the assignment of Foundation Objects to employees in Chapter 9.

SAP provides a packaged integration to replicate these Foundation Objects to SAP ERP Organizational Management (OM) infotypes and to replicate the assignment to employees. Delta replication of organizational data is supported.

Prerequisites

The following prerequisites must be met to fulfill this integration:

▸ SAP_BASIS 700 SP 18 or higher

▸ SAP_APPL 600 SP 15 or higher

▸ PA_SE_IN 100 SP 11 or higher

Integration Process

Once Employee Central is set up, all configuration of the packaged integration (such as infotype mapping and assigning BAdIs) is performed in the middleware and in SAP ERP. Within SAP ERP, configuration is performed in the IMG via menu path PERSONNEL MANAGEMENT • INTEGRATION WITH SUCCESSFACTORS EMPLOYEE CENTRAL • REPLICATING DATA FROM EMPLOYEE CENTRAL TO SAP ERP • REPLICATING ORGANIZA-TION DATA.

The integration process is as follows:

1. The integration middleware calls SAP SuccessFactors APIs (see Section 19.8) to retrieve the data.

2. Data conversion and transformation is performed as necessary in the middleware.

3. The data is sent to SAP ERP, where it's processed by one of the inbound web service interfaces:

    ▸ `OrganisationalStructureReplicationRequest_In`

    ▸ `JobReplicationRequest_In`

    ▸ `PositionReplicationRequest_In`

    ▸ `EmployeeOrganisationalAssignmentReplicationRequest_In`

4. The data is written to staging area in SAP ERP.

5. Scheduled programs write data from the staging area to the database:

    ▸ `RH_SFIOM_PROC_ORG_STRUC_RPRQ`

    ▸ `RH_SFIOM_PROC_EE_ORG_ASS_RPRQ`

Figure 19.8 illustrates this data flow.

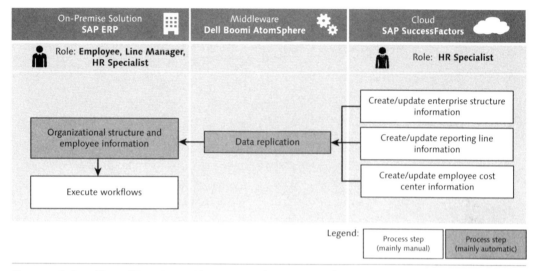

Figure 19.8 Data Flow of Foundation Object Data and Assignments from Employee Central to SAP ERP

Foundation Objects and Field Mapping

Table 19.5 lists the Foundation Objects that are replicated to SAP ERP and their corresponding objects.

Foundation Object	Object	Object Type
Business Unit	Organizational Unit	O
Division	Organizational Unit	O
Department	Organizational Unit	O
Job Classification	Job	C
Position	Position	S

Table 19.5 Foundation Objects Mapping between Employee Central and SAP ERP

Table 19.6 shows the Foundation Objects and corresponding fields are part of the standard organizational data integration.

Organizational Data	Fields
Business Units, Divisions, and Departments	▸ Code (HRP1000-OBJID) ▸ Start Date (HRP1000-BEGDA) ▸ End Date (HRP1000-ENDDA) ▸ Name (HRP1000-STEXT) ▸ Parent (HRP1000-SOBID) ▸ Description (HRT1002-TLINE)
Job Classifications	▸ Job Code (HRP1000-OBJID) ▸ Start Date (HRP1000-BEGDA) ▸ End Date (HRP1000-ENDDA) ▸ Job Title (HRP1000-STEXT) ▸ Description (HRT1002-TLINE)
Positions	▸ Code (HRP1000-OBJID) ▸ Start Date (HRP1000-BEGDA) ▸ End Date (HRP1000-ENDDA) ▸ Title (HRP1000-STEXT)

Table 19.6 Organizational Data Fields

The following employee assignments are part of the standard employee data integration:

▸ Department (assigned to the employee's position in Infotype 1001)

▸ Division (assigned to the employee's position in Infotype 1001)

▸ Business Unit (assigned to the employee's position in Infotype 1001)

▸ Job Classification

▸ Position

▸ Cost Center (assigned to the employee's position in Infotype 1001)

▸ Manager (using position-to-position relationship in Infotype 1001)

For Foundation Objects, specific logic is related to certain fields based on the similarities and differences between the two systems. These fields include the following:

▸ **Language-dependent name fields**
Replication of language-dependent name fields is supported and uses the LANGU fields in Infotype 1000 to store the different country-specific values for each object.

- **Parent fields**
  Due to the nature of the organizational structure, the middleware determines the Organizational Unit parent object based on the following rules:

  - If a Department has a parent Department, then this parent Department is the parent.

  - If a Department doesn't have a parent but has a Division assigned, then the Division is the parent.

  - If a Division has a parent Division, then this Division is the parent.

  - If a Division doesn't have a parent but has a Business Unit assigned, then the Business Unit is the parent.

  Note that Business Unit cannot have a parent in Employee Central and therefore will not have a parent in SAP ERP.

- **Custom objects**
  If custom objects are used in the organization structure (e.g., Sub-Department), then they can be replicated by implementing BAdI EX_SFIOM_KEY_MAP_ENH_ORG_STRUC.

- **Custom associations**
  If the associations in Employee Central are configured differently than the standard (e.g., a Division's parent is a Department), then the middleware must be configured to read the associations as they are configured in Employee Central.

- **Object relationships and employee assignments**
  Object relationships and employee assignments use standard logic in Infotype 1001 and therefore leverage the RSIGN, RELAT, SCLAS, and SOBID fields to store the parent–object relationship.

- **Job Relationships**
  Relationships defined in the Job Relationships portlet can be replicated by implementing BAdI EX_SFIOM_ADAPT_EE_ORG_ASSGNMNT.

- **Position Management in Employee Central**
  Position is a required object for an employee in SAP ERP. If Position Management is not used in Employee Central, then a position will be created in SAP ERP by the integration.

- **Custom fields**
  Custom fields are not replicated as standard but can be mapped by implementing BAdI EX_SFIOM_PROC_CUSTOMER_FIELDS.

▶ **Country-specific Job Classification fields**
Country-specific Job Classification fields are not replicated as standard but can be mapped by implementing BAdI `EX_SFIOM_PROC_COUNTRY_FIELDS`.

Mappings for Foundation Objects replicated to Employee Central are stored in key mapping table `SFIOM_KMAP_OSI` in SAP ERP, which determines the object ID written to the OBJID field of Infotypes 1000, 1001, and 1002. This ID is used in case Foundation Object codes are not in the format required by SAP (i.e., an eight-digit numeric code with leading zeroes). Upon the first replication, the mapping table should be maintained with all mappings if no new organizational units need to be created (i.e., data has been migrated from SAP ERP to Employee Central). BAdI `EX_SFIOM_KEY_MAP_ENH_ORG_STRUC` can be used to automate the mapping of object IDs.

Additional Resources

For more information on the organizational data integration, field mappings, and BAdIs, refer to the *Replicating Organizational Data from Employee Central to SAP ERP* integration guide found at *http://help.sap.com/hr_integration* under the heading SUCCESSFACTORS AND SAP ERP: CORE HYBRID HCM. In addition, information on maintaining and monitoring the integration can be found in the *Maintaining Organizational Data Replication from Employee Central to SAP ERP* integration guide found at the same location.

19.2.4 Cost Center Data

In most cases, SAP ERP FI-CO is the system of record for cost center data. However, this cost center data is needed in Employee Central so that an employee can be assigned a cost center and so that a cost center can be assigned to a Department if required.

SAP provides a packaged integration to replicate cost centers from SAP ERP FI-CO to Employee Central. The data is replicated via middleware to Employee Central, and the source data can be replicated to the middleware either via IDoc technology or via a flat file (CSV). Delta replication of cost center data is supported.

Prerequisites

The following prerequisites must be met to fulfill this integration:

▶ SAP_BASIS 700 SP 18 or higher

▶ SAP_APPL 600 SP 15 or higher

▶ ODTFINCC 600 SP 10 or higher

Integration Process

Once Employee Central is set up, all configuration of the packaged integration (such as infotype mapping and assigning BAdIs) is performed in the middleware and in SAP ERP. Within SAP ERP, configuration is performed in the IMG via menu path CONTROLLING • INTEGRATION OF SAP ERP CO MASTER DATA WITH SUCCESS-FACTORS EMPLOYEE CENTRAL.

The integration process is as follows:

1. Data replication is triggered via scheduled jobs:

   ▸ If replication is via IDoc technology, then Report RBDMIDOC runs in SAP ERP (usually as a scheduled job), followed by Report ODTF_REPL_CC.

   ▸ If replication is via a flat file, then Report ODTF_REPL_CC_CSV runs.

2. Data conversion and transformation is performed as necessary in the middleware.

3. The data is written to Employee Central. Records are created, edited, or delimited as required based on the data sent from SAP ERP FI-CO.

Figure 19.9 illustrates this data flow.

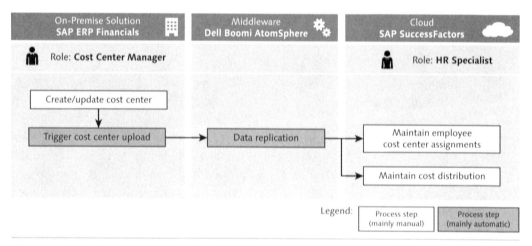

Figure 19.9 Data Flow of Cost Centers from SAP ERP FI-CO to Employee Central

Figure 19.10 shows the two different technology options.

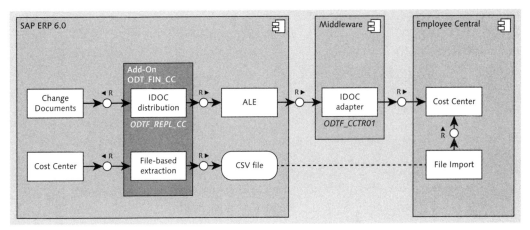

Figure 19.10 Technology Options

Field Mapping

The following Cost Center object fields are part of the standard cost center data integration:

- externalCode
- Start Date
- End Date
- Status
- Name
- Description
- ExternalObjectID

When ALE technology is used, change pointers are set up to trigger replication changes to cost center data. IDocs are created based on the change pointers and are sent to the middleware to be converted to Employee Central format before being sent to Employee Central.

Due to the nature of customer landscapes and external systems, cost center IDs can be replicated from a mapping table in SAP ERP FI-CO (PAOCFEC_KMAPCOSC), or the cost center ID to be used in external systems can be replicated to the External-ObjectID field of the Cost Center object in Employee Central.

In some instances, customers may have multiple systems that contain nonunique cost center IDs. In order to modify the mappings of the cost center IDs in each

SAP ERP FI-CO system, the BAdI `ODTF_CC_REPLICAT_IDOCS_MODIFY` can be implemented. There are two implementations; one implementation for IDoc replication (`ODTF_CO_REPL_IDOC_COST_CENTERS`) and one implementation for flat-file replication (`ODTF_CO_REPL_IDOC_COST_C_CSV`).

> **Additional Resources**
>
> For more information on the details of the integration, field mappings, and BAdIs, refer to the *Replicating Cost Centers from SAP ERP to Employee Central* integration guide found at *http://help.sap.com/hr_integration* under the heading SUCCESSFACTORS AND SAP ERP: CORE HYBRID HCM.

19.2.5   Employee Central Payroll

Employee Central Payroll is based on SAP ERP Payroll, and therefore integration between Employee Central and Employee Central Payroll uses the employee mini-master integration covered in Section 19.2.2. SSO can be set up between Employee Central and Employee Central Payroll so that infotype mash-ups can be accessed and the pay slip can be displayed.

> **Additional Resources**
>
> For more information on the details of the integration, field mappings, and BAdIs, refer to the *Employee Central Payroll* handbook found at *http://help.sap.com/hr_integration* under the heading SUCCESSFACTORS AND SAP ERP: CORE HYBRID HCM.

Integration exists between Employee Central and Employee Central Payroll in three other areas:

- Time Sheet
- Time Off
- Payroll results in Employee Central Payroll

We'll take a look at these areas now.

Time Sheet Integration

When using the Time Sheet functionality, the valuated time data can be replicated to Employee Central Payroll so that employees can be paid based on the time data that they entered into the system. We covered the Time Sheet feature in Chapter 10.

SAP provides a packaged integration to replicate valuated time data from Employee Central to Infotype 2010 in Employee Central Payroll. This packaged integration also updates the Data Replication Monitor in Employee Central.

Once Employee Central is set up, mapping of a Time Type Group to a Time Pay Type Code is performed in Employee Central Payroll in the IMG via menu path Personnel Management • Integration Settings for SuccessFactors Employee Central Payroll • Assignment of Code Values • Define Mapping of External Code Value Lists to Internal Code Value Lists.

The integration process is as follows:

1. The integration middleware calls the OData API in SAP SuccessFactors (see Section 19.8) to retrieve data.

2. Data conversion, mapping, and transformation is performed as necessary in the middleware.

3. The data is sent to Employee Central Payroll, where it's processed by the inbound web service interface `EmployeeTimeECToERPRequest_In`.

4. The data is written to Infotype 2010.

Figure 19.11 illustrates this data flow.

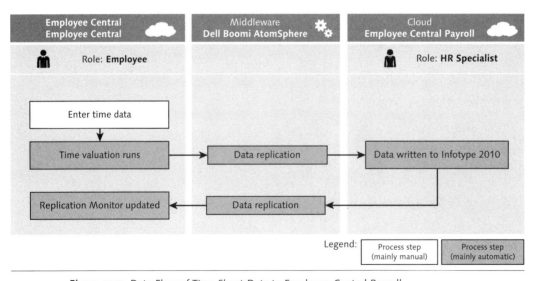

Figure 19.11 Data Flow of Time Sheet Data to Employee Central Payroll

Table 19.7 shows the Time Sheet data and corresponding fields are part of the standard Time Sheet data integration.

Time Sheet Data	Fields
Data Replication Proxy	▸ externalCode
	▸ Worker
	▸ Company
Employee Time Sheet	▸ Person ID external (PA2010-PERNR)
	▸ Approval Status
Employee Time Valuation Result	▸ Booking Date (PA2010-BEGDA)
	▸ Booking Date (PA2010-ENDDA)
	▸ Time Pay Type (PA2010-LGART)
	▸ Hours (PA2010-ANZHL)
	▸ Cost Center (ASSOB-KOSTL)

Table 19.7 Time Sheet Fields

In addition, during replication, the value of PA2010-AWTYP is set to ECTVR for each record created through the integration.

Additional Resources

Information on integrating Time Sheet with Employee Central Payroll can be found in the *Integrating Payroll Time Sheet with Employee Central Payroll* integration guide found at *http://help.sap.com/hr_integration* under the heading SUCCESSFACTORS AND SAP ERP: CORE HYBRID HCM.

Time Off Integration

When using the Time Off functionality, the resulting absence data can be replicated to Employee Central Payroll so that employees have the appropriate deductions made from their vacation/PTO, sick leave, and other time off balances on their pay slip. We covered the Time Off feature in Chapter 10.

SAP provides a packaged integration to replicate time off from Employee Central to Infotype 2001 in Employee Central Payroll. This packaged integration also updates the Data Replication Monitor in Employee Central.

Once Employee Central is set up, various settings (such as disabling Infotype 2001 checks, defining Absence Types, disabling work schedule checks, etc.) are performed in Employee Central Payroll in the IMG via menu path TIME MANAGEMENT • TIME DATA RECORDING AND ADMINISTRATION. Other configurations are performed in Transaction SM30 and in the IMG via menu path PERSONNEL MANAGEMENT • INTEGRATION SETTINGS FOR SUCCESSFACTORS EMPLOYEE CENTRAL PAYROLL • ASSIGNMENT OF CODE VALUES.

The integration process is as follows:

1. The integration middleware calls the OData API in SAP SuccessFactors (see Section 19.8) to retrieve data.

2. Data conversion, mapping, and transformation is performed as necessary in the middleware.

3. The data is sent to Employee Central Payroll, where it's processed by the inbound web service interface `EmployeeTimeECToERPRequest_In`.

4. The data is written to Infotype 2001.

Figure 19.12 illustrates this data flow.

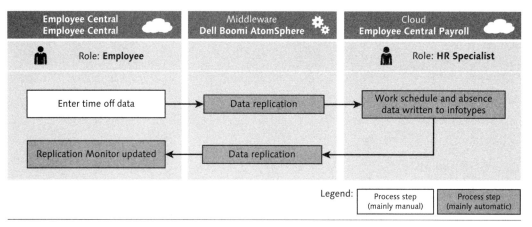

Figure 19.12 Data Flow of Time Sheet Data to Employee Central Payroll

The following data and corresponding EMPLOYEE TIME fields are part of the standard Time Sheet data integration:

▸ User (PA2001-PERNR)

▸ Approval Status

- Start Date (PA2001-BEGDA)

- End Date (PA2001-ENDDA)

- Quantity in Days (PA2001-ABWTG)

- Quantity in Hours (PA2001-STDAZ)

- Time Type (PA2001-AWART)

- User ID

- Company of user

In addition, during replication, the value of PA2001-AWTYP is set to ECTOF for each record created through the integration.

Additional Resources

Information on integrating Time Off with Employee Central Payroll can be found in the *Employee Central Payroll and Time Off* handbook found at *http://help.sap.com/hr_integration* under the heading SuccessFactors and SAP ERP: Core Hybrid HCM.

Payroll Results Export

When using Employee Central Payroll, you can export payroll results from the system to be imported into Employee Central. This enables you to perform comprehensive reporting in Employee Central Advanced Reporting. We covered Employee Central Advanced Reporting in Chapter 17.

SAP provides a report in Employee Central Payroll to export the payroll results from logical database PNP to a flat file (CSV). This flat file of data can then be imported into Employee Central manually or via integration middleware.

Once Employee Central Payroll is configured, wage types must be configured for a Subapplication in the IMG via menu path Personnel Management • Integration Settings for SuccessFactors Employee Central Payroll • Data Extraction of Payroll Results. Additional configuration is required in Employee Central to configure a business rule to map payroll run types and wage types.

The integration process is as follows:

1. Report PAOCF_EC_ExportPayrollResults runs to export the payroll results (usually as a scheduled job).

2. The report is uploaded to Employee Central via middleware or through manual import in OneAdmin.

3. The data is written to the Employee Payroll Run Results object.

4. Data is replicated into the Employee Central Advanced Reporting Operational Data Store (ODS).

Figure 19.13 illustrates this data flow.

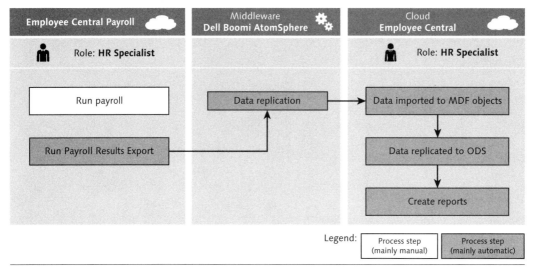

Figure 19.13 Data Flow of Payroll Data to Employee Central Advanced Reporting

Report PAOCF_EC_ExportPayrollResults enables cumulated results, detailed results, or both to be exported for the Subapplication of wage types that was defined in the IMG. After the file has been exported, it can be imported manually through OneAdmin in EMPLOYEE FILES • IMPORT AND EXPORT DATA. Automated import via middleware requires manual configuration of middleware.

Additional Resources

For more information on the Payroll Results Export, refer to the *Setting up Payroll Results Export* chapter of the *Employee Central Payroll* handbook found at *http://help.sap.com/hr_integration* under the heading SuccessFactors and SAP ERP: CORE HYBRID HCM.

19.2.6 SAP Identity Management

As part of enterprise-wide identity and security policies, many SAP customers use SAP Identity Management (IDM). Although Employee Central is the system of record for employee data, SAP IDM is the system of record for identities and their privileges.

As of SAP IDM version 8.0, an SAP SuccessFactors Connector is available to integrate Employee Central and SAP IDM. Two identity propagation scenarios are covered by the connector:

▸ Initiated from SuccessFactors

▸ Initiated from SAP IDM

> **Additional Resources**
>
> You can read more about SAP IDM in *SAP Security and Risk Management* by Mario Linkies and Horst Karin (2nd edition, SAP PRESS, 2010) and in *Authorizations in SAP Software: Design and Configuration* by Volker Lehnert and Katharina Stelzner (SAP PRESS, 2010).

Once Employee Central is set up, package `com.sap.idm.connector.sfsf` needs to be imported in SAP IDM Developer Studio, a repository created, and the initial job load performed.

The integration process is as follows:

1. SAP IDM calls the OData API in SAP SuccessFactors (see Section 19.8) to retrieve employee and permission data.

2. Data is stored in the Identity Store.

3. Data is provisioned to an LDAP directory server (e.g., Microsoft Active Directory), an AS Java system (e.g., SAP Enterprise Portal), and an AS ABAP system (e.g., SAP ERP system).

4. Permission data is sent back to SAP SuccessFactors.

Figure 19.14 illustrates this data flow.

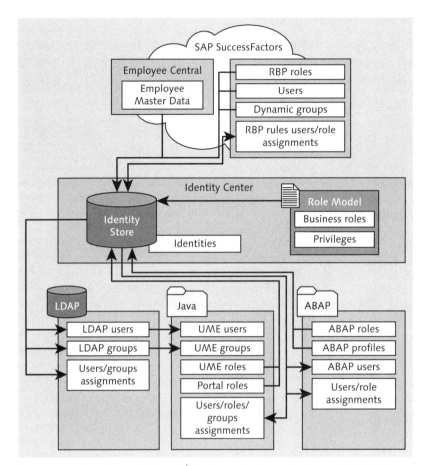

Figure 19.14 Data Flow of Integration between Employee Central and SAP IDM

As mentioned previously, there are two methods for identity propagation, which are usually triggered for activities such as a Hire, Job or Position Change, or Termination. SAP IDM can be configured to determine whether it's the leading system for role and attributes assignment.

When Employee Central is the leading system, identity propagation is initiated from Employee Central to SAP IDM. The RBPs assigned to users in SAP SuccessFactors are leveraged by SAP IDM, as shown in Figure 19.15.

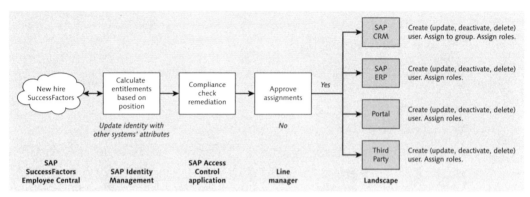

Figure 19.15 Process Flow when Employee Central is System of Initiation

When SAP IDM is the leading system, then identity propagation is initiated from SAP IDM. In this scenario, the SAP SuccessFactors RBP framework is leveraged to create users and assign them to roles in SAP SuccessFactors, as shown in Figure 19.16.

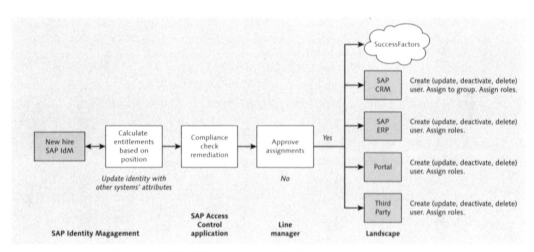

Figure 19.16 Process Flow when SAP IDM is System of Initiation

SAP IDM can generate usernames and passwords for users with configurable formats for both usernames and passwords. This information is configured in the SAP IDM Developer Studio.

19.2.7 Side-by-Side

As we discussed in Chapter 1, Section 1.12, a Side-by-Side deployment model is needed in some scenarios for some organizations to maximize investment in SAP ERP HCM while leveraging core HR in the cloud. This deployment model requires bidirectional data, process, and UI integration to achieve a seamless user experience.

To integrate SAP ERP HCM and Employee Central in the Side-by-Side deployment model, SAP provides packaged integrations that are used alongside existing packaged integrations. Data replication can be performed either through a flat file (CSV) or middleware integration. The employee data, organizational data, and cost center data packaged integrations that we covered in Section 19.2.2, Section 19.2.3, and Section 19.2.4 are leveraged in the Side-by-Side Consolidated deployment model to replicate data from Employee Central to SAP ERP.

In this section, we will focus on the packaged integration provided for the Side-by-Side Distributed deployment model as well as the UI mash-ups used in the Side-by-Side Consolidated deployment model.

Prerequisites

The following prerequisites must be met to fulfill this integration:
- SAP_BASIS 700 SP 18 or higher
- SAP_APPL 600 SP 15 or higher
- PA_SE_IN 100 SP 11 or higher

Integration Process

Once Employee Central is set up, all configuration of the packaged integration (such as infotype mapping and assigning BAdIs) is performed in SAP ERP in the IMG via menu path PERSONNEL MANAGEMENT • INTEGRATION WITH SUCCESSFACTORS EMPLOYEE CENTRAL • REPLICATING AND MIGRATING DATA FROM SAP ERP TO EMPLOYEE CENTRAL.

The integration process is as follows:

1. The integration middleware calls SAP SuccessFactors APIs (see Section 19.8) and SAP ERP web services to retrieve the data.

2. Data conversion and transformation is performed as necessary in the middleware.

3. Data is replicated between SAP ERP and Employee Central, depending on the scenario (in some scenarios, bidirectionally).

Figure 19.17 illustrates this data flow.

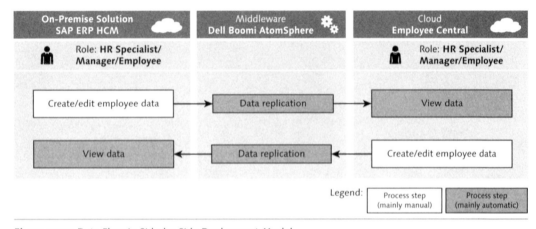

Figure 19.17 Data Flow in Side-by-Side Deployment Model

The Side-by-Side Distributed approach is focused on bidirectional replication of data, which makes the scenario much more complicated. Care must be taken to ensure that data mastered in each system is view-only within that system so that it can only be changed in the system of record for that data. This ensures data consistency between systems.

Talent Hybrid Scenario

If a Talent Hybrid scenario existed prior to using Employee Central (i.e., employees mastered in SAP ERP HCM are replicated to SAP SuccessFactors for talent management processes), then there are additional configurations required to ensure data consistency between systems.

The Side-by-Side Consolidated deployment model supports replication of most employee entities in Employee Central. For the latest list of replicated entities, refer to the *Integrating SAP ERP with Employee Central in a Side-by-Side Deployment Model* integration guide found at *http://help.sap.com/hr_integration* under the heading SUCCESSFACTORS AND SAP ERP: SIDE-BY-SIDE HCM. At the time of writing (December 2015), the following actions are supported:

- Hire
- Rehire
- Transfer
- International Transfer
- Global Assignment
- Concurrent Employment
- Termination

Field Mapping

When setting up employees in Employee Central, it's important that you use the following key field mappings:

- `user-id`
  Personnel number (PERNR)
- `username`
  Personnel number (PERNR)
- `person-id-external`
  Central Person object ID (object type CP)

Figure 19.18 shows the mapping of these objects.

BAdI `EX_ECPAO_EMP_USYID_PRN_UNM_MAP` can be used to modify the mapping for the `user-id` and `username` fields. `person-id-external` is a direct field mapping.

Template groups are used to assign the field mappings between SAP ERP HCM and Employee Central. Two sample template groups are provided in SAP ERP HCM with standard mappings, although customers can create their own template groups as required to modify mappings. The five fields listed in Table 19.8 are considered standard fields and cannot be mapped in the template groups.

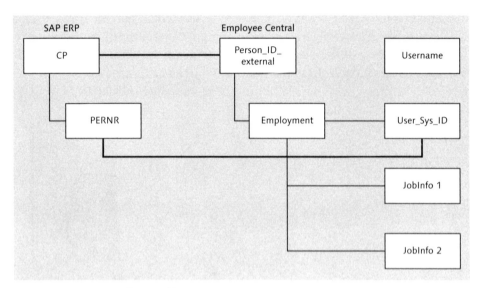

Figure 19.18 Mapping of Key Fields

SAP ERP HCM	Employee Central
Personnel number (PERNR)	`user_id`
Central Person object ID	`person_id_external`
Hire Date (from Infotype 0041)	`start_date`
First Hire Date (from Infotype 0041)	`originalStartDate`
Manager (from table `ECPAO_EE_MGNR`)	`manager_id`

Table 19.8 Standard Fields in Side-By-Side Integration

Two reports are provided to trigger data replication, which should be run in this order:

1. ECPAO_OM_OBJECT_EXTRACTION

2. ECPAO_EMPL_EXTRACTION

Both reports support both flat file replication and middleware replication. In general, these reports should be scheduled as jobs to run periodically. Delta replication is supported by using Report RBDMIDOC to generate change pointers, which can be scheduled to run periodically prior to jobs for the above-mentioned reports running. For the Side-by-Side Consolidated deployment model, UI integration exists so that Employee Central can be used as the central hub for managers and employees. It enables Web Dynpro applications to be run inside Employee Central to perform actions on employees who are mastered in SAP ERP HCM. Figure 19.19 shows an example of a Web Dynpro application being used inside Employee Central to perform an action on an employee mastered in SAP ERP HCM.

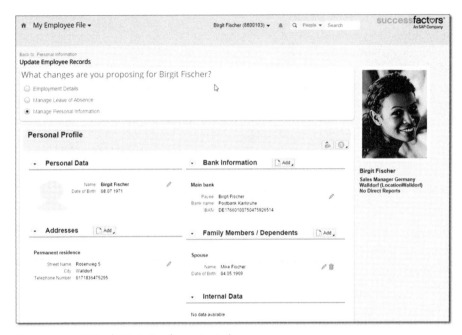

Figure 19.19 UI Mash-Up in Employee Central

19.2.8 SAP Business ByDesign

SAP Business ByDesign is SAP's ERP solution for small and medium enterprises (SMEs). It includes a strong suite of financial solutions and other processes that require employee data.

For customers using Employee Central and SAP Business ByDesign, they need to replicate employee data from Employee Central into SAP Business ByDesign. For customers using SAP Business ByDesign for only financial processes and who use Employee Central for HR processes, they can leverage a predefined integration scenario provided by SAP. The integration uses a direct web services connection between the two systems, so no middleware is required.

Once SAP Business ByDesign and Employee Central are set up, all configuration of the packaged integration (such as setting up the communication layer and the scope) is performed in SAP Business ByDesign in the work center BUSINESS CON-FIGURATION • IMPLEMENTATION PROJECTS.

The integration process is as follows:

1. SAP Business ByDesign sends cost center data to the SAP SuccessFactors APIs (see Section 19.8) via web services.

2. SAP Business ByDesign calls the SAP SuccessFactors APIs (see Section 19.8) to retrieve employee data and reporting relationships via web services.

This data flow is represented as a process integration in Figure 19.20.

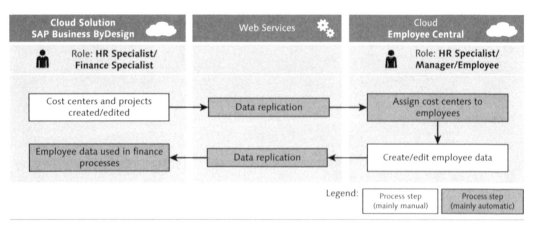

Figure 19.20 Data Flow between Employee Central and SAP Business ByDesign

In this scenario, there are two considerations:

1. Company data is maintained in both systems manually.

2. SAP Business ByDesign is the system of record for cost centers.

Code mapping is required between the systems to ensure mapping of business objects. The integration supports extensibility, meaning that custom fields in either system can be mapped with standard or custom fields in the other system.

Additional Resources

For more information on the details of the integration, field mappings, BAdIs, and minimum requirements and prerequisites, refer to the *Integrating SAP SAP Business ByDesign and SuccessFactors Employee Central* integration guide found at *http://help.sap.com/hr_integration* under the heading EMPLOYEE CENTRAL AND SAP SAP BUSINESS BYDESIGN.

Now that we've covered the integrations between SAP ERP and Employee Central, let's move on to integrations with third-party solutions.

19.3 Integration with Third-Party Solutions

As mentioned in Section 19.1.1, SAP provides packaged integrations for third-party systems, service providers, and business process outsourcing (BPO) providers (see Figure 19.21).

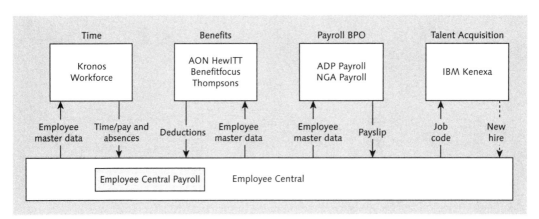

Figure 19.21 Third-Party Integrations for Employee Central

We'll run through each of these scenarios in this section of the chapter.

19.3.1 Time and Attendance

SAP provides two packaged integrations to integrate Employee Central for time and attendances:

- WorkForce Software EmpCenter
- Kronos Workforce Central

Both packaged integrations provide mappings for employee data replication from Employee Central to the target system as well as absence data and remuneration data from that system to Employee Central Payroll.

SAP also provides a standard time and attendance integration template that can be used to integrate Employee Central with other time and attendance systems, which we will cover in Section 19.9.

For both packaged integrations, the following data is replicated from Employee Central to the target system:

- Personal Information
- Phone Information
- Email Information
- Job Information
- Employment Details
- Recurring Pay Components

For the WorkForce Software EmpCenter integration, the following data is also replicated:

- Biographical Information
- Address Information
- Compensation Information

As part of each packaged integration, absence data and remuneration data can be replicated to Employee Central Payroll. This requires configuring the Absence Types and Remuneration Wage Types in the Employee Central Payroll system prior to executing integration.

Figure 19.22 shows the data flow for the packaged integrations.

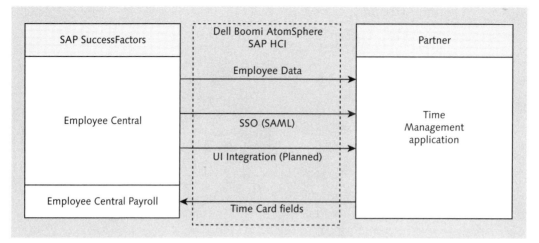

Figure 19.22 Data Flow for Time and Attendance Integrations

SSO is configurable between Employee Central and both systems, as well as with Kronos Workforce Ready. The configuration steps are defined in the implementation guides, except for the SSO with Kronos Workforce Ready, which is described in the *Implementing Single Sign-On with Kronos Workforce Ready Implementation Handbook*.

A UI mash-up is available for both the WorkForce Software WebClock and the Kronos Widget. This UI mash-up enables either the WebClock or the Kronos Widget to be accessible on the SAP SuccessFactors HOME page as a tile. Figure 19.23 shows the WORKFORCE SOFTWARE WEBCLOCK tile. These elements are configured as per the steps found in the *Embedding WorkForce Software EmpCenter Web Applications in Employee Central Integration Guide* for the WorkForce Software WebClock or the *Embedding Kronos Widgets in Employee Central Integration Guide* for the Kronos Widget.

> **Additional Resources**
>
> For more details on these packaged integrations—including implementation steps and in-depth detail of mappings—refer to the *Employee Central and WorkForce Software Integration Guide* for WorkForce Software EmpCenter integration and the *Employee Central and Kronos Workforce Central Integration Handbook* for Kronos Workforce Central integration, both available at *http://help.sap.com/hr_integration* under the heading EMPLOYEE CENTRAL AND THIRD-PARTY TIME AND ATTENDANCE VENDORS. The other handbooks mentioned in this section can also be found here.

Figure 19.23 WorkForce Software WebClock

19.3.2 Benefits

SAP provides three packaged integrations to integrate Employee Central with three different benefits providers:

- AON Hewitt
- Benefitfocus
- Thomsons Online Benefits

Each of the packaged integrations provide mappings for employee data replication from Employee Central to the target system as well as benefits data from that system to Employee Central Payroll.

SAP also provides a standard benefits integration template that can be used to integrate Employee Central with other benefits systems, which we discuss in Section 19.9. For all of the packaged integrations, the following data is replicated from Employee Central to the target system:

- Biographical Information
- Personal Information

- Phone Information
- Email Information
- Address Information
- Employment Information
- Compensation Information
- Recurring Pay Components
- National ID Card

In addition, the packaged integration for AON Hewitt and Thomsons Online Benefits replicates Job Information. The packaged integration for Benefitfocus replicates Emergency Contacts Information in addition to the data listed previously.

As part of each packaged integration, benefits data can be replicated to Employee Central Payroll for processing 401(k) accounts and other types of saving plans or for creating wage deductions and additional payments for health, insurance, credit, disability, and FSA plans. Depending on the type of savings plan, data is replicated to Infotype 0169 or 0171 in the Employee Central Payroll system. Deductions and additional payments are replicated to Infotypes 0014 and 0015, respectively. Wage Types must be configured to map pay code information, benefits, and deductions.

Figure 19.24 shows the data flow for the Benefitfocus packaged integration. This data flow is the same for the AON Hewitt and Thomsons Online Benefits packaged integrations.

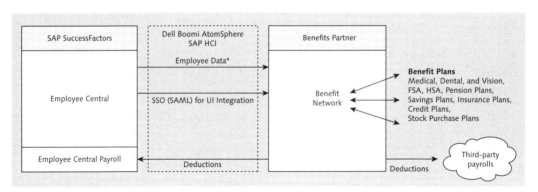

Figure 19.24 Data Flow for Benefits Integration

SSO is configurable between Employee Central and Benefitfocus and between Employee Central and Thomsons Online Benefits. The configuration steps are defined in the respective implementation guides.

Additional Resources

For more details on the packaged integrations—including implementation steps and in-depth detail of mappings—refer to the appropriate integration guide found at *http://help.sap.com/hr_integration* under the heading EMPLOYEE CENTRAL AND THIRD-PARTY BENEFITS VENDORS:

▸ *Employee Central and Aon Hewitt Core Benefits Administration*

▸ *Employee Central and Benefitfocus*

▸ *Employee Central and Thomsons Online Benefits*

19.3.3 Payroll BPO

SAP provides three packaged integrations to integrate Employee Central with three different payroll BPO providers:

▸ ADP GlobalView

▸ NGA euHReka

▸ NGA Payroll Exchange

Both ADP GlobalView and NGA euHReka are hosted versions of SAP ERP Payroll and therefore use the packaged integrations discussed in Section 19.2.5. We will not discuss them in this section of the chapter. The packaged integration for NGA Payroll Exchange provides mappings for employee data replication from Employee Central to NGA Payroll Exchange for processing of payroll.

SAP also provides a standard payroll integration template that can be used to integrate Employee Central with other payroll systems, which we will cover in Section 19.9.

For the NGA Payroll Exchange packaged integration, the following data is replicated from Employee Central to NGA Payroll Exchange:

▸ Biographical Information

▸ Personal Information

▸ Phone Information

- Email Information
- Address Information
- Employment Information
- Compensation Information
- Recurring Pay Components
- Non-Recurring Pay Components
- National ID Card
- Direct Deposit/Payment Information
- Work location address (from the Location Foundation Object)

Figure 19.25 shows the data flow for the ADP GlobalView packaged integration, which includes pay slip display in Employee Central. Figure 19.26 shows the NGA euHReka packaged integration data flow.

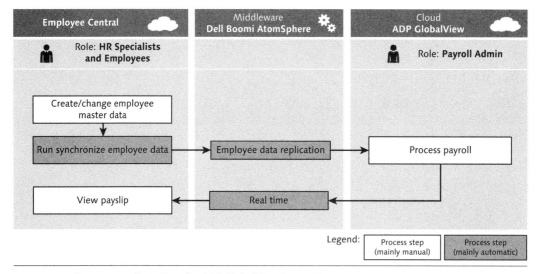

Figure 19.25 Data Flow for ADP GlobalView Integration

Additional Resources

For more details on the NGA Payroll Exchange packaged integration—including implementation steps and in-depth detail of mappings—refer to the *Employee Central and NGA Payroll Exchange* integration guide found at *http://help.sap.com/hr_integration* under the heading EMPLOYEE CENTRAL AND THIRD-PARTY PAYROLL VENDORS.

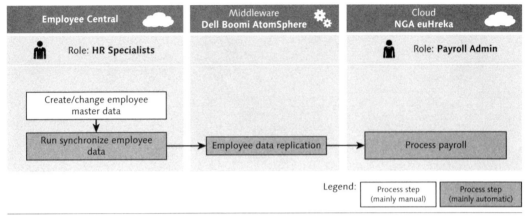

Figure 19.26 Data Flow for NGA euHReka Integration

19.3.4 Microsoft Active Directory

SAP provides a packaged integration to integrate Employee Central with Microsoft Active Directory in order to create and disable user accounts in Active Directory based on the hiring and termination of employees in Employee Central. The integration does not support rehire, transfer, data changes, or activating an inactive account in Active Directory.

For the packaged integration, the following data is replicated from Employee Central to the Microsoft Active Directory when a user is created:

▸ Biographical Information

▸ Personal Information

▸ Phone Information

▸ Email Information

▸ Job Information

During the integration, the middleware fetches data from Employee Central for all employees created since the last transmission, sends the data to Active Directory to create the accounts, records the date of transmission, and records any errors in the middleware log. Figure 19.27 illustrates the data flow for this integration. Disabling a terminated user follows a similar process.

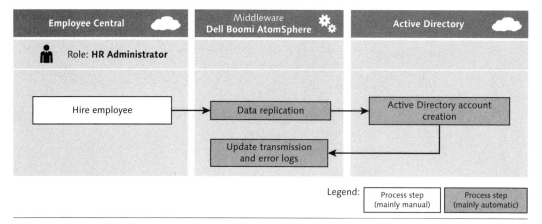

Figure 19.27 Data Flow for Microsoft Active Directory Integration

---

Additional Resources

For more details on the packaged integration—including implementation steps and in-depth detail of mappings—refer to the *Employee Central and Microsoft Active Directory* integration guide found at *http://help.sap.com/hr_integration* under the heading EMPLOYEE CENTRAL AND MICROSOFT ACTIVE DIRECTORY.

19.3.5 IBM Kenexa Talent Management Suite

Two packaged integrations are provided to integrate Employee Central and IBM Kenexa Talent Management Suite for performing recruiting-related activities:

▶ Job Code Default Data (JCDD)

▶ Requisition Field Association (RFA)

The packaged integration for JCDD provides replication of Job Classification Foundation Object data from Employee Central to IBM Kenexa Talent Management Suite so that job requisitions can be created based on Job Classifications. Figure 19.28 illustrates the data flow for the integration.

Additional Resources

For more details on the packaged integrations—including implementation steps and in-depth detail of mappings—refer to the *Employee Central and IBM Kenexa Job Code Default Data (JCDD)* and *Employee Central and IBM Kenexa Requisition Field Association (RFA)* handbooks available at *http://help.sap.com/hr_integration* under the heading EMPLOYEE CENTRAL AND THIRD-PARTY RECRUITMENT VENDORS.

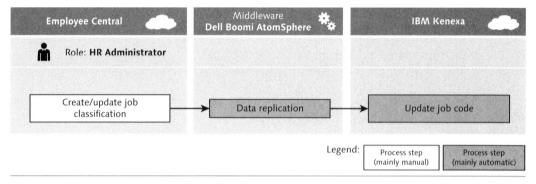

Figure 19.28 Data Flow for IBM Kenexa Talent Management Integration

The packaged integration for RFA provides the replication of Foundation Object associations from Employee Central to IBM Kenexa Talent Management Suite so that data in job requisitions can remain synchronized with Employee Central. This includes the follow associations:

▶ Business Unit > Division

▶ Division > Department

▶ Company > Location

As shown, SAP provides a variety of third-party integrations to further customize an organization's scenario.

19.4 SAP SuccessFactors HCM Suite Integration

Although the SAP SuccessFactors HCM Suite is an integrated suite, there are certain configurations needed to define the data mapping and how the integration between Employee Central and some other modules of the suite work together. The primary touch points that require some degree of configuration and/or data mapping are as follows:

▶ User Data File/Employee Profile

▶ Compensation and Variable Pay

▶ Recruiting

▶ Onboarding

▶ Succession Planning

We'll run through these now.

19.4.1 User Data File

Certain data is synchronized from Employee Central to the User Data File (UDF) on a real-time basis as standard, such as Name, Manage, Department, and so on. This is called HRIS Sync and is covered in Chapter 1, Section 1.10.

The Employee Profile, all of the talent applications, and ad hoc reporting leverage employee data from the UDF.

19.4.2 SAP SuccessFactors Compensation and Variable Pay

When using Employee Central, SAP SuccessFactors Compensation and SAP SuccessFactors Variable Pay leverage the Pay Components or Pay Component Groups and their assignment to employees directly from Employee Central. Variable Pay also reads employment history data from Employee Central. Compensation process results are written back to Compensation Information as effective-dated Pay Component changes.

Figure 19.29 shows the data flow between Employee Central and Compensation, as well as the types of data flows and integrations that are used. You can see that the Rules Engine is mentioned, because rules are created in the Rules Engine that define eligibility for compensation and/or variable pay plan access and entitlements.

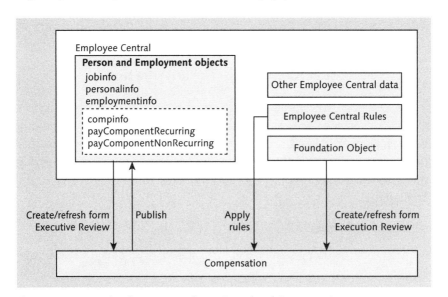

Figure 19.29 Data Flow between Employee Central and Compensation

The mapping of Pay Components or Pay Component Group objects and fields to a compensation form and its fields is configured in the compensation plan XML. Typically, this work would be performed by a Compensation specialist with input and guidance from an Employee Central specialist. For Variable Pay, the process is similar. The only real difference is that employee history is also read by Variable Pay in addition to the other data read in the Compensation integration.

Additional Resources

For more information on the integration and configuration, refer to the *EC-Compensation Integration* section in the *Compensation (Implementation Guide)* found at *http://service.sap.com/sfsf* under COMPENSATION MANAGEMENT. You can also find some detailed blogs on the topic on SAP Community Network (SCN) at *http://scn.sap.com/community/erp/hcm*.

For more information on Variable Pay, refer to the *Variable Pay and Employee Central (Integration Guide)* found at *http://service.sap.com/sfsf* under VARIABLE PAY.

19.4.3 SAP SuccessFactors Recruiting

The way in which Employee Central and SAP SuccessFactors Recruiting interact is common to the way in which most integrations work between these types of processes. Recruiting reads job and position data from Employee Central, and new hire data is fed to Employee Central to prefill and accelerate the new hire process. When SAP SuccessFactors Onboarding is used as well, this hire data flows to Employee Central via Onboarding.

Once an employee is hired in Employee Central, his or her user ID is sent back to the Candidate Profile. Figure 19.30 shows the PENDING HIRES screen, from which recruited or onboarded employees can be hired into Employee Central.

Requisitions in Recruiting can be created for a position in the position org chart. Integrating these two applications for new hire data focuses on field mappings in transformational XML. Reading job and position data from Employee Central is more automated.

Additional Resources

For more information on the integration and configuration, refer to the *Employee Central (RCM to EC Integration)* section in the *Recruiting Management (Implementation Guide)* found at *http://service.sap.com/sfsf* under RECRUITING. You can also find some detailed blogs on the topic on SCN at *http://scn.sap.com/community/erp/hcm*.

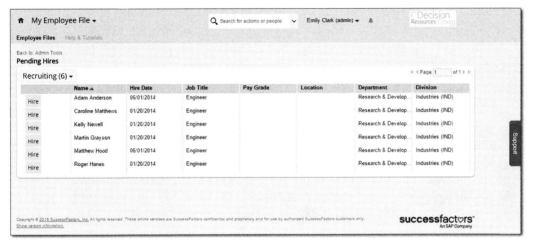

Figure 19.30 Pending Hires Screen

19.4.4 SAP SuccessFactors Onboarding

Similar to the new hire data flowing from Recruiting to Employee Central, Onboarding replicates prehire/candidate data to new hire transactions in Employee Central. Onboarded employees will be available for hire in the PENDING HIRES screen in Employee Central that you saw in Figure 19.30. A field mapping is made with transformation XML.

Additional Resources

For more information on the integration and configuration, refer to the *Onboarding, Recruiting Mgmt & Employee Central (Integration)* handbook found at *http://service.sap.com/sfsf* under ONBOARDING.

19.4.5 SAP SuccessFactors Succession Planning

Integration of Employee Central with Succession Planning occurs via Position Management. Position data is read from the Position Generic Object in the MDF to enable position-based succession planning. Succession plans can be built against positions, and the position-based structure is built based on position relationships.

Now that we've discussed actual integration topics, let's begin to take a look at the different features and functionality that support creating integrations. We'll start by looking at the Integration Center.

19.5   Integration Center

In the Integration Center, business users and administrators can build and deploy simple, pattern-based, outbound flat file integration files in a guided workflow. Integrations can also be monitored here (both job statuses and error messages), and the Template Catalog provides templates to be used to get up and running with your integrations quickly.

The Integration Center can be used not only to build the integration data structure but also to schedule a job to export data to an SFTP, from which it can be picked up by a middleware platform or the target application. File encryption is also supported. Any data that is accessible through the OData API can be used in the Integration Center. This covers most of the Employee Central objects and all the Generic Objects that have the API VISIBILITY field set to EDIT or VIEW.

The layout and order of the output file can be defined in the Integration Center, and filter conditions can be applied to select only the right set of required data. Simple manipulations and calculations of data can be performed, value lookup tables can be used for data mapping, and so on.

Figure 19.31 shows the basic process flow for creating an integration.

Figure 19.31 Process Flow for Creating an Integration

Figure 19.32 shows the homepage of the Integration Center, which can be accessed in OneAdmin via COMPANY SETTINGS • INTEGRATION CENTER.

Figure 19.32 Integration Center

The Execution Manager in the Integration Center enables you to check jobs and errors (see Figure 19.33).

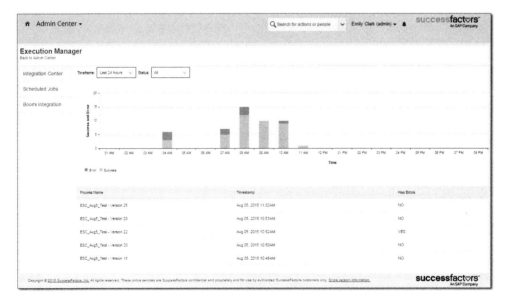

Figure 19.33 Execution Manager

19.6 External Event Framework

The External Event Framework—also known as Intelligent Services—is an event-based Service Event Bus (SEB) that enables a *publisher* (e.g., Employee Central) to raise an *event* (e.g., a manager change or new hire) that is sent to one or more *subscribers* (e.g., another SAP SuccessFactors application, an integration middleware, or a third-party application).

Events can be configured for a publisher using the Event Center in Next Gen Admin, which can be accessed either from the EVENTS CENTER tile or via COMPANY SETTINGS • EVENTS CENTER. Please note that that Event Center is not available in the regular or legacy versions of OneAdmin.

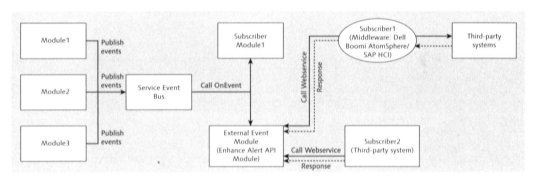

Figure 19.34 Notification Flow of the External Event Framework

Figure 19.34 shows the notification flow of the External Event Framework. The process is as follows:

1. Data is changed in Employee Central (the publisher), which triggers an event to be published to the SEB.

2. The SEB triggers an event to either another SAP SuccessFactors application or to the External Event module.

3. If an event goes to the External Event module, it will trigger an integration either to middleware or to a specific system, depending on what subscribers are configured.

Figure 19.35 shows the Event Center homepage. The homepage shows all of the events in the system along with the number of subscribers (hovering over the number lists the subscribers) and the number of events raised in the past seven days. A large number of standard events are offered in the system, and more will be added periodically by SAP SuccessFactors to extend the offering.

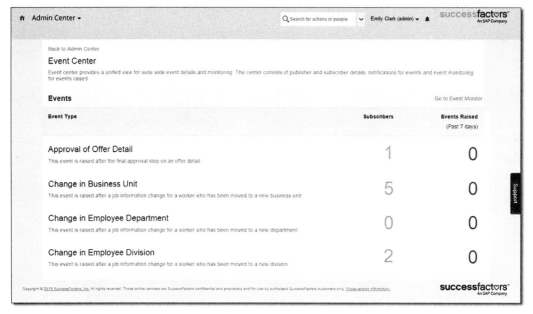

Figure 19.35 Event Center

Typical events cover many common changes to an employee's information, such as business unit, division, department, location, job, or manager. Hire, rehire, and termination are also available, as well as Time Off. Another event that can trigger processes occurs when an employee becomes a manager of one or more employees for the first time.

Selecting an event takes you to the EVENT DETAIL screen, where you can see the configuration of the event. Here, you can see the notifications that get sent to the SEB, the publishers of the events, and which applications subscribe to those events. Figure 19.36 shows the EVENT DETAIL screen of a CHANGE IN MANAGER event.

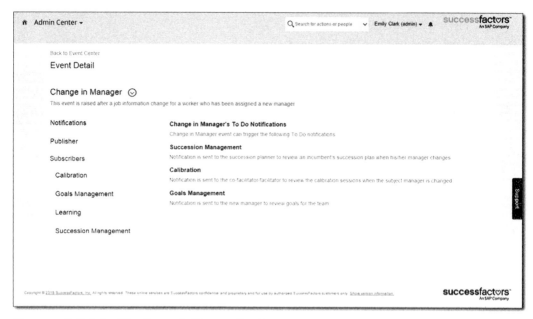

Figure 19.36 Details of the Change in Manager Event

Additional Resources

For more information on using and configuring the Extension Center, refer to the *External Event Notifications (Implementation Guide)* found at *http://service.sap.com/sfsf* under FOUNDATION (INCLUDING APIs).

19.7 Adapters

Adapters for building integrations with Employee Central and other systems are available in SAP PI, SAP HANA Cloud Integration, and Dell Boomi AtomSphere. The purpose of the adapters is to provide an easier way to build integration content and mappings within each middleware to accelerate the construction of integrations. They work with both the SFAPI and the OData API, both of which we will cover in Section 19.8. All adapters support the full range of operations for each API and manage session handling.

SAP introduced two adapters for SAP PI—the SuccessFactors SFAPI Adapter and SuccessFactors OData Adapter—with SAP Process Integration, connectivity add-on 1.0. You can find more details at *http://help.sap.com/nw-connectivity-addon101*.

19.8   APIs

SAP SuccessFactors contains two APIs that can be used for integrating Employee Central with other systems. The purpose of the integration and the platform used determine which of the following two APIs to use:

- OData API
- Compound Employee API (CE API)

You can use APIs when custom integrations need to be created. They typically aren't used for data migration. Table 19.9 highlights which API to choose based on your needs.

OData API	CE API
▶ RBP-based user access	▶ Field-level delta
▶ Custom and extension applications	▶ Snapshot of data
▶ Update Employee Central data	▶ Modified employees only
▶ Consume MDF data	▶ Only read and not write data
▶ Access a wide range of employee data	▶ No OData capabilities

Table 19.9 OData API vs. Compound Employee API

SAP provides all documentation on SAP SuccessFactors APIs at *http://help.sap.com/hr_api*.

We'll now take a look at each API and its use cases.

19.8.1 OData API

The OData API is the core API provided to integrate Employee Central with other systems. The packaged integrations provided by SAP leverage this API, and it contains deep functionality for querying, updating, and purging data in Employee Central. The OData API is built on the Open Data (OData) Protocol v2.0, a standardized protocol for creating and consuming data.

The OData API supports most of the entities in Employee Central, plus Generic Objects and Platform entities, such as users, permissions (RBPs), and To Do list items. The latest list of entities that are exposed to the OData API can be found in the following handbooks located at *http://help.sap.com/hr_api*:

▶ *Employee Central OData API Reference Guide*
▶ *OData API Reference Guide*

API calls to the OData API are made via a HTTP call, which can be triggered from a middleware platform or any other application that supports the OData protocol and can make OData calls to the OData API. Multiple operations are available for each entity:

▶ Create, query, or update data
▶ Select, order, filter, skip, top, format, or expand queries
▶ Create, update, or delete links between entities
▶ Navigate between related entities

The latter option enables you to use navigation properties to reach related entities. For example, the National ID Information entity (`PerNationalID`) and Job Information entity (`EmpJob`) can be queried through the person entity (`PerPerson`). This means that you can build a query to retrieve a complete dataset of employee data and related object data, including Foundation Object, Generic Object, and picklist data. Let's take a look at an example query to help us understand how this might work in practice.

In the `PerPerson` query shown in Listing 19.1, a dataset for employee Carla Grant is being queried from Employee Central. The query includes data such as national ID, first name and last name, email address, hire date, pay group, all pay components, location, person Id, and date of birth.

```
PerPerson?$filter=personIdExternal+eq+'cgrant1'&$select=nationalIdNav/
cardType,nationalIdNav/nationalId,personalInfoNav/
firstName,personalInfoNav/lastName,emailNav/emailType,emailNav/
emailAddress,employmentNav/startDate,employmentNav/compInfoNav/
payGroup,employmentNav/compInfoNav/empPayCompRecurringNav/
payComponent,employmentNav/compInfoNav/empPayCompRecurringNav/
paycompvalue,employmentNav/jobInfoNav/
location,personIdExternal,dateofBirth&$expand=
nationalIdNav,personalInfoNav,emailNav,employmentNav,employmentNav/
compInfoNav,employmentNav/compInfoNav/
empPayCompRecurringNav,employmentNav/jobInfoNav
```
Listing 19.1 Query of PerPerson Object to Extract Data about an Employee

The OData API can be audited and managed within OneAdmin, once the features have been permissioned as per the *HCM Suite OData API* handbook. There are four options available in OneAdmin under COMPANY SETTINGS:

▸ API AUDIT LOG
  Captures payload details for the last 10,000 API calls.

▸ MANAGE API OPTION PROFILE
  Manages settings for creating new users.

▸ ODATA API DICTIONARY
  Provides information on all entities exposed to the OData API.

▸ ODATA API METADATA REFRESH AND EXPORT
  Enables all OData entities to be refreshed after configuration changes are made.

Additional Resources

For more details on how to use the OData API, refer to the *HCM Suite OData API* handbook (called the *OData API Programmer's Guide* handbook on *http://help.sap.com/hr_api*).

19.8.2 Compound Employee API

The CE API is a web services–based API that uses the SOAP protocol to extract employee data from Employee Central. It is read-only and therefore cannot be used to update data within Employee Central. The primary use case of the CE API is to replicate a snapshot or delta of employee data from Employee Central to payroll and/or benefits systems. As a result, the CE API does not read historical or future-dated records, although it does read changes to employee data within the time period being extracted. It can read multiple changes made in one day.

The CE API is used by packaged integrations to replicate employee master data to SAP ERP and Employee Central Payroll and to third-party benefits, time and attendance, and payroll systems. The Employee Delta Export—which we'll look at in Section 19.10—also uses the CE API.

CE API Entities

The CE API supports most Employee Central entities. For the latest list of entities, please refer to the *Compound Employee API—Supported Fields* handbook found at *http://help.sap.com/hr_api*. For the latest list of supported operators for each field and other information regarding queries, refer to the *Implementing the Compound Employee API* handbook found at *http://help.sap.com/hr_api*.

The CE API uses a subset of traditional SQL to extract data. It uses the following SQL statement format to extract data:

```
SELECT <fields> FROM <entity> WHERE <conditions> ORDER BY <fields>
```

Unlike traditional SQL, no joins, subselect queries, or calculations are possible. In most cases, the FROM clause is FROM CompoundEmployee, but for the user entity it will be FROM user. The WHERE clause supports the following operators:

▸ AND and OR logic operators

▸ =, >, >=, <=,

▸ IS NULL/IS NOT NULL

▸ LIKE/NOT LIKE

▸ IN/NOT IN

Listing 19.2 provides an example statement to extract Person Information and Job Information for employees whose company is SAP and whose data was modified after January 1, 2016.

```
SELECT person, job_information
FROM CompoundEmployee
WHERE company='SAP'
AND last_modified_on > to_datetime ('2016-01-01','YYYY-MM-DD')
```

Listing 19.2 SQL Statement to Retrieve Data about Employees in Company 'SAP'

The CE API can be audited and monitored within OneAdmin, once the features ACCESS TO SFAPI AUDIT LOG and ACCESS TO SFAPI METERING DETAILS have been permissioned for the user under the MANAGE INTEGRATION TOOLS permission category. Like the OData API, the CE API uses the API Audit Log that can be found in OneAdmin via COMPANY SETTINGS • API AUDIT LOG. In addition, the API Metering Details option found in OneAdmin via COMPANY SETTINGS • API METERING DETAILS provides analytics on API usage over the last thirty days.

> **Additional Resources**
>
> For more details on the CE API, refer to the *Implementing the Compound Employee API* handbook and *Compound Employee API—Supported Fields* reference document at *http:// help.sap.com/hr_api*.

19.9 Standard Integration Templates

To build integrations with payroll, benefits, or time and attendance systems not covered by the packaged integrations quickly, SAP provides three standard integration templates. A template exists for each of the three process: payroll, benefits, and time and attendance.

Each template uses the Employee Central Compound API and Dell Boomi Atom-Sphere to export employee data from Employee Central in CSV format for employees for whom that data has changed since the last transmission and to send the resulting CSV file to the target system. The templates provide generic logic and process modules to build templates that can be executed in the middleware. They require some custom logic and effort, depending on the requirements of the target system.

Each of the templates is designed to export a selection of employee data, including:

▶ Biographical Information
▶ Personal Information
▶ Address Information
▶ Phone Information
▶ Email Information
▶ Employment Information
▶ Job Information
▶ Compensation Information
▶ Recurring Pay Components

Each template may also export some other employee data. For example, the benefits standard integration template also includes Dependents Information, Manager Information, National ID Card Information, and Pay Group Foundation Object data.

Figure 19.37, Figure 19.38, and Figure 19.39 each show the data flow for the standard integration template for time and attendance, payroll, and benefits, respectively.

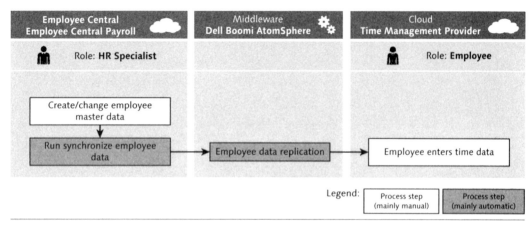

Figure 19.37 Data Flow of Time and Attendance Standard Template

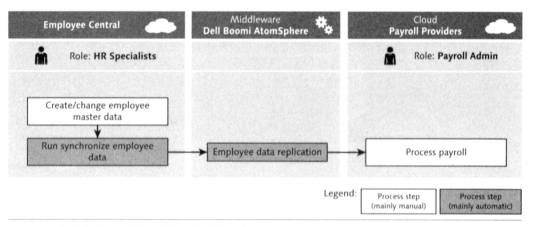

Figure 19.38 Data Flow of Payroll Standard Template

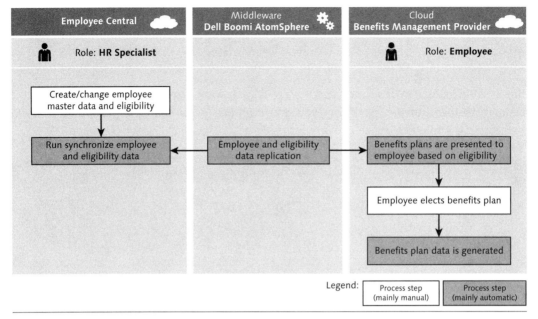

Figure 19.39 Data Flow of Benefits Standard Template

Additional Resources

For more details on the standard integration templates—including implementation steps and in-depth details of mappings—refer to the appropriate integration guide found at *http://help.sap.com/hr_integration*:

▶ *Standard Integration Template for Employee Central and Third-Party Time and Attendance Vendors*

▶ *Standard Integration Template for Employee Central and Third-Party Payroll Vendors*

▶ *Standard Integration Template for Employee Central and Third-Party Benefits Vendors*

Refer to Section 19.8.2 for details on the CE API.

19.10 Employee Delta Export

The Employee Delta Export exports employee master data from Employee Central in CSV format so that it can be used in payroll systems. It provides a delta of employee data changes (i.e., it only provides data changes since the last run of the export) that considers both future-dated and retroactive changes of employee data, as well as including deleted data that must be actioned in the target system (for example, deletion of a Pay Component) and hires and terminations.

The Employee Delta Export is comprised of an add-in for Microsoft Excel and two Microsoft Excel spreadsheets that provide the configuration and provide the layout of the data that is exported from Employee Central; one spreadsheet provides all data in three sheets (new employees, changed employees, and terminated employees), while the other spreadsheet provides data as one sheet per person and employment object.

The add-in and two spreadsheets can be downloaded from OneAdmin via REPORTING • EMPLOYEE DELTA EXPORT. The Employee Delta Export leverages the Employee Central HRIS SOAP API in order to export the data from Employee Central into the workbooks. Because of this, RBPs are not respected and all data that matches the filter criteria defined within the Employee Delta Export spreadsheet will be retrieved from Employee Central.

The output data is written to the spreadsheets with several columns to identify changes. The Status column shows whether the record is new, changed, a new segment (for elements that store multiple different records for an object, such as National ID or Work Permit), or has been deleted. For many fields, a column exists to show both the old value and the new value.

The standard-delivered Employee Delta Export spreadsheets can be extended to include custom columns or calculated columns and to remove columns not used.

Additional Resources

For more details, refer to the *Using the Employee Delta Export Add-In for Microsoft Excel* user guide found at *http://help.sap.com/hr_ec* under the USER GUIDES heading.

19.11   Employee Central Payroll Integration

Employee Central Payroll—which we covered in Chapter 15—can be integrated with many systems, particularly the time and attendance and benefits applications that we covered in Section 19.3.1 and Section 19.3.2. For all customers, BSI TaxFactory SaaS is used by Employee Central Payroll for calculation of US employees' withholding taxes, and integration is available with BSI eFormsFactory for employees to maintain withholding and other tax details. We will cover both the web services and BSI integration in this section.

In addition, a web service exists for Employee Central Payroll to transfer benefits information from benefits providers to the infotypes in Employee Central Payroll.

19.11.1 BSI

SAP provides three types of integration with BSI solutions:

▸ Data integration between Employee Central Payroll and BSI TaxFactory SaaS

▸ SSO between Employee Central and BSI eFormsFactory

▸ Replication of changed personnel numbers to BSI eFormsFactory

The integration with BSI TaxFactory SaaS works by direct web service communication between the two solutions. A payroll run in Employee Central Payroll triggers communication with BSI TaxFactory SaaS to calculate employees' withholding taxes. Employee Central Payroll passes all of the taxable wages and information over to BSI TaxFactory SaaS, and BSI TaxFactory SaaS returns the tax amount.

For BSI eFormsFactory, users access BSI eFormsFactory directly from the PAYROLL INFORMATION screen in Employee Files by selecting WITHHOLDING TAX FORMS in the TAX portlet. Employee and company data is replicated from Employee Central Payroll to BSI eFormsFactory by using Report RPCPAYUS_CLD_NOTIFY_BSI, which should be scheduled within the Employee Central Payroll system.

Figure 19.40 shows the data and transaction flow for BSI integration.

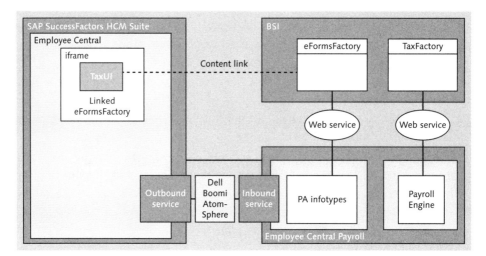

Figure 19.40 Data and Transaction Flow for BSI Integration

For more details, refer to the *Employee Central Payroll and BSI SaaS Solutions* handbook found at *http://help.sap.com/hr_integration* under the heading EMPLOYEE CENTRAL PAYROLL AND THIRD-PARTY VENDORS.

19.11.2 Web Services

Benefits information can be replicated from benefits providers to the infotypes in Employee Central Payroll using a standard-delivered web service. The web service interface `EmployeeBenefitsVendorDataUpdateRequestConfirmation_In` is provided to enable HTTP requests to post data to Employee Central Payroll and to provide the sender with a HTTP response.

For more details, refer to the *Web Service for Updating Employee Central Payroll* handbook found at *http://help.sap.com/hr_integration* under the heading EMPLOYEE CENTRAL PAYROLL AND THIRD-PARTY VENDORS.

19.12 Summary

In this chapter, we covered the ins and outs of Employee Central's integrations, the packaged integrations provided by SAP, the different APIs available, and other tools that can be used to ensure that the integration between Employee Central and other HR and non-HR systems runs smoothly. With many options and accelerators comes many choices, but also many benefits. The roadmap and available packaged integrations evolve every quarter, so customers will find more and more options as time goes by. Even if your scenario is not covered by a packaged integration, the tools available in the suite will enable you to quickly build an integration to suit your needs.

This chapter concludes our journey across SAP SuccessFactors Employee Central. In the next chapter, you'll find the conclusion to what we hope has been an enjoyable and informative publication.

Employee Central is a complete, end-to-end core HR platform that can provide value, simplicity, and efficiency. The processes, features, and functionality available makes it a viable option for organizations of all sizes.

Conclusion

As you've seen throughout this book, Employee Central is a complete and robust core HR system for managing an enterprise. Although some features are further along in their development trajectory than others, the overall set of features can support a number of business processes and scenarios of varying complexities.

Employee Central is a flexible system with strong extensibility capabilities. Although flexibility is a core strength, it can also provide too many options and too many ways of doing things. Strong guidance, decisiveness, and a holistic view of enterprise-wide process and technology architecture are required for an optimal implementation.

In many places in this book, we would've like to have delved deeper into one topic or another. However, the aim was not to regurgitate information already available in the implementation or integration handbooks, but neither was it our intention to skip over some technical aspects of using or implementing features. In addition, with quarterly releases, it didn't make sense to cover information in the book that is likely to change on a regular basis, so we've referenced some ever-changing resources during the book and in the latter section of this conclusion.

It's a fine balance to compile all of the moving parts and especially tough to deliver all of the content in "only" 500 pages or so. We do hope, however, that what we have managed to include has been insightful and went above and beyond information found in other sources. Where possible, we've tried to reference those other sources to ensure you can find the information you need if that information is not included in this title.

Recap

We covered a lot of content within the book and made sure to include some reference to most functionality within the Employee Central application. We started off by looking at the basic concepts of Employee Central (see Chapter 1) before reviewing implementation steps and considerations (see Chapter 2). Many of the concepts found in these two chapters were expanded upon as we progressed through the book.

In Chapter 3 through Chapter 7, we aimed to provide foundational information for Employee Central. This included permissions in an Employee Central context, events, employee statuses, workflows, extensibility, Foundation Objects for master data, positions, and data imports.

From Chapter 8 on, we began looking at the key functionality and operation of Employee Central. This began with employee data, employee administration, and organization management before moving onto Time Management, benefits, Global Assignments, Contingent Workforce Management, mass changes, advances and deductions, letter generation, concurrent employment, pension payouts, the pay scale structure, and more. We also looked at reporting capabilities, mobile functionality, and the Employee Central Payroll feature.

Finally, we tackled integration in a mammoth, final chapter of the book. We looked at the SAP strategy in an Employee Central perspective as well as the technology options. We then ran through the packaged integrations available as standard, the standard integration templates, API options, the external event framework, and other features provided to enable data and process flow between systems.

Just reading those last few paragraphs goes to show what breadth of capabilities there are in Employee Central and how you can apply such capabilities to your business.

Further Resources

There are a multitude of resources available to Employee Central customers and partners. These resources cover different needs, ranging from technical documentation to customer communities. Typically, they center on the following sites:

- SAP Help Portal (*http://help.sap.com*)

- SAP Service Marketplace (*http://service.sap.com*)

- SuccessFactors Community (*http://community.successfactors.com*)

- SAP Community Network (*http://scn.sap.com/community/erp/hcm*)

For SAP employees and partners, there are three other sites of interest:

- SuccessFactors Partner Portal (*https://partners.successfactors.com*)

- SAP PartnerEdge (*https://partneredge.sap.com*)

- SAP Jam (*https://jam4.sapjam.com*)

We'll run through these now.

SAP Help Portal

On the SAP Help Portal, there are a number of places that provide documentation pertinent to Employee Central. There are three main sites:

- *http://help.sap.com/hr_ec*
  Provides Employee Central handbooks and implementation guides.

- *http://help.sap.com/hr_integration*
  Offers integrations handbooks for packaged integrations and other integrations for Employee Central and other SAP SuccessFactors applications to integrate with third-party systems and SAP ERP.

- *http://help.sap.com/hr_api*
  Identifies the APIs available for integrating SAP SuccessFactors with other systems.

The handbooks provide a lot of detail to understand how the system works and how to configure it.

SAP Service Marketplace

Many of the handbooks mentioned in the previous section are also available on SAP Service Marketplace at these URLs:

- *http://service.sap.com/ec-ondemand*
  Employee Central handbooks and implementation guides.

- *http://service.sap.com/sfsf*
  Handbooks for other modules; the handbooks found in the Foundation section contain useful handbooks for modules related to Employee Central and APIs.

- *http://service.sap.com/roadmaps*

- The SAP SuccessFactors HCM Suite roadmap is publicly available on SAP Service Marketplace. Click on PRODUCT AND SOLUTION ROAD MAPS and then select LINE OF BUSINESS. The SAP SuccessFactors roadmap can be found in the PRODUCT ROAD MAPS section towards the bottom of the screen.

- *http://service.sap.com/rds*
  There are several Rapid-Deployment Solutions (RDS) available for SAP SuccessFactors, details of which can be found here. To navigate to the SAP SuccessFactors RDS packages, look under LINE OF BUSINESS and select the appropriate RDS under HUMAN RESOURCES (SAP SuccessFactors RDS have *Cloud* in brackets after the name).

SAP SuccessFactors Community

SAP SuccessFactors customers and partners can access the SAP SuccessFactors Community, which provides a wealth of resources, information, communications, and forums for customers to stay up-to-date with the latest information, ask questions, and raise enhancement requests. Access the SAP SuccessFactors Community via *http://community.successfactors.com*; access is granted exclusively to customers and partners.

The key communications released through the SAP SuccessFactors Community are the quarterly releases information and the yearly release schedules. Other important information is also posted, so it is recommended to make this a must-visit site on a regularly basis.

In addition, SAP has made it known that the Employee Central product management team reviews enhancement requests on a weekly basis. This is a key tool to request enhancements to the solution directly with the product team.

Cloud Learning Center

Customers and partners that have a SuccessFactors Community user account can also access the Cloud Learning Center. Here, they can find a number of trainings for each SAP SuccessFactors application, including Employee Central, Dell Boomi

API training, and Metadata Framework (MDF). To access these, log in to the Cloud Learning Center (*https://sa.plateau.com/learning/user/login.do*) with your SAP SuccessFactors Community user credentials. The different curricula can be accessed within the SUCCESS ACADEMY LEARNING PATHS portlet.

Typical trainings for Employee Central include the following:

- **SuccessFactors Employee Central Project Team Orientation**
  This is an important orientation training that is recommended to be taken by all project team members at the beginning of the implementation.

- **SuccessFactors Employee Central Administration**
  This course provides information on administering Employee Central.

- **Employee Central Payroll for HR Administrators**
  This course provides information on administering Employee Central Payroll.

- **Employee Central: Job Aids**
  This enables a user to download a set of job aids that can be used to support end users.

SAP Community Network

The SAP Community Network (SCN) is the official user community of SAP and has more than two million members. For Employee Central, the SAP ERP HCM space (*http://scn.sap.com/community/erp/hcm*) contains a significant and growing collection of blogs, documents, and forum posts.

The *SuccessFactors: Useful Resources and Documents* document is a popular collection of blogs and articles on SAP SuccessFactors—including many on Employee Central—that you can access via *http://scn.sap.com/docs/DOC-41539*.

LinkedIn

LinkedIn boasts a number of different groups covering various SAP SuccessFactors topics. For Employee Central, the most relevant group is the *SuccessFactors Employee Central* group (*https://www.linkedin.com/grp/home?gid=7461662*). For more general SAP SuccessFactors information, the *SAP HCM and SuccessFactors* group (*https://www.linkedin.com/grp/home?gid=4278743*) is another popular group.

Twitter

Twitter can be a great source for the latest news, information, blogs, and articles relating to SAP SuccessFactors. The @SuccessFactors handle and #SuccessFactors hashtag offer good ways to stay informed. In addition, the hashtags for the SuccessConnect and SAP Insider HR conferences can also provide the latest information announced during these conferences. The hashtags change yearly, but often follow the pattern of #sconnectXX (where XX is the two-digit year) and ##HRXXX (where XXXX is the year of the conference).

You can also follow authors Luke Marson and Murali Mazhavanchery via their handles, *@lukemarson* and *@murzen*, respectively.

Other Resources

Other useful sources of information, videos, and articles include the following:

- **SuccessFactors YouTube channel**
  https://www.youtube.com/user/SuccessFactorsInc
- **SearchSAP**
  http://searchsap.techtarget.com/resources/SAP-HR-management
- **SAP experts**
  http://sapexperts.wispubs.com/HR
- **SuccessFactors blog**
  http://blogs.successfactors.com/blogs/business-execution

Summary

In this book, we covered a plethora of processes, approaches, features, and functionality for implementing, using, and maintaining Employee Central in your organization. As noticed, the page count could be significantly higher given the breadth of functionality available in the system. Although this publication is the comprehensive guide, there is so much more we would love to have included.

This finally concludes our tour of the robust and deep Employee Central. The solution enables full end-to-end employee lifecycle management and integrates into the SAP SuccessFactors HCM Suite. There are also integration capabilities provided to make sure Employee Central can speak to any system and exchange data as needed.

The key takeaway from all of this is that Employee Central is a process enabler primarily. It's designed to support your business and to enable enhanced simplicity in HR and employee operations. The innovation through quarterly releases means that you can continue to evolve HR as new features are introduced that can be used to make your HR organization more effective.

The Authors

Luke Marson is a C-level leader, architect, principal consultant, and globally-recognized expert for SAP SuccessFactors HCM suite solutions and is a Certified Professional in Employee Central. In addition to being an author, writer, speaker, and go-to individual on HCM and SAP SuccessFactors topics, he is also an SAP Mentor program alumni and an America's SAP Users' Group (ASUG) volunteer. In his current role, Luke delivers strategy, advisory, roadmap, integration, and consulting services to SAP ERP HCM and SAP SuccessFactors customers and also provides strategic guidance and expertise to support various HCM initiatives.

He has delivered more than 40 projects in multiple countries across North and Central America, Europe, the Middle East, and Asia to organizations of various sizes (up to 240,000 employees) and types in different industries and sectors, including oil and gas, defense, retail, manufacturing, the public sector, telecommunications, and media. He is an active Twitter user (*@lukemarson*); a regular writer and blogger on SAP SuccessFactors, HCM in general, cloud, and various thought leadership topics; and an active contributor to the SAP Community Network (SCN). He has also contributed to numerous articles, reports, and podcasts for SAPinsider magazine, SAPexperts, SearchSAP, CIO Review, and other publications. Luke has spoken at numerous events internationally and in various webinars and podcasts.

Murali Mazhavanchery is the senior director of product management at SAP focusing on Employee Central design and development. He has over 15 years of HRIS project management experience. Murali has been around HR functionality for all his professional life. In his past roles, he was an industrial relations manager, an HCM systems implementation consultant, and has now transitioned to building software.

Rebecca Murray is an experienced HCM consultant and a partner at Cultiv8 Consulting. She specializes in the design and integration of HRIS and talent management solutions including both SAP ERP HCM and SAP SuccessFactors. Rebecca has completed numerous global and multi-national implementations in both SAP ERP HCM and SAP Success-Factors and is considered a thought leader in the field of Employee Central.

Combining her specialized knowledge with her love for teaching and learning, Rebecca teaches Employee Central Academy classes for SAP Education and actively participates in planning the course's content. She is a HR Advisor for SAPexperts and she speaks widely on her experiences at industry conferences and trade shows around the globe. Rebecca holds a bachelor's degree in computer engineering and a master's degree in business administration. She is an SAP SuccessFactors Certified Professional Consultant in Employee Central and a Dell Boomi AtomSphere Certified Process Developer.

Index

▶ SuccessFactors: what it is, how it works, and what it can do for you

▶ Explore the SuccessFactors suite for your entire HR workflow

▶ Simplify business processes in Employee Central and other SuccessFactors modules

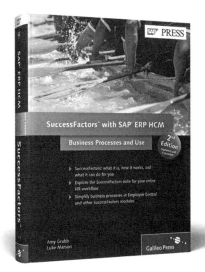

Amy Grubb, Luke Marson

SuccessFactors with SAP ERP HCM

Business Processes and Use

Looking to better your HR workflow? Discover the potential of SuccessFactors, SAP's HR cloud solution, with this introductory guide. Updated and revised, this edition covers new integration packages, additional SAP HANA Cloud Platform information, details on the Metadata Framework, and a look into the new Job Profile Builder. Discover what SucessFactors is, how it works, and what it can do for you.

644 pages, 2nd edition, pub. 11/2014
E-Book: $59.99 | **Print:** $69.95 | **Bundle:** $79.99

www.sap-press.com/3702

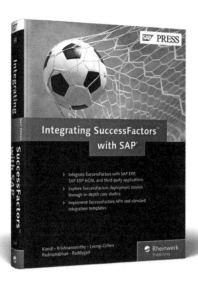

Interested in reading more?

Please visit our website for all new
book and e-book releases from SAP PRESS.

www.sap-press.com